*Third Edition*

# PERSUASION & INFLUENCE IN AMERICAN LIFE

**Gary C. Woodward**

*College of New Jersey*

**Robert E. Denton Jr.**

*Virginia Polytechnic Institute and State University*

WAVELAND

PRESS, INC.

Prospect Heights, Illinois

For information about this book, write or call:

Waveland Press, Inc.
P.O. Box 400
Prospect Heights, Illinois 60070
(847) 634-0081

**Credits**

Calvin and Hobbes 137, 227; © Watterson. Reprinted with permission of Universal Press Syndicated. All rights reserved.
CATHY 70, 104, 159, 231, 289; © Cathy Guisewite. Reprinted with permission of Universal Press Syndicate. All rights reserved.
DOONESBURY 8, 310, 411; © 1996 G. B. Trudeau. Reprinted with permission of Universal Press Syndicate. All rights reserved.
THE FAR SIDE 64, 66, 219; © 1985 & 1986 FarWorks, Inc./Dist. by Universal Press Syndicate. Reprinted with permission. All rights reserved.
National Gallery of Art 362; used by permission.
Tribune Media Services 77, 101, 334; used by permission.
WALNUT COVE 63, 300; King Features Syndicate, Inc., world rights reserved.

**Photo Credits**

The Bettman Archive 35, 44, 329
*Chicago Tribune* 23, 77, 131, 158, 184, 196, 214, 216, 220, 233, 237, 249, 261, 324, 336, 346, 369, 395, 396, 419
*Seinfeld* photo reprinted by permission of Castlerock Productions 210
U.S. House of Representatives 41

Copyright © 1996, 1992, 1988 by Waveland Press, Inc.

ISBN 0-88133-905-9

Printed in the United States of America

7  6  5  4  3  2

# Contents

## 3 The Advocate and the Manipulation of Symbols  57

## PART II FOUR PERSPECTIVES ON THE NATURE OF PERSUASION  83

## 4 Persuasion and Reasoning  85

# **5**  Credibility and Authority

# **6**  The Psychology of Persuasion

# 7 Social Bases of Persuasion

# PART III  THE CONTEXTS OF PERSUASION

# 8 Interpersonal Persuasion

# 9 Public and Mass Persuasion 247

# 10 Advertising as Persuasion 283

# 11   Political Persuasion 321

# PART IV   ISSUES AND STRATEGIES OF MESSAGE PREPARATION 361

# 12   Ethical Considerations of Persuasion 363

## 13  Constructing and Presenting Persuasive Messages    393

# Preface to the Third Edition

We began this project in 1986 with an eye toward creating a different kind of book. We wanted to write a description of persuasive settings, processes, and messages that would be readable but accurate. Our goal was to answer questions that active learners without any previous exposure to the subject would find interesting and useful. Several ground rules were established. We thought the book should be as nontechnical as possible, summarizing research findings and scholarly conclusions, but avoiding extensive jargon. We wanted to talk about persuasion processes by using a variety of specific instances, including detailed case studies as well as briefer illustrations. Our intention was also to place the study of persuasion in the context of both its Western intellectual tradition and its pivotal role in the political culture of the United States. Additionally, we wanted to draw upon a variety of vital contexts, redressing the tendency in some books of shunning political and social settings in favor of illustrations from the sometimes more obvious and more trivial worlds of advertising and public relations.

Our third edition adheres to these goals, but it also updates them. We have maintained the basic chapter organization of the previous edition, changing various sections to say things more clearly, update research, and provide newer examples and illustrations. This edition, for example, considers persuasion in the 1992 and 1994 national elections. It also recognizes enormous changes in the growth of more specialized media, such as cable television, and in the added importance of subjects such as contemporary feminist thought and the continuing debate over "political correctness." In some cases we have abandoned obscure examples that betray the fact that at least one of the authors grew up in the age of the Hoola-Hoop and the Edsel. But we have avoided the temptation to strip away historical references contained in previous editions that we judge to be of lasting relevance to modern readers.

So this edition, like its predecessors, remains only partly a textbook. The eclectic mix of theories, applications, recommendations, and analyses in these pages is meant to provoke discussion and further analysis. By its nature, persuasion is an inexact and highly fluid process. Those of us who teach this subject understand less than we might like to confess. We hope this book frankly and effectively introduces a number of ideas, theories, and observations that reflect our interest in communicating both the illusive and fascinating dimensions of persuasion and influence.

## Plan of the Book

This text is divided into thirteen chapters within four broad sections. Part I addresses how persuasion serves as a vehicle for social change and how human symbols are given shared meanings. Part II discusses four major approaches to the process of influence: philosophical, character-centered, psychological, and sociological. Part III is an examination of the many varieties of political and commercial persuasion that engulf us daily. Two chapters discuss the special features of communication unique to both intimate and large settings. Two others describe the most recognized applications of persuasion in modern life: advertising and politics. Part IV opens with a chapter that explicitly reviews some of the special ethical issues that confront various types of advocates. It is followed by a final chapter that provides practical guidelines for preparing and delivering messages, including those presented in formal speeches and other forms of media.

Each chapter concludes with questions for self-study, which allow readers to determine if the ideas and concepts contained in the chapters have been understood. Intermixed with the questions are suggestions for putting ideas and strategies to work on specific projects. The projects may be adapted to the reader's needs and to course-related assignments. Each section of the book also ends with a list of additional resources for readers wishing to explore certain topics more extensively.

## Acknowledgments

The authors are indebted to many colleagues and students who have contributed ideas and suggestions for the three editions of this text. Charles Stewart and Carol Rowe asked challenging questions and made a number of helpful editorial recommendations throughout the preparation of the manuscripts. Many others contributed specific comments and a variety of useful materials. They include Paul Frye, J. Justin Gustainis,

Harold Hogstrom, Maryanne Kehoe, John Makay, Jack McCullough, Janette K. Muir, Beth Waggenspack, and Paula Wilson. The authors are also grateful to many instructors around the country who have shared their experiences in using this text.

Teaching at a public institution means that writing must always compete for time with many other responsibilities. Robert Denton would like to thank his colleagues at Virginia Polytechnic Institute and State University, his patient co-author, and his insightful editor. Gary Woodward acknowledges the support of the College of New Jersey Faculty Research Committee. Both also thank their students, past and present, who have made the teaching of persuasion a challenge and a pleasure.

Gary C. Woodward
Robert E. Denton, Jr.

# 1

# Persuasion and Influence
## An Introduction

## OVERVIEW

- Influence and Attitudes
    Four Introductory Cases
        Advertising: Selling and Unselling
        Advocating a Dangerous Form of Religion
        Persuasion and the Politics of Peace
        Persuasion in Everyday Life
    What These Cases Suggest
        Message and Advocate Intertwined
        Persuasion as an Amoral Process
        Unpredictability
        Frequently a Private Rather Than Public Process

- Persuasion as a Subject for Study
    The Love-Hate Relationship
    The State of Our Knowledge
        Our Limited Ability to Predict Persuasion Effects
        Pattern of Minimal Effects
        The Importance of Limited Effects

- Three Types of Communication
    Pure Information
    Pure Expression
    Pure Persuasion

- Persuasion Defined

- Questions and Projects for Further Study

- Notes

- Additional Reading

> To insist upon the importance of language may seem like battering at an open door. But there are times when it is necessary not to flinch from the obvious. In the society to which we belong, talking and listening, reading and writing, are so constantly present that familiarity blunts perception of the extraordinary character of such activities.[1]
>
> —Max Black

It was a short moment in the proceedings of the Senate, but an interesting one. A freshman from Illinois—the Senate's only African-American member—spoke out against a pending vote. In the course of a single impassioned speech, she defeated one of that body's most powerful members.

The occasion was Senator Jesse Helms' quiet introduction of an amendment that would have extended federal recognition of the confederate flag as the symbol of a women's organization called the Daughters of the Confederacy. What he had not bargained for was the angry response his "routine" amendment would provoke from Carol Moseley Braun, who argued that the symbol was offensive to African-Americans whose ancestors had been slaves. She noted that the Daughters of the Confederacy may do good works in serving various charities. "If they choose to wave the Confederate flag, that certainly is their right." But the symbol so closely tied to slavery should not be "underwritten, underscored, adopted, approved by this United States Senate."[2] Braun's speech came after Helms had successfully maneuvered a 52 to 48 test vote on his amendment.

Soon after her speech, however, support began to erode for renewal of the design patent for the organization. A Rhode Island senator noted that "rarely on this floor are votes changed by words," but that was precisely what was happening as members began to gather again in anticipation of a second vote. Braun angrily denounced the confederate flag as a symbol of the civil war where we "fought to try to preserve our nation, to keep the states from separating themselves over the issue of whether or not my ancestors could be held as property, as chattel, as objects of trade and commerce in this country."[3] In the course of a hot July afternoon, she convinced 27 of her colleagues—northern and southern—to change their votes. In the end, the Helms amendment went down to defeat, 75 to 25.

The study of persuasion is intrinsically fascinating as well as truly essential. The process of influencing others has been perhaps the most studied and analyzed of all social activities. How do we change beliefs? What makes us susceptible to or immune from constant attempts to persuade us to accept ideas, products, and people? How do demagogues manipulate people to deny their beliefs and to accept an action that imposes personal hardship or violates their self-interest? People have been asking such questions since the infancy of democratic government in ancient Greece. The study of the ebb and flow of influence reveals fundamental characteristics about human nature.

Communication is the lifeline of our existence. It is a medium unique to humans; it permits us to express the vital, invisible qualities of who we are and what we believe. In contrast to the rest of the living world, we establish a sense of our "place" by the way we define ourselves and the ways others define us. However bravely the child repeats the age-old aphorism, "Sticks and stones may break my bones, but words can never hurt me," the reverse is closer to the truth. Words and their non-verbal symbolic counterparts do hurt. We use them against our enemies and for our friends. We give language the awesome responsibility of carrying our judgments to others. Words convey praise, blame, guilt, and joy. Persuading others to see a corner of our world as we see it is a basic human need. The simple designation of "F" on a student's final exam can inflict its own kind of severe pain. We are rarely indifferent to the efforts of others to transform what we think and believe, and we are never unconcerned about our own efforts to have others share our agenda of interests, concerns, and values. Persuasion is the process that constantly negotiates this give and take.

## Influence and Attitudes

Persuasion does not present itself in one easily discernable form. It occurs in a diverse range of contexts ranging from simple exchanges of opinions with friends to elaborate debates extended over years. Efforts to manipulate attitudes may grow from one or two persons to encompass vast audiences interconnected by the mass media. A speaker from Amnesty International may try to win support from a small handful of listeners on a college campus. By contrast, the Media-Advertising Partnership for a Drug-Free America may reach 40 million television viewers with one ad during a prime time television show. Persuasion may originate within organized groups such as the National Organization for Women or the American Civil Liberties Union, or it may start with the efforts of individuals. Persuaders may be as well-financed as the Mobil Corporation or the AFL-CIO, or as resource-poor as a small band of homeowners fighting the decisions of a local zoning board. The range of human contacts that require skillful persuasion is nearly endless. As citizens in an open society, we cannot escape the responsibility for organizing or participating in public persuasion. As individuals functioning in a web of personal relationships, we similarly face the necessity of negotiating an enormous range of close contacts within the family, in community institutions, and at work.

## Four Introductory Cases

Life is filled with moments that call for persuasion, compromise, and agreement. We begin our study with an examination of four diverse kinds of persuasive circumstances.

### Advertising: Selling and Unselling

Advertising is a common and lucrative form of influence. Billions of dollars are spent each year to find purchasers for countless goods and services. The advertising-based industries in the United States are the big consumer products companies, their advertising agencies, and the mass media that depend on the sale of space and time for their revenues. A four-color, one page advertisement in a national magazine may sell for $80,000, and one thirty-second, prime-time, network television commercial may cost $500,000.

In the history of American advertising, few products have provoked more controversy than cigarettes. Although they are not advertised in the broadcast media, they represent a major buyer of space in magazines and newspapers. As the 1990s began, about 58 million adult Americans continued to smoke, despite repeated warnings by surgeon generals and most sectors of the medical community. While there is evidence that cigarette use has begun to decline, the most loyal consumers of tobacco still include poorer populations in general and black males in particular. In 1989 nearly half of all African-American men were regular customers, supported in part by extensive tobacco advertising on billboards in large cities and in magazines such as *Jet* and *Ebony*.[4] In the early months of 1990, the decision of one manufacturer to launch a new brand aimed at this target group set off a flurry of charges and countercharges.

The conflict began when R. J. Reynolds announced its intention to set up a six-month plan for test-marketing a new brand of menthol cigarettes in Philadelphia. "Uptown" was scheduled to be introduced with the usual publicity that accompanies the launch of a new product. Billboard space was leased, advertising commitments were purchased in African-American newspapers and other media in Philadelphia, and projections were released indicating that the company hoped to push its market share up several points from its current level of 28.6 percent.[5] Uptown was also part of a larger plan by R. J. Reynolds to end a slide in cigarette sales to competitors and to improve its market performance as the new owner of the food giant, Nabisco.

What followed, however, was a corporate nightmare that combined negative publicity with a bruising countercampaign. Plans for the Uptown advertising blitz were widely reported in the national press, some of whom noted that the company had targeted African-American males because of their loyalty to menthol-flavored brands of cigarettes. Complaints about the plan originated among black and other ethnic

*In the history of American advertising, few products have provoked more controversy than cigarettes. Critics charge that "Joe Camel" targets the young.*

leaders in Philadelphia, spread to the city's local media, and soon were voiced by a cabinet member. Dr. Louis Sullivan, then secretary of health and human services, angrily denounced RJR-Nabisco for "deliberately and cynically" focusing on African-American males for what he described as the "culture of cancer."[6] In a public letter fired off to the president of the company, Sullivan noted that "cigarettes are the only legal product on the market that are deadly when used exactly as intended," resulting in 390,000 deaths a year. He followed up this letter several days later with a speech in Philadelphia that criticized companies who seek "profits at the expense of the health and well-being of our poor and minority citizens."[7]

Plans to introduce Uptown were quietly shelved, but accusations against the tobacco industry increased with a $28 million anti-smoking campaign that began several months later in California. Two years earlier, California's voters had approved a 25-cent tax on packages of cigarettes to finance advertising on radio and television which would go beyond the usual health warnings about tobacco use. The campaign would attack the industry itself. One spot dubbed "subliminal" featured a photo montage of familiar cigarette ads and logos from magazines and sporting events. Another ad directed to African-Americans used rap music to emphasize what California's director of health services described as the "selective exploitation of minorities" and the "selling of suicide."[8] The lyric used in this ad began, "We used to pick it; now they want us to smoke it." The most potent and most controversial ad of the campaign used actors to portray cigarette executives engaged in a strategy session scheming to find new ways to lure new smokers for their product.

By 1994 it became evident that what had started out as small skirmishes between specific tobacco companies like R. J. Reynolds and various public agencies was turning into a full-scale public relations war. Life imitated art when top executives of leading tobacco companies were called to testify before a House subcommittee about whether cigarette makers manipulated the level of nicotine in cigarettes. The companies presented a unified front in denying research into the addictive nature of nicotine.

In California, the tobacco industry was losing ground. Smoking in the state was down by 30 percent, due at least in part to its combination of taxes and anti-smoking ads. Use by teens had also leveled off, in contrast to most of the rest of the country. States as diverse as Virginia and Colorado began looking to the California experience as a model for their own campaigns.[9] For their part, some of the tobacco companies decided to give up on the war for public opinion and focus instead on quieter forms of lobbying. R. J. Reynolds, for example, focused its efforts on state legislatures, attempting to lobby members to back only modest tax increases on cigarettes and softer regulations on smoking. Their goal

The full-scale public relations war between tobacco companies and their critics has many forums. One of the most prominent is the print media. Newspapers and magazines report the most recent allegations and counter-allegations. Tobacco companies purchase full page advertisements to discuss nicotine levels in cigarettes, underage smoking, and the dangers of bureaucratic control.

was to work against strong anti-smoking actions that had gained approval in cities like Los Angeles and San Francisco.

Persuasive encounters over the use of tobacco range from the interpersonal (differing opinions over cigar smoking at a football game, for example) to well-financed advertising campaigns to class-action lawsuits. The multilayered complexities surrounding the subject of smoking require substantial knowledge of persuasion—whether as the persuader or the persuadee. Growing tobacco is not only legal but is subsidized by the United States government. For thirty years, that same government has required companies to label their product as dangerous to consumers' health and has banned certain forms of advertising. Tobacco interests contribute millions of dollars to election campaigns. Members of Congress have failed to end tobacco subsidies and have not enacted legislation authorizing the FDA to regulate tobacco—yet restrictions on a legal product are increasingly common. The emphasis shifts but the controversies do not subside. The "Uptown" campaign was derailed by interests who perceived it as exploiting minorities. Since that time, the focus has shifted to protecting the young.

In March 1996 the Liggett Group (the smallest U.S. tobacco company) broke ranks with other tobacco companies and agreed to settle *Castano*, a class-action lawsuit. For twenty-five years, Liggett will pay 5 percent of its pretax income—up to $50 million—into a fund to pay for programs to help people stop smoking. Liggett will also adopt the government's proposed advertising and marketing restrictions on underage smoking.[10] The settlement was the first breach in the united front previously presented by tobacco interests. The persuasive effects of Liggett's compromise remain to be seen. Will the public perceive Liggett as a responsible company attempting to contribute to the public good? Will it view Liggett's actions as self-serving and opportunistic (if the other companies continue to fight the class-action suit and win, Liggett will

**DOONESBURY**

DOONESBURY © 1996. G. B. Trudeau. Reprinted with permission of Universal Press Syndicate.

benefit—and will have gained some good-will at little cost)? Did Liggett perceive that circumstances had changed dramatically with class-action suits and several states suing tobacco companies over Medicaid costs for treating smokers? The high-stakes debate continues.

### Advocating a Dangerous Form of Religion

Persuasion affects our lives for good or ill. We rightly assume that most advocates have honorable intentions. When they do not and when their insensitivity is matched by their success, disaster may follow.

The remote South American nation of Guyana was the scene of an American tragedy in 1978. An American evangelist, driven by an intense sense of persecution, directed a large group of followers to commit mass suicide. It was the final act of persuasion in what had been a long and increasingly desperate road for Jim Jones and his followers.

Jones was considered unorthodox in his California evangelist days, but similar to other evangelists who mingled politics and religion. He was especially popular among the poor because his indignation toward "exploiters" and the rich struck a responsive chord. The mission he established attracted members through activities and services designed to make them feel special and different. Like David Koresh—the Waco, Texas, fundamentalist whose compound was attacked and eventually destroyed by the FBI in 1993—Jones was a powerful leader. He used his pulpit to preach not only a religious doctrine but also long diatribes against the secular culture outside. Also like Koresh, Jones grew increasingly strident and isolated.[11] He began to make every issue a personal one and every member a part of his own private crusade. He cultivated a following by cleverly mixing his gospel of social change with carefully orchestrated demonstrations of support. Members were required to give their money and personal allegiance to "The Father." For Koresh and his Branch Davidians in Waco the price of their isolation and identification with a zealous leader would be the loss of 87 lives in a fiery holocaust. For the residents of Jonestown, the losses were even more staggering: 912 followers were shot or took their lives in one mass suicide.

The remote Guyana village was an unusual spot for an American religious commune, but Jones must have realized that a leader's control is enhanced when his or her followers' dependence is increased though physical isolation. Jones sold his jungle location as a place free from persecution and victimage. "I am preparing a promised land for you in Jonestown," he said. "When you get there all of your tribulations will be over. There will be no need for discipline when you get away from the capitalistic society of America. There you will be able to love and be loved."[12]

According to one member of the People's Temple, Jones' "only source of pleasure was observing his followers' total devotion to him."[13] He became obsessed with his control over the inhabitants of the new village. Members were publicly beaten and humiliated. Bizarre marathon meetings were held in which he revealed his belief that he was the target of assassination plots. He began preaching with a gun at his side and erupting into tirades when a member tried to leave a meeting. These were ominous signs of his growing paranoia.

After hearing complaints from members of families that relatives were being held against their wishes, California Congressman Leo Ryan decided to visit the Guyana village with several members of the press. His visit pushed Jones to a deadly state of paranoia and rage. In poor health himself, he calmly planned the demise of his commune and everyone in it. After ordering the assassination of Ryan and several reporters, he persuaded and coaxed almost one thousand people to commit the ultimate act of self-destruction. Many willingly gave doses of a fruit drink laced with poison to themselves and to their children, while others were murdered by Jones' bodyguards. A tape recorder left running preserved the bizarre final moments:

> So my opinion is that you be kind to children and be kind to seniors and take the potion like they used to take it in ancient Greece, and step over quietly, because we are not committing suicide. It's a revolutionary act. We can't go back, and they won't leave us alone. They're now going back to tell more lies, which means more congressmen. And there's no way, no way, we can survive.[14]

Jones' power to persuade his followers to commit suicide remains a partial mystery. The basic impulse to live should defeat even the most manipulative of persuaders, but we must not overlook the fact that the murder/suicide was only a last step in what had been an incremental process begun years earlier. From its start, the People's Temple had fostered the principle of personal obedience. Members of the church were more than followers of a set of religious beliefs. They were disciples of Jim Jones. Had he been a different person, they might have benefited from their identification with him because persuasion is both a social and rational process. The attraction to the idea of the People's Temple—a mission apart from society—became fatally tied to the magnetic personality of Jones. Like David Koresh, he had attracted supporters first to his ideas, then to his isolated mission, and finally to their deaths.

### Persuasion and the Politics of Peace

Woodrow Wilson was one of America's most eloquent presidential orators. He built much of his long public career around his faith in the power of persuasion, but he overestimated even his considerable skills. His last attempt to shape public opinion left history with a fascinating case study of the clash between politics and principle.

Wilson reluctantly led America into World War I against Germany in 1917. It was difficult to commit Americans to fight in a Europe that was splintered by age-old factions and disputes. The United States had been an island of peace preoccupied with its western expansion and newfound wealth; European quarrels seemed distant and petty. The 1915 attack and sinking of the liner *Lusitania* near the Irish coast pushed the Western Hemisphere closer to war. Nearly 1,200 passengers perished— victims of new submarine technology and a willingness by the Allies to mix civilians with military cargo. Eventually German submarine attacks on other ships in the Atlantic forced Wilson to declare war.

World War I was a brutal and bitter conflict. The machine gun changed the technology of war, exposing long lines of soldiers to instant death. Army officers sent to the front to lead battalions of foot soldiers rarely returned alive. The possibility of an armistice began to emerge only after staggering losses developed on all sides. The world had never witnessed such concentrated fighting and killing; 8.5 million soldiers and 28 million civilians were killed.

As early as 1918 Wilson began to grapple with the problem of finding a way to assure peace in Europe. The final form of his proposal consisted of "Fourteen Points" to be applied to a negotiated settlement. In a dramatic address before Congress, Wilson announced his plan to save the world from future "force and selfish aggression." The fourteen principles included a call for a ban on secret treaties, absolute freedom of the seas, the removal of Germans from Belgium and other countries, the removal of economic controls between nations, and evacuation of foreign troops from Russia. Wilson's highest goal was Point Fourteen: "a general association of nations must be formed under specific covenants for the purpose of affording natural guarantees of political independence and territorial integrity to great and small states alike."[15] His objective was to establish a world organization devoted to peace to be known as the League of Nations.

Germany was finally defeated, but the bitter fighting had exacted a heavy political cost. The German government soon accepted Wilson's Fourteen Points as a basis for an armistice, but the Allies were reluctant to settle for anything less than enormous financial reparations. Reflecting concerns that have still not completely subsided in much of Europe, Britain and France did not want to see a prosperous neighbor reemerge to their east. Leaders in both nations felt that the war had forced them to sacrifice the lives of the best and brightest of an entire generation. For his part, Wilson believed—probably naively—that a nonpunitive American solution could be imposed on the European political landscape.

Wilson faced two enormous dilemmas—both rooted in his need to change attitudes. One problem was how to win over the Allies to accept a peace that did not further humiliate the defeated Germany. The other was how to get the American Senate to ratify the idea of a world organization dedicated to peace. In spite of his best efforts, Wilson failed on both counts. The Allies forced Germany to pay a heavy price economically and geographically, and Wilson accepted far less than the original

*Woodrow Wilson hoped to persuade the public that the League of Nations was essential to secure world peace.*

ideals embodied in the Fourteen Points. The ultimate irony, however, is that the resulting Treaty of Versailles probably assured a future war. Germany's resentment made it ripe for a dangerous form of nationalism to develop under Adolph Hitler's Nazi Party.

Wilson's greatest political defeat was his failure to secure Senate ratification of the treaty establishing the League of Nations. He could not convince two-thirds of the Senate to accept his plan and was unwilling to compromise and accept an amended proposal. Instead he took his case to the American people, hoping to persuade the public that the League was essential and thereby force the Senate to ratify the proposal. His faith in his power to override his opponents by direct appeals to the American public was a classic presidential ploy.

On September 3, 1919, he left Washington on a train that would take him 8,000 miles in 22 days and permit him to deliver countless speeches in favor of the League. Radio was still too new to offer an alternative to the grueling trip. Wilson's reluctance to work with the Senate leadership cost him dearly. After an impassioned speech in Colorado, he suffered a stroke and returned to Washington partially paralyzed.[16]

Wilson's enemies in the Senate—William Borah, Henry Cabot Lodge, and others—remained unmoved by pleas for American participation in the League of Nations. They argued that there could be no participation without compromise. The once energetic Wilson was unwilling to alter his vision for the league and spent the last months of his presidency completely immobile in a corner bedroom of the White House. It was a sad end to a supremely proud man.

America did not join the League, and a true world organization never developed from the ruinous battles and treaties of World War I. The divisions that had created war remained, and Germany was forced against Wilson's wishes to accept harsh terms of peace. A line from one of Wilson's last speeches in favor of the League proved prophetic:

> I can predict with absolute certainty that within another generation there will be another world war if the nations of the world do not concert the method by which to prevent it [and in that struggle] not a few hundred thousand fine men from America will have to die, but as many millions as are necessary to accomplish the final freedom of the world.[17]

### Persuasion in Everyday Life

The cases we have reviewed so far involve organizations or powerful institutions: a major corporation, a church, and the presidency. Organizations as large as these have the resources to affect large numbers of people with the same message; however, no overview of the process of persuasion would be complete without noting that everyday life is filled with attempts at influence. Sociologist Erving Goffman has a remarkable ability for seeing the subtle patterns of influence in the activities of ordinary life. He notes "that when an individual appears before others he [or she] will have many motives for trying to control the impression they receive of the situation."[18] In routine exchanges with others, we want to be liked and to have our ideas accepted. We want others to show a regard for our feelings and for the values which serve as the anchors for our actions. As Goffman reminds us, children, teachers, parents, close friends, employees, employers, spouses, lovers, and co-workers all have strategies for projecting their interests to those with whom they come in contact. Since we perform many of these roles simultaneously, we are constantly faced with the need to make our actions and attitudes acceptable to others. Every role we play carries a number of possible strategies for influencing others. In words, gestures, and small signs, we leave a trail of cues that are meant to guide the responses of our audiences. No moment in the routine events of the day is too small to be devoid of persuasion. Many instances of "impression management" collected by Goffman have become classic accounts of what could be called "micro-persuasion." His reference to George Orwell's account of the routine strategies of restaurant waiters is a favorite:

> It is an instructive sight to see a waiter going into a hotel dining room. As he passes the door a sudden change comes over him. The set of his shoulders alters; all the dirt and hurry and irritation have dropped off in an instant. He glides over the carpet, with a solemn priest-like air. I remember our assistant maitre d'hotel, a fiery Italian, pausing at the dining room door to address his apprentice who had broken a bottle of wine. . . . ''Tu me fais—Do you call yourself a waiter, you young bastard? You a waiter! You're not fit to scrub floors in the brothel your mother came from . . .'' Then he entered the dining room and sailed across it dish in hand, graceful as a swan. Ten seconds later he was bowing reverently to a customer. And you could not help thinking, as you saw him bow and smile, with that benign smile of the trained waiter, that the customer was put to shame by having such an aristocrat to serve him.[19]

Life is full of such moments. Any novel or film could be studied for all of the small but significant cues that are performed to elicit acceptance or approval. We ''read'' and perform such acts so routinely that we tend to forget how essential they are in oiling the machinery of everyday interaction. Consider, for example, how the following conventional situations invite the use of various persuasive strategies:

- You have a second job interview with a firm that seems interested in you. However, they have expressed some concern about your lack of experience. You need to reassure members of the interview team.

- The appeals panel of the city planning board has allowed a member of your family just three minutes to challenge their decision prohibiting the addition of a room on your existing home.

- A close friend decides to go home after her last Friday class and casually announces to friends over lunch that she will hitchhike along the 45-mile stretch of lonely interstate highway to reach her parents' house.

- A driver has been pulled over by a police officer for going a few miles over the posted speed limit while passing a slow truck.

- A friend has been in a deep depression for days. You would like him to see a counselor, but you don't want to ''interfere.''

- You are broke. The prospect of eating oatmeal for dinner until the next paycheck arrives is too much to bear. But you do have some affluent friends . . .

- You are an officer in a campus organization which needs new members, and you know where good prospective candidates are. It is just a matter of getting them to join.

- As a part-time salesperson paid on commission, every sale increases the amount of your monthly paycheck. You attempt to locate a method for detecting serious buyers from more casual and time-consuming ''browsers.''

- You have agreed to canvass several neighborhoods on behalf of a candidate for Congress. The problem is what to say to members of households as they come to their front doors.

We could suggest an endless list of similar settings, some involving only brief segments of a busy day and others that are more structured and sustained. All represent instances that illustrate how the normal patterns of daily life require attempts to influence others. Moreover, in contrast to stereotypes of persuasion, it is interesting to note that some of these instances suggest that influence is not always driven by selfish motives but often by a passion for ideas or a genuine concern for the welfare of others.

## What These Cases Suggest

### Message and Advocate Intertwined

We chose the cases in the first part of this chapter for their diversity. Even so, they share features that give recognizable form to attempts to change attitudes. All remind us that persuasion is a symbolic act that inevitably focuses on advocates as well as messages. In persuasion, the person communicating matters a great deal. Messages do not stand alone; consumers weigh both the credibility of advocates as well as the quality of their messages. Wilson felt that his presidential prestige could command a following sufficient to produce a constructive peace. With terrible efficiency, Jim Jones and David Koresh used their popularity to attract followers to their increasingly demented ideas.

### Persuasion as an Amoral Process

These examples also remind us that the process of attempting to change attitudes is neither inherently good nor bad. Each case must be considered on its own merits. The self-centered evangelism of Jim Jones and David Koresh is alarming. R. J. Reynolds' advertising campaign raises questions about the ethics of promoting a product with known health risks, an issue compounded by the fact that the targeted group already exhibited high instances of stress and health-related problems. Wilson's failed attempts, however, illustrate a series of persuasive events that might have prevented a second war. His quest for a nonpunitive peace still offers some tantalizing "ifs": if only he had been more flexible, if the Senate had been more supportive, if the Allies had not given Germany justifications for revenge. Persuasion may spring from selfish motivations or altruistic ones. We may gain money or prestige from our abilities to influence others, or—at the other extreme—we may act out of a genuine regard for the welfare of those we seek to influence. Although we may harshly judge much persuasion as "propaganda" or "manipulation," we could cite countless instances from personal experience where persuasion has served as a "therapeutic" form of communication—helping rather than exploiting.

### Unpredictability

Taken together, these cases also serve as a reminder of how unpredictable persuasion is. Sophisticated marketing plans and huge advertising budgets may not be enough to guarantee acceptance of a new form of controversial product. The situation Wilson faced was far more complex than R. J. Reynolds', and the hindsight of history suggests that Wilson hoped to do too much. He wanted to activate world opinion around his Fourteen Points, but even the fine-tuned messages of a respected expert orator were no match for deep-seated attitudes and opinions. Most clearly, the tragedies of Jonestown and Waco present an enormous puzzle. Those events carry a grim fascination; we struggle to understand how one person can engineer and manipulate such lethal doses of persuasion. We assume that no amount of influence could give legitimacy to·acts of mass suicide.

### Frequently a Private Rather Than Public Process

Finally, the first three cases should not distract us from the fact that persuasion is as much personal as it is institutional. We often dwell on dramatic, headline-making attempts because such instances serve as obvious and interesting illustrations. Ultimately, the persuasive options that presidents, advertisers, and social activists face are very similar to the options the rest of us must also consider. Persuasion that organizations produce is not very different in form from the day-to-day communication we have with friends, co-workers, and family. Indeed, it is within the context of our own immediate contacts that the most significant attitudes are shaped. As Philip Zimbardo, Ebbe Ebbesen, and Christina Maslach have noted,

> It is impossible to overestimate the extent to which you are influenced daily to be the kind of person other people want you to be. "Tastes" in food, dress, art, music, friends, hobbies, and other things are acquired through subtle interpersonal influence processes. . . . The language you speak, your dialect, pronunciation, hand gestures, body semantics, and displays of affection or temper are all the products of how people communicated in your family, neighborhood, and cultural subgroup.[20]

# Persuasion as a Subject for Study

## The Love-Hate Relationship

The variety of cases we have cited—commercial, religious, political, and "interpersonal"—reminds us that the study of persuasion attracts as well as repels. On the one hand, few questions are more intriguing than, "What makes people change their minds or alter the ways they act?" We have a natural curiosity about the ways we manipulate and influence others and how others do the same to us. Through the ages, persuasion has often exposed the darker side of human nature. In fiction and in fact, the manipulative "con artist" represents a common form of villain, whether he is selling cars or ostensibly saving souls. Villainous persuaders remind us that persuasion can succeed for all the wrong reasons. Examine lists of classic or current films. You could easily construct a rogue's gallery of stock characters who cynically exploit the fears and vanities of ordinary people—many of whom seem too ready to agree and too willing to suspend their judgment in favor of the blandishments of a glib persuader.

However, as we will explore in the next chapter, a society that confronts the realities of persuasive practice—including negative aspects—provides its citizens with a valuable service. Analyzing the forms of influence that are common to modern life is the first step in acquiring an effective form of self-defense. Knowing when a good case has been made is as valuable as knowing when it has not. Knowing how to shape events is a critical step in gaining control over our lives. The Greek philosopher Aristotle wisely emphasized knowledge of persuasive practice as a kind of survival skill:

> It is absurd to hold a man ought to be ashamed of being unable to defend himself with his limbs, but not of being unable to defend himself with speech and reason, when the use of rational speech is more distinctive of a human being than the use of his limbs. And if it be objected that one who uses such power of speech unjustly might do great harm, that is the charge which may be made against the things that are most useful, as strength, health, wealth. . . .[21]

Persuasion confers power. By putting our knowledge of it to work, we force others to share this power. Knowledge of persuasive practice provides us with the opportunity to leave our imprint on events, both big and small.

## The State of Our Knowledge

Persuasion is one of the oldest topics studied and taught in Western civilization. Aristotle was among the first great teachers of the subject. Writing one of the first texts devoted exclusively to persuasion, he believed that advocacy should be a central concern in democratic societies. *The Rhetoric* discusses the nature of attitudes, audiences, psychological appeals, and logical fallacies; it represents one of the first attempts to outline the psychology of audiences. For example, Aristotle noted that all messages should be constructed with the "character" of an audience in mind—their common traits and patterns of thought. To affect an audience of "young men," for instance, the persuader must understand their collective psychology, including some of the following traits:

> While they love honor, they love victory still more; for youth is eager for superiority over others, and victory is one form of this. They love both more than they love money, which indeed they love very little, not having yet learnt what it means to be without it. . . . They look at the good side rather than the bad, not having yet witnessed many instances of wickedness. They trust others readily, because they have not yet often been cheated.[22]

As will become apparent as you read this book, persuasion is not a subject that yields simple conclusions or easy explanations. The state of our knowledge is limited by several important conditions.

### Our Limited Ability to Predict Persuasion Effects

Aristotle wrote his text over three hundred years before the birth of Christ. Despite all of the effort that we have devoted to the subject over the last two thousand years, we still know little about the exact processes that govern attempts to influence others. We have theories but no "laws" of human persuasion. We can speculate that certain kinds of appeals may affect certain audiences under specific circumstances, but we are a long way away from a "science" that allows predictions with a high degree of certainty. Because human behavior is infinitely complex and varied, individuals do not react in consistent and predictable ways. Our knowledge of persuasion allows us only to note tendencies that may be observed in larger numbers. As you read this book, you may often find that a persuasion model does not fully account for the way *you* might behave in a given situation. For example, we cannot determine if a certain kind of anti-smoking appeal will work on a particular person, or if a few viewers of a violent and anti-social film will internalize what they have seen. All individuals carry their own special forms of psychological ballast that allow them to weather challenges to their beliefs in unpredictable ways. We can, however, estimate an appeal's probable effects on a national audience.[23]

### A Pattern of Minimal Effects

It is also important to remember that persuasion is not an easy or sudden process. Attitudes and behaviors are difficult to change. When change does occur, it evolves very slowly and almost always over a significant period of time. When we think of persuasion we often think of unusual and dramatic moments: Jim Jones in Guyana or the sudden confessions and conversions of characters in television's popular melodramas. We have an entire vocabulary that is used to account for such moments of apparent instant conversion. "Brainwashing," "indoctrination," "mind control," "subversion," and "subliminal persuasion" are only a few. In the 1930s and 1940s, for example, it was widely held that Hollywood was vulnerable to subversion by a few stratgically placed Communists who could easily gain control over the American mind through positions as union leaders, writers, and directors. One president of the powerful Screen Actors' Guild, Ronald Reagan, came to such a view. "The Communist plan for Hollywood," he noted, "was remarkably simple." Part of it would be "to gradually work into the movies the requisite propaganda attitudes . . . to soften the American public's hardening attitude toward Communism."[24]

If persuasion were only so predictable. The dramatic and sudden collapse of the Soviet system after 1986 speaks to a tougher truth. Even a society that had allegedly mastered the techniques of political propaganda—from official Komsomols for teens to nearly complete control of the mass media—could not hold back a yearning for political reform and a different kind of society.

Every student of persuasion needs to keep the "law of minimal effects" in mind. Even apparently fluent and effective messages will usually produce only minimal effects on their intended audiences.

## The Importance of Limited Effects

Even if persuasion effects are usually minimal, they are not insignificant. In the fields of politics and marketing, for example, it is useful to think of what we call the "6 percent rule." If only 6 percent of all buyers of a product or voters on election day choose other options, enormous change is possible. Many elections turn on differences between candidates that are less than 6 percent. In our recent past, such a change in the popular vote would have denied John F. Kennedy the presidency. The same difference would have given a 1968 victory to Hubert Humphrey over Richard Nixon, and probably would have resulted in a defeat for Bill Clinton in 1992.[25] The study of persuasion thus requires us to look for subtle causes and effects in order to determine what changes people and to measure the extent of these changes. While the biologist can study a specimen of diseased tissue to discover what caused an infection, the student of persuasion deals with a less certain kind of knowledge. The physical world may reveal its secrets willingly, but the mysteries of human thought are far more difficult to pinpoint. Even so, virtually all of the social sciences and professions have attempted to deal with how communication and persuasion affect their fields. Political scientists study campaigns; sociologists assess the effects of friendship and group membership; psychologists study "behavior modification"; mass media analysts track the ebb and flow of public opinion on an infinite variety of issues; schools of business offer courses in "marketing" or sales; and many of us participate in self-help groups designed to change aspects of our lives. Persuasion touches every part of our world, whether we seek money, support, friendship, conversion, or power.

# Three Types of Communication

We talk or write in order to accomplish something, even if our objective is not always fully conscious. As a result, it is useful to classify forms of human interaction that imply different intentions.

Broad but useful distinctions can be made among three types of communication: pure information-giving, pure expression, and pure persuasion. Although virtually every message type contains elements of all three, their theoretical differences are revealing.

## Pure Information

Information-giving involves the relating of facts or information where the communicator's interest is primarily in the receiver's understanding. Information givers want to be sure the receiver heard and comprehended the data that was cited. A stranger giving directions to a visitor from out of town, the Directory Assistance operator passing along a phone number, and a Weather Service report are examples of pure information-giving. Communicators of pure information may not be especially interested in how we respond beyond having us comprehend the message. With this objective, we are free to accept or reject what is said.

## Pure Expression

Pure expression is characterized by a desire to speak one's mind rather than have others agree or disagree, act or not act. We may want to unload our anger, joy, anxieties, or fears merely for the sake of the release it provides. Pure expression gives our feelings an outward form, but it is undertaken more for the pleasure it gives us than for those who overhear it. Many expressions can make us feel better: lecturing the family dog for eating the furniture, cheering on the home team, or denouncing the doctor in *General Hospital* who cheats on his faithful wife. Giving our inward feelings outward expression can be its own reward. What we say is not intended to elicit a reaction from someone else but to give vent to a rapid succession of feelings.

## Pure Persuasion

Pure persuasion is different and more complex than information-giving and expression. It involves a new dimension: a concern with how our ideas or actions will affect someone else. The persuasive message is calculated to be believed, not merely understood. It is intended to alter someone's attitudes or actions. If a listener says, "I understand what you are saying, but I do not accept it," the information giver who has no personal stake in acceptance or rejection of a message may be satisfied. The persuader, however, looks for signs of commitment and approval, and perhaps evidence of the persuadee's willingness to use the new ideas as a reference point for future thought and conduct.

In reality, these forms often overlap. For example, statistics on automobile seat belt use indicate that wearing belts saves lives. These numbers are—in a simple sense—pieces of information. It is also easy to imagine a persuader using them with the intention of gaining support for state-imposed fines on individuals who refuse to wear seat belts. If a listener responds by saying that he or she understands the statistics, the persuader might ask impatiently, "Yes, but do you accept my conclusion?" Advocates want commitment as well as understanding. We often hear the expression, "Here are the facts, take them or leave them," from teachers, journalists, and others. That expression usually conceals the hope that we will not only "take" the facts but will accept the larger visions of the world that they imply. A good deal of persuasion occurs under the pretext of information-giving. Most of us are not as indifferent as we may seem to how others accept our statements. As we note in chapter 7, all of us are motivated to find a secure place within the enormous maze of immediate contacts that make up our lives. We want to be liked, so we seek approval for our feelings and frustrations. The urge to have others identify with our attitudes and values runs deep.

Does this mean that all communication is persuasive? Have the authors fallen into the "expert's disease" of describing their subject as the inevitable center of the universe? To both questions, we give a qualified no.

Communication and persuasion are not interchangeable terms. Not all communicators have as their primary goal the listener's acceptance of the legitimacy and importance of their messages. Scientists and journalists, for instance, may have more simple informational goals. Even so, persuasion is a far more common process than may at first be evident. We frequently do want our messages to change the way others think, act, and feel. It may be the exception rather than the rule when a communicator feels genuine indifference about how a message affects us. Even in the seemingly light-hearted world of prime-time television, we should view statements by producers that they are "merely" producing entertainment with suspicion. This is not because there is an effort to conceal political or social messages in benign content. Rather, it is probably impossible to construct a televised fantasy without promoting some basic assumptions: for example, that doctors are healers first and businessmen second, that the police uphold rather than manipulate the law, or that families have the capacity to solve their toughest domestic problems.

## Persuasion Defined

Most definitions of persuasion are similar, although some emphasize processes more than specific outcomes. In an unusual departure from both forms, Daniel O'Keefe declines to define the concept at all, noting that any definition sets up boundaries that are partially arbitrary.

Instead, he describes a number of features that are almost always found in typical or "paradigm" cases of persuasion. The norm of such messages includes having a specific goal in mind, achieving it through the use of language or symbols, and producing "a change in the mental state of the persuadee." O'Keefe also notes that true persuasion implies "some measure of freedom (free will, free choice, voluntary action)." Forcing others to act is not the same thing as truly persuading them.[26] Erwin Bettinghaus begins his study of the subject by observing that a persuasive situation involves "a conscious attempt by one individual to change the attitudes, beliefs, or the behavior of another individual or group of individuals through the transmission of some message."[27] Similarly, Herbert Simons describes persuasion as primarily "a process of communication designed to modify the judgments of others."[28]

We endorse all of these traits, but with several special emphases. The important qualifier offered by Bettinghaus that persuasion may affect behavior as well as judgments and attitudes is especially relevant. A message may affect a person's feelings, behaviors, or both. We may induce someone to act differently (for example, to taste what seems like an awful kind of food) but not fundamentally affect the way they feel. Conversely, persuasion may create internal changes that are not readily seen in the way a person acts. Internal attitudes and external acts are different but equally valid outcomes of persuasive attempts. In addition, we would slightly amend the definitions of persuasion by Simons and Bettinghaus to include the possibility of **strengthening** existing attitudes and actions in addition to modifying or changing them. While persuasion is most apparent when a transformation of some sort occurs within an individual, an exclusive emphasis on change overlooks the pervasive role of communication which is intended to prevent the erosion of support. As most advertisers know, the most effective persuasive strategies are essentially defensive. It is easier to reassure a listener's faith in what is already accepted than to urge change to something new. Advertising is often a strategy to protect a product's present market share. The rituals of the church and the political campaigns of heavily favored incumbents do much the same. An exclusive emphasis on persuasion as an offensive tool (that is, against "old" actions or attitudes)

*Politicians work to heighten positive feelings—to provide encouragement to maintain current opinions.*

*Tribune* photo by Jose More

ignores the elaborate efforts of many persuaders to keep things as they are, to keep the lid on a simmering pot rather than encouraging it to boil over. For instance, many people who attend political rallies at election time already believe in the candidacy of the speakers. Rallies heighten positive feelings (or make them less dormant) and may guarantee continuity by providing reasons against changing attitudes. Like the advertisements we have heard thousands of times for McDonald's or Chevrolet, persuasion often serves to keep feelings stable. The fact that positive feelings already exist does not necessarily relieve the persuader of the need to maintain them.

Thus, we define persuasion as a process composed of five constant dimensions.

## THE PERSUASIVE PROCESS

Persuasion is

1. the process of preparing and delivering
2. verbal and nonverbal messages
3. to autonomous individuals
4. in order to alter or strengthen
5. their attitudes, beliefs, or behaviors.

Our definition covers a range of desired outcomes including reinforcing or changing attitudes and affecting the ways people think as well as act. With O'Keefe, we also note that persuasion is directed to autonomous individuals who have the freedom to reject or accept the appeals of advocates. The first clause of our definition emphasizes the processes of planning as well as presenting persuasive messages. We think a complete understanding of persuasion necessarily includes considering the art and technique of influence, not just its outcomes. In order to understand how the processes of influence work, it is necessary to apply theories of persuasion to practical problems. While it may be possible to appreciate music without being a musician, we doubt if it is possible to appreciate persuasive communication fully without actually understanding the strategic thinking that goes into its preparation.

Obviously, the study of this complex topic is not simple. In spite of the plethora of self-help books, pop-psychology tracts, and simple "recipes for success" that offer instruction on changing our lives and the lives of those around us, the assumption that one individual or group can discover simple nostrums for altering thought and action is largely a myth. The realities of all human encounters are too complex to be reduced to formulas. If it is to be understood at all, the process of persuasion requires an open mind and a capacity to live with conditional rather than certain truths. The study of persuasion requires mental gymnastics that can balance a sensitivity to language with an appreciation for the immensely varied and elusive patterns of human thought.

## Questions and Projects for Further Study

1. As this chapter suggests, persuasion comes to us through many channels: advertising, face-to-face encounters. and news reports about issues and advocates. Try to audit your own exposure to these sources of persuasion in one day. Keep a written log recording the number and types of advertisements you hear or see in newspapers, magazines, and broadcasts. Keep a record of the news and information sources you see and hear which contain bits and pieces of persuasive messages (for example, a film clip in a newscast in which a doctor warns viewers about the dangers of some product or activity). Note how frequently conversations with others contain requests for your agreement, time, or money.

2. The case of Uptown cigarettes raises questions about the limits of legitimate persuasion. In particular, is advertising of potentially harmful (but legal) products the right of a company or should advertisers be held to a different standard? What responsibilities do

consumers bear for making their own judgments about such targeted advertising?

3. Some analysts have suggested that Jim Jones was a more effective persuader in the remote jungle in Guyana than in the United States. What differences are evident in the two settings which might explain the increased allegiance of his followers in remote Jonestown? How do less dramatic changes in settings (such as moving from home to a college campus) affect individuals?

4. Woodrow Wilson's successors now travel to their destinations on Air Force One rather than by train. What other technologies make the "whistle stop" tour unnecessary or ineffective? Do listeners and viewers who only read printed remarks know as much about a president as those who see the chief executive "in the flesh"?

5. Look through a magazine, newspaper, or this text for statements that first appear to be informational but actually argue for a particular point of view. In the examples you find, how is the persuasive intent hidden from the casual reader? How can persuasion be concealed as "information"?

6. As the Jonestown case suggests, strong leadership may bring misery upon those who succumb to it. Identify other examples of destructive persuasion. Identify positive cases that suggest persuasion can be a constructive process. Compare your examples with a friend.

7. The authors suggest that it may be possible to change someone's behavior but not necessarily his or her attitudes. Describe a scenario where this might occur. Also attempt the reverse: a scenario where attitudes may change but not a person's actions.

8. Using examples of your own choice, probe the five features of the authors' definition of persuasion. How adequate are they? Does the definition fail to account for certain kinds of persuasion?

9. In this chapter the authors have noted that persuasion is generally an unpredictable process. Cite several reasons why it is difficult to predict if and how specific individuals will be persuaded by a particular message.

## Notes

[1] Max Black, *The Labyrinth of Language.* New York: Mentor, 1969, p. 12.

[2] Adam Clymer, "Daughter of Slavery Hushes Senate," *New York Times,* July 23, 1993, p. B6.

[3] *Ibid.*

[4] Anthony Ramirez, "A Cigarette Campaign Under Fire," *New York Times,* January 12, 1990, p. D4.

[5] *Ibid.*

[6] Philip J. Hilts, "Health Chief Assails a Tobacco Producer for Aiming at Blacks," *New York Times*, January 19, 1990, p. A1.

[7] *Ibid.*, p. A20.

[8] Bradley Johnson, "Anti-Smoke Torch Flickers," *Advertising Age*, April 16, 1990, p. 66.

[9] B. Drummond Ayres, Jr., "Philip Morris on Offensive in California," *New York Times*, May 16, 1994, pp. A1, A12.

[10] *Chicago Tribune*, March 15, 1996, Section 1, p. 24.

[11] Comparisons between Jones and Koresh abound. See, for example, Melinda Liu and Todd Barrett, "Hard Lessons in the Ashes," *Newsweek*, May 3, 1993, p. 31.

[12] Jones quoted in Jeannie Mills, *Six Years With God*. New York: Times Books, 1979, p. 317.

[13] *Ibid.*, p. 319.

[14] Jones quoted in James Reston, Jr. *Our Father Who Art in Hell*. New York: Times Books, 1981, p. 324.

[15] Wilson, Address to Congress, January 8, 1918, in *The Politics of Woodrow Wilson*, ed. August Heckscher. New York: Harper, 1956, p. 306.

[16] Samuel and Dorothy Rosenman, *Presidential Style: Some Giants and a Pygmy in the White House*. New York: Harper and Row, 1976, pp. 256–59.

[17] Wilson quoted in *Ibid.*, p. 258.

[18] Erving Goffman, *The Presentation of Self in Everyday Life*. New York: Anchor, 1959, p. 15.

[19] *Ibid.*, pp. 121–22.

[20] Philip G. Zimbardo, Ebbe B. Ebbesen and Christina Maslach, *Influencing Attitudes and Changing Behavior*, Second Edition. Boston: Addison-Wesley, 1979, p. 1.

[21] *The Rhetoric*, trans. by W. R. Roberts in *The Basic Works of Aristotle*, ed. by Richard McKeon. New York: Random House, 1941, p. 1328.

[22] *Ibid.*, p. 1404.

[23] See, for example, Melvin L. Defleur and Everette E. Dennis, *Understanding Mass Communication*, updated 1996 Edition. Boston: Houghlin Mifflin, 1991, pp. 571–79.

[24] Ronald Reagan, *Where's the Rest of Me?* New York: Karz, 1981, p. 163.

[25] The 1992 election was made more complex by the presence of Ross Perot, who got 19% of the popular vote. However, obviously, a 6% switch from one candidate to another could happen if only 3% of the voters changed their minds.

[26] Daniel J. O'Keefe, *Persuasion: Theory and Research*. Newbury Park, CA: Sage, 1990, pp. 15–16.

[27] Erwin B. Bettinghaus, *Persuasive Communication*, Fifth Edition. Fort Worth, TX: Harcourt Brace, 1994, p. 6.

[28] Herbert W. Simons, *Persuasion: Understanding and Practice*, Second Edition. New York: Random House, 1986, p. 24.

# Additional Reading

Aristotle, *The Rhetoric*, trans. by W. R. Roberts in *The Basic Works of Aristotle*, ed. by Richard McKeon. New York: Random House, 1941.

Erwin P. Bettinghaus, *Persuasive Communication*, Fifth Edition. Ft. Worth, TX: Harcourt Brace, 1994.

J. A. C. Brown, *Techniques of Persuasion: From Propaganda to Brainwashing*. New York: Penquin, 1972.

Erving Goffman, *The Presentation of Self in Everyday Life*. New York: Anchor, 1959.

George N. Gordon, *Persuasion: The Theory and Practice of Manipulative Communication*. New York: Hastings House, 1971.

Daniel J. O'Keefe. *Persuasion: Theory and Research*. Newbury Park, CA: Sage, 1990.

Herbert W. Simons, *Persuasion: Understanding, Practice, and Analysis*, Second Edition. New York: Random House, 1986. (Boston: Addison-Wesley, 1976).

Philip G. Zimbardo, Ebbe B. Ebbesen, and Christina Maslach, *Influencing Attitudes and Changing Behavior*, Second Edition. Boston: Addison-Wesley, 1977.

# Origins of
# Persuasive Practice

# I

On one level, persuasion is an unavoidable human tendency. On another, it is a hard-earned and precious political right. Like all forms of communication, persuasion depends on the uniquely human attribute of symbol-using. The natural inclination to influence each other works best if we select the "right" symbols to guide thought and action. A universal feature of skillful persuaders in every corner of the world is their sensitivity to the socially constructed meanings that are triggered by words and symbols. Language and symbols rule our mental lives; they shape our perceptions of what we "know," what we believe, and what we disdain or desire. Symbols represent the basic materials of communication available to every advocate in every kind of society. In order to understand how persuasion in the United States works, we believe that it is also necessary to rediscover the political and social milieu that sanctions the right to engage in public persuasion. Advocacy in our society is grounded on more than a single requirement to master language. It rests on the shared belief that constructive conflict and public debate have important roles in transforming and renewing vital institutions. Chapter 2 begins with a look at some of these important but often neglected beliefs. In chapter 3 we go on to review the vital role that symbol-using plays in all forms of persuasion.

# 2

# The Advocate in
# an Open Society

## OVERVIEW

We can never be sure that the opinion we are endeavoring to stifle is a false opinion; and if we were sure, stifling it would be an evil still.[1]

—John Stuart Mill

Persuasion is a universal feature of human life. In every society, influence directed to co-workers, family members, and friends is part of the fabric of daily existence. Some persuasive opportunities are available only to members of democratic institutions or societies: cultures and groups where many decisions are subject to the prior approval of public opinion. The essential idea of a democracy is that power is shared by a variety of citizens who are, at various times, both the initiators and the recipients of influence. This intimate link between democracy and persuasion is the subject of this chapter.

## The Rushdie Affair and the Open Society

In the winter of 1989, a story surfaced that could have come out of the fiction of a Robert Ludlum novel, but it was chillingly true. The leader of a nation publicly called for the murder of a writer, with a promise of a $5 million reward to the "patriot" who successfully carried out the execution. The object of this death threat was British author Salman Rushdie. His 1988 book, *The Satanic Verses,* enraged Iran's spiritual leader, the Ayatollah Ruhollah Khomeini.

Khomeini was regarded by many Americans as a dangerous foe and an unexpected political phenomenon. The aging fundamentalist had accomplished what few political or religious leaders thought was possible in modern times, engineering a 1979 political revolution that would give enormous power to a minority of elderly religious clerics. One of the first products of his revolution, the humiliating and protracted taking of American hostages, dominated the 1980 presidential campaign. Ten years later, the death sentence on Rushdie again dramatized the enormous schism separating East and West.

In the 1980s Iran was essentially a medieval theocracy. Some of its fervent Shiite leaders saw the revolution as a chance to purge their culture of the Western "modernism" forced upon it by Shah Reza Pahlavi. After his overthrow, conservative clerics, who had long decried ties to the "great satan" of the United States, vowed to establish a true Islamic state based on the centuries-old doctrines and customs of ancient Islam.[2] Like all religious beliefs, Islamic precepts are subject to wide varieties of interpretation. Under Khomeini's influence, Iranian society became far less tolerant and more totalitarian than other predominantly Islamic states.

Iran changed from a monarchy out of touch with its people to a closed society smothered by clerics who would not—and perhaps could not—relinquish their dogmatism. The national identity was tied to a dogma that rejected anything that carried a Western imprint—including traditions of political and ideological tolerance. Any remnants of the rich Iranian past that suggested tolerance, experimentation, or change were rejected. Coercion replaced dialogue, and conformity extinguished much of the nation's diversity.

The primary function of religious teachings in every society is to prescribe moral and immoral behavior for individuals. In our society, obedience to these doctrines is a matter of personal choice, a fact reflected in the First Amendment clause guaranteeing freedom of religion. The sacred and the secular are separated in many societies. A very different culture results when sacred beliefs are codified into constitutional law. When religious doctrine becomes official state doctrine, the freedom of individuals can be swept aside in a tide of righteous certainty. In modern Iran, members of dissident sects have been executed, exiled, or officially ignored. Most of the nation's courts, mass media, and schools are closely monitored by Shiite clerics.[3] Some issues of state are still vigorously debated in Iran's parliament and newspapers, but Iran's theocracy requires a high level of obedience on issues ranging from foreign policy to matters of how women should dress. In large cities, patrols of vigilantes impose conformity on various citizens who may have strayed beyond attitudes or actions deemed appropriate to the goals of the revolution. One group, the sisters of Zaynab, patrol the streets in special cars and pounce on unsuspecting offenders guilty of the slightest improper exposure.[4]

In this context, it is easy to see why Rushdie became the focus of Khomeini's fury. His book is a fantasy about immigrants told partly through the dreams and events that beset its principal characters, two Indian actors named Gibreel and Saladin. Most of it has very little to do with religion, although it is filled with the musings of its protagonists about the sometimes jarring differences between Anglo-American and Eastern cultures.

In two chapters Rushdie describes Gibreel's dream about a religion that has obvious similarities with Islam. The middle-aged actor, a not very devout Muslim living in the fictitious London enclave of Brickhall, dreams about a worldly and calculating faith inspired by a prophet named "Mahound." His fantasy parallels the Islamic belief that the Koran is the literal word of God passed on to the prophet Mohammad by the angel Gabriel. In Gibreel's fantasy, a character named Salman is fed up with a religion of arbitrary rules and obvious hypocrisies:

> Amid the palm-trees of the oasis Gibreel appeared to the Prophet and found himself spouting rules, rules, rules, until the faithful could scarcely bear the prospect of any more revelation, Salman said, rules about every damn thing. . . . It was as if no aspect of human existence was to be left unregulated, free. The revelation — the recitation — told the faithful how much to eat, how deeply they should sleep, and which sexual positions had received divine sanction. . . . And Gibreel the archangel specified the manner in which a man should be buried, and how his property should be divided, so that Salman the Persian got to wondering what manner of God this was that sounded like a businessman. This was when he had the idea that destroyed his faith, because he recalled that of course Mahound himself had been a businessman, and a damned successful one at that, a person to whom organization and rules came naturally . . .[5]

The book's title is itself a reference to the Islamic belief that the devil actually set out to trick Gabriel by having Muhammad include "satanic" verses as part of the holy word of the Koran.[6]

By October of 1988 the novel had been banned by the Indian government, and its sale was restricted in Saudi Arabia, Pakistan, and Egypt. Khomeini then decided to issue his own proclamation. In February 1989, one of his aides read the ominous death sentence on Rushdie, his publishers, and potentially anyone who was involved in its sale. The message to "all proud Muslims of the world" was delivered over Iranian radio by an aide:

> The author of *The Satanic Verses* book — which has been compiled, printed, and published in opposition to Islam, the Prophet, and the Koran — and all those involved in its publication who were aware of its content, are sentenced to death.[7]

Khomeini's action was defended by the president of Iran as "an irrevocable dictum."

The threats to Rushdie shocked the Western literary world. Devout Muslims, editorialized the *New York Times*, "have every right to denounce his novel, but they offend civilization when they clamor for his death."[8] He was soon given 24-hour police protection and moved from his home to a series of secret safe houses. The offices of Viking/Penguin, Rushdie's publishers, also beefed up their security. In response to phone threats that came to many booksellers, hundreds of individual stores — including two chains: B. Dalton and Walden Books — initially removed *The Satanic Verses* from their shelves.[9] Even after Khomeini's death in June of 1989, the author continued to receive new warnings from clerics in Iran.

The Rushdie affair had clearly challenged some of the most cherished values held in the West. Did any author's words deserve such condemnation? Is there ever a legitimate reason to censor a writer's criticism, even when his ideas or beliefs are unpopular? None of these questions would produce unanimous agreement in any society. Indeed, debates

*Salman Rushdie responded to protests against his* Satanic Verses *by asserting that without the freedom to challenge all orthodoxies, freedom of expression ceases to exist.*

about what constitutes permissible discussion — most recently in the areas of music, photography, and religion — have flared up in the United States.[10] Most residents of democracies expect that the bounds of social and religious comment will be broadly drawn. An open society is likely to produce ideas that occasionally offend or challenge mainstream beliefs. It is an article of faith in liberal democracies that a culture is often enriched by such diversity. "What is freedom of expression?" Rushdie asked in a *Newsweek* essay after one year in hiding. "Without the freedom to offend, it ceases to exist. Without the freedom to challenge, even to satirize all orthodoxies, including religious orthodoxies, it ceases to exist."[11]

## Tolerance, Democracy, and Persuasion: Early Debates

Humankind has long struggled with the question of how much conformity should be forced upon individuals within a society. Since humans are by nature social and since living together requires common rules (i.e., whether to drive on the left or the right side of the road, whether criticizing others will be a crime, whether children shall be required to attend school), governments have always sought to impose laws and policies that civilize daily life. In a totalitarian system, the price of citizenship is often enforced silence. In a more open society, institutions and governments depend on public discussion and the legitimacy that public support provides.

Since the first glimmerings of democracy in Greece 800 years before the birth of Christ, there have been strong disagreements about the "best" forms of social organization. Teachers and philosophers in the earliest civilizations groped with questions about the degree to which people needed to be led and guided by strong rulers. To what extent should the rules and choices that bind us to the community be self-imposed? Who should govern the activities of the individual in the culture: the individual, or those who act in the name of the society and the state? These questions hold no great mystery for us today. We are nurtured from childhood in the values and attitudes of individualism, tolerance, freedom of thought and speech. We assume that we have the right to influence others, just as they have the right to attempt to persuade us. We routinely believe that everyone has the option to attempt to make claims upon our loyalties: to sell us soap, to encourage us to vote for a candidate for Congress, to speak out against a foreign policy decision of our government. Collectively, these are rights of expression: rights to praise, criticize, seek supporters, as well as the right to resist such appeals. They are so familiar to us that we take them for granted.

## Plato and the Sophists:
## The Feud over the Value of Public Opinion

Societies which tolerate a wide range of individual freedoms are the exception rather than the rule. Those who have argued against permitting dissent and vigorous public debate have had powerful allies. The great philosopher Plato is perhaps the most important traditional opponent of democracy and self-government. A brief sketch of his reasoning reveals several key ideas that still have credibility today.

Plato spent much of his adult life at his academy on the edge of Athens arguing that democratic states were bound to fail. He thought ordinary people were incapable of making decisions about their communities because they lacked the intelligence and thorough training necessary for decision making. Plato felt that democracies were governed by mobs unable to separate rhetoric from reason.[12] Few citizens were capable of discriminating between the thoughtful judgments of the well-trained leader — described in *The Republic* as the "philosopher king" — and the irrational "pandering" of the well-trained persuader. Because the democratic leader owed his power to the people, he would play to their fears and fantasies rather than to the more important needs of the nation. The leader chosen by popular will would substitute flattery of the "mob" in place of true wisdom. To Plato, leaders guided by public opinion were bound to be as misguided as teachers who let their pupils decide what should be taught.

Plato's view, however, did not go unchallenged. A prolonged debate over the wisdom of democracy developed between him and other teachers who traveled through the city-democracies along the coasts of Greece, Sicily, and Italy. Plato was among the few philosophers of his era to write down what his intellectual adversaries thought. He was deeply troubled and frustrated by the activities of these independent tutors whom affluent parents hired to educate their male children. (The enlightenment of the Hellenic world ended short of including women, slaves, and the impoverished as full citizens—even in democratic Athens.) Among the first tutors was Corax, who taught public speaking skills to citizens who needed to improve their persuasive abilities in legal and political settings. Plato scorned Corax and other itinerant teachers, who were collectively known as Sophists. We suspect that he disliked them partly because they worked outside of the prestigious intellectual center of Athens and partly because they accepted fees on a pay-per-lesson basis. Plato was particularly irked that virtually all of these teachers taught the techniques of persuasion—techniques that were potentially dangerous. His dislike of the Sophists was so strong that he named some of the weak-thinking characters in his dialogues after several of them. It is a tribute to Plato's prestige that the term "sophistic" still survives as a label of scorn for people who play too loosely with truth and fact.

The case of Gorgias is especially interesting. In a famous dialogue against the practice of teaching persuasion, Plato writes parts for his own honored teacher, Socrates, and his democratically inclined opposite, Gorgias. In the dialogue, Gorgias is portrayed as a fifth-century-B.C. version of a shady used car salesman. He is no match for Socrates' superior wisdom.[13] The real Gorgias was born in Sicily but taught and gave performances in many cities, including Olympia, Delphi, and Athens.[14] Like all Sophists, he taught many different subjects but always the art of persuasion. According to W. C. Guthrie, "a special feature of his displays was to invite miscellaneous questions from the audience and give impromptu replies." To his credit, "he saw the power of persuasion as paramount in every field, in the study of nature and other philosophical subjects no less than in the law-courts or the political arena."[15] Like many of his contemporaries, Gorgias believed that the freedom to speak in defense of opinions and beliefs required skill in knowing how to hold an audience's attention and how to shape their attitudes.

Plato took issue with Gorgias and other Sophists on several important points. Most basically, they disagreed about the certainty of truth and the importance of public opinion. Plato believed that most issues that invited persuasion had a single best or "true" answer. Beauty, for example, was not in the eye of the beholder, but closer or farther from the ideal of *perfect* beauty. Likewise, he felt that large concepts such as justice were not tied to individual values or specific circumstances, but to "perfect" (and perhaps unknowable) forms. We might fall short of actually knowing all that can be discovered about an idea, but better knowledge is always possible. Seriously considering what other people think, he felt, was simply a wasted detour from the path of truth. Since there is perfect truth, perfect justice and perfect beauty, the best life is spent working toward perfection rather than the lure of popular approval.

The Sophists believed that many questions of public dispute were not solvable by application of rigorous reasoning; they were better determined by appeals to public opinion. For instance, the question of who would be most qualified to lead a government could not be settled by reference to one single standard. There may be no single "true" choice, but a range of acceptable options based on the specific interests and priorities of different people. One leader may be better for one group but not for another. On policy issues, "good" solutions may change as public attitudes change. If we apply this principle to a contemporary issue, we could argue that a policy of giving out automatic jail terms to convicted drug users is "good"—whatever its merits in curbing the sale and use of illegal substances—as long as it continues to enjoy public support. Given this view, there is no way that individual facts or truths can substitute for how we *collectively* feel about an idea. As members of groups, we have values that lead us to certain kinds of preferences. The *pluralism* of societies composed of mixed racial, religious, and ethnic groups leads us to recognize that others may have their own good reasons for disagreeing with us on topics as diverse as prayer in public schools and the rights of mothers and fetuses under state abortion laws. In democracies, public attitudes are and should be formed by reference to the consensus that emerges (or sometimes fails to emerge) when our values and attitudes are subject to public debate.

For the Sophists, and for democracies in general, public opinion is everything. Perhaps the clearest statement to that effect came from Protagoras, who offered a convenient declaration which could serve as a seven-word definition of democracy. He said "*Man is the measure of all things . . .*"[16] In matters that affect the collective welfare of a society, the people should be left with the power to judge what is just, true, and fair for themselves.

The concept that "man is the measure" is useful in two senses. First, it implies that many issues that spark public persuasion and controversy are about *preferences* rather than truths or ultimate answers. In a decision as trivial as which brand of soap to buy, or as important as a decision to speak against a colleague's proposal, the final choice is personal and unique to our situation. What we think and how we feel determines how we act. The Sophists felt that no quest for absolute truth could remove the responsibility of making choices from a politician, a legislature, or the electorate. Groups and constituencies have different answers and attitudes that may be addressed and changed by outsiders. They made the common-sense observation that most answers to complex problems cannot be rendered totally "false" or useless for all people at all times.

Second, the idea that "man is the measure of all things" can serve as a refreshing reminder that, ultimately, persuaders must have faith in the good sense of an audience to locate both the wisdom and the "puffery" that comes with public debate. Plato's student, Aristotle, seemed to find the right middle ground. He opened his persuasion text by stating a belief in the ultimate soundness of public opinion formed by exposure to various sides of a dispute. Persuasion, he noted, "is useful because things that are true and things that are just have a natural tendency to prevail over their opposites . . ."[17] People, he felt, can judge for themselves. In closed societies where decisions are reserved for the few, there will be hostility to competition from others and the "unofficial" explanation of events. The totalitarian leader can be expected to claim that a variety of viewpoints will "confuse" and "bewilder" the ordinary public. The democrat, in contrast, shares the populist's faith that the public can find its own best answers in the give and take of full and vigorous discussion.

## America Emerges: The Debate Renewed

Colonial America inherited a strong intellectual tradition in favor of the individual's right to engage in public persuasion. The French roots of the Enlightenment, the ideas of British thinkers such as John Milton and John Locke, and the steady increase in the powers of Britain's Parliament all had their liberalizing effects. From these European origins, the colonists had acquired a belief in the "natural rights" of man— freedoms given eloquent expression in the Bill of Rights and the Declaration of Independence. Underpinning these liberties was faith in reason and the freedom necessary to give human logic its rightful reign.

In addition to their philosophical reasons, citizens of the colonies had the more practical goal of establishing local democratic governments to replace the frequently indifferent colonial administrations. They wanted to be able to confront those who were legislating decisions—an impossibility when the seat of authority was in London. After the War of Independence, they designed independent states and adapted the basic principles and models of the governments that they had known in Europe. They attempted to secure for themselves what England had provided for its own citizens: local government and direct access to the legislative process. They also had pragmatic reasons for breaking with England. Many families had come to the new world years earlier as religious dissidents, most notably Baptists, Quakers, and Catholics. They sought safety in their adopted land by creating governments that were tolerant of their differences. Liberty to speak out or to practice a religion different from one's neighbor was a kind of self-protection. By moving to the establishment of a confederation of states to replace rule by a monarchy, the newly independent Americans attempted to assure that decisions affecting their lives would be subject to public discussion rather than private dictate.

The actual task of inventing a government in the late 1780s was not as easy as it might have seemed. The founders of the United States had to deal with one of the questions that divided Plato and the Sophists: how strong a role should persuasion and public opinion play in setting policy?

Among the most eloquent voices heard was Thomas Jefferson's. As the unofficial philosopher of American independence and writer of its declaration, he expressed enormous faith in the ordinary citizen and favored local governments with direct ties to the "grass roots." Jefferson is remembered for his strong opposition to a centralized federal government, but his belief in the wisdom of the common person and localized governance was not universally shared. Other founders such as James Madison and Alexander Hamilton had limited faith in how free citizens would ultimately exercise their liberty. They argued for the need to balance the dangers of "factions" against broad individual freedoms. They feared the "turbulence and contention" of pure democracies. "Factions"—their code word for angry citizens who could rise up and replace a ruling party or group by force or majority rule—had to be checked. "So strong is this propensity of mankind to fall into mutual animosities," noted Madison, "that where no substantial occasion presents itself the most frivolous and fanciful distinctions have been sufficient to kindle unfriendly passions."[18] Madison and other founders wanted to protect land and property owners from mob rule and unchecked public opinion. Jefferson wrote the Declaration's words, "all men are created equal," but few of his colleagues were willing to accept the idea that each should have an equal say in the society and its government. They wanted an orderly and stable society, something not necessarily guaranteed in one-person-one-vote democracies.

So the colonists settled on a safer alternative that provided a layer of insulation between the supposedly unpredictable passions of ordinary citizens and the cooler reasoning of those who would probably run the government. They formed a *republic*, not strictly a government "*of* the people" but a government of representatives who would be elected to act *for* the people. Even after the Constitution was adopted in 1789, only the members of Congress could vote for a president, and citizen voting was restricted to white male landowners. On the whole, the Constitution was intended as much to protect wealth and property as to insure the natural rights of the citizens who warred against the British.

Speaking for many others, Madison noted that "a pure democracy" was "no cure for the mischiefs of faction."[19] For him, a republic was a safe refuge from rapid changes in public opinion. Even to this day, the Senate of the United States functions as an institution of republican government. Senators are insulated from the public's wrath for six years at a time, and each state has two senators rather than representation based on population. The House of Representatives is more democratic: members represent districts of roughly equal size and must face voters every two years. Even in the hallmark of open societies, there was suspicion of the power of the persuader. The fear that freedom of expression could combine with pure democracy to produce unwanted change was very real among the designers of American government. They believed in popular democracy and public persuasion, but only to

*In the House of Representatives members represent districts of roughly equal size and must face voters every two years.*

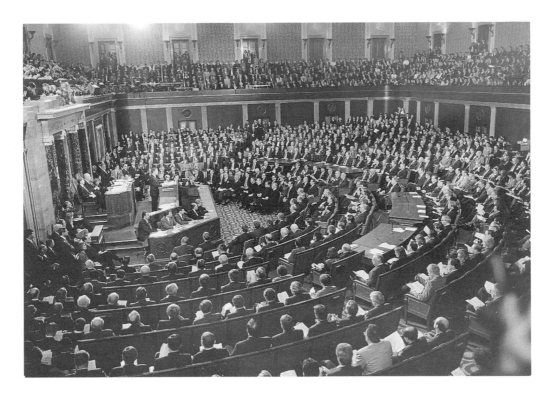

a point. Most were less certain than Jefferson who wrote that "government degenerates when trusted to the rulers of the people alone. The people themselves are therefore its only safe depositories."[20]

# The Nature of "Open" and "Closed" Societies

The British philosopher Karl Popper noted that "the open society is one in which men have learned to be to some extent critical of taboos, and to base decisions on the authority of their own intelligence."[21] A society is open when it permits discussion, dissent and criticism, when it makes argumentation and conflict part of the normal functioning of its institutions. A society is closed when its leaders determine that differing viewpoints are unnecessary and dangerous. Open societies not only tolerate free expression, they act upon the reverberations of public opinion. They guarantee the right to debate matters as diverse as religion, politics, and public policy. They sponsor genuine elections, frequently use juries rather than judges to decide cases, encourage competing voices in a variety of mass media, and foster competition among companies and products. Individuals are treated as free agents and may seek to change their status, improve their education, or alter governmental actions. Most importantly, they may organize into groups and use a wide variety of protected communication forums to seek these changes.

No society meets all of these standards. Openness is always a matter of degree. Only the most powerful Greek men had a say in public affairs. And Popper's own England—while providing the primary model for parliamentary democracies—was for many years controlled by a self-selected upper-class elite. The "old boy" network in government was largely populated by the children of the wealthy, trained in expensive private schools and channeled to the universities of Oxford or Cambridge. Even the United States has imposed restrictions on those who seem to favor "dangerous ideas." One human rights organization, for example, estimates that over 350,000 foreign citizens have been barred from visiting the United States in the 1980s, many for espousing the wrong political views.[22] Congress recently limited such practices, but the State Department may still turn down a visa request without justifying its decision.

## The Technological Push toward Openness

Freedom of expression is the machine that drives an open society. A totalitarian system sees decentralized public communication as a threat. To regulate the flow of information is to control the thoughts and ideas of citizens who might be enlightened by a variety of sources. Prior to the sweeping changes brought on by *glasnost* in the late 1980s, Soviet managers regarded the everyday photocopy machine and the video cassette recorder as potentially dangerous technologies. Such devices decentralize the flow of information, making "unofficial" points of view easy to duplicate without scrutiny for its "ideological correctness." Businessmen who used to work in the Soviet Union remember the periodic appearance of "the hammer man," a worker whose only job was to destroy photocopying machines ready for the junk pile. He always made certain that an old copier was rendered useless.[23] George Orwell's *1984* paints a similar picture of a society which sacrificed personal freedom for rigid certainty, a state which outlawed public debate in favor of centralized control of ideas and conduct — from which there was no legitimate dissent. An efficiently run "Ministry of Truth" kept citizens in a form of induced sleep.[24]

Orwell's dark vision was of a society where technology came under the exclusive control of oppressive regimes. The evolution of modern communications methods has not gone in that direction, although the new technologies do require some level of economic success. In this age of nearly universal phone service, the "fax" letter, e-mail, and easy video "uplinks" to satellites, it is now harder than ever for governmental authorities to maintain their citizens in isolated islands of limited information. "Official" ideas and "approved" versions of events are now increasingly challenged by the electronic dissemination of information that easily circumvents arbitrary political boundaries. Pro-democracy students who confronted the Chinese leadership in May of 1989 were initially helped in their Tiananmen Square protests by sympathetic journalists who beamed pictures to China's 400 stations.[25] When their cause was crushed, scores of foreign news organizations were able to circumvent the Army and continued to send out stories and pictures about the crackdown to the rest of the world. In the brutal days of repression that followed, some of the student leaders were kept abreast of events with the help of electronic mail messages sent by supporters from distant parts of the globe.

Similarly, the remarkable disintegration of the single-party dictatorships in the Soviet Union, East Germany, Poland, and elsewhere were unquestionably hastened by the increased speed with which information about the relative affluence and freedom of neighboring democracies became known. East Europeans exposed to frequent doses of broadcast and videotaped television grew steadily more impatient with the slow pace of political and economic change in their own countries. Inevitably, ever higher tides of electronic information finally swamped efforts by the old regimes to control it. Images of Western materialism especially helped plant the seeds of dissolution that later produced popular uprisings in favor of economic reforms.[26]

*This image was telecast internationally during the 1989 student unrest in China as a symbol of a citizen confronting totalitarian repression.*

## The Marketplace Theory

By whatever medium it arrives, persuasion is ultimately the tool that allows a society to renew itself. An open society is not only marked by a tolerance for differences but by the desire to see differences translated into constructive and peaceful change. The result is that new and sometimes unpopular ideas are given the chance to be heard, making government only one of a competing array of voices. Oliver Wendell Holmes counseled "that the ultimate good desired is better reached by free trade in ideas—that the best test of truth is the power of the thought to get itself accepted in the competition of the market."[27]

In an open society the presence of debate, propaganda and selling—the verbal battles of all the "factions" that James Madison worried about—gives individuals a basis for countering the power that resides in institutions and governments. In the best of circumstances, it gives them the chance to be more than cogs in someone else's wheel.

## How "Open" Is American Society?

The right to free speech—the right to persuade—is alive and well in the United States. However, it is not an absolute right, nor is it assured by a perfect marketplace for ideas. In this section we briefly examine a number of examples that suggest how far we sometimes are from the abstract ideal of free expression.

---

### Figure 2.1

### The First Amendment

The United States Constitution was written in 1787. Many delegates from the states wanted assurances that the new government it established would preserve individual liberties. Ten Amendments, also known as "The Bill of Rights," were finally adopted and took effect in 1791. Even though the wording of the First Amendment is straightforward and unequivocal, Congress, the courts, and public agencies have all placed restrictions on where Americans may meet, speak, and write.

Amendment 1: Congress shall make no law respecting an establishment of religion, or prohibiting the free exercise thereof; or abridging the freedom of speech, or of the press; or the right of the people peaceably to assemble, and to petition the Government for a redress of grievances.

---

## Governmental Controls

The first and most important amendment to the Constitution states that "Congress shall make no law . . . abridging the freedom of speech or of the press . . ." Recent history, though, is littered with examples of advocates who have been punished for the "crime" of speaking out. Since World War I, thousands of citizens have been jailed for distributing pamphlets against war, advocating the overthrow of the government, protesting against the military draft, marching against racial segregation, and joining unpopular political causes.[28] Authorities have used laws against libel (uttering "false" and defamatory accusations), trespassing, spying, disturbing the peace, marching without a permit, and impeding a criminal investigation to stifle dissent. Here are just a few representative instances that point to a variety of governmentally sanctioned curbs on the flow of ideas:

- In 1987 various libraries around the nation discovered that they were the objects of an FBI program to secure the library-lending records of foreigners. Libraries in 12 states had been asked to turn over records to the FBI so that the agency could determine if certain books had been used by persons "hostile to the United States," presumably citizens from the Soviet Union. In response, the American Library Association adopted a "Policy of Confidentiality of Library Records," but it also left open the possibility of negotiations with the FBI.[29]

- In 1963 civil rights leader Martin Luther King and 3,300 other African-Americans were arrested in Birmingham, Alabama, for parading without a permit. In most urban areas it is illegal to carry out a public protest without a permit from municipal or police officials. In Dr. King's words, "there is nothing wrong in having an ordinance which requires a permit for a parade. But such an ordinance becomes unjust when it is used to maintain segregation and to deny citizens the First-Amendment privilege of peaceful assembly and protest."[30]

- In 1990 record store owner Charles Freeman was convicted of selling obscene material in the form of a record by the rap group 2 Live Crew. At the same time, retailers in Alabama, Tennessee and Texas also faced obscenity charges for sale of the album.[31]

- In the late 1970s, the village of Orem, Utah, served a criminal summons on the owner of the town's only bookstore. The shopkeeper's offense was selling four books: *A Clockwork Orange, The Symbol, Last Tango in Paris,* and *The Idolators.* Local Ordinance 210 established a "Commission of Decency" to seek out obscene books, as well as teachers who assigned such materials to their classes.[32]

- From the outset of the 1991 war in the Persian Gulf, the United States' military command set down a series of restrictive rules for news reporters covering the conflict. During both World War II and the Vietnam War, reporters often had wide latitude to move around and visit particular locales and battlefield sites. The rules enforced by the Pentagon were generally much more restrictive, sometimes beyond the understandable need to protect the lives of troops involved in the conflict. Reporters were restricted from many battlefield locations, and they generally had to conduct interviews in the presence of military public affairs officers. Most ominous of all, stories produced by pool reporters had to be cleared by military censors.[33]

- The Supreme Court recently issued a decision limiting the rights of high school journalists to publish articles on social issues. The case arose when students at Hazelwood East High School in St. Louis prepared two articles that were pulled from the paper before it could be printed. One of the articles dealt with teen pregnancy; the second was a well-written discussion of the impact of divorce on children. Justice Byron White wrote in the majority opinion that school officials had the authority to exercise control over the style and content of student journalists. In his dissent from the Court's decision, Justice William Brennan noted that the interests of school administrators should not be used to justify the suppression of ideas they may find "embarrassing" or "distasteful."[34]

Issues that involve challenges to freedom of expression frequently require choices between competing values. In many similar instances, courts and legislatures have weighed the ideal of free expression and freedom of the press against the desire for a peaceful and orderly society. Because advocates for causes have often created inconveniences such as traffic jams or angry crowds, careful vigilance is necessary to be sure that such problems do not become a pretext for curtailing the right to persuade.

## Access to Governmental Information

Not surprisingly, the flow of information from government to the public is another area where ideals and actualities clash. A society is open to the extent that information flows freely between government and the public. "We began our society," notes press critic Ben Bagdikian, "on the principle that government exists legitimately only with the consent of the governed and that consent without significant information is meaningless."[35]

Americans generally have more access to government sources than the citizens of most other nations. Under the sweeping Freedom of Information Act (which in 1974 became a major tool for the press and the Congress to gain access to government files), federal agencies are obligated to handle requests for all kinds of information. Documents could be labeled "classified" only with good cause. The motive behind the act was the democratic idea that the public has a right to know what its government knows—with obvious exceptions such as the names of spies and certain military secrets.

However, over the years the act has been eroded by presidents and the Congress, sometimes with the apparent objective of concealing embarrassing information. For example, by 1984 Congress had denied public access to information

> submitted by manufacturers of hazardous products to the Consumer Product Safety Commission; unclassified information submitted to the Department of Energy about the production and transportation of nuclear materials; the records of professional review . . . organizations that review medical practices of institutions relying on medicaid funding . . . and information about nuclear research . . .[36]

There have been enough cases in America's recent past—the Watergate affair, Iran-Contra, and the Pike Congressional report, to name just three—to raise questions about how willing government agencies are to share what they know. During the Watergate affair, the

Nixon administration concealed information about the activities of several employees involved in spying on the Democratic Party's national headquarters. In 1986 Oliver North and others altered or destroyed documents that linked the Reagan administration to the sale of weapons to insurgents in Nicaragua—a sale specifically prohibited by Congress.[37] And in 1976, the Pike Committee report detailed secret and often illegal activities conducted in other countries by the Central Intelligence Agency. These activities became known only because someone within the Congress violated congressional rules and "leaked" the material to the press.[38] Battles over governmental secrecy will continue, primarily because large numbers of Americans have come to expect that popular government should mean open government.

## Corporate Controls

When the inventors of the Constitution incorporated the Bill of Rights, the idea of freedom of expression was easily defined. People were free to say or publish what they wanted. Our world is now very different. The flow of information occurs less as a private matter between individuals than as a process that often involves corporate participation. The privately owned mass media in the United States have increasingly replaced the back fence, the church, and the town meeting as forums in which issues of the day are discussed. In turn, they are supported by corporations who buy advertising space to reach potential consumers. With some exceptions, these advertisers are reluctant to underwrite the kinds of persuasion that may provoke public debate. They pay enormous fees to reach large audiences. One million dollars for 60 seconds in prime time television is not unusual. For such high stakes, the advertisers want to entertain and to reassure audiences rather than to inform and to provoke them. Few corporate sponsors are interested in subsidizing television programs that question or attack the audience's judgments or attitudes; the risk is too great.

Compared to our counterparts in the late 1700s and early 1800s, our knowledge of the world owes less to our neighbors and daily contacts than to the wealth of sources that come via the commercial media. Without question, our lives are enriched by ready access to the products of the nation's publishers and broadcasters, but many of these essentially private sources of information have inherited a power that the first citizens of the United States could not have envisioned. Increasingly, major corporations—rather than governments or individuals—now play a major role in encouraging and sometimes impeding the flow of information. Corporate controls on ideas occur in a variety of ways, as the following cases illustrate.

- A recent book completed by two experienced writers was suddenly cancelled by its publisher when it was learned that the book would suggest a link between the publisher and a company involved in organized crime. The book, *Connections: American Business and the Mob*, was dropped by Little, Brown and Company, a subsidiary of what is now Time-Warner, even after it had been featured in pre-release publicity. Executives of the parent company said the book was not cancelled because it would embarrass their company. Others in the publishing industry have observed that the timing of the cancellation made it difficult to accept that explanation.[39]

- Because of the way American copyright law is written, it is illegal for writers to quote song lyrics or more than a line or two of dialogue from a play or film. The law makes no significant distinction between performing a work—where the case for payment of a royalty makes sense—and quotation of a work simply for the purpose of analysis and discussion. Some authors and publishers generously grant permission to quote from their works. Others are much less willing to allow citation of their ideas. The result, notes writer and musician Gene Lees, is that "many lyrics are virtually immune to published analysis, much less criticism."[40]

- Corporations selling products often have far more money to reach their audiences than groups offering useful public information. In 1989, for example, the McDonald's Corporation spent over *one billion* dollars (one thousand million) just on advertising and promotion.[41] In the same period, the Federal Government's Consumer Information Center was given a budget of slightly more than one million dollars to provide information to consumers.[42]

- In 1982 CBS decided to pull the plug on the hour-long *Lou Grant* show for reasons that are still in dispute. The network claimed that the program about the staff of a Los Angeles newspaper had lost too much of its audience. There is also evidence that the politics of its star, veteran actor Ed Asner, was also a factor. Even before he became president of the Screen Actors' Guild, Asner had become a critic of American policy in El Salvador, a supporter of Poland's Solidarity Party, and a critic of another former SAG president, Ronald Reagan. Asner's views to some extent matched those of the crusty and concerned editor he played in the program, and advertisers began to complain. Kimberly Clark—the manufacturer of Kleenex and other products—stopped advertising on the program because of Asner's politics. After receiving 13 letters of protest from consumers, another sponsor—Vidal Sassoon—asked CBS to intervene. Sassoon's president noted that the company did not wish to be associated with any controversial political issues.[43]

- In 1982 a reporter at the *Dallas Morning News* was fired because of a story that had appeared in the paper about a local bank. The reporter wrote that the Abilene National Bank was about to fail, following a number of other cash-short savings institutions in the 1980s. The bank's president demanded the firing, even though the story was accurate. Two weeks later, federal examiners took over the Abilene National Bank, but the reporter was not rehired.[44]

• In a 1995 decision to censor itself, CBS decided to alter a segment of its popular *60 Minutes* dealing with the cigarette industry. The segment included an interview with a former Brown and Williamson Tobacco Corporation employee. Lawyers for the network advised cancellation of the interview because they feared that a nondisclosure agreement he had made with his employer might produce a lawsuit against CBS. Brown and Williamson had given no indication it would bring a suit, and attorneys doubted that a media outlet could be successfully prosecuted for interviewing such an employee.[45] Even so, an earlier suit brought against ABC by another tobacco company apparently made the network cautious. The segment eventually aired in 1996 after CBS was soundly criticized.

To be sure, the best of the mass media can be remarkably independent of the pressures and views of advertisers, but the constant need for high ratings and large circulation numbers is always a factor in the ways ideas are distributed. The founding fathers could not anticipate that public information would be so heavily tied to information industries dominated by major publishing and broadcasting chains. Their idea of popular government was to disperse rather than to centralize influence.

## The Growing Gap between Free Speech and True Access

Today when we talk of "democracies" we mean something vastly different from what the early Greeks and the American colonists had in mind. The first Mediterranean democracies were frequently limited to individual cities. Aristotle said the ideal state is where "the land as well as the inhabitants . . . should be taken in at a single view."[46] He meant that popular government could work only if limited to a group of people meeting in one place at one time. The designers of the American colonies thought in slightly bigger terms and located colonial legislatures within easy reach of a state's citizens. With these limited spaces and populations in mind, the designers of the First Amendment in 1791 talked about freedom of speech and of the press in a literal way. The standard means of public communication then were simpler. Debate and discussion were largely conducted in local village newspapers, and speeches were delivered in courthouses, churches, and state legislatures. We wonder how the early Americans would react to electronic forums such as ABC's *Nightline* or the *Oprah Winfrey Show* that reach millions of viewers spread over an entire continent.

In short, the forces of influence that act upon modern Americans are increasingly centered in national rather than local institutions. Because of these changes, many critics have asked if the First Amendment itself is in need of an amendment: a new right of access to the mass media, which have replaced the town hall and the local newspaper as major opinion-leading sources of news. They argue that freedom of expression is only meaningful to the extent that citizens have access to significant numbers of listeners or readers. As First Amendment scholar Jerome Barron put it:

> In the contemporary life of ideas, the victories and defeats of politics and the fortunes of intensely important issues are resolved in the mass media. . . . Our constitutional guarantee of freedom of press is equipped to deal with direct and crude governmental assaults on freedom of expression, but is incapable of responding to the more subtle challenge of securing admission for ideas to the dominant media.[47]

Barron suggests that the idea of freedom of expression has been rendered impotent. There may be romance in the image of the ordinary citizen standing up for his or her convictions at a town council meeting, but the real battleground of public opinion has shifted to the broadcaster and the large daily newspaper. The ideal of freedom of speech, he argues, must now include some sort of means for citizen access to the forums now dominated by the television networks, major newspapers, and corporate advertisers. Letters to the editor, cable public access channels, and standard news interviews are all vehicles for opening up the mass media to the views of their consumers. Many students of the First Amendment believe that these measures still fall short of giving persuaders genuine opportunities to shape local public opinion. Today, notes George Gerbner, corporations can almost act as "private governments," with the power to buy access to the mass media as the virtual equivalent of the right to operate a private "ministry of culture."[48]

## Summary

Throughout history people who have built nations or studied existing societies have disagreed about whether the power of persuasion—left in the care of ordinary people—can result in decisions that will show intelligence and civility. The choices we make as individuals and as citizens of a nation may never satisfy critics who dislike the power of public opinion and distrust its wisdom. But of this we are certain, the greater the diversity of choices within a nation, the more it *needs* vigorous public discussion. The role of the advocate in American society is basic. Few of us would risk giving up the franchise that allows us to attempt to influence others.

   It is also important to note that the freedom to persuade implies special responsibilities in addition to special privileges. The whole idea of the marketplace carries obligations for advocates as well as the society of which they are a part. Persuaders must use their protected rights of freedom of speech and freedom of the press well and wisely. As we noted in chapter 1, the abuse of an audience's openness can lead to disasters similar to those that occurred in Jonestown, Guyana. For their part, powerful leaders and the mass media should be willing to share their near-monopolies of the channels of communication with less powerful individuals and organizations. The freedom to persuade is rendered meaningless if it does not include the opportunity for ordinary citizens to have access to opinion leaders and audiences.

## Questions and Projects for Further Study

1. One of the current battlegrounds over freedom of expression in the United States centers on shopping malls. Some state courts have denied advocates the right to distribute campaign and issue-centered materials at malls, noting that they are private property. Others have taken a more liberal view, concluding that the shopping mall has become "main street." Contact the management of a mall near you and ask about its policy regarding distribution of materials. As an alternative, explore the question with a campus faculty member (in a law or criminal justice department) who is familiar with this issue.

2. A reader with a comprehensive knowledge of the Middle East may find our book's discussion of the Rushdie affair biased against non-Western ways of thinking and Islamic sensitivities. Others may disagree. To what extent should we view the values expressed in the First Amendment as "universals" that could be profitably adopted by all nations?

3. The right to freedom of expression is easiest to defend when we consider the cause to be a "good" one, but free speech issues often develop from more unpopular roots. In 1977, for example, the American Nazi Party decided to hold a parade and make speeches in Skokie, Illinois. The northern suburb of Chicago has a large Jewish population, many of whom are survivors of Hitler's infamous World War II death camps. If you were the judge presented with Skokie's request to issue an injunction *against* the march, what would you decide? Try to defend your decision to another member of the class. Look at Nat Hentoff's book *The First Freedom* to find out what actually happened.

4. In *The Republic*, Book VIII, beginning at section 554, Plato describes the problems in democratic governments. Read the pages of this section, consider his arguments, and prepare a short summary of his complaints against democracy. Use his analysis as the basis of a paper or a short oral summary presented to other members of your course.

5. After the war against Iraq in 1991, many journalists complained about heavy restrictions against reporting of military actions imposed by all of the governments involved, including the United States. Officials in the Pentagon forcefully argued that reporting restrictions were necessary to avoid passing on valuable information to Iraq about troop movements and damage estimates. Many members of the press argued that controls were much more extensive and designed to minimize the likelihood that the audience at home would see the horrors of war firsthand. Examining the sources cited on this event in this chapter, defend or attack the general reporting "ground rules" imposed during this brief war.

6. Some large cable television companies operate "public access" channels. Contact a local station and ask if they allow access programming and facilities. Ask them to explain how these items work and how they have been used in the past.

7. Students of the First Amendment have argued that some social innovations that eventually find their way into the mainstream start out as part of a "radical" movement. Many ideas and policies we now take for granted, such as the progressive income tax, federal regulation of industries, and women's suffrage initially came from "fringe" groups in the United States. Cite one or two recent examples of ideas or policies that needed First Amendment protections in order to gain acceptance.

8. In this chapter, Thomas Jefferson is described as a democratic hero, a strong believer in liberty and self-determination, yet Jefferson owned slaves. Explain this apparent irony (or hypocrisy). A good place to start is the chapter on Jefferson in Richard Hofstadter's popular book *The American Political Tradition*.

9. Develop a questionnaire that can be completed by other students. In the questionnaire, list various kinds of persuasive events, such as a speech on campus against registering for the draft, the marching of Nazi Party members, the campus appearance of speakers representing an unusual religion, and so on. Design your questions so you can determine how much freedom of expression respondents are willing to tolerate. After asking a representative sample of people to respond to your questions, review the tabulated results.

# Notes

[1] John Stuart Mill, *On Liberty*, ed. by Currin V. Shields. New York: Bobbs-Merrill, 1956, p. 21.

[2] Said Amir Arjomand, *The Turban for the Crown: The Islamic Revolution in Iran*. New York: Oxford, 1988, pp. 91–133. For general background on the primacy of Islam in the political life of most Middle East states see G. Hossein Razi, "Legitimacy, Religion, and Nationalism in the Middle East," *American Political Science Review*, March 1990, pp. 69–85.

[3] Arjomand, p. 170. For a discussion of continuing tensions within Iran see also, Nikola B. Schahgaldian, "Iran After Khomeini," *Current History*, February 1990, pp. 61–64, 82–84; and Philip Shenon, "Khomeini's Tomb Attracts Pilgrims," *New York Times*, July 8, 1990, p. 8.

[4] Arjomand, p. 170.

[5] Salman Rushdie, *The Satanic Verses*. New York: Viking, 1989, pp. 363–64.

[6] Daniel Pipes, "The Ayatollah, the Novelist, and the West," *Commentary*, June 1989, p. 11.

[7] *Ibid.*, p. 12.

[8] "The Ghost of Khomeini," editorial in the *New York Times*, June 18, 1990, p. A20.

[9] See Edwin McDowell, "'Satanic Verses' Is Removed From Shelves by Book Chain," *New York Times*, February 17, 1989, pp. A1, A12.

[10] For example, in early 1990 a Florida court had banned a rock album by a popular "rap" group, and an Ohio grand jury charged the director of Cincinnati's Contemporary Arts Center with displaying the allegedly obscene photographs of Robert Mapplethorpe. See Robert D. McFadden, "Shock Greets Banning of a Rap Album," *New York Times*, June 8, 1990, p. A10; and Harry Anderson, "The Battle of Cincinnati," *Newsweek*, April 16, 1990, p. 27. In addition, in June of 1990 Vatican officials told Roman Catholic theologians that they did not have the right to publicly dissent from official church doctrines. See Peter Steinfels, "The Vatican Warns Catholic Theologians Over Public Dissent," *New York Times*, June 27, 1990, pp. A1, A5.

[11] Rushdie, "A Pen Against the Sword," p. 53.

[12] Karl R. Popper, *The Open Society and its Enemies*, Vol. 1, Fifth Edition. Princeton: Princeton University Press, 1966, p. 42.

[13] The dialogue is called *The Gorgias*. For an interesting modern analysis of Plato's attacks on Gorgias and the teaching of persuasion see Robert M. Pirsig's best-selling biographical novel, *Zen and the Art of Motorcycle Maintenance*. New York: William Morrow, 1974, especially Part IV.

[14] W. C. K. Guthrie, *The Sophists*. Cambridge, England: Cambridge, 1971, p. 270.

[15] *Ibid.*, p. 272.

[16] *Ibid.*, p. 183.

[17] Aristotle, *The Rhetoric* in *The Basic Works of Aristotle*, ed. by Richard McKeon. New York: Random House, 1941, p. 1327.

[18] Alexander Hamilton, James Madison, and John Jay, *The Federalist Papers*, ed. by Clinton Rossiter. New York: Mentor Books, 1961, p. 79.

[19] *Ibid.*, p. 81.

[20] Jefferson quoted in Page Smith, *Jefferson: A Revealing Biography*. New York: American Heritage, 1976, p. 157.

[21] Popper, p. 202.

[22] Frank J. Prial, "Big Growth Disclosed in List of Barred Aliens," *New York Times*, June 23, 1990, p. 24.

23 Philip Taubman, "The Kremlin Worries That Too Many Know Too Much," *New York Times*, January 26, 1986, p. 22E.

24 George Orwell, *1984*. New York: New American Library, 1961, pp. 5–7.

25 See Mark Hopkins, "Watching China Change," *Columbia Journalism Review*, September/October, 1989, pp. 35–40.

26 For a specific example of increased flow of information across a political and cultural border see Jackson Diehl, "East Europe on Cultural Fast Forward," in *Media Reader*, ed. by Shirley Biagi. Belmont, CA: Wadsworth, 1989, pp. 340–42. General patterns of international communication are discussed in Hamid Mowlana, *Global Information and World Communication*. New York: Longman, 1986, pp. 19–92.

27 Holmes quoted in Jerome A. Barron, *Freedom of the Press for Whom?* Bloomington: Indiana University, 1973, p. 320. The emphasis is ours.

28 Howard Zinn, *Disobedience and Democracy: Nine Fallacies on Law and Order*. New York: Vintage, 1968, pp. 67–87.

29 Gene Lanier, "Libraries Invaded by the FBI" in *The Free Speech Yearbook*, Volume 27, 1989, ed. by Raymond S. Rodgers. Carbondale: Southern Illinois Press, 1989, pp. 68–74.

30 Martin Luther King, Jr., "Letter From Birmingham Jail" in *The Rhetoric of No*, Second Edition, ed. by Ray Fabrizio, Edith Karas, and Ruth Menmuir. New York: Holt, Rinehart and Winston, 1974, pp. 301–2.

31 Juliet Dee, "Heavy Metal, Rap, and the First Amendment" in *Free Speech Yearbook*, Vol. 31, ed. by Dale A. Berbeck. Carbondale: Southern Illinois University Press, 1994, p. 113.

32 Nat Hentoff, *The First Freedom*. New York: Delacorte Press, 1980, pp. 296–97.

33 See "Notes and Comment," *New Yorker*, February 4, 1991, p. 21; and Malcome W. Browne, "The Military vs. The Press," *New York Times Magazine*, March 3, 1991, pp. 27–30, 44–45.

34 Donna A. Demac, *Liberty Denied: The Rise of Current Censorship in America*. New York: Pen American Center, 1988, pp. 18–19.

35 Ben H. Bagdikian, "Preface" in Donna A. Demac, *Keeping America Uninformed: Government Secrecy in the 1980s*. New York: Pilgrim, 1984, p. ix.

36 Demac, *Keeping America Uninformed: Government Secrecy in the 1980s*. New York: Pilgrim, 1984, p. 77.

37 For an account of the Iran-Contra affair see Jane Mayer and Doyle McManus, *Landslide: The Unmaking of the President, 1984–1988*. Boston: Houghton Mifflin, 1988, pp. 317–55.

38 For an account of this incident see news reporter Daniel Schorr's narrative in his *Clearing the Air*. New York: Berkeley, 1978, pp. 187–225.

39 Roger Cohen, "Killed Book is Haunting Time-Warner," *New York Times*, April 16, 1990, pp. D1, D8.

40 Gene Lees, "Irving Berlin: It Wasn't All Blue Skies," *New York Times Book Review*, July 1, 1990, p. 25.

41 "McDonald's Ad Spending Tops $1 Billion," *Advertising Age*, April 16, 1990, p. 57.

42 "Fiscal 1990 HUD, VA, Agencies," *Congressional Quarterly*, July 22, 1989, p. 1865.

43 Todd Gitlin, *Inside Prime Time*. New York: Pantheon, 1983, pp. 3–11.

44 Ben H. Bagdikian, *The Media Monopoly*, Third Edition. Boston: Beacon, 1990, p. 37.

45 Bill Carter, "*60 Minutes* Order to Pull Interview in Tobacco Report," *The New York Times*, November 9, 1995, pp. A1, B15.

[46] Aristotle, p. 1284.

[47] Barron, p. 4.

[48] George Gerbner, "Ministry of Culture, the USA, and the 'Free Market of Ideas'" in *Media Reader*, ed. by Shirley Biagi. Belmont, CA: Wadsworth, 1989, pp. 335–39.

## Additional Reading

Jerome A. Barron, *Freedom of the Press for Whom?* Bloomington: Indiana University, 1973.

Ben Bagdikian, *The Media Monopoly*, Third Edition. Boston: Beacon, 1990.

Donna A. Demac, *Liberty Denied: The Rise of Current Censorship in America*. New York: Pen American Center, 1988.

Nat Hentoff, *The First Freedom*. New York: Delacorte Press, 1980.

Richard Hofstadter, *The American Political Tradition and the Men Who Made It*. New York: Knopf, 1973.

George Orwell, *1984*. New York: New American Library, 1961.

Daniel Pipes, *The Rushdie Affair: The Novel, the Ayatollah, and the West*. New York: Carol Publishing Group, 1990.

Robert M. Pirsig, *Zen and the Art of Motorcycle Maintenance*. New York: William Morrow, 1974.

Plato, *The Republic*, Book VIII, trans. by W. H. D. Rouse in *Great Dialogues of Plato*, ed. by Eric Warmington and Philip Rouse. New York: Mentor, 1956.

Karl R. Popper, *The Open Society and Its Enemies*, Vol. 1, Fifth Edition. Princeton: Princeton University Press, 1966.

Thomas L. Tedford, *Freedom of Speech in the United States*, Second Edition. New York: McGraw-Hill, 1993.

# 3

# The Advocate and the
# Manipulation of Symbols

## OVERVIEW

- ■ The Nature of Language
    - Signs
    - Symbols
    - Meaning
    - Functions of Language
- ■ Language, Interaction, and Reality
    - The Creation of Reality through Interaction
    - "Self" as a Product of Interaction with Others
    - Society as a Product of Interaction with Others
- ■ Political Uses of Language
    - Common Political Language Devices
        - Labeling
        - Doublespeak
        - Euphemisms
        - Jargon
        - Bureaucratese
        - Inflated Language
        - Slanting
- ■ Summary
- ■ Questions and Projects for Further Study
- ■ Notes
- ■ Additional Reading

> And however important to us is the tiny sliver of reality each of us has experienced firsthand, the whole overall "picture" is but a construct of our symbol systems.[1]
> —Kenneth Burke

On the evening of April 29, 1974, President Richard Nixon went on television to put the Watergate scandal behind him and to prove that he had nothing to hide. He asserted that for more than a year he attempted "to get to the bottom of the matter and that the truth should be fully brought out—no matter who was involved. . . . I want there to be no question remaining about the fact that the President has nothing to hide in this matter. . . ." As evidence, Nixon offered transcripts of critical conversations he had privately recorded in the White House. Very little time passed before it became evident that Nixon's "slice of reality" bore no resemblance to the public's perception of the same events.

It took just four days for the *New York Times* to publish the text of the tapes for all to read. Over three million copies were sold in one week. Among the revelations of the transcripts were the frequent use of unprovoked obscenities. Historian Theodore White wrote that the tapes "spoke in a vulgarity of language, an indecision of tone and a profanity of such commonness as to make the imaginative level of Lyndon Johnson's obscenities seem artful by comparison."[2] Robert Strauss, Democratic National Committee Chairman, declared, "I'm embarrassed to have our kids read this and think it's part of the life I'm in."[3] With the release of the transcripts, public support for the president eroded. Two weeks after release of the transcripts, 49 percent of the public endorsed Nixon's impeachment.[4]

Interestingly, the transcripts did not contain any offending words. Rather, the manuscript was full of parentheticals stating "adjective deleted" or "expletive deleted." It was up to the reader to fill in the "dirty words." The inserts drew attention to the frequency of profanity and fueled the public's imagination. Sixteen years later, Nixon wrote that the disclosure of his use of profanity was unfortunate, although "as a matter of fact, most people [use it], at one time or another—especially in Washington. But since neither I nor most other presidents has ever used profanity in public, millions were shocked. I have heard other presidents use very earthy language in the Oval Office, but none of them had the bad judgment to have it on tape. If they did, the tapes are still tucked snugly away—as they should be."[5]

Of course, Nixon was not the only president to use profanity and vulgarity in the White House. Harry Truman was given to call people he did not like SOBs, and Lyndon Johnson's daily conversations were peppered with profanities. Even Jimmy Carter stimulated some controversy by using the words "screw" and "shack up" in an interview in *Playboy* magazine in the 1976 presidential campaign.

Times change. The phrase "kicking ass" became a George "Bushism" in 1984. After a vice-presidential debate with candidate Geraldine Ferraro, Bush told an official of the International Longshoremen's Association that he had "tried to kick a little ass." When the remark was picked up by a television microphone, Bush later explained that the phrase is "an old Texas football expression. . . . and I stand behind it. That's the way I talk, so get it accurate."[6] In December 1990 before the War in the Gulf, Bush told members of Congress that if there was a war, Saddam Hussein was "going to get his ass kicked." After the cease-fire, Bush noted that Hussein had indeed gotten properly "kicked."[7] During the conflict, "kick ass" t-shirts were popular and the phrase was frequently used in magazine stories and on radio.

President Clinton is viewed by the public as affable, warm, caring, and friendly. However, an exposé of the Clinton presidency by author Bob Woodward surprised the public and caused some controversy by revealing Clinton's quick anger, shouting matches and personal attacks on staff members. His tirades are as intense and extreme as those of the legendary Lyndon Johnson. David Gergen (former communications director), when witnessing his first Clinton tirade, shared that he was stunned. "He had never quite seen an adult, let alone the president, in such a rage."[8] A subsequent book by Elizabeth Drew also noted Clinton's quick temper expressed in a full range of street profanities and common vulgarities. There is a kind of "petulance" to his temper. "Compared to many men his age, or even younger, he didn't seem quite grown up."[9] Profanity, by definition, violates accepted custom and language. Profanity today has become rather commonplace and much more accepted. For some observers, President Clinton simply reflects the style and language of his generation and the times in which we live.

Profanity provides a good illustration of the symbolic aspects of language. It disengages the word from its "dictionary" meaning, attaches emotional fervor to it, and links behavior with socially disapproved constructs. As a result, it can induce powerful reactions from those who hear it. In this chapter, we are going to investigate the nature of language, to identify the elements of language and meaning, to consider how language allows us to create the realities upon which we act, and to consider political uses of language.

# The Nature of Language

Human language is a marvelous and powerful tool. Most of our early education in language emphasizes the meaning of words, their placement in sentences, and how sentences form paragraphs. Language, however, is far more than a collection of words and rules for proper usage. Language is the instrument and vehicle for human action and expression. How important language is to us can perhaps best be illustrated by contrasting the "extentional world" with the "intentional world." The extentional world is the world of our senses, the world we know through firsthand experiences. You know the room you are sitting in—the precise color of the walls, the texture of the carpet, the comfort of the chair—because you are there. The intentional world, however, is the world of language, words, and symbols. We know this world by what we read and are told. Perhaps you have never been to Europe, but you could describe many European things, people, and places because of what you have read or have been told by others. We know a great deal about the Civil War (the culture, the issues, the battles) not because of firsthand experience but because of what we have read. When you think about it, our firsthand experiences are very limited. For most of us, the world we know and understand is based upon what we are told and what we read rather than what we experience.

Language can describe direct experience as well as past and future events; it can detail the reality confronting us or images of possibilities that do not yet exist; it is capable of transmitting both true and false messages with equal skill. Theorists often use the terms *signs, symbols* and *meaning* to explain the capacity of language to accomplish all this. While there is debate over the terminology,[10] it is useful to explore some of the definitions since they provide insights that are helpful both for choosing language to convey a persuasive message and for dissecting messages received.

## Signs

Both Ernst Cassirer and Susanne Langer make a distinction between signs and symbols. Langer describes a sign as a natural indication of the existence of a condition. Lightning is a sign that a thunderclap will be heard; fever is a sign of an illness; the tapping of a beaver's tail is a sign of danger. A sign is a symptom of a particular happening; the two are linked by a direct relationship. Symbols do not have any such natural association with what they signify. In her words, signs announce objects, whereas symbols induce conceptions of objects.[11]

Another useful distinction about signs is their one-to-one relationship with what they signify. While stop signs are not a "natural" occurrence, they do have a simple meaning once learned. They do not invite interpretation. They signal a required behavior.

C. S. Pierce divides signs (a category he uses to name *all* human signifying activity) into icons, indices, and symbols.[12] Icons are replicas of what they represent; they resemble, in some way, the objects they stand for—the universal symbols for male and female restrooms, crosses displayed in churches, or maps or territories. An index signifies an object

*Signs have a one-to-one relationship with what they signify.*

by having been affected by it; there is a cause and effect relationship—dark clouds and high winds are an index of thunderstorms. Icons and indices have some connection with the objects they represent that is not purely arbitrary. As discussed below, Pierce categorized arbitrary signs as symbols.

## Symbols

Cassirer described three aspects of a symbol: it stimulates sensation; it stands for something other than itself, and the relationship between the symbol and what it stands for is conventional not natural.[13] Pierce labelled symbols as arbitrary signs because the relationship between an object and its symbol depends on the thought (the *interpretant*) which links them. Ferdinand de Saussure divided linguistic signs (which Cassirer and Langer would have labelled symbols) into two parts. He referred to the initial sensation—the psychological imprint—as the signifier. The mental concept triggered by the signifier is the signified.[14]

Symbols, in contrast to signs, may have many relationships to the thing signified. Your name is a symbol that stands for or represents you. A minister is a symbol and stands for or represents a specific set of beliefs, values, and modes of conduct. Words are symbols that are conventionally agreed upon to represent certain things. Words are convenient symbols. They simplify the amount of information needed to communicate about something. We need only say "chair," and we know that it is an item upon which we sit. We do not need to describe and explain that a "chair" is an item with a seat, back, and legs that support one's weight. Symbols are flexible, arbitrary, and culturally learned.

## Meaning

The relationship between a symbol and the thing it represents is what we call meaning. There is not a one-to-one relationship between symbols and meanings. Ogden and Richards devised the semantic triangle to articulate the relationship of the symbol, object, and meaning.[15] Their relational diagram distinguishes among the elements of "thought," "symbol," and "referent."

As you can see, the simple diagram (Figure 3.1) represents a very complex and varied process. At the apex of the triangle is the reference or thought which the speaker has of an object or event. At the bottom right of the triangle is the referent or actual object. The symbol, at the bottom left of the triangle, abstractly stands for the object. It is important to note that there is no direct connection (thus, the dashes) between the symbol used and the referent. The only connection is through the thought. In other words, thought, symbol, and referent do not represent an equation. Meanings exist in people not in the symbols themselves. Two individuals could see the same referent—a sleek convertible parked at the curb—use the same symbol (''Corvette'') and have two radically different thoughts: ''dream car'' versus ''overpriced, uncomfortable piece of fiberglass.''

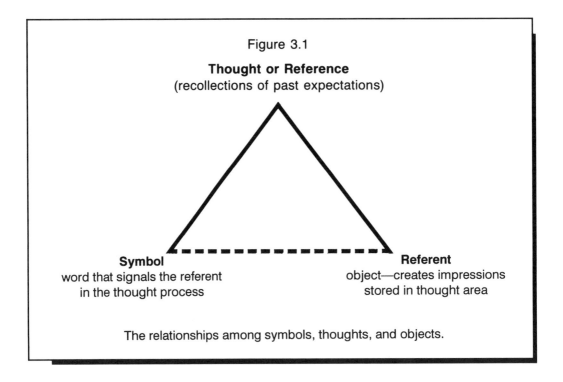

Figure 3.1

**Thought or Reference**
(recollections of past expectations)

**Symbol**
word that signals the referent
in the thought process

**Referent**
object—creates impressions
stored in thought area

The relationships among symbols, thoughts, and objects.

The process of using signs and symbols to represent things is called signification. Umberto Eco divides this process into four interrelated steps:

1. objects in the world
2. signs (meaning anything which designates something other than itself)

3. a repertoire of responses
4. a set of corresponding rules

Symbols are created as we develop an ever-expanding set of responses to stimuli. For there to be commonality and understanding, rules evolve to govern the structure of human communication. Words, as symbols, are arbitrary; they are created by humans and have significance only when two or more people agree to some general interpretation of the symbol. Everyone assumes the meaning of "chair" is clear, yet your mother may visualize a Queen Anne chair, while your father thinks of a big, comfortable recliner. Thus, words and symbols, even ordinary ones, have multiple meanings. In fact, the five hundred most frequently used words in the English language have more than fourteen thousand

## WALNUT COVE

*The symbols we create in response to stimuli are arbitrary; meanings of words change over time.*

meanings assigned to them.[16] If simple concepts have so many interpretations, imagine the possible difficulty with abstract concepts such as freedom, equality, or liberty.

We can subdivide meaning into two categories. *Denotative meanings* refer to formal, dictionary, agreed-upon meanings for words. The relationship between the word and its meaning is generally universal, informative, and describes essential properties of the referent. In this context, the word "chair" denotes an object upon which one sits. The denotative sense of most profanity, if analyzed literally, would have little application to the situations in which it is used. It is the *connotative meanings* of words that provide positive or negative overtones. In this sense, the relationship between the word and the object are individual, personal, and subject to interpretation. If we say that an individual "sits in the chair of power," we mean more than the object upon which the

*Gary Larson has an uncanny ability to dissect the complexities (and absurdities) of human language and behavior. Perhaps his degree in communication from Washington State University sharpened his unique perspective. Here he provides a fanciful illustration of connotative vs. denotative meaning.*

THE FAR SIDE © FarWorks, Inc./Dist. by Universal Press Syndicate.

"Fuel . . . check. Lights . . . check. Oil pressure . . . check. We've got clearance. OK, Jack—let's get this baby off the ground."

person sits. For us, the eagle means more than a bird, the flag more than a piece of cloth, and a cross more than a piece of wood. As a result, words can have positive and negative meanings simultaneously. For some people, abortion is murder. For others, it is a constitutional right.

The meaning of words change over time. A "bad" suit may imply an ugly, ill-fitting suit for your parents. To your peers, however, it may mean a sharp, good-looking suit. Today, if something "rocks," it means it is "awesome," or "cool," or "neat," depending upon your age. The greeting, "Hey dude," popularized by Bart Simpson, may be interpreted as "cool" or sarcastic depending upon the age of the speaker, the reference group, or the tone of delivery.

Two other aspects of meaning are important to note. Human use of symbols allows us the capacity to see what might be as well as to see what is not. Burke referred to humans as "inventors of the negative." There is no negative in nature; the negative is a creation of language—it is a concept with no referent in the physical universe.[17]

Arthur Asa Berger asks, "Have you ever wondered why it is that often when you think of a word, the opposite of the word pops into your head? . . . It is because meaning is relational. Nothing means anything in itself and everything means something because of some kind of relationship in which it is embedded."[18] Berger continues his explanation by pointing out that rich has meaning only if we know what poor means; large is useful only as compared to small. He cites Saussure's belief that "concepts are purely differential and defined not by their positive content but negatively by their relations with the other terms of the system."[19]

The ability to see negative relationships has a companion image. We make choices about categories to which a new stimulus belongs—we decide it is not one thing but has similarities to another. We make connections between the world of the senses and the world of symbols. This is the basic process of language—connecting symbols to experience.[20] Ernesto Grassi used the term *ingenium* to describe the human ability to see relationships.[21] The metaphor is an example of how *ingenium* operates in language. Aristotle long ago analyzed the usefulness of metaphor. He described it as uncovering relationships not previously seen. Cicero used a metaphor to "illuminate" how metaphors operate. He said metaphors act as lights in providing insight into relationships.[22] In seeking meaning, we need to be aware of both positive and negative relationships.

Context plays an important role in establishing the meaning of symbols. I. A. Richards believed symbols have meaning because they have previously been members of a context which affected us as a whole. Words later serve as substitutes for the part of the context missing from subsequent similar experiences.[23] He used the term comparison fields to refer to the contexts of previous experiences that color the meaning of the present experience. Effective communication requires common experiences—an abundance of shared comparison fields so that the

*Words substitute for missing context—but only when comparison fields are shared!*

THE FAR SIDE © FarWorks, Inc.

**"Hang him, you idiots! Hang him! . . . 'String-him-up' is a figure of speech!"**

experience which occurs in the hearer's mind matches the experience in the speaker's mind. Human communication is really a "stirring-up" process rather than a "transmitting" process. Contextual factors that influence meaning include: the social status of speakers, the social conventions governing the speech act, the physical and social-cultural environments, and previous discourse between the parties.

There are several conclusions we can generate about the relationship between symbols and the things symbolized:

1. Meanings are in people, not in words. Words evoke different meanings in different people. They are relative and are based on shared experiences and common culture. As Dan Rothwell asserts, "When we treat words as things, it is tantamount to eating the menu rather than the food."[24]

2. As society and culture change, so do common meanings of words and their acceptable usages. The words "colored," "Negro," "Black," "Afro-American," and "persons of color" have referred to the same ethnic group during the past half-century, and each word has varied in degree of acceptability.

3. No word is inherently "good" or "bad." Society defines morality, and language is used to justify it. The acceptability of words is culturally determined.

We will explore each of these implications further as we continue our discussion of language.

# Functions of Language

Language is an organized, agreed-upon, yet arbitrary system of symbols for communication. According to Ann Gill, there are several criteria for a language.[25] First, any language involves the production of physical stimuli in some channel of communication. Humans create sounds or "marks" receivable by auditory, tactical, or visual channels. Second, the stimuli created must be reproducible and receivable by a distinct group of people. In other words, a language system requires more than one person. Interaction, and hence communication, involves an exchange of symbols. Third, the stimuli exchanged between two or more people must impact or affect the listener. There is some reaction or response resulting from the exchange. Finally, all language systems have some nonrandom rules governing the language system. Rules include syntax, punctuation, and grammar.

Language serves four basic functions. First, language is a practical tool for getting things done. Each language system allows us to share information and to express desires. It allows us to function as a unit—to build, to create, and to destroy. Language is our primary means of relating to the environment and to others; language habits reflect our personality and emotional states. Through language, then, we organize reality and seek security and information. Language is the "infrastructure" of human culture.

Second, language facilitates thought and creativity. An interesting question is whether our behavior is a function of the language we speak or the reverse. According to Benjamin Lee Whorf, the linguistic system a people uses shapes their ideas and guides mental activity.[26] The argument, known as the "Whorfian Hypothesis," states that "the structure of a culture's language determines the behavior and habits of thinking in that culture."[27] The environment may lead a particular culture to develop special modes of thinking. For example, Eskimos have many words to describe the numerous kinds and conditions of snow while we have only a few. Aztecs have only one word for our "cold," "ice," and "snow." The limits and boundaries of our world are the limits and boundaries of our language.

Language is based on human experience. It is a way to "name" happenings and to establish categories that differentiate particular stimuli. At one extreme, we may argue that each word is simply a name of a category of experience, because most languages do share thousands of common categories. For example, the English word "horse" is the French word "cheval" and the German word "pferd." Some categories of language, however, are untranslatable. The reasons may be grammatical, semantical, or experiential. Each language system provides special ways of communicating about experiences; those specific ways of communicating create unique needs, responses, ways of thinking and, ultimately, behavior.

Language is not just a collection of names for objects and ideas; it colors and shapes the reality perceived. As Ann Gill points out, some concepts are beyond our grasp because we have no signifier for them.[28] Without the signifier there is no signified. She creates the word *dewonks* to symbolize humans in their teens missing teeth. If dewonks became commonly accepted usage tomorrow, we would see dewonks frequently, even though yesterday we were not aware of them.

Third, language is a key element in shaping society. If we are, as Aristotle proclaimed, "social animals," then language allows us to be so. Through language we define social roles and rules of behavior; our behavior is often regulated more by words than by physical force. S. I. Hayakawa has noted that language has the same relationship to experience as a map does to an area of land.[29] A map is a pictorial representation of the territory. To be useful, it must be accurate and current. If not, we might get confused, lost, or even injured. Thus, it is important that a map reflect precisely the physical territory it represents. This is also true for language. Our language system must reflect accurately the extentional, empirical world. If our language is not precise, others may be confused or hurt. Misunderstanding may even escalate to violence. When the symbols of "liberty," "equality," and "equal opportunity" do not reflect the real world experience of some citizens, the consequences can be devastating. In 1852 Frederick Douglass, an ex-slave, was invited to commemorate the signing of the Declaration of Independence in Rochester, New York. He began by asking:

> Fellow citizens, pardon me, allow me to ask, why am I called upon to speak here today? . . . Are the great principles of political freedom and of natural justice, embodied in that Declaration of Independence, extended to us? . . . The blessings in which you, this day, rejoice are not enjoyed in common.

Confusion and violence occurred because Douglass' words did not match the expectations of the audience on that occasion. Hitler described a world unacceptable to other nations and war followed. Patrick Henry articulated the importance of liberty for people that resulted in a commitment to arms. In each case, language was the vehicle for social, collective action.

Finally, language links the past with the present and makes civilization possible. We can record our ideas, thoughts, plans, and discoveries for future generations. We can then build upon our knowledge and experiences. Isolated, alone, and unable to communicate through words, we would have to rediscover again and again the making of fire, the use of tools, the treatment of disease, and so on. We are, therefore, a product of all who have preceded us. Human knowledge grows because we can record and transmit past knowledge. We do not need to start our education again each day because we can benefit from centuries of knowledge and experience.

## Language, Interaction, and Reality

### The Creation of Reality through Interaction

Why are so many different classes offered on the college curriculum? Most academic endeavors are attempts to understand the nature and social behavior of human beings. Formal education is a process of presenting a variety of perspectives from which to study or view reality. Sociology, psychology, communication, history, science, politics and the humanities, to name only a few, present perspectives that individuals may use to interpret their worlds. We live in both a symbolic and physical environment. Symbolic reality is an interpretation of physical reality. A tree exists in nature. When we paint a picture of it or attempt to describe it, our interpretation is a reflection of that reality.

Language is the "vehicle" for sharing meanings and interpretations. Before a response to a situation can be formulated, the situation must first be defined and interpreted. We *construct* meanings, *define* situations, and *provide* justifications for behavior. Hence, communication and interaction with others give "meaning" to the world and create the reality toward which we respond and act. We alone can create, manipulate, and use symbols to control our behavior and the behavior of others.

Cassirer explained that humans live in a different reality than the physical world of sensation.[30] Humans live in a symbolic universe. Language, myth, rituals, art, music, and religion are some of the threads that weave the tapestry of our experience. We often see only symbolic reality; physical reality can be overwritten by symbolic experiences. We don't deal with an actual object—we deal with our perception of it which has been influenced by a myriad of previous symbolic experiences. In

*Humans are so steeped in symbolic experience that they often deal only with perceptions—their finely constructed versions of reality.*

CATHY © Cathy Guisewite. Reprinted with permission of Universal Press Syndicate.

Kenneth Burke's words, humans are separated from the "natural condition by instruments of their own making."[31]

Our view of the world may change as our symbol system is modified through interaction. Meanings of symbols are derived from interaction in rather specific social contexts. New interaction experiences may result in new symbols or new meanings for previous symbols. Consequently, one's understanding of the world may change. In the 1960s when black Americans were challenging years of white domination and discrimination, language played an important role in transforming perceptions of society. A "brother" was a fellow black person and "black power" represented group identity, pride, and self-awareness. The movement redefined the heritage of "Negro" into "Afro-American," reinforced a positive self-concept of "Black is Beautiful," and declared a new political activism.

## "Self" as a Product of Interaction with Others

Who are you? What are you? Why do you like and dislike certain things? Why do you believe the things you believe and take the positions on issues you take? The answer lies in your personality as a social product that grows out of communicating with others. From birth, we send out signals for others to confirm, deny, or modify. We interpret the signals sent back by people hoping to determine who we are and where we fit. We gradually discern our status, our strengths, and our weaknesses. Through communicating with others, we become "somebody" and have opportunities to change ourselves.

The "self" actually becomes a social object that we share with others in communication. We come to "know" self in interaction with others. Throughout our lives we isolate, interpret, and define ourselves. The self literally becomes a separate entity to be modified, evaluated, and reinforced in interactions with others. Our perception of the world, how the world perceives us, and how we perceive ourselves depends upon our contacts with other people.

## Society as a Product of Interaction with Others

Throughout our interactions, we learn what is good or bad, right or wrong. In discovering self, we identify, isolate, and assume socially defined roles. We form attitudes—likes and dislikes of people, places, or things—through interaction with others. As we form various attitudes, we also develop beliefs—what we know to be true about our world of people and objects. As we organize and test our attitudes through interaction, we establish values that provide general guidelines for behavior. Values are the core elements which help us interpret reality; they form the basis of how we judge or evaluate issues and concepts. For example, is loyalty more important than personal gain?; is war always wrong?; is honesty always good? Social control is not solely a matter of formal governmental agencies, laws, rules, and regulations but a direct result of citizens identifying and internalizing the values of a group. Values become essential to our self-esteem and act to support the social order.

In addition to creating expectations of behavior, symbols create social sanctions (for example, war as God's will) or function as master symbols or "god terms" (to die for freedom). Our nation sent troops to the Persian Gulf to ensure "freedom" for the Kuwaiti people and to stop the spread of "dictator aggression." We are told that MX missiles are the "peace-keepers" of the future. When followers, through socialization, have been taught "significant" symbols which uphold social order, they require leaders to "play" defined roles. Leaders must create and use symbols that unite and transcend individual and collective differences. Leaders articulate positions of superiority, inferiority, and equality; they persuade us through symbols of power, majesty, and authority.

We have certainly drawn a rather large circle in our discussion. We started with the role of language in defining and discovering ourselves and concluded with demonstrating how language maintains social order. It is useful to examine further the role of social interaction and language as a function of governing. While our focus in chapter 11 is on the forms of political persuasion. Our concern here is how language structures our social relationships within a democracy and how leaders of society use language to define and interpret reality to provide a rationale for future collective action.

## Political Uses of Language

Language is not just reserved for the honorable and skilled. This human tool is available to all—the good and bad, the kind and cruel, the generous and selfish. It is, therefore, open to abuse as freely as it is to proper usage. Umberto Eco summarized semiotics in terms which have application to a number of areas, including political communication.

> Semiotics is concerned with everything that can be taken as a sign. A sign is everything which can be taken as significantly substituting for something else. This something else does not necessarily have to exist or to actually be somewhere at the moment in which a sign stands for it. Thus semiotics is in principle the discipline studying everything which can be used in order to lie. If something cannot be used to tell a lie, conversely it cannot be used to tell the truth; it cannot in fact be used "to tell" at all. I think that the definition of a "theory of the lie" should be taken as a pretty comprehensive program for a general semiotics.[32]

The substance of the information the language conveys, the setting in which the interaction occurs, and the explicit or implicit functions the language performs determine whether or not language is political. According to Paul Corcoran, the very essence of language is political. "Language in the broadest sense—ordinary conversation, symbolic expression, the grammar of social and sexual roles, the maintenance of customs and institutions, the transmission of cultural norms from generation to generation—is inevitably political because it prescribes, constrains, socializes, reinforces, and conserves the status quo."[33]

Political language is often designed to evoke *reaction*, not thoughtful response. Political language can be a creative instrument to stimulate passion and commitment. To control, manipulate, or structure the audience's interpretation is the primary goal of politics in general. Political discourse involves a struggle over meaning, status, power, and resources.[34] A successful politician, then, will use rather specific linguistic devices to reinforce popular beliefs, attitudes, and values. Politicians generally avoid complex issues, positions, or arguments.

Doris Graber identifies five major functions of political language: information dissemination, agenda-setting, interpretation and linkage, projection for the future and the past, and action stimulation.[35] Information is shared in many ways with the public in political messages. The most obvious, of course, is the sharing of explicit information about the state of the nation. Such dissemination of information is vital to the public's understanding and support of the political system. This is especially true in democratic nations where the public expects open access to the legislative debates and decision making of government officials. But the public, being sensitized to uses of language, can obtain information from what is *not* stated, *how* something is stated, or *when* something is stated. Often, especially in messages between nations, the public must read between the lines of official statements to ascertain proper meanings and significance of statements. Such inferences are useful in gauging security, flexibility, and sincerity. Sometimes the connotations of words communicate more truth than the actual statements. Are our relations with China "open," "guarded," or "friendly"? There are times when the very *act* of speaking can communicate support, sympathy, or strength. Thus, the decision to speak rather than the words spoken conveys the true meaning of the rhetorical event.

The topics politicians choose to discuss channel the public's attention. The agenda-setting function of political language works as follows. Before "something" can become an issue, a prominent politician must first articulate a problem to bring the issue to public attention. The issue can be a longstanding concern (poverty), one that needs highlighting (status of American education), or created (health care "crisis"). Political language establishes a national agenda by controlling the information disseminated to the public. Within this realm, there is always a great deal of competition because only a limited number of issues can maintain public interest. While certain topics may be critically important to a person, party, faction, or group, the same topics may be perceived as meaningless or even harmful to other factions, persons, or groups.

For example, in the fall of 1993, President Clinton launched the health care debate with a special address before a joint session of Congress. He reported that the nation faced a "health care crisis." Interestingly, the president did not define the issue as one of quality of technology, knowledge, care, or the skill of medical professionals. Rather, the speech centered around the theme of "security"—security in the knowledge that health care, as one of our most "basic needs," can never be taken away. Clinton proclaimed that the American health care system "is too uncertain and too expensive, too bureaucratic and too wasteful. It has too much fraud and too much greed." The insurance industry and many large businesses challenged the president's views and definition of our health care system. These opponents argued that there was no "crisis." They emphasized the quality of American health care and the need to preserve choice among health care providers.

The act of calling the public's attention to an issue defines, interprets, and manipulates the public's perception of the issue. Figure 3.2 identifies President Clinton's principles for health care reform. Although the principles are general and open to broad interpretation, the highlighted words illuminate the attempt to define a complex problem in terms the public would accept and approve. As will be discussed in chapter 11, the public eventually rejected President Clinton's definition and interpretation of the health care system.

Control over the definition of a situation is essential in creating and preserving political realities. Participants in election primaries, for example, all proclaim victory regardless of the number of votes received. The top vote-getter becomes the "front runner." The second-place winner becomes "the underdog" candidate in an "uphill battle." The third-place candidate becomes a "credible" candidate and alternative for those "frustrated" or "dissatisfied" with the "same old party favorites."

---

### Figure 3.2
### Bill Clinton's Principles for Health Care Reform

1. **Security**—"those who do not now have health care coverage will have it; and for those who have it, it will never be taken away."

2. **Simplicity**—"our health care system must be simpler for the patients and simpler for those who actually deliver health care—our doctors, our nurses, our other medical professionals."

3. **Savings**—"we're spending over 124 percent of our income on health care—Canada's at 10; nobody else is over nine. Reform must produce savings in this health care system."

4. **Choice**—"Americans believe they ought to be able to choose their own health care plan and keep their own doctors. We also believe that doctors should have a choice as to what plans they practice in."

5. **Quality**—"to preserve and enhance the high quality of our medical care."

6. **Responsibility**—"we need to restore a sense that we're all in this together and that we all have a responsibility to be a part of the solution."

Source: "Address of the President to the Joint Session of Congress," *Weekly Compilation of Presidential Documents*, September 22, 1993, 1836–1846.

A great deal of political language deals with predicting the future and reflecting upon the past. Candidates forecast idealized futures under their leadership and predict success if their policies are followed. Some predictions and projections are formalized in party platforms or in major addresses such as inaugurals or state of the union speeches. Nearly all such statements involve promises—promises of a brighter future if followed or Armageddon if rejected. Past memories and associations are evoked to stimulate a sense of security, better times, and romantic longings. An important function of political language, therefore, is to link us to past glories and to predict a successful future in order to reduce uncertainty in an increasingly complex world.

Finally, and perhaps most importantly, political language mobilizes society and stimulates social action. Language serves as the stimulus, means, or rationale for social action. Words can evoke, persuade, implore, command, label, praise, and condemn. Although political language is similar to other uses of language, it also articulates, shapes, and stimulates public discussion and behavior about the allocation of public resources, authority, and sanctions.

## Common Political Language Devices

It should be obvious by now that the connotative, personal, interpretive meanings of words are potentially the most dangerous and easily abused. Words can be both descriptive and evaluative. As a result, a specific reality is constructed toward which we act and react. It is useful for us to identify some of the more common ways language is used to evoke specific responses in people.

### Labeling

Defining and labeling stimuli and elements in our environment make life easier. Labels tell us what is important about an object and what to expect; socialization prescribes how we should act or interact with the object defined. Labeling also forces us to make judgments and evaluations, which causes the potential for abuse. It is easier to kill a "gook" or "jap" than a human being. Labeling an action as communistic or socialistic produces negative connotations in America. How should we characterize the government's bailout of the Chrysler Corporation or the numerous savings and loan associations? What is government's role in terms of subsidies to the poor or social security? Are these examples of socialism? Perhaps. Although we value the concepts of capitalism, free enterprise, and democracy, none of these concepts exist in a pure form. Certainly, however, if government officials had described the saving of Chrysler as a socialistic solution, the legislation probably would have failed.

The 1994 congressional elections resulted in a Republican Party majority in the House of Representatives for the first time in forty years. Newt Gingrich, a former history professor from Georgia, became the speaker of the House and called for nothing less than an American renewal. He is credited with reinvigorating the Republican Party. Throughout the 1980s, Congressman Gingrich served as the nation's leading conservative lightning rod and gained a reputation as a razor-tongued, oratorical streetfighter. As a strategic thinker, he has a strong appreciation for the power of ideas and words. In 1990 as president of a Republican group known as GOPAC, Gingrich prepared a list of "positive governing words" and their opposites for distribution to supporters.[36] A large list of colorful adjectives, nouns, and adverbs were supposedly screened by market researchers to locate those that would have special potency with voters. The result: lists of terms of praise and condemnation that potential candidates and campaign workers could use in their local campaigns. A letter mailed to party workers entitled "Language: A Key Mechanism of Control" noted that many politicians had expressed the wish that they "could speak like Newt."

The recommendations of GOPAC included the following. Characterize yourself and your own record with terms like: *moral, proud,* and *hard work.* Words GOPAC recommended as useful to "define our opponents" included: *liberal, shallow,* and *self-serving.*

When the group's mailing became public, Democrats noted that it was typical of conservative Republicans to find ways to use old smears like "traitor" or "betray" against their opponents. GOPAC's Chairman, Bo Callaway, cautioned recipients of the list against using the negative terms in the wrong context. "A word that might be well justified in a particular context," he noted, "would be inappropriate in other contexts."

Labeling works because it renders judgment by making positive or negative associations. For example, how we act toward and perceive an individual differs greatly if we are told the person is inquisitive or nosey, cool or frigid, reflective or moody, thorough or picky, forgetful or senile.

## Doublespeak

In 1971, members of the National Council of Teachers of English passed two resolutions aimed at studying and publicizing the "dishonest and inhumane use of language."[37] The resolutions resulted from the growing concern about the manipulation of language by government and military officials in characterizing and reporting the Vietnam War. A year later, the NCTE created the Committee on Public Doublespeak to monitor and combat the misuse of public language by government, public, and corporate officials. By 1974 the committee began publishing a newsletter that later evolved into the *Quarterly Review of Doublespeak* and presenting a Doublespeak Award for "language that is grossly deceptive, evasive, euphemistic, confusing, or self-contradictory and which has pernicious social or political consequences.''[38]

Doublespeak, according to William Lutz, is ''language which pretends to communicate but really does not.''[39] It is saying one thing but meaning something else. It confuses or hides the true meaning or intent of the communicator. It conceals or prevents thought. Such usage of language is certainly not helpful or informative; it is destructive. Doublespeak is not the result of careless grammar or sloppy thinking. Rather, it is the intentional use of language to mislead, to distort, and to corrupt. Such language threatens democracy and breeds contempt, suspicion, cynicism, and public distrust.

Lutz identifies four kinds of doublespeak: euphemisms, jargon, bureaucratese, and inflated language.[40] It is useful to discuss each of these in relation to public policy.

*Euphemisms* are words or phrases designed to avoid negative or unpleasant reality. We use euphemisms to be courteous and sensitive to the feelings of others. For example, instead of referring to someone as ''fat,'' we use full-figured, husky, portly, or healthy, to name only a few. Within the realm of politics, however, euphemisms are used to

---

*This cartoon satirizes the use of the euphemism ''downsizing'' and illustrates how slanting attempts to mask or recast situations.*

## MacNelly's view

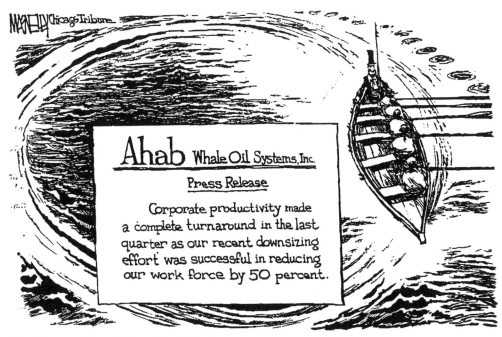

Reprinted by permission: Tribune Media Services

mislead, cover up, or avoid sensitive issues, problems, or positions. During the Gulf War in 1991, civilian casualties were referred to as "collateral damage" and American casualties resulting from allied forces as "friendly fire." Such terminology is less unpleasant than the reality of our bombs killing innocent women and children or our soldiers being killed by fellow troop members.

*Jargon* is the specialized language created for specific functions by those of a trade, profession, or group. The use of jargon is really an efficient way to communicate with group members. The problem arises, however, when individuals outside the group attempt to understand or participate in communication with group members. In effect, such language usage discourages interaction and may also confuse or hide the truth. The need to conduct a "needs assessment" (a survey) in order to develop an adequate "evaluation tool" (a test) for those who will manage a "transportation component" (a bus) certainly sounds like a complex and expensive project. Legal documents are full of jargon. They require "special" interpretations which make us dependent on attorneys for help, advice, and action. The medical profession also relies heavily on specialized jargon to communicate. Notice how such usage reduces interference from those outside the inner circle and acts as an inhibitor to full, open discussion.

*Bureaucratese* is the piling on of complex and compound words and sentences that, upon analysis, say very little. It is a combination of using specialized jargon within complex, rambling sentence structures. In 1986 the recipients of the Doublespeak Award by the NCTE were NASA, Morton Thiokol, and Rockwell International for their written and oral testimony in relation to the *Challenger* space shuttle disaster. To

---

### Figure 3.3

### A Letter from the U.S. Tariff Commission to the Administrative Conference of the U.S.

---

This is in reply to your letter concerning the "data-gathering and processing systems of this agency having to do with administrative proceedings."

The problems and considerations therein presented, together with ancillary ramifications, have been carefully analyzed in conjunction with manipulative and nonmanipulative factors relative to administrative equilibrium. Our conclusions, while tentative and perhaps unsuited to peripheral institutionalization, suggest in marked degree, a sub-marginal coefficient of applicability vis-a-vis the activities of the Commission, and have thus been deemed an appropriate basis for nonactional orientation toward the questionnaire accompanying your letter.

Please advise us if further information is needed.

illustrate, when an official of NASA was asked if the performance of the space shuttle had improved with each launch, he responded:

> I think our performance in terms of the liftoff performance and in terms of orbital performance, we knew more about the envelope we were operating under, and we have been pretty accurately staying in that. And so I would say the performance has not by design drastically improved. I think we have been able to characterize the performance more as a function of our launch experience as opposed to it improving as a function of time.[41]

The testimony of another official included:

> The normal process during the countdown is that the countdown proceeds, assuming we are in go posture, and at various points during the countdown we tag up the operational loops and face-to-face in the firing room to ascertain the facts that project elements that are monitoring the data and that are understanding the situation as we proceed are still in the go direction.[42]

*Inflated language* is language designed to make the common appear uncommon, the ordinary seem extraordinary. To achieve this effect, usage of euphemisms, jargon, and bureaucratese are essential. Renaming is the most common way to make everyday things more important or impressive. Examples abound: "environmental engineers" instead of garbage collectors, "sales associates" instead of store clerks, or "maintenance engineers" instead of custodians, to name only a few. While the above examples may enhance worker esteem, what about calling a concentration camp a "pacification center," a military retreat a "tactical withdrawal," tax increases a "revenue enhancement," or governmental lies "selective deniability." The result is confusion and misrepresentation.

---

### Figure 3.4
### Ways to Characterize Lying

| | |
|---|---|
| lie | falsehood |
| white lie | barefaced lie |
| fib | terminological inexactitude |
| deception | dancing on the edge of the truth |
| plausible denial | misinformation |
| misrepresentation | tactical omission |
| diversion | anomaly |
| abnormal aberration | misstatement |
| slight exaggeration | stretch the truth |
| misunderstanding | inaccuracy |

*Slanting* is a form of outright misrepresentation where a particular implication is suggested by omitting certain crucial information. For example, a politician may proclaim that more people are employed today than ever before in our nation's history while the *percentage* of people employed might well be lower than ever before. During the Gulf War in 1991, Americans were shown videos by the military of the pinpoint accuracy of our "smart bombs." After the war, published Air Force estimates revealed that 70 percent of the "ordinance" dropped on Iraq missed their targets. Thus, without lying, the information presented could create a different impression than the facts warrant.

## Summary

We began this chapter by considering the impact of presidents using questionable language. For some, the use of profanity raises questions about sincerity, credibility, integrity, and even morality. For others, it demonstrates that leaders are human just like the rest of us. The reaction to profanity reminds us that perceptions of the same event can vary dramatically. Language reveals a great deal about the speaker and the listener—and the society in which they live.

Symbols are human inventions. They have meaning or significance only when, through experience or agreement, we interpret them. Through language, we construct reality which influences our behavior. Through interaction with others, we come to know who we are, how we fit in, and what we are supposed to do.

Finally, we investigated the nature of political language. We saw how language can be used to control us, to confuse us, and to hide information from us. Human communication can never fully capture reality because it is fundamentally a process of selection, interpretation, and symbolism. All communication is, however, purposeful. Thus, we must not only focus on the structure of arguments or the evidence provided but also on the language used to define or describe reality.

## Questions and Projects for Further Study

1. Why does it matter if we say a glass is half full or half empty?
2. Think of words or expressions that have clear meanings for you but may not be clear to your parents. Why?
3. What is your greatest strength? How do you know?
4. What is your greatest weakness? How do you know?
5. Give an example of how you define "self" through an interaction you've had with another or others.

6. Do you stop at a stop sign even if no one is around? Why?

7. What does the term "freedom" mean to you? What does the term "equality" mean to you?

8. Prepare a list of five words to describe the United States, China, and Iraq. How do the lists differ? Why?

9. Go to the library and find the stockholders' report for a large company. Identify examples of jargon, euphemisms, double-speak, and bureaucratese.

10. Select several magazine print ads and analyze the language of the ads. What promises are implied? What does the ad *not* tell you?

# Notes

[1] Kenneth Burke, *Language as Symbolic Action*. Los Angeles: University of California Press, 1966, p. 5.

[2] Theodore White, *Breach of Faith*. New York: Atheneum, 1975, p. 297.

[3] *Ibid.*

[4] *Ibid.*, p. 298.

[5] Richard Nixon, *In the Arena*. New York: Simon & Schuster, 1990, p. 90.

[6] Beverly Beyette, "Hey, If George Bush Can Say It, It Must be OK," *Roanoke Times and World-News*, Monday, March 11, 1991, Section 3, pp. 1 and 3.

[7] *Ibid.*, p. 1.

[8] Bob Woodward, *The Agenda*. New York: Simon & Schuster, 1994, p. 278.

[9] Elizabeth Drew, *On the Edge*. New York: Simon & Schuster, 1994, p. 96.

[10] For a succinct summary of signs, symbols and signification, see *Rhetoric and Human Understanding* by Ann Gill. Prospect Heights, IL: Waveland Press, 1994, pp. 6–17.

[11] Gill, p. 9.

[12] *Ibid.*, p. 15.

[13] *Ibid.*, p. 7.

[14] *Ibid.*, p. 16.

[15] C. Ogden and I. A. Richards, *The Meaning of Meaning*. New York: Harcourt Brace Jovanovich, 1923.

[16] Dan Rothwell, *Telling It Like It Isn't*. Englewood Cliffs, NJ: A Spectrum Book, 1982, p. 13.

[17] Sonja K. Foss, Karen A. Foss, and Robert Trapp, *Contemporary Perspectives on Rhetoric*, Second Edition. Prospect Heights, IL: Waveland Press, 1991, p. 189.

[18] Arthur Asa Berger, *Signs in Contemporary Culture: An Introduction to Semiotics*. Salem, WI: Sheffield, 1989, p. 173.

[19] *Ibid.*

[20] Foss, Foss, and Trapp, p. 155.

[21] *Ibid.*, 154.

[22] *Ibid.*

[23] *Ibid.*, p. 37.

[24] Rothwell, p. 48.

[25] Gill, p. 28.

[26] See "The Function of Language Classifications in Behavior" by John Carroll and Joseph Casagrande in *Communication and Culture* by Alfred Smith. New York: Holt, Rinehart & Winston, 1966, p. 491.

[27] Stephen Littlejohn, *Theories of Human Communication*, Fifth Edition. Belmont, CA: Wadsworth, 1996, p. 196.

[28] Gill, p. 21.

[29] S. I. Hayakawa, *Language in Thought and Action*, Third Edition. New York: Harcourt Brace Jovanovich, 1972. p. 27–30.

[30] Gill, pp. 9–10.

[31] Foss, Foss, and Trapp, p. 198.

[32] Umberto Eco, *A Theory of Semiotics*. Bloomington: Indiana University Press, 1976, p. 7.

[33] Paul E. Corcoran, "Language and Politics" in *New Directions in Political Communication*, eds. David Swanson and Dan Nimmo. Newbury Park, CA: Sage, 1990, p. 70.

[34] *Ibid.*

[35] Doris Graber, "Political Languages" in *Handbook of Political Communication*, eds. Dan Nimmo and Keith Sanders. Beverly Hills: Sage Publications, 1981, pp. 195–224.

[36] See Michael Oreskes, "For GOP Arsenal, 133 Words to Fire," *New York Times*, September 9, 1990, Section One, p. 30.

[37] William Lutz, "Resolutions" in *Beyond Nineteen Eighty-Four*, ed. William Lutz. Urbana, IL: National Council of Teachers of English, 1989, p. ix.

[38] *Ibid*, p. xii.

[39] William Lutz, "Notes Toward a Definition of Doublespeak" in Lutz, p. 4.

[40] *Ibid*, pp. 4–9.

[41] See appendix B in Lutz, p. 202.

[42] *Ibid.*

## Additional Reading

Herbert Blumer, *Symbolic Interactionism: Perspective and Method*. Englewood Cliffs, NJ: Prentice Hall, 1969.

Robert E. Denton, Jr. and Gary Woodward, *Political Communication in America*, Second Edition. New York: Praeger, 1990.

Joseph DeVito, *Human Communication*, Sixth Edition. New York: Harper Collins, 1994.

Hugh Duncan, *Symbols in Society*. New York: Oxford University Press, 1968.

Murray Edelman, *Constructing the Political Spectacle*. Chicago: University of Chicago Press, 1988.

Sonja Foss, Karen Foss, and Robert Trapp, *Contemporary Perspectives on Rhetoric*, Second Edition. Prospect Heights, IL: Waveland Press, 1991.

Ann Gill, *Rhetoric and Human Understanding*. Prospect Heights, IL: Waveland Press, 1994.

S. I. Hayakawa, *Language in Thought and Action*, Third Edition. New York: Harcourt Brace Jovanovich, 1972.

Kathleen Hall Jamieson, *Eloquence in an Electronic Age*. New York: Oxford University Press, 1988.

Robin Lakoff, *Taking Power: The Politics of Language*. New York: Basic Books, 1990.

David Swanson and Dan Nimmo, eds., *New Directions in Political Communication*. Newbury Park, CA: Sage, 1990.

# Four Perspectives on the Nature of Persuasion

# II

In this section we look at four different ways scholars and analysts have traditionally accounted for the process of influencing others. As rhetorical theorist Trevor Melia has noted, every field of knowledge provides a different way to explain the same human events. Like four peaks surrounding a valley, each of the perspectives in this section offers one vantage point from which to view the varied terrain of persuasion. All can be used to look at the same kinds of messages. The individual traditions and assumptions of each lend specific observations for the specialized landscape of this very complex human process. Each chapter in this section provides an important perspective but, inevitably, an incomplete one. Just as an observer on one mountaintop sees a valley that is slightly "different" from the same valley seen by someone else a few miles away, these perspectives offer unique and sometimes contradictory conclusions.

Chapter 4 examines persuasion from a rationalistic point of view, summarizing some of the invaluable criteria that help us determine when assertions are worthy of our belief. Chapter 5 looks at the important roles that various forms of power and authority play in gaining assent. Chapter 6 explores various psychological processes that may occur when attitudes are challenged or changed. It describes several extremely useful models that predict what happens "inside" receivers faced with change-inducing appeals. Chapter 7 focuses on the social perspective that accounts for the formation of attitudes in groups within society.

# 4

# Persuasion and Reasoning

## OVERVIEW

- ■ Understanding Practical Arguments
- ■ Reasoning Processes: Basic Distinctions
    - Analytic Arguments and Practical Enthymemes
    - Demonstration and Argumentation
    - Factual and Preferential Claims
    - Implied and Stated Components of Arguments
    - Reasoning to Discover and to Defend
    - Finding Good Reasons for Claims
- ■ Common Examples of Defective Reasoning
    - Ad Hominem
    - False Cause
    - Non Sequitur
    - Circular Argument
    - Excessive Dependence on Authority
- ■ How Persuasion and Logical Argumentation Differ
    - Are Arguments either Logical *or* Emotional?
    - Persuasion's ''Self-Interest'' and Argumentation's ''Public Interest''
- ■ Summary
- ■ Questions and Projects for Further Study
- ■ Notes
- ■ Additional Reading

Plato said that the worst fate that can befall a man is to become a misologist, a hater of reason; for him it was clear that since man is essentially reasonable, when he ceases to reason he ceases to be a man. I happen to believe this unfashionable doctrine. . . . I also believe that when any society loses its capacity to debate its ends and means rationally, it ceases to be a society of men at all and becomes instead a mob, a pack, or a herd of creatures rather less noble than most animals.[1]

—Wayne C. Booth

The scene is a meeting between two long-time adversaries who have aired their differences in front of national television audiences many times. On one side sits William F. Buckley, publisher of the *National Review*. He has devoted much of his life to the defense of self-sufficiency and freedom of choice, virtues which he believes have sustained America through its industrial and political expansion. Buckley's darting eyes and the tapped drumbeats of his pencil presage the verbal combat that is about to start. He relishes his reputation as a fearless debater and a reliable defender of political conservatism. On the other side sits his friend and nemesis, John Kenneth Galbraith. Galbraith comes across as a professorial Jimmy Stewart; his affability speaks more of his rural Ontario origins than his position as a distinguished Harvard economist and advisor to Democratic presidents. Galbraith delights in politely ransacking the political principles that have furnished Buckley's world. He uses his slow prairie drawl to camouflage his argumentative weapons of humor, understatement, and irony; a combatant often is slow to realize how severely he or she has been gored by this seemingly genteel academic. These two old friends are at it again, assailing each other's different attitudes about the responsibilities that governments and individuals have in American life. Another episode of *Firing Line* begins:

Galbraith: I suppose that the oldest of the conservative clichés is that assistance to people in caring for their health, and providing them with better housing and jobs, and preventing inflation denies liberties to the people at large. I've always thought, Bill—although I've never myself experienced it— that one of the most constricting things that one can experience is to be without a job and without money. This must have an *enormously* adverse effect on liberty. And so your feeling that anybody who addresses himself to that problem is *limiting* liberty is something I confess I've never been able to understand. But there's so much in your point of view that I've never been able to understand that I don't want to single that out.

Buckley:   Well, a lot of people who are now without money would not be without money if the tax collector were to return some of what he took away. I think it's very hard to say to somebody from whom you take a couple of thousand dollars a year in taxes when he is heavily mortgaged that you are doing him any particular service in virtue of taking that money from him. It's all very well to say, "We will look after other people's schooling; we will look after other people's health; we will look after other people's psychological problems," but philosophical rigor requires you to say, "In order to do this, we shall *take* from other people."

Galbraith:   I don't deny that for a moment. I don't deny that—

Buckley:   You don't stress it.

Galbraith:   No, I *would* stress it. But I would say that one of the great civilizing influences of my lifetime and indeed of the whole period since 1913 has been the leveling effect of the progressive income tax. If the progressive income tax had not been inaugurated—incidentally, by a Republican President, President Taft—the extremes of income that would have developed would have been an enormously disturbing influence on the economy; and perhaps that tax is the single most important conserving and conservative force in the modern society. One of the things that best helps the poor and the deprived to bear life is to hear the occasional screams of the rich.[2]

This exchange captures several of the key attributes of persuasive reasoning considered in this chapter. Persuasion reaches its highest plane when advocates submit their views for comparative analysis and public inspection. The most advanced and honorable forms of persuasion are those that weigh the comparative merits of ideas. Although Buckley and Galbraith have relatively little new to say with respect to their political and social differences, their commitment to subject their opinions to analysis and possible refutation is an important benchmark by which much persuasion should be judged.

In addition, this exchange is a reminder that rationality is not a simple binary concept. Practical arguments are not easily judged as wrong or right, valid or invalid. Arguments work for different audiences in different ways. What is logical for one group may be illogical for another, with no absolute means for determining "correct" and "incorrect" modes of reasoning. It is also apparent that individuals are not always willing to commit the necessary mental energy to the task of determining whether conclusions have significant rational justifications.[3] At times, our reasons for accepting persuasive messages are more personal and eclectic than strictly "logical." A message presented in the context of a television or

*An advertisement that attracts the attention of one audience may not
have the same appeal for others. Our reasons for accepting persuasive
messages are more personal and eclectic than strictly "logical."*

Reprinted with permission of Toyota Motor Sales, U.S.A., Inc.

magazine advertisement may be attractive to us even in the absence of
reasons that we could articulate or defend to others.

Despite these important caveats, persuaders will often be unsuccessful
if they fail to recognize the important role of rationality in persuasion.
Using a number of examples, we will define reasoning, examine some
of its basic patterns, and suggest ways to estimate how these patterns
vary in their power to command assent. In addition, we will identify
common logical mistakes made by persuaders and will close with several
basic observations on the differences between "public" argumentation
and "private" appeals.

# Understanding Practical Arguments

Reasoning, notes Stephen Toulmin, Richard Rieke, and Allan Janik, "is a collective and continuing human transaction, in which we present ideas or claims to particular sets of people within particular situations or contexts and offer the appropriate kinds of 'reasons' in their support."[4] When we reason with others, we attempt to establish connections that link our claims to corresponding ideas or evidence that make our claims seem plausible or true. In the context of controversy, claims are assertions, vulnerable to challenge, that we hope we can convince others to accept. Some claims are never stated in public because we feel we do not have the rational means to defend them; we may privately believe prejudicial sterotypes like "the French are lazy" or the "Irish drink too much." When we publicly express our conclusions, we enter the realm of reasoning because we assume that our assertions will be able to withstand the critical scrutiny of others. Phrases such as "I know . . . ," "It's true that . . . ," "I believe . . . ," and "It would be difficult to doubt . . ." all carry a tone of certainty that implies we can provide evidence to back up our views. Statements that go on to support such claims are called premises.

Aristotle was among the first to put practical reasoning at the center of persuasion theory. He criticized other teachers of persuasion in ancient Greece for presenting "but a small portion of the art," neglecting the important role that practical reasoning plays in winning converts. "Persuasion," he noted, "is clearly a sort of demonstration" that depends on a sequence of logically related statements or arguments. "A statement is persuasive and credible either because it is directly self-evident or because it appears to be proved from other statements that are so." Aristotle called these arguments containing implied facts or judgments supplied by the listener *enthymemes* and noted that they "are the substance of rhetorical persuasion."[5] We will have more to say about the special nature of enthymemes shortly, but first it is important to point out several key differences between "formal" arguments used by logicians and the everyday, "practical" arguments used in persuasion.

# Reasoning Processes: Basic Distinctions

## Analytic Arguments and Practical Enthymemes

The reasoning of "formal" logic is very different from the informal evaluations of ordinary life. Formal logic starts with the ideal of the analytic argument, where claims necessarily follow from a series of premises. An argument is "analytic" when its conclusion absolutely follows from its premises.[6] In this kind of ironclad reasoning sequence,

*This advertisement demonstrates Toyota's commitment to American labor. It answers unstated concerns that Toyota is a foreign company by providing good evidence of its investment in local industries.*

# BUYING

## quality

# PARTS

## is not a

# FOREIGN

## idea to us.

OVER THE last five years, Toyota in America has purchased more than $20 billion in parts and materials from 510 U.S. suppliers.* Today, more than half the Toyota vehicles sold in America are built at our plants in Kentucky and California. Local investment that contributes to America's place in the global economy - it all makes good sense, in any language.

*Toyota Avalon. Built in Georgetown, Kentucky.*

*INVESTING IN THE THINGS WE ALL CARE ABOUT.* **TOYOTA**

*Some parts that go into our American-built vehicles are purchased overseas. For more information about Toyota in America visit our web site at http://www.toyota.com/antenna/usa.html or write Toyota Motor Corporate Services, 9 West 57th Street, Suite 4900-S8, New York, NY 10019*

Reprinted with permission by Toyota Motor Corporate Services of North America.

the claim is "necessary" rather than "probable" because acceptance of the premises dictates acceptance of the conclusion. Although the circumstances of real life rarely allow us to construct valid and true analytic arguments, this ideal provides a tantalizing model for persuaders. Mathematics provides the easiest language for the writing of analytic arguments because—unlike ordinary language—mathematical symbols are completely unambiguous. They are *denotative*; their meanings are clearly defined and closed to differing interpretations. For example, the expression

$$2 + 5 = 7$$

is analytic because its conclusion (the sum of 7) necessarily follows from its premises (universally accepted definitions of what "2," "5," and " + " mean). Similarly, the equation

$$(3 \times 6^2 / 4) - 25 + 8 = 10$$

uses a rigid logic that leads to an unchallengeable result. Anywhere in the world, a mathematically competent person (whether socialist or capitalist, Catholic or Muslim) could be expected to reach the same correct conclusion by applying universally accepted rules and premises. We can also use letters rather than numbers to represent analytic arguments. For example:

1. If A then B.
2. A.
   Therefore,
   B.

In this argument—sometimes also called *deductive* or *syllogistic*—the relationship defined in the first premise ("If A is present then B is also present") sets up a reasoning sequence that leads irreversibly to the claim. We can substitute ordinary language in place of letters or numbers.

1. If Harry decides to visit Europe this summer, Jan will go with him.
2. Harry has decided to go.
   Therefore,
   Jan will also be in Europe this summer.

The most interesting characteristic of valid analytic arguments is that there is no way to deny the force or potency of their claims if you accept the soundness of their premises. The prospect of developing a series of statements with a built-in certainty has attracted scholars and scientists for hundreds of years. The idea of asserting a series of statements of fact or judgment which cannot be refuted is extremely alluring. Philosophers from Descartes to Bentham hoped that mankind would benefit from a logic that used known premises to reach unchallengeable conclusions. They were intrigued by the possibility that people could move beyond the "fictions," "falsehoods," and exceptions common to ordinary discussion. As "a system of necessary propositions which will impose itself on every rational being," the idea of the valid analytic argument promises timelessness and absolute truth.[7] To these philosphers this was more than an idle scholarly pipedream; a logic as universal as the logic of mathematics—if it could be found or invented—would be a valuable pathway that could save the human race from wars and other destructive forms of conflict.

The **force**, or built-in potency, of analytic arguments has intrigued persuaders for similar reasons. Just as we do not argue about the answers to basic math problems (an answer is either right or wrong), analytic arguments used in actual persuasive situations would make the conversion of listeners or readers a simple matter of explaining ironclad relationships. It is hardly surprising, therefore, that in many persuasive statements we see the general form of analytic arguments, even if their actual force is less than their form implies. For example, consider an argument made several years ago by Meir Kahane, the controversial head of the Jewish Defense League who was later murdered while attending a meeting in New York City.

> A Jewish state is one with a majority of Jews who can
>   establish their own sovereignty.
> A democracy allows non-Jews to become a majority and
>   turn Israel into a non-Jewish state. (Therefore,)
> The idea of a 'democratic Jewish state' is nonsense.
>                             (Thus,)
> For the sake of survival, let us carry out. . . the removal
> of the Arabs in the land of Israel to their own Arab lands.[8]

While this example has a superficial certainty that makes it seem like an analytic argument, the premises themselves are not necessarily true. For example, is the idea of a democratic Jewish state really—to quote Kahane—"nonsense"? Is the character of Jewish Israel destroyed by having non-Jews within its borders? History suggests that efforts to make religious and political boundaries conform can create enormous misery. Kahane apparently missed the parallel between his own assertions and those made by the leaders of Nazi Germany whom he despised. The Nazis also had a "solution" for removing "foreign" elements from their own "pure" citizens. His argument has a clear-cut logic, but his premises are hardly true or self-evident.

The problem with this case is symptomatic of two difficulties in developing analytic arguments on persuasive topics. The first difficulty results from the fact that ordinary language is such an important carrier of personal and cultural values; unanimous agreement is difficult if not impossible to achieve. The further we stray from purely denotative languages, such as mathematics, the less likely we are to locate valid analytic arguments that deal with the complexities of the real world. Language is less precise than numbers. The symbols, "2" and "%," for example, have single, stipulated meanings. By contrast words like "is," "because," and "cannot" may seem to define precise relationships, but actually fall far short. The definitions of numbers or signs with invariant meanings, such as in computer languages like BASIC or Fortran, are in the symbols. As we noted in chapter 3, the meanings of expressive words reside within us—not just in denotative definitions. Language carries our values and evokes personal feelings. In certain contexts we may feel good or bad, angry or pleased about subjects represented with words like "sovereignty," "democracy," "clever," or "lustful." It would be extremely odd to hear that a friend "liked" the number "7" better than "2" or grew angry at the sight of a percent sign. However it does not surprise us that thousands of years of human history have failed to produce agreement about what constitutes a "democracy" or even "truth" itself.[9]

A second reason for the difficulty in making "airtight" analytic arguments is that most persuasive statements do not apply to all cases, categories, or people. The claim "all As are Bs" is easy to state and manipulate as an abstract expression, but it is much more difficult to make comparable categorical assertions that would help settle real human differences. People, groups, and cultures are rarely all of anything. In the realm of human affairs, the only statements that can be made without citing important exceptions are either obvious (water is necessary to sustain life) or trivial (all children had parents).

This is where the concept of the enthymeme comes in. Aristotle shrewdly noted that the enthymeme was "sort of" analytic, because ordinary persuasion finds its premises in the "probable" existing opinions of audiences rather than in the categorical truths (the "alls" and "if-thens") of formal logic.[10] He noted that the conclusions of enthymemes are contingent on audience acceptance; they are not certain. Because enthymemes spell out logical relationships based on generally accepted opinions,[11] they must be at least partially judged by how well the persuader has used audience beliefs as premises for persuasion. Here, for example, is an enthymeme that Aristotle cites to show how to argue from generally accepted beliefs to persuasive claims:

> Thus it may be argued that if even the gods are not omniscient, certainly human beings are not. The principle here is that, if a quality does not in fact exist where it is more likely to exist, it clearly does not exist where it is less likely.[12]

Or, in a simpler diagrammatic form:

Premise: Even the gods are not perfect.
Premise: (Since the gods are better than people,)
  Claim: Certainly human beings are not perfect.

Note that the premise "the gods are not perfect" is a statement of social belief, not (at least for us) a truth for which there could be universal agreement. Even so, the reasoning sequence in this practical argument "makes sense" if the implied premise is accepted.

## Demonstration and Argumentation

We can approach the distinction between formal arguments and practical enthymemes from another useful perspective. A mathematics problem is a demonstration because its final sum is self-evidently true. The process of how to perform the computations may require demonstration, but the transformation of the various operations into a conclusion is "beyond discussion." No one deliberates over claims that are self-evident by definition or direct observation. In contrast, argumentation is not so much concerned with truth as with the possible agreement of readers or listeners. We may argue a point to a hostile audience using a wide variety of reasoning skills, but we know that we cannot sweep away all of their doubts in the same way that we can correct an incorrect math problem. As Aristotle noted, practical reasoning works from "opinions that are generally accepted." Demonstrations work from basic premises where it would be "improper to ask any further for the why and wherefore of them."[13] There are no universal procedures for "demonstrating" conclusions such as "the United States is the most open society on earth." We may argue this point successfully before many audiences, but there is no way to make claims that will be immune from potential disagreement. Practical persuasion is thus always subject to the acceptance of a particular audience. In locating persuasive ideas to build arguments, we meet our audiences "on the ground . . . of their own convictions."[14]

## Factual and Preferential Claims

Another distinguishing feature of arguments is whether they contain claims of fact or claims of judgment. Generally speaking, the force of an argument based on a claim of judgment will not be as great as that of a reasoning sequence in support of a claim of fact. Facts hold the possibility of being proven true or false. In contrast, judgments express priorities, preferences, or values that differ from individual to individual.

We frequently mistake judgmental for factual claims, thereby overestimating how much "proof" is needed and underestimating how much disagreement can be expected. The word *is* in a claim sometimes creates the problem. Is and other indicative verb forms (i.e., *was* and *were*) have an aura of finality that makes judgmental claims seem as provable and timeless as known "facts." For instance, the statement "Thomas Jefferson was a better president than Abraham Lincoln" is not a statement of fact. As applied to the presidency, *better* can be legitimately defined in different ways. One person may rank a president's performance on foreign policy decisions higher than domestic policies; someone else may reverse priorities. By contrast, factual claims are statements that hold the promise of being demonstrated true or false, regardless of your own beliefs.[15] Here are some examples:

It costs $390,000 to buy 30 seconds of ad time on *Seinfeld*.

There are ice caps on the planet Mars.

Water at sea level boils at 210° F.

Sirhan Sirhan killed Senator Robert Kennedy in 1968.

David Letterman spent most of his broadcasting career with NBC.

Smoking increases a person's chances of contracting lung cancer.

The *Los Angeles Times* is the nation's largest newspaper.

Deaths from automobile crashes have decreased in the last ten years.[16]

All of these statements share the possibility of being shown conclusively right or wrong. We say "possibility" because the available evidence is sometimes insufficient to discover the truth about actual events. For example, we know (it is an unchallenged fact) that the baby of aviation hero Charles Lindburgh mysteriously disappeared from his family's home. We also know that a carpenter, Bruno Richard Hauptmann, was convicted of kidnapping the baby in a 1935 trial and was later electrocuted. However there are still doubts that Hauptmann committed the crime.[17] Persuasion frequently involves factual claims in widely varying situations: the courtroom (Hauptmann was probably innocent), the physical sciences (some deep sea plants do not need sunlight to flourish), and on social issues (children watching violent television programs imitate the violence they see).

The most common claims in the realm of persuasion are preferential.[18] These cannot be proved or settled by citing supporting facts, nor can they be known in the same way that we "know" the truth of a statement such as, "Texas was once a part of Mexico." A judgmental claim involves assigning personal preferences to persons, objects, or laws. The words we use in these claims indicate how we feel about what we are describing. The object of our attention is good, bad, worthwhile, dangerous, or desirable, reflecting our (and often our culture's) preferences about what is right or wrong, decent or indecent, moral or immoral, important or insignificant. Consider these samples:

The American system of higher education is the best in the world.

Robin Williams is a comic genius.

Deaf grade school students should be required to learn hand signs.

As a network, CBS has been mismanaged in the last ten years.

Catholicism is superior to other forms of Christianity.

Republicans do a better job of managing the nation's economy.

College students should spend a year performing national service.

Insurance companies unfairly discriminate against young drivers.

Maine's Arcadia National Park is a hiker's paradise.

Note that in every statement, some word gives a judgmental "spin" to the claim. Words like *better, should, good, superior,* and *unfairly* express feelings about the qualities of ideas or objects. While we can "prove" to the satisfaction of most reasoning people that "smoking increases a person's chances of contracting lung cancer"—a valid cause and effect factual claim with ample proof to support it—we cannot with the same certainty "prove" that "Catholicism is a superior form of Christianity."

This is not to say that the old axiom that you can't argue about religion and politics is correct. We inevitably will debate our preferences with others; preferences are the basis of most of the laws and codes by which we live. Yet it is unreasonable to expect that argumentation will put all contrary positions to rest in the way that DNA testing may "prove" that an accused person was present at a crime scene. Communicators frequently forget that "differences of opinion" are not necessarily resolved by appealing to "the facts." Determinations of what is right and wrong, best or worst, are debatable because people are different. As Kenneth Burke has noted, the temptation may be great, "but we cannot call a man illogical for acting on the basis of what he feels to be true."[19]

## Implied and Stated Components of Arguments

Many times logical relationships that lead to assertions hardly need to be explored at all, as when we make passing comments about noncontroversial subjects. The claim that "it is too hot today" is usually accompanied by obvious evidence (high temperature, humidity, or bright sun) that makes it unnecessary to provide supporting reasons. If pressed, however, we could make the reasoning behind almost any assertion explicit by writing down all relevant claims and premises. Our complete argument about the weather might include a *factual premise* (the thermometer reads ninety-two degrees) and a judgmental premise that "interprets" the significance of the facts (ninety-two degrees is, by my definition, too hot). This argument diagrammed as an enthymeme could be represented in simple form:

Factual Premise: The thermometer reads ninety-two degrees.
Judgmental Premise: (implied but not stated) A temperature of ninety-two is too hot.
(Therefore . . .)
Claim: It is too hot today.

Persuasion, of course, is neither so formal nor so simple. We rarely debate the weather. When persuasion occurs, routine and noncontroversial observations are rarely the focus. Our feelings are often involved, along with our sense of status and self-esteem. Arguments from everyday life often have many preferential and factual premises that reflect deeply held priorities, values, and opinions. As in our simple example, it is often unnecessary to make all of the premises (and sometimes even the claims) of our arguments explicit. We can count on our listeners to supply parts of the reasoning sequence, because speakers and listeners frequently share similar assumptions about what evidence implies.

Because vital parts of many arguments exist as unstated premises rather than overt reasons, shrewd persuaders should work to tap agreement with unstated premises. The arrest and trial of O. J. Simpson, for example, triggered a torrent of public discussion about spouse abuse. In one instance, an observer on National Public Radio asked several rhetorical questions where the implied answers were perhaps less interesting than the unstated premise behind them. To paraphrase her, "Do men talk to other men about domestic violence?" "Shouldn't men feel like they have a responsibility to help stop it?"[20] Perhaps men as a class have been too silent about violence directed toward women. However, the unstated assumption behind this premise would not find universal acceptance. The implication is that people of one gender have some responsibility for the actions of others of the same sex. In simplified form:

> Premise: Men do not show enough concern about domestic violence.
>
> Premise: (an implied bridge to the claim) People of one gender have an obligation to deal with the dysfunctional actions of others of the same sex.
>
> Claim: Men should help stop domestic violence.

Some form of these premises had to be supplied by listeners to answer yes to the rhetorical questions. Yet the unstated portion of the argument hinges on a gender responsibility that seems illogical and unobtainable. In specific terms, does any man or woman share such a gender responsibility? Does one's mother share responsibility for the actions of all irresponsible women, whether they are drug dealers, child abusers, or television celebrities? Should one's father share the guilt of serial murderers, rapists, or pandering talk-show hosts? Any useful exploration of the responsibility for dysfunctional behavior in society must involve far more elements than categories of gender.

Consider a second example where the keys to an argument lie in unstated, rather than stated, assumptions. In a media feeding-frenzy that continued well into his presidency, Bill Clinton was repeatedly probed by reporters about his personal life, including his fidelity, his activities twenty years earlier as a student, and his performance as governor of Arkansas. No subject, though, provoked more comment or ridicule than his response to a question during the 1992 presidential campaign about whether he had ever smoked marijuana. A New York television reporter raised the question, noting that Clinton had been evasive in the past, saying only that he had "not broken any state laws." Very well, she thought, if not in the United States, did he smoke pot as a student in England? The candidate responded that "when I was in England, I experimented with marijuana a time or two." He then added, "And I didn't like it, and I didn't inhale, and I didn't try again."

The statement provoked a flurry of reports and jokes, as well as heated defenses of the candidate. It became evidence for two very different kinds of arguments, both of which depended on unstated but vital assumptions. For some, such as veteran political writers Jack Germond and Jules Witcover—while his actions as a student were "no big deal," his statement was symptomatic of "evasion" and "dissembling"—in their words, "revealing of Clinton's habit of trying to minimize something that might hurt him politically"[21]

The campaign thus dealt with a continuing "character" argument raised by the press and the opposition, as in this abbreviated example:

Factual Premise:  Clinton smoked pot, but tried to minimize the event.

Factual Premise:  Clinton similarly conceded but minimized problems in his marriage, his anti-war views while in England, etc.

Therefore . . .

Judgmental Claim:  (often implied, but not stated) Clinton lacks the character to be president.

Phrase to condense the argument: "Slick Willie"

For supporters and undecided voters, a very different argument emerged from the coverage of character issues. For them, the problem with the campaign was not the candidates but the media, which seemed to be setting its collective agenda from the front pages of "trash" tabloids and their voyeuristic television counterparts. When Clinton appeared on *Donahue*, for example, he was subjected to half an hour of questions building on the above argument. After reviewing the marijuana statement and other issues, Donahue noted that "Part of the 'Slick Willie' problem is caused by what some analysts see as your ability to deflect questions and to give answers which really don't speak—." Clinton interrupted. "I don't believe I or any other decent human being should have to put up with the kind of questioning you're putting me through." Many in the audience agreed. They later cheered the assessment of one young woman in the studio audience: "I think, really, given the pathetic state of most of the United States at this point—Medicare, education, everything else—I can't believe you spent half an hour of airtime attacking this man's character. I'm not even a Bill Clinton supporter, but I think this is ridiculous."[22] From this frame of reference, if there was a question of character in the campaign, it was with a press that was viewed as parasitic and increasingly invasive. This partly implied and partly explicit argument can be easily summarized:

Judgmental Premise:  Campaign coverage has been driven by "revelations" of questionable relevance.

Judgmental Premise:  Clinton has been the victim of a distorted news agenda.

Judgmental Claim:  (sometimes stated, sometimes implied) Much of the news media has cheapened the political process.

Phrase to condense the argument: "Junk Journalism"

In the first argument Clinton was the issue. In the second—especially among supporters of the Democratic candidate—the media became the issue. In both cases, Americans went to the polls dealing with a wealth of arguments to sort out—complicated by the task of sorting out implied components of the stated arguments.

## Reasoning to Discover and to Defend

It follows from what we have said that reasoning is used to rationalize ideas as well as to discover them. We can employ the processes of logical demonstration to discover what we did not know. For example, the numbers in our checkbook may be calculated to reveal that we are overdrawn at the bank. Similarly, computers use advanced programs and vast amounts of information to calculate everything from shifts in the earth's crust to the movements of hurricanes. When we learn how to program a computer or use existing software, we have harnessed elaborate reasoning sequences (computer codes and logic) that will extend our knowledge beyond its present limits. The reasoning of argumentation, however, more commonly defends what is already known or believed. As a persuader on a given topic, your view is more or less fixed; what you hope to alter is the attitude of your listeners. This form of practical reasoning, notes Toulmin and his colleagues, is "not a way of arriving at ideas but rather a way of testing ideas critically." Argumentative reasoning

is concerned less with how people think than with how they share their ideas and thoughts in situations that raise the question of whether those ideas are worth sharing. It is a collective and continuing human transaction, in which we present ideas or claims to particular sets of people with particular situations or contexts and offer the appropriate kinds of "reasons" in their support.[23]

This is not to suggest that persuasion is simply rationalization. The quality of persuasion cannot be very good if, at some point, reasoning is not also employed as a tool of discovery. Aristotle's teacher, Plato, made the telling point that elaborate efforts at persuasion without equally intense efforts to discover the "best" or "true" will result in the exploitation rather than enlightenment of an audience.[24] When we wonder if celebrities actually use the services they endorse in advertisements, we are using this principle. An endorsement is suspect if a celebrity has made no effort to discover the worth of the product or service.

## Finding Good Reasons for Claims

A useful guide for judging whether a premise works is to consider whether it is a "good reason" for supporting a claim. We have described reasoned persuasion as the support of claims with relevant premises, stated or implied. These premises will contain various principles, conclusions, and forms of evidence relevant to an argument. According to Karl Wallace, "Good reasons are a number of statements, consistent with each other, in support of an ought proposition or a value-judgment."[25] They provide explanations that the persuader believes will elicit widespread agreement from an audience. The anticipated agreement is based on the fact that good reasons frequently summarize what members of a society already accept as true or "right." The following are two examples of media-related preferential claims and their "good reason" premises:

Claim: Companies that direct advertising to very young children are engaged in unethical conduct.

Reason: Young children lack sufficient sophistication to "discount" for the "puffery" in advertising.

Reason: Ethical persuaders, by definition, will not exploit gullible audiences who lack the ability to weigh the motives of communicators.

Claim: Congress should consider restricting the sale of American-owned media to foreign interests.

Reason: Foreign owners of American media frequently lack the pluralist outlook that is the lifeblood of American society.

Reason: Foreign media buyers may impose their own cultural and political standards on the "American" books, films, and music they control.

Reason: The Japanese owner of MCA/Universal noted that he "could never imagine" producing films that would reflect negatively on Japan.[26]

You may agree or disagree with these arguments, or find fault with one or more of the good reasons. There are times when one person's "common sense" is another's irrationality. Even so, you can usually sense when you have located reasons that will hold up under public scrutiny. Your impression of whether a statement will gain acceptance is an inexact but invaluable guide in determining the strongest defenses that can be made for claims.

Practical reasoning frequently boils down to "common sense." When you isolate the premises that you intend to use in support of a claim, your "sense" of what works is largely based on the ideas you hold in "common" with others in the culture. An individual's rationality is partly the outcome of years of socialization in the culture. Learning is the lifelong process of acquiring norms about what goes with what, what fits, and what contexts are friendly or hostile to certain ideas.

Interestingly, humor is one important cultural vehicle for celebrating the threshold where sense becomes nonsense. Humorists deliberately set out to offend the norms and expectations of logic. Our laughs serve

## SHOE

*Humor works because it turns our expectations upside down and exposes our vulnerabilities.*

as signs that we hold membership in the society of the sane. A complaint made against Mozart by another composer in the 1984 film *Amadeus* is funny because it violates expectations. A defect of Mozart's music, he said solemnly, was that it had "too many notes." It is obviously an odd standard (that is, outside the norms of the culture) to assess music in terms of the number of notes in a piece, but the comment was writer Peter Schaffer's astute way of showing how an insecure person might grasp for any reason, even a bad one. In chapter 13, we will show how the search for good reasons can be put to work in constructing persuasive speeches and messages.

## Common Examples of Defective Reasoning

Textbooks that address reasoning almost uniformly attempt to provide readers with the logician's equivalent of the Rock of Gibraltar—some sturdy reference point to simplify the problem of navigating between "good" and "bad" reasoning. If we know what "good" reasoning is, then it follows that there must be systematic ways to classify "bad" reasoning. "A fallacy," notes philosopher Max Black, "is an argument which seems to be sound without being so . . ."[27] Fallacious arguments frequently suggest more than they deliver, using the grammar and verbal patterns associated with argumentation but without the genuine linkages that should exist between claims and "supporting" statements.

Before we identify several common forms of fallacies, a major qualification needs to be noted. Given the diversity of experiences and values that exist in all audiences, it would be foolhardy to presume that fallacies are uncovered as easily as incorrect mathematical calculations. As we have noted, not only do audiences have different standards for assessing the appropriateness of arguments, but reasoning patterns useful in one context may be inappropriate in another.

## Ad Hominem

This commonly cited fallacy is argument directed against persons rather than against their ideas. A series of 1990 television commercials by some New York area Oldsmobile and Pontiac dealers ridiculed the physical stature of Japanese people, as well as their extensive foreign real estate holdings. Those advertisements fit the category of ad hominem. As the *New York Times* editorialized, "Disputing the cost or quality of Japanese cars is fair game; attacking their makers is not."[28] There can be little doubt that automobiles ought to be sold on their features rather than through vague appeals to racial stereotypes. The issue is less clear when we do need to make decisions about an individual's capacity to perform under various circumstances. For example, as we have seen, individuals may differ on the relevancy or irrelevancy of a political candidate's private life. Since governmental officials are elected to make many decisions beyond those that can be presented in a campaign, you may feel that a candidate's character and personal affiliations are indeed relevant in determining fitness for office. But for others, such an emphasis on private actions is used largely for political points, a way to attack a person without dealing with his or her ideas. Fallacies like ad hominem must be analyzed with careful attention to the context in which they are applied.

## False Cause

A persuader who has fallen victim to false cause assumes that because two related events have occurred together, one has probably caused the other. Millions of readers and filmgoers worldwide believe that the paragon of perfect reasoning is Arthur Conan Doyle's famous detective, Sherlock Holmes. When the available evidence of a murder seems to indicate to readers that the butler did it, the more thoughtful Holmes invariably finds the true cause. Blows that could not have been made by a right-handed person, bodies that have been dead too long, and footprints left in a rug are only a few of the clues that have allowed the master sleuth to sort out real from false causes.

The child who notes that a rooster always crows before the morning sun may conclude that it is the rooster who calls the sun. He or she has made the same mistake as the angry constituent who once complained to his congressman that federal statutes mandating Daylight Savings Time would result in "too much sun" for his garden. Each wrongly assumed that it was possible for living creatures to violate the physical laws that govern the solar system. Likewise, most Americans still identify the Great Depression of 1929 with the stock market crash on October 24 known as "Black Thursday." Stock prices plunged dramatically and made paupers out of many former millionaires. Actually, the crash was more a symptom of the weak 1929 economy than a cause of it. There were many reasons for the depression—too much consumer debt, overproduction, unstable foreign money systems, and so on. Stock speculation was only the most visible sign of the economic house of cards that eventually collapsed as the 1920s ended.[29]

A final example of false cause comes from the social sciences. For many years, it was almost an automatic reflex in educational circles to assume that television viewing by young children decreased their interest in reading. In fact, some studies now suggest that television may encourage literacy in certain children, particularly slower learners.[30] There are few simple correlations that link the use of any medium to other kinds of behaviors, but new evidence on how people use television may force us to rethink assumed but unjustified assertions.

CATHY © Cathy Guisewite. Reprinted with permission of Universal Press Syndicate.

## Non Sequitur

A non sequitur is when a conclusion does not follow from the reasons that have been cited. When talk-show host David Letterman reads one of his famous "top ten lists," he is usually in the realm of the non sequitur. One of his ten reasons for leaving General Electric's NBC in favor of CBS, for example, was, "I've stolen as many GE bulbs as I can fit in my garage."[31]

Most non sequiturs have at least superficial connections that link claims to supporting "reasons," but under closer examination the connection is insufficient or downright inconsistent. Consider the wording of an advertisement for Alka-Seltzer Plus Cold Medicine, as reported by *Consumer Reports*.[32] In fine print, the ad notes that the "product may cause drowsiness; use caution if operating heavy machinery or driving a vehicle." The same message also contains testimony from Harold "Butch" Brooks, a truck driver, who notes, "When I'm out on the road, bad weather, bad cold, my load's still gotta go, so I rely on Alka-Seltzer Plus." The whole ad is a non sequitur; the sum total of its claims do not fit together. Its basic inconsistency is similar to the strange reasoning used on a package of D-Con, which proudly announces that the poison is made from a "scientifically balanced blend of natural ingredients."

Targeting advertisements to locate non sequiturs is equivalent to shooting fish in a barrel. When we read beer ads that imply beer drinking is the key to sociability or automobile ads that imply a new car will create respect and envy, we know that such product claims cannot stand up to logical scrutiny. The more dangerous non sequiturs are those that arise in debates on important social issues and in the rhetoric that is offered in defense of an official action. One of the most valuable services political reporters and analysts perform is to expose the sometimes confused reasoning of policy makers in government. Before his death in 1990, *The New Republic*'s Richard Strout always had a good ear for political statements that said less than they first seemed, as in the campaign speeches of Dwight Eisenhower:

> He has an effective little trick of non sequitur in which he begins, "I do not think this," and after developing at length what he does not think, says suddenly and positively as though in a burst of confidence, "But I do think this," and comes out with the answer to quite a different question.[33]

## Circular Argument

Sometimes the reasons cited for a claim are little more than a rewording of the claim. What are offered as supporting premises are really just restatements, which give the appearance of more support than actually exists. Ad slogans such as "When you're out of Schlitz you're out of beer" and "When you say Budweiser, you've said it all"[34] have the structure of sentences that progress from one idea to another but actually start and end with the same idea. Parents regularly use this form of argument on their children in the familiar retort "Do it because I said so." What follows after "because" is essentially a duplicate of what preceded. Circular arguments can cut short public debate on pressing issues by narrowly focusing on only unchallengeable claims. By August of 1968, for example, the United States had committed 541,000 troops to the Vietnam War. Many leaders in Congress and in the Johnson and Nixon Administrations argued that because we were so deeply committed to the defense of South Vietnam, we should stay to see the war through to a successful conclusion. Even those who regretted having become involved in an Asian land war felt that the enormous human and economic costs already expended prohibited a withdrawal of forces. Because the deaths and misery had to serve some higher need, a quagmire of circular reasoning developed. The fact of being at war became its own justification for delaying our departure from Vietnam until the fall of South Vietnam in 1975. By that time, over 58,000 American lives had been lost.[35]

## Excessive Dependence on Authority

It is a legitimate pattern of reasoning to support a persuasive claim by citing the expertise of like-minded authorities. Excessive dependence on authority, however, sometimes results in the premature conclusion of discussion. As Toulmin, Rieke, and Janik have noted, "Appeals to authority become fallacious at the point where authority is taken as closing off discussion of the matter in question. No further evidence is considered; the authority's opinion has settled the matter once and for all."[36]

Persuasion frequently implies the question, have I heard enough to change my mind? The answer, if only one source has spoken, should usually be, not yet. Sometimes, however, a single source may have the power to change someone's mind or motivate them to act. There is no shortage of experts—real or self-styled—who are prepared to argue that they should have the last word. Sometimes history has demonstrated that they could not have been more wrong. RCA pioneer David Sarnoff at one time thought it unlikely that Americans would accept advertising as a basis for the new and emerging broadcast industry. Some aviation engineers once believed that no plane or pilot could survive a flight beyond the speed of sound. More than a few Hollywood studio executives of the early 1920s doubted that film audiences would really want to hear their favorite actors talk.

Presidents, ministers, influential teachers, and therapists represent a few of the authorities who are sometimes consulted for what amounts to total documentation of a claim or a decision. Even excellent scholars can sometimes overstate the case for one kind—their kind—of perspective. Consider the implications behind the following sentence found in a psychology text: "It is interesting to note that when ordinary people try to understand behavior, they are acting as naive psychologists."[37] With the use of the word *naive*, the authors make the subtle assumption that "ordinary" people should not attempt to understand the diverse ways in which humans act. Only the real authorities (academic psychologists) have the necessary qualifications. The sentence thoughtlessly excludes the varied and valuable insights into the nature of human action given to us by playwrights, sociologists, journalists, novelists, and scores of others. Phrases like, "He said so, and that's enough for me," "The only person I trust said . . . ," or "She has the advanced degree, so she must know what she is saying" are clues to attitudes that have been accepted on the slender thread of only one other's advice. In chapter 5 we will examine in more detail persuasion based on such appeals to authority.

## How Persuasion and Logical Argumentation Differ

Thus far, we have shown how a claim supported by reasonable premises can lead to persuasion. We labeled this single logical unit an "argument" and noted that Aristotle discovered forms of argumentation (enthymemes) that routinely appear in most types of persuasion. Does it follow that we can use the words *persuasion* and *argumentation* interchangeably? Is persuasion always subject to the rules of practical reasoning? Philosophers and social scientists have debated these questions for years, but raising them is more than an empty academic exercise. How you answer them says a great deal about how you think you can influence others. Answering yes to both implies that persuasion should always involve the use of "good reasons." Answering no suggests that factors other than reasoning can and should influence what people believe. We close this chapter with an explanation of why we think persuasion is more than the construction of reasoned arguments, vital though they are. We start by noting a common misconception: that persuasion depends more on emotional than on rational responses.

## Are Arguments either Logical or Emotional?

In *The Rhetoric*, Aristotle identified three forms of "proof" available to the persuader: logical, emotional, and ethical (what others know or think about us).[38] Although he did not specifically note that the presence of one meant the absence of another, popular usage of these categories has had that effect. Ask the average person to analyze an advertising "pitch" or a pamphlet from a group seeking social change. Predictably, he or she will come up with a variation of Aristotle's distinction. Some parts of the message will be identified as containing "logical" reasons and other parts as containing "emotional" appeals. Among experts who study messages closely, the wording may be fancier, but the implication that logic and emotion are opposites is still present. A law school professor regrets that "emotion can activate any behavior which has not been inhibited by reason."[39] An expert on political communication similarly notes that the statements of most politicians are "nothing more than emotional appeals."[40] We think, however, it is a mistake to assume that the presence of emotion indicates the absence of logic.

The problem with this common distinction is that reason and emotion are not opposites but complementary processes. A sense of reasoned justification usually increases our emotional attachment to ideas. When we feel that we have a strong case for a point of view, our sense of urgency in communicating that commitment is enhanced. Think about your experiences with the emotion of anger. Your anger can develop in proportion to the "good reasons" you have for it. Reasoning motivates our emotions. Our emotions are often the product of intensely felt and often very logical relationships. "Revenge films" that may be widely criticized for their "mindless violence" (*Death Wish*, *RoboCop*) are careful to make their villains so evil and cruel that their deaths at the hands of the enraged heroes seem justified. The misplaced distinction between "reason" and "emotion" thus fails to provide a way to separate persuasion from argumentation, but it does turn us toward the right direction.

## Persuasion's "Self-Interest" and Argumentation's "Public Interest"

Persuasion and argumentation can differ both in the types of reasoning that are present and in the kinds of reasons that are offered in support of claims. All persuasion must provide a series of incentives or reasons for winning the approval of audiences, but not all legitimate persuasion involves "good reasons." As we have noted, the good reasons that occur in arguments are made with the hope that a wide diversity of people might also sense their reasonableness. By contrast, while persuaders frequently employ rational argumentation, they also rely on their abilities to use appeals to personal wants and needs.

The distinction between persuasive appeals and argumentative good reasons is revealing. As we will discuss more fully in chapter 6, all of us have personal needs for affection, for approval from others, for high self-esteem, and so on. We can be motivated by appeals that promise to satisfy these needs. However, when we present arguments for the approval of audiences, we know that our reasoning must often move beyond individual needs in order to win the approval of the public as a whole. For example, in a courtroom jurors are sometimes cautioned by a judge to ignore attempts at flattery directed to them by lawyers eager to win their cases. Appeals to an individual juror's private needs (the need for approval, the need to belong, and so forth) are as out of place in the courtroom as they are in argumentation's "court of reason" based on the accumulation of facts and evidence.[41] Yet, persuasion frequently depends on just such identification—on efforts to recognize and appeal to individual needs and motivations. For instance, one of the most successful advertising slogans used by McDonald's was the jingle, "You deserve a break today." It was an attractive persuasive appeal, but it was not much of an argument. The slogan struck a chord of self-interest by implying that a trip to McDonald's was a way to get out of the kitchen and, at the same time, give oneself a reward. "I do deserve a break" was the anticipated response. A long-used slogan for FTD Florists offered the same kind of persuasive appeal. "When you care enough to send the very best" was effective because it made the purchase of flowers a certification of excellence. Both of these slogans successfully appealed to the need most of us have to raise our self-esteem, but neither slogan was meant to provide information about the merits of their products. Good reasons are explanations we would accept as equally relevant to others as to ourselves. Appeals, by contrast, are statements that "work" because they favorably motivate us as creatures with fundamental needs. One reason advertising is so effective on television is that it reaches the viewer as a private rather than a public person. We accept advertising appeals made to us in our homes that we might reject as a member of a "live" audience. It is revealing that a commercial viewed passively at home is sometimes greeted by groans of disbelief when shown to an audience gathered in a theater. To put our point another way, while persuasion can employ reasoning from facts and general opinions, it also reaches individuals by appeals to subjective and personal needs that have no firm basis in public opinion.

This distinction between argumentation and persuasion is admittedly imprecise, but it is important. It explains why the understanding of the process of influence is as much the study of individual psychology as the logic of argumentation. It also reminds us that communication is an activity with layers of meanings. As recipients of messages, we are capable of assessing claims with the collective interests of others in mind, but we also consider ideas more personally. Wayne C. Booth, whose observations opened this chapter, reminds us that not all of our attitudes can be subject to rational argument.

> As a university professor I am committed to the supreme professional standard of rationality: insofar as I am an honest professor, worthy of my own respect, I am sworn to change my mind if and when someone shows me that there are good reasons to change my mind. But both as a man who loves art and literature that I cannot fully explain, and as a human being who holds to many values the correctness of which I cannot easily prove with unanswerable rational arguments, I know how much of my life is not readily explicable at the court of what is usually called reason.[42]

Our beliefs cannot always be measured by what we can support with good reasons, as a final example illustrates. Several years ago, network television was saturated with an advertisement for a cream that promised to remove "ugly age spots." Like most cosmetic ads, it promised a way to purchase greater satisfaction about the way we appear to others. The commercial for Porcelana cream opened with four middle-aged women playing a card game. One of the women is obviously ill at ease as she looks down at her hands holding the cards. We hear her say to herself, "These ugly age spots; what's a woman to do!" Obviously, Porcelana is ready to come to her rescue.

From an argumentative point of view, the commercial is hopelessly flawed. Would friendships be at stake merely because a person had a few spots on her hands? Of course not, but the woman's anxiety and embarrassment has a certain dramatic plausibility. Based on just a few seconds of the commercial, we can believe that there are people like us who are anxious to be accepted by their friends and may believe that even minor blemishes could put them at risk. The commercial appeals to the very private fear of rejection that most of us experience from time to time. To dismiss it as "irrational" is to miss the point. The appeal to fear of rejection is not intended to stand up under the close scrutiny that we give arguments containing good reasons. The appeal evokes subtle and fragile feelings that are not easily allayed. One can argue that using the cream will not help maintain friendships, but that does not deny the strong possibility that some users of the product may feel better in the knowledge that they have taken a step to improve their personal appearance. We have missed something important if we fail to recognize that there is a strong rhetorical component to our personal sense of well-being.

## Summary

In this chapter we looked at the role that reasoning plays in persuasion. For our purposes, we defined reasoning as the process of supporting controversial claims with premises that function as good reasons. Reasons are good when we believe that they are as sensible for others as they are for ourselves. Reasoning may be the basis of the humor and information exchanged by two adversaries on a television talk show, or it may aspire to be the basis of a political campaign.

We have also noted that there is a great deal of misunderstanding about reasoning and about what it can and cannot do. For example, not all persuasion utilizes good reasons because sometimes the most direct route to attitude change is by appealing to private but powerful motivations, such as a person's need to feel wanted by others. These individualized appeals are not necessarily "irrational emotions" or "unreasonable" grounds for forming attitudes, but neither are they the kinds of statements that can stand up as reasons that would help shape a consensus of support in a public gathering. Advertising is full of motivating appeals, which frequently have the effect of allowing people to reward themselves or sanction a certain feeling. Topics of greater consequence, such as efforts to reconstruct the guilt or innocence of a defendant in a trial, demand more rigorous defenses. Some of the claims and premises of arguments may involve judgments that can never be fully argued away, others may be factual and possibly yield tests to prove their accuracy.

Using the pioneering writings of Aristotle as a guide, we looked at the unique features of practical arguments called enthymemes. Enthymemes have two special features that make them different from the formal "analytic" arguments used by scientists, mathematicians, and logicians. First, the claims in enthymemes, are "probable" or "preferable," since they deal with practical subjects for which demonstrations of fact are usually impossible. Second, usually one or more of their parts (claims or premises) may be implied rather than stated; enthymemes typically build from what an audience already believes or accepts. They build on underlying assumptions the audience will readily supply. Like all forms of reasoning, enthymemes can be made up of premises of dubious quality. In fallacies like ad hominem, false cause, non sequitur, and circular argument, the premises of some arguments may present only the illusion rather than the reality of logical support.

Reasoning can create a sense of indisputable power drawing listeners or readers to a predetermined conclusion. Being aware of potential misrepresentations and false linkages in arguments is the first crucial step in resisting unreasonable appeals and in avoiding such problems in our own persuasive messages.

## Questions and Projects for Further Study

1. Locate an argumentative essay written by a newspaper columnist. After studying the column, summarize the claims and premises the author has used. Be careful to look for implied as well as stated premises. Make a judgment about the quality and adequacy of the author's arguments.

2. Observe one of the adversarial exchanges between William F. Buckley and one of his guests on his show or on any television news/talk program (for example, NBC's *This Week With David Brinkley*, ABC's *Nightline*, or PBS's *McNeil/Lehrer Newshour*). Identify the extent to which each advocate is able to communicate "good reasons" in defense of his or her position.

3. Using examples from magazine advertisements, locate and explain messages that contain fallacies mentioned in this chapter: ad hominem, false cause, non sequitur, circular argument, and excessive dependence on authority.

4. This chapter describes practical reasoning by comparing several categories of opposites. Briefly explain the differences between each of the following contrasting terms, indicating which term identifies a characteristic of practical reasoning:

    demonstration vs. argumentation

    reasoning to discover vs. reasoning to defend

    analytic arguments vs. enthymemes

5. Explain the statement in this chapter that "the most interesting characteristic of analytic arguments is their potency or force." Construct a simple argument with two premises and a conclusion that illustrates an analytic argument.

6. In this chapter we note that one of the most common mistakes people make with regard to reasoning is the mistaken assumption that they can "prove" a claim of judgment. Cite your own examples of claims of preference and claims of fact. Why is a claim of judgment not provable with the same certainty as a claim of fact?

# Notes

[1] Wayne C. Booth, *Now Don't Try to Reason With Me*. Chicago: University of Chicago, 1970, p. 22.

[2] William F. Buckley, Jr., *On the Firing Line*. New York: Random House, 1989, pp. 293–95.

[3] For a discussion on audience motivations to seek out logical relationships in persuasion, see Daniel J. O'Keefe, *Persuasion: Theory and Research*. Newbury Park, CA: Sage, 1990, pp. 96–116; see also our discussion in chapter 4 on shortcuts and the discussion of elaboration liklihood theory in chapter 6.

[4] Stephen Toulmin, Richard Rieke, and Allan Janik, *An Introduction to Reasoning*. New York: Macmillan, 1979, p. 9.

[5] Aristotle, *The Rhetoric*, in *The Basic Works of Aristotle*, ed. by Richard McKeon. New York: Random House, 1941, p. 1325.

[6] See Stephen Toulmin, *The Uses of Argument*. London: Cambridge University, 1964, pp. 125–35.

[7] Chaim Perelman and L. Olbrechts-Tyteca, *The New Rhetoric: A Treatise on Argumentation*, trans. by John Wilkinson and Purcell Weaver. Notre Dame, IN: University of Notre Dame, 1969, p. 2.

[8] Meir Kahane, "Annex, Expel," *New York Times*, July 18, 1983, reprinted September 30, 1990, Sec 4a, p. 14.

[9] For further discussion of this point, see Richard Weaver, *The Ethics of Rhetoric*. Chicago: Henry Regnery, 1953, pp. 7–9.

[10] Lloyd Bitzer, "Aristotle's Enthymeme Revisited," *Quarterly Journal of Speech*, December 1959, pp. 399–408.

[11] Aristotle, *Topics*, in McKeon, p. 188.

[12] Aristotle, *The Rhetoric*, in McKeon, p. 1421.

[13] Aristotle, *Topics*, in McKeon, p. 188.

[14] *Ibid.*, p. 189. For further discussion of the differences between demonstrations and arguments, see also Perelman and L. Olbrechts-Tyteca, pp. 13–14.

[15] A good case has been made by "Sociologists of Knowledge" and others that very little knowledge about human affairs is completely free of our own values. In a practical way, however, certain obvious facts are largely free of subjective interpretations. The reader interested in how social values can shape what we claim to "know" might start with Peter L. Berger's and Thomas Luckmann's *The Social Construction of Reality*, New York: Doubleday, 1967.

[16] *Guinness 1984 Book of World Records*. New York: Sterling, 1984, p. 340.

[17] For a convincing case arguing Hauptmann's innocence, see Ludovic Kennedy, *The Airman and the Carpenter*. New York: Viking, 1985.

[18] Ray Anderson and C. David Mortensen, "Logic and Marketplace Argumentation," *Quarterly Journal of Speech*, April, 1967, p. 150.

[19] Kenneth Burke, *Permanance and Change*. Indianapolis, IN: Bobbs-Merrill, Library of the Liberal Arts, 1965, p. 85.

[20] Letter broadcast on "Weekend Edition," National Public Radio, July 2, 1994.

[21] Jack W. Germond and Jules Witcover, *Mad as Hell: Revolt at the Ballot Box, 1992*. New York: Warner, 1993, pp. 273–274.

[22] *Ibid.*, p. 276.

[23] Toulmin, Rieke, and Janik, p. 9.

[24] See Weaver, pp. 11–12, and Plato's Phaedrus, trans. by R. Hackforth, Indianapolis, IN: Bobbs-Merrill, Library of the Liberal Arts, 1952, pp. 119–22.

[25] Karl R. Wallace, "The Substance of Rhetoric: Good Reasons," in *Rhetoric of Our Times*, ed. by J. J. Auer. New York: Appleton-Century-Crofts, 1969, p. 287.

[26] See David E. Sanger, "Politics and Multinational Movies," *New York Times*, November 27, 1990, pp. D1, D7.

[27] Max Black, "Fallacies," in *Readings in Argumentation*, ed by Jerry M. Anderson and Paul J. Dovre. Boston: Allyn and Bacon, 1968, p. 301.

[28] "Sell Cars, Not Racism," Editorial, *New York Times*, July 19, 1990, p. A22.

[29] Geoffrey Perrett, *America in the Twenties: A History*. New York: Touchstone, 1982, pp. 384–90.

[30] See, for example, Michael Morgan, "Television Viewing and Reading: Does More Equal Better?" *Journal of Communication*, Winter, 1980, pp. 159–165.

[31] Joshua Hammer and Harry Waters, "Good Night, Dave," *Newsweek*, January 24, 1993, p. 62.

[32] "Selling It," *Consumer Reports*, April, 1986, p. 279.

[33] Richard L. Strout, *TRB: Views and Perspectives on the Presidency*. New York: Macmillan, 1979, p. 109.

[34] Ivan L. Preston, *The Great American Blow Up*. Madison, WI: University of Wisconsin, 1975, p. 18.

[35] This is admittedly a simplification of a very complex issue. There were obviously many reasons for the American commitment to support the South Vietnamese. One reporter who has written extensively on both the early and later phases of our involvement is David Halberstam, whose first book, *The Making of a Quagmire*, New York: Random House, 1965, points to the dilemmas brought on by heavy military involvement in a land war. His second book, *The Best and Brightest*, New York: Random House, 1972, partially reconstructs the circular reasoning behind what became the United State's "no win" situation.

[36] Toulmin, Rieke, and Janik, p. 17.

[37] Philip G. Zimbardo, Ebbe B. Ebbesen, and Christina Maslach, *Influencing Attitudes and Changing Behavior*, Second Edition. Reading, MA: Addison-Wesley, 1977, p. 73.

[38] Aristotle, *The Rhetoric*, Book I, Chapter 2.

[39] Gray L. Dorsey, "Symbols: Vehicles of Reason or of Emotion?" in *Symbols and Values: An Initial Study*, ed. by Lyman Bryson, Louis Finkelstein, R. M. McIver, and Richard McKeon. New York: Cooper Square, 1964, p. 445.

[40] Murray Edelman, *The Symbolic Uses of Politics*. Chicago: University of Illinois Press, 1967, p. 137.

[41] A similar distinction is sometimes made between "persuasion" that moves us intellectually and "conviction" that moves us personally. See Perelman and Olbrechts-Tyteca, pp. 26–31.

[42] Booth, p. 20.

## Additional Reading

Ray Lynn Anderson and C. David Mortensen, "Logic and Marketplace Argumentation," *Quarterly Journal of Speech*, April 1967, pp. 143–51.

Wayne C. Booth, *Now Don't Try to Reason With Me*. Chicago: University of Chicago, 1970.

William F. Buckley, Jr., *On the Firing Line*. New York: Random House, 1989.

Gary Lynn Chronkite, "Logic, Emotion, and the Paradigm of Persuasion," *Quarterly Journal of Speech*, February 1964, pp. 13–18.

Howard Kanane, *Logic and Contemporary Rhetoric: The Use of Reason in Everyday Life, Seventh Edition.* Belmont, CA: Wadsworth, 1995.

Chaim Perelman and L. Olbrechts-Tyteca, *The New Rhetoric: A Treatise in Argumentation*, trans. by John Wilkinson and Purcell Weaver. Notre Dame, IN: University of Notre Dame, 1969.

Stephen Toulmin, Richard Rieke, and Allan Janik, *An Introduction to Reasoning.* New York: Macmillan, 1979.

Karl R. Wallace, "The Substance of Rhetoric: Good Reasons," in *The Rhetoric of Our Times*, ed., by J. J. Auer. New York: Appleton-Century-Crofts, 1969.

# 5

# Credibility and Authority

## OVERVIEW

- The Essential Role of Credibility
- The Multidimensional Aspects of Authority
- The Three Meanings of Credibility
  Ethos and the Idea of Good Character
  The Rational/Legal Ideal of Credibility
  Source Credibility as Believability
  Credibility Reconsidered
- Four Source-related Persuasion Strategies
  Prestige and Legitimation
  Mystification
  The Charismatic Persuader
  Authoritarianism and Acquiescence
- Summary
- Questions and Projects for Further Study
- Notes
- Additional Reading

> There could be no mistaking he was a great man—he looked like one, talked like one, was treated like one and insisted that he was one.[1]
> —John Kennedy describing Daniel Webster

# The Essential Role of Credibility

The game of "fictionary" requires only a small group of participants, pens, some sheets of paper, and a good dictionary. For each round of the game, a different person in the group looks through the dictionary and selects a word which the other members do not recognize. In one game among four friends, the word chosen was "halation." Three members of the group made up what they hoped would be plausible definitions and gave them to the holder of the dictionary, who had written down the real meaning of the word. That member convincingly read each of the definitions. The players then voted for what they thought was the proper meaning. Was it a condition of progressive baldness affecting animals and advanced primates; the effect of hearing an echo in a large space; the presence of a strong odor coming from the breath of a mammal; or a blurring of the edges of a light area on a photograph? Few participants in this game were sure they could detect the "right" definition, for which they would receive one point. (The person who chooses the word gets five points if no one guesses the correct meaning. Other players receive one point every time someone else chooses their bogus definition.)

"Fictionary" can be characterized as a blind search for credibility. Within the words and structure of the definitions, there may be clues that can be used to determine which one is authentic. Working against that possibility is the equal likelihood that other participants in the game will be skillful con artists. That is, their deception may lead other players into the trap of accepting a definition that will have more plausibility than accuracy. With almost any group of players, it is surprisingly difficult to determine the authoritative dictionary definition (in our example, the photography definition was correct). The issue of what to believe is even more difficult when it is not possible to know whom to believe.

The power to persuade is often contingent on assessments of the credibility or authority of a source. Even though we frequently pay lip service to the "integrity of ideas" or the "impartiality of facts," there is no doubt that the credibility of a communicator can be decisive in winning supporters.

This chapter considers how sources use personal characteristics to increase the prospects for successful persuasion. After a brief reminder about the difficulties in assessing credibility, the first half of this chapter explores three very different perspectives that account for how persuasive authority is established and communicated to audiences. The second half concludes with an extended examination of four related settings that are useful in understanding how certain advocates can dramatically affect audiences.

# The Multidimensional Aspects of Authority

The power that one individual exerts over another comes from many nonrhetorical contexts. As Andrew King notes, the ability to control another person may include physical or psychological threats, the assignment of official authority to one person or group, or the initiation of control through personal or secret action.[2] Our attention in this chapter is primarily on the power that flows from a persuadee's conviction that someone else has a legitimate claim to special knowledge or expertise.

As we shall see, the processes that accompany complying with a "superior" or more knowledgeable source are anything but simple. Three cautions need to be kept in mind. First, as with many patterns of persuasion, the multidimensional concept of authority is a reminder that there is an enormous gap between the questions that we raise and the relatively incomplete answers current research is able to provide. Power relationships between people are fascinating, but they are rarely reducible to simple formulas. Indeed, understanding questions about how authority operates may be more important than the partial answers now available. Persuasion theorists are constantly reminded that the mysteries of human behavior cannot be revealed with the clarity that comes with discoveries in the physical world. The physical sciences provide concrete findings not easily duplicated in studies of human action. We may be able to predict when and where an overloaded bridge will yield to the weight of a superior force; we are far less able to predict when an individual will yield to the claims of another person. Second, it is important to remember that the power to persuade applies to both individuals and to groups. Sometimes it makes more sense to talk about the specific credibility of one individual, such as the president of the United States or a speaker in a persuasion course. At other times, it is more relevant to consider the credibility of a group or an organization, as in a poll that asks Americans to estimate if moral and ethical standards are higher in big corporations or higher in the federal government. Finally, our emphasis on messages should not overshadow the fact that many of our relationships require certain responses. Human interaction often occurs in hierarchical frameworks that dictate compliance.

Sometimes what looks like persuasion is simply a veil that covers the necessity for inferiors and superiors to act out their roles. We like to think of ourselves as free agents able to exercise choice in a wide range of situations, but established relationships that exist with parents, employers, mentors, and others may mean that the power structure in a given setting communicates more than any specific message.

## The Three Meanings of "Credibility"

"Credibility" is a pivotal term in the study of persuasion, but those who use it frequently have different—if equally valid—meanings in mind. In a general sense, estimates of credibility involve assessing how the response of a given audience is affected by *who* a persuader is. For some, credibility means good character. For others, it is a synonym for truthfulness. Social scientists apply a third meaning to the term: it is a trait identified with a source who is believable to others, even if the source is "immoral" or "wrong." As we shall see, these three perspectives sometimes blend together. At other times, each one presents an opportunity to explore the different ways used by sources to achieve persuasive goals.

### Ethos and the Idea of Good Character

One of the oldest terms associated with the qualities of an advocate is the Greek word, *ethos*. For Aristotle, ethos was one of the three major forms of influence. He wrote in *The Rhetoric* that the ideal persuader should put the audience in the right emotional frame of mind (pathos), state the best arguments (logos), and have the right kind of character (ethos). The persuader "must not only try to make the argument of his speech demonstrative and worthy of belief; he must also make his own character look right.[3]

Aristotle labeled the components of good character as good sense, good moral character, and goodwill. "It follows," he noted, "that anyone who is thought to have all three of these good qualities will inspire trust in his audience.[4] "Good sense" and "good moral character" center on an audience's perception that a persuader's judgments and values are reasonable and justified. It is obvious that if the persuader seems to see the world in the same terms as the audience—a world in which "good" people are easily separated from less trustworthy people—they will be inclined to accept the speaker's evidence and conclusions. Add in the element of "goodwill"—the important idea that the persuader seems to have honorable intentions toward the audience—and we have a sense of what kinds of advocates are likely to be successful.

## Character Judgments in Everyday Life

We "read" every social setting for cues about the motives and competence of strangers as well as acquaintances. All interpersonal contact requires a degree of trust. Whenever someone encourages us to part with our money or to alter our attitudes, we want to be certain that our faith in them will not be abused.

In a book that describes his cross-country motorcycle travels *as well* as the deeper journey into his mind, Robert Pirsig provides examples of how we assess the abilities and sensibilities of people who present themselves as knowledgeable. At another level, Pirsig's *Zen and the Art of Motorcycle Maintenance* is also an eye-opening description of the confrontation between the Sophists and Plato discussed in chapter 2. In one revealing instance, he describes the credibility-revealing behavior of two uninvolved and distracted mechanics who had been asked to diagnose a strange noise coming from the engine of his motorcycle.

> The shop was a different scene from the ones I remembered. The mechanics, who had once all seemed like ancient veterans, now looked like children. A radio was going full blast and they were clowning around and talking and seemed not to notice me. When one of them finally came over he barely listened to the piston slap before saying, "Oh yeah. Tappets."[5]

Pirsig eventually paid a $140.00 repair bill for services that failed to remedy the engine problem. He later discovered that the noisy piston was caused by a damaged twenty-five cent pin accidentally sheared off by an equally careless mechanic. "Why," he wondered, "did they butcher it so?" What evidence did they provide that indicated they were less than fully competent mechanics?

> The radio was the clue. You can't really think hard about what you're doing and listen to the radio at the same time. Maybe they didn't see their job as having anything to do with hard thought, just wrench twiddling. If you can twiddle wrenches while listening to the radio that's more enjoyable.

> Their speed was another clue. They were really slopping things around in a hurry and not looking where they slopped them. More money that way. . . .

> But the biggest clue seemed to be their expressions. They were hard to explain. Good-natured, friendly, easygoing—and uninvolved. They were like spectators. You had the feeling they had just wandered in there themselves and somebody had handed them a wrench. There is no identification with the job. No saying, "I am a mechanic." At 5 P.M. or whenever their eight hours were in, you knew they would cut it off and not have another thought about their work. They were already trying not to have any thoughts about their work on the job.[6]

Pirsig argues that a good mechanic is a person who can match the precise tolerances of machinery with an equally precise and analytic mind. The ethos of an expert mechanic has little to do with "wrench twiddling," but a great deal to do with cultivating a skill for problem solving.

## Assessing the Character of Advocates

Ethos is the personal or professional reputation the persuader brings to the persuasive setting or constructs in the process of communicating. We usually have little difficulty recognizing the general traits of credibility. We identify high ethos sources as fair, trustworthy, sincere, reliable, and honest. Their knowledge about a subject may be seen as professional, experienced, and authoritative, and their manner of presentation may be perceived as energetic, active, open-minded, objective, bold, or decisive.[7]

Political candidates are especially challenged by the press to establish their character. Was Bill Clinton "so political," as the joke ran, that if asked to name his favorite color he would answer "plaid?"[8] Were the incomplete sentences and botched syntax of George Bush symptomatic of a hollow intellect?

No public figure from our recent past has shown more skill in using ethos-building devices than former President Ronald Reagan. He became a public figure nearly fifty years ago in the entertainment industry—first as a radio announcer, then as a Warner Brothers actor, and finished the Hollywood phase of his career as president of the powerful Screen Actors' Guild. He moved on to serve as a spokesperson for General Electric, visiting hundreds of offices and factories and giving countless speeches in praise of GE and American free enterprise. It was from his GE forum that he successfully rose to the governorship of California and later to the presidency in 1980.

Even as governor, however, Reagan knew his background was not necessarily a political asset. Audiences were suspicious of a person who had made a career in the fantasy world of film and television. Many wondered how a person who was good at taking direction and reading someone else's lines could master the demands of the presidency. His responses to these attacks on his ethos were masterful. He made his background seem more appropriate and urgent to the world of politics than many would initially judge. Consider how he started an address to a California press club in 1961, before his move into electoral politics. At the time, he was known only as a "nice guy" actor and former president of the actors' union.

> It must seem presumptuous to some of you for a member of my profession to stand here and attempt to talk on problems of the nation. We in Hollywood are not unaware of the concept many of our fellow citizens have of us and our industry. We realize that our merchandise is made up of tinsel, colored lights and a large measure of make-believe.[9]

*In this advertisement, all the traits of high ethos are evident: trustworthiness, sincerity, reliability, experience, and honesty.*

*Denzel Washington*

❝He stood about five-foot, nine-inches tall, but he was a giant. Billy Thomas. He ran the Boys & Girls Club where I grew up. Now, I know today it's different. Young people face problems I never even had to think about.

But that's why now, more than ever, *we need* the Boys & Girls Club. It's a positive place where thousands of people like Billy Thomas help young people succeed. Does it work? It did for me.❞

## 1 - 8 0 0 - 8 5 4 - C L U B

**BOYS & GIRLS CLUBS**
OF AMERICA

**The *Positive* Place For Kids.**

By identifying and labeling the audience's likely assumptions about the mythical world of Hollywood, Reagan served notice that he was under no illusions about his occupation. His self-effacing description of his career was candid and fair minded, but he substantiated his theme of encroaching control of government by pointing out that Hollywood itself was on the front lines of a vital struggle. As he saw it, the key battleground was in Hollywood's important and powerful unions.

> However, a few years ago "a funny thing happened to us on the way to the theatre." Ugly reality came to our town on direct orders of the Kremlin. Hard core party organizers infiltrated our business. They created cells, organized Communist fronts, and for a time, deceived numbers of our people, who with the best intentions, joined these fronts while still ignorant of their true purpose. The aim was to gain economic control of our industry. . . . The men in the Kremlin wanted this propaganda medium for their own destructive purposes.[10]

In countless speeches like this one, Ronald Reagan presented himself as more than an actor. His speeches joined art and politics. While we judge that his fears of Soviet influence were largely unjustified, there is no question his ethos as a former president of the Screen Actors' Guild gave his works additional weight.

## The Rational/Legal Ideal of Credibility

A second major way of estimating the quality of sources is through the use of formal guidelines for judging expertise and reliability. From the rational/legal perspective, statements or views deserve to be believed if their sources meet certain general standards for accuracy and objectivity. As described by Robert and Dale Newman, a source is credible if "worthy of belief"—telling the truth "with no concern as to whether any specific audience or reader will in fact believe it."[11]

The difference between a persuader's ethos and his or her rational credibility rests on objective criteria that exist apart from the beliefs of people in specific settings. Only an audience can determine if a certain persuader has "good character," hence, high ethos. But the legal rules for judging sources are constructed to apply to all audiences. Members of a jury, for example, may have strong suspicions that a defendant of a different social background is guilty of the charges brought against him or her. Under courtroom guidelines for assessing sources, they are obliged to disregard their personal preconceptions in favor of the rules of evidence before them. The witness who is outwardly most like them (in dress, ethnicity and education level, for example) may only be capable of giving "hearsay" (overheard or secondhand) evidence. Under the legal rules governing sources, hearsay testimony will be discounted by a judge in favor of statements from an eyewitness, even if the lifestyle of the eyewitness is alien to most of the members of the jury.

The challenge of rising above one's own prejudice to see the raw truth is a dilemma posed in the popular American novel *To Kill a Mockingbird*. In Harper Lee's story, an all-white jury in the 1930s is asked to believe that a black man, Tom Robinson, is innocent in the alleged rape of a white woman. As the story unfolds, it becomes clear that the charge is unfounded. Lee describes a young and disturbed woman who coaxes Robinson into her house, kisses him, and then tries to erase the guilt by claiming that she had been assaulted. The story pits the nation's most

### On the Line: A Reporter's Credibility

A vivid drama of credibility surfaced in the tense weeks of air assaults at the beginning of the war with Iraq in 1991. The center of the controversy was reporter Peter Arnett who, along with his crew from Cable News Network, covered the opening moments of the war from a hotel room in Baghdad.

Arnett had covered countless harrowing incidents for the Associated Press in Vietnam. He won a Pulitzer Prize in 1966 and a reputation for being a "soldier's reporter"—a correspondent who could dramatize the agonies, defeats, and ambiguities of close combat. His steady character was admired by the men and women he covered and by his fellow journalists. He was perceived as tough but low-keyed, a risk-taker but not foolhardy. Arnett left Southeast Asia only after President Lyndon Johnson identified him as a "troublemaker" and a Communist, hinting that his wife was a collaborator with the North Vietnamese. After a grueling stint in El Salvador, the native New Zealander joined CNN.

In 1991 the veteran correspondent was one of the few remaining journalists in Baghdad. The relentless bombing campaign against Iraq went on for days, with Arnett reporting under heavy Iraqi censorship. Damage to military targets could not be shown; troop movements could not be reported. Hints of local hostility to Hussein were taken out of videotaped interviews. Arnett always indicated that his reports had been screened by local officials. Even so, when he reported on the destruction of what Iraqi officials described as a baby formula factory, the switchboards at CNN lit up. Callers complained by the hundreds. Didn't he know that the American military was targeting only military sites and that the Pentagon had asserted that the factory was really a chemical plant? Why did he allow himself to be used? Senator Alan Simpson went even further. Arnett was not just another reporter for an American network, Simpson hinted at something much darker. In the Wyoming Senator's words, Arnett was a "sympathizer" with Iraq, and—repeating Lyndon Johnson's old charge—perhaps a Communist with ties to repressive and anti-American governments.

The Senator later apologized for both assertions, but not for his belief that Arnett's reports were biased in favor of Iraq and against official Pentagon reports. The battle over the reporter's credibility had momentarily cooled but was far from settled. As Arnett said at a reception at Washington's National Press Club, "I've taken some flak. So what else is new."

See: William Prochnau, "If There's a War, He's There," *New York Times Magazine*, March 3, 1991, pp. 31–31, 34.

honored values of fair play and justice against the worst impulses of our past. The sympathetic figure of defense attorney Atticus Finch (played in the 1963 film by Gregory Peck) tries valiantly to point out that no objective review of the evidence can lead a thinking person to a verdict of guilty. In his stirring summation he concludes, "I am confident that you gentlemen will review without passion the evidence you have heard, come to a decision, and restore this defendant to his family."[12] But the jury of white men accepts the dubious testimony of the witnesses for the prosecution, seeing only what its collective prejudices dictated: that a black man stepped out of his place in a rigid social hierarchy. From the moment Tom Robinson was charged, the narrator tells us, he was guilty "in the secret courts of men's hearts."[13]

What standards should have guided the jury? In the practice of law, guidelines for determining the quality of a source are relatively straightforward, although they are always harder to apply to specific cases than to summarize in the abstract. They involve two fundamental questions—one concerning ability and one pertaining to probable objectivity.

## Ability

How do we determine if someone has the ability to tell the truth or to make intelligent observations about a specific subject? The first crucial test spotlights the need to measure the extent to which an "authority" has been in a position to observe. In many walks of life, from legal proceedings to the reconstruction of historical events, we routinely estimate the credibility of claimants based on their expertise. Were they eyewitnesses to events or did they get information secondhand from another source? Do they have the training, experience, access to information, and knowledge to know what to look for? Can testimony of one source be supported by others with knowledge in a similar area?

In 1990 Iben Browning, an expert on the earth's climate, predicted a massive earthquake along the New Madrid fault in southern Missouri. He based his prediction on the questionable assumption that the moon's relatively close proximity to the earth would trigger shifts in the earth's crust. Very few seismologists had faith in Browning's conclusions, pointing out that a background in climatology does not qualify someone to determine how earthquake faults will behave on specific days.[14] Americans who evacuated their schools and homes in response to Dr. Browning's predictions would have been better served by the counter-vailing arguments of genuine authorities.

True expertise should be consulted. However, healthy skepticism warns that even sources that may have the ability to make sound judgments will not always be reliable. There are times when even a genuine expert may have an overriding reason to ignore or to overlook what accumulated knowledge should indicate.

## Objectivity

The second crucial factor in rational and legal discussions of credibility involves estimates of objectivity. Not only must we ask if a source has the ability to tell the truth and to make expert judgments but also if the source is free from an overriding bias that could cancel out the advantages of expertise. In a practical way, objectivity is a trait we identify in sources who are able to set aside personal values or prejudices as reference points for understanding an event. While complete objectivity is impossible, interpretations of reality can still be rendered with high degrees of accuracy and fairness. Such objectivity is rightly prized in a source.

Determining that a certain source lacks objectivity is not simply a matter of labeling a person "deceptive" or "fraudulent." It is natural to see the world from a self-interested viewpoint. We expect personal investments to shape the comments and responses of groups and individuals. CBS does not routinely praise NBC's television programs; political candidates usually see faults rather than strengths in the activities of their rivals.

We can judge a source's relative objectivity by determining the amount of willingness or reluctance. The Newmans note that the idea of reluctant testimony is based on a sturdy old principle: "It is assumed that sane individuals will not say things against their own interests unless such testimony is true beyond doubt." Sources are reluctant when they take positions that go against their own interests, hence, "the greater the damage of his own testimony to a witness, the more credible it is."[15] For instance, consider the statement of a police chief from a large metropolitan area (Oakland, California) who admitted that his department "blew it" for failing to follow up on certain kinds of rape cases. By largely ignoring rapes committed against drug users and prostitutes prior to 1990, the chief belatedly conceded that his department failed to provide equal protection. Was the chief's admission credible? Because admitting errors or mistakes is not something a person or group would do without good cause, there is little reason not to conclude that justice had been unevenly dispensed in Oakland. As one advocate for the rape victims noted, "An easier way [out for the police] would have been for them to try to fix the numbers or make excuses."[16]

Willing testimony, by contrast, always supports the testifier's existing interests and perceptions. By definition, willing sources make claims that tend to confirm judgments or facts that are flattering or self-serving. It is thus difficult to place much faith in their conclusions without corroboration from less biased sources. One year after the large oil spill from an Exxon tanker in Alaska's Prince William Sound, for instance, Exxon was reporting to its shareholders that the effects of the spill would be short-lived. The breaching of the massive tanker Exxon *Valdez* in March of 1989 had produced a storm of public protest and pleas for tougher rules governing standards for huge tankers and their crews. Citing the conclusions of biologists apparently paid by the company, Exxon noted that by the summer of 1990 "the area has retained its natural beauty; there are abundant signs of plant and animal life, and recovery is well under way on even the most severely impacted beaches."[17] A careful observer of evidence would probably conclude that the measure of the rate of recovery in Prince William Sound would be better served by independent experts rather than those "commissioned" by a corporation with a need to repair its tarnished image. Indeed, by 1994, federal and state scientists had concluded that Exxon's experts had been too optimistic.[18]

In reality, the gap between the willing and the reluctant source is an unbroken continuum that is heavily weighted at the willing end of the scale. Reluctant testimony is understandably rare. The task of audiences searching for advocates worthy of belief is to find high-ability sources who, though perhaps not completely reluctant, are at least not so deeply tied to one fixed point of view that they are incapable of seeing merit and truth in circumstances antithetical to their own positions.

## Source Credibility as Believability

A third perspective on credibility comes from comparatively recent experimental studies on the formation of attitudes. The redefinition of credibility as believability received support in the important work of psychologist Carl Hovland in the early 1950s and spawned hundreds of studies examining the range of source-related traits that can affect audience acceptance of a message.[19]

### Source Credibility as Audience Acceptance

In some ways, scientific interest in the personality traits of advocates was an updating of Aristotle's interest in the attributes of the persuasive speaker. As we have seen, the idea of ethos implies an idealized view of the advocate as someone with "good character" and strong virtue. In contrast, social psychologists—struck by the dramatic effectiveness of Hitler and many other demagogues within the first half of the twentieth century—separated the analysis of an advocate's effectiveness from his or her ethical obligations. They noted that although a persuader might be believed by a particular audience, he or she might still be unworthy of belief by more traditional standards. In the words of one set of researchers, "Credibility and like terms do not represent attributes of communicators; they represent judgments by the listeners."[20]

We think both views are valuable. The newer tradition of focusing on what audiences think and what they will accept is useful for describing certain situations. For example, there is no other way to explain Adolph Hitler's ability to persuade than to consider his credibility in a descriptive sense. The prescriptive standards outlined by Aristotle and others would not acount for Hitler's successes with his audiences.

### Measuring Source Credibility: Problems and Selected Research

A 1951 study of audience responses to high- and low-credibility sources by Hovland and Weiss is considered a classic.[21] The researchers asked students at Yale to complete opinion questionnaires that measured the students' attitudes on four different topics. After completing the questionnaires, students were given pamphlets arguing pro and con positions on four areas. All the students read identical opinions on the four issues. The students were then randomly subdivided into different groups. Hovland and Weiss assigned sources with obvious high or low credibility to various positions. For the question "Can a practicable atomic-powered submarine be built at the present [1950] time?", the opinion was attributed to different sources for different groups of students. One group was told that the opinion they were reading was from the Russian daily, *Pravda*. Another group was told that the source was the widely respected physicist, J. Robert Oppenheimer. Another topic was whether the popularity of television would decrease the number of movie theaters in operation. Again, the opinion on this subject was attributed to a high-credibility source for some (*Fortune Magazine*) and a low-credibility source for others (a movie gossip columnist). The study was designed to hold every variable constant except for the sources who had allegedly made the comments.

Would the attributions make a difference? Would there be greater attitude change from the groups who believed in the integrity of their sources? Not surprisingly, many of the respondents agreed with opinions when they were attributed to high-credibility sources. Oppenheimer and *Fortune*, for example, were ranked as more believable than *Pravda* and the columnist. Did high credibility translate into greater agreement with the source? The answer was a qualified yes. The experimenters measured shifts in attitudes by comparing the results of the initial questionnaires with the results of attitude surveys conducted after the experiment. The net change in attitudes was not enormous, but it was always greater for readers of "trustworthy" sources.[22] Even so, other analysts who have studied and replicated this research have since noted that

> in order to demonstrate a measurable effect upon attitudes, the researchers had to create extreme differences in communicator credibility that, nevertheless, gave only a slight edge to the credible source in producing attitude change. In real-life situations, where the naturally existing differences between communicators would be much less extreme, would there still be the same enhancement of the communication by virtue of its attribution to a slightly more credible source? Some of the data suggest there would not.[23]

The problems involved in designing precise experimental studies are far too complex to be outlined here.[24] The important point is to realize that source credibility has many relevant dimensions. It is difficult to reduce a many-sided concept to just one measurable dimension. "One persistent theoretical problem," notes Arthur Cohen, "is that of disentangling the main components of credibility. Is it expertness or trustworthiness, perception of fairness or bias, disinterest or propagandistic intent, or any combination of factors which is responsible for the effects of credibility on attitude change?"[25] Sources can be studied by focusing on one special dimension (dress, sex, age, perceived intelligence, the decision to include both sides of an argument) or on a broader identity (a writer for the *New York Times*, a representative of the United States government, a member of the chamber of commerce, or a felon). We may link communicator traits to the content of a message, as has been done in studies of how the race of a speaker affects attitudes on the subject of racism.[26] Other traits may be topic-neutral, as when listeners are asked to classify sources as honest, aggressive, crude, sincere, or boring.[27] Even the simplest communication setting contains a multitude of variables and people with different expectations and experiences reacting to a message in diverse ways. It is hardly surprising that efforts to "control" for all of these factors have tended to raise more questions than answers.

In spite of these limitations, some useful observations have come from research into the believability of sources. The following summary represents several well documented conclusions about how the credibility of sources is judged by audiences.

1. *For many people, high credibility means trustworthiness.* Receivers are more willing to accept what a persuader says if they believe that his or her intentions are honorable. Trustworthy sources are seen as people who will not abuse their access to an audience. Audiences who believe that they are being used, deceived, or carelessly misled will pay little attention to an advocate's ideas.

2. *Similarities between communicators and audiences do not necessarily pave the way for influence.* Researchers have sometimes found that listeners judge similar sources "as more attractive than dissimilar sources."[28] Most of us would expect as much. Some recent research has cast doubt on the view that "attitude similarity" translates into positive attraction toward a persuader.[29] The fact that there is prior agreement between people on a range of topics does not guarantee that they will more easily influence each other.

3. *Physical attractiveness increases a persuader's chances with audiences of the same and opposite sexes.* While intense audience involvement with a subject is usually more important, a number of researchers who have studied audience reactions to persuaders have concluded that attractive, well-dressed, and well-groomed

advocates are likely to be more successful than "unattractive persuaders."[30]

4. *Most surveys of audience attitudes indicate that the high pre-scriptive standards for judging sources (as noted in our previous discussion of rational standards) are not routinely applied.* Many audiences can be induced to believe sources with questionable credibility. Persuaders who state the origins of their information generally do not fare any better than less candid advocates.[31]

5. *Experimenters on credibility have discovered that audiences seem to learn information regardless of a source's reliability.*[32] Thus, a political campaign commercial on television may teach the viewer more about the political views of a candidate than an objective news report with ostensibly higher credibility.[33] We absorb views regard-less of our assessments of the quality of the teacher.

6. *Perceptions of credibility may matter less over time than the message itself.* Demonstrating what is sometimes called the "sleeper effect," some studies have shown that people tend to forget their initial impressions of an advocate while retaining at least a general sense of the point of view expressed. The work of Carl Hovland and others has pointed out that "the increased persuasion produced by a high-credibility source disappears. Similarly, the decreased persuasion produced by a low-credibility source vanishes."[34]

7. *When compared with radio, newspapers, and magazines, tele-vision retains the greater believability, especially as a news source.*[35] Although studies looking at the mass media in the aggregate provide only general impressions, television consistently ranks high as a believable medium.

8. *The needs of receivers often override extensive consideration of a persuader's credibility.* The acceptability of a source is sometimes based on factors far removed from rational source credibility criteria. Gary Cronkhite and Jo Liska ask, "Do listeners always attend to public and television speakers because they consider the sources to be believable? Sometimes that is the reason, of course, but persuasion in such formats also proceeds as a matter of mutual need satisfaction." At times, "likability, novelty, and entertainment are valued more highly" than traditional standards of competence and trustworthiness.[36]

## Credibility Reconsidered

As we have seen, the qualities which make a given source attractive to a particular audience have been the subject of much speculation. We have outlined three perspectives. For the early Greeks, who first systematically thought about the role of the advocate in persuasion, credibility was inherent in the quality of a person's character. A good persuader had to be a good and virtuous person. For logicians and historians, credibility resides in sources who have high expertise and reasonable objectivity. To social scientists who are concerned with how attitudes are formed, source credibility means believability, and it is determined by the standards of an audience rather than the logician or expert. Figure 5.1 presents a brief summary of these perspectives.

---

### Figure 5.1

**Three Perspectives on Credibility**

| Prescriptive | | Descriptive |
|---|---|---|
| **1.** | **2.** | **3.** |
| *Ethos* as "good character" | *Legal* Standards for Judging Sources | *Behavioral* Studies of Believability |
| Good sense<br>Good moral character<br>Goodwill, etc. | Ability to make accurate observations<br>Objectivity (more reluctant than willing) | Trustworthiness<br>Honesty<br>Expertise<br>Smilarity to receivers |

---

# Four Source-related Persuasion Strategies

Although a message often stands or falls on the weight of its ideas and arguments, this is not the case with the four strategies discussed below. Each represents a dimension of persuasion that depends as much on an advocate's attributes as on the ideas presented. The use of a source's prestige to make ideas acceptable, the use of "mystifying" language to protect a source's power, the exploitation of charisma as a basis for leadership, and the sometimes dangerous substitution of appeals to authority in place of open, idea-centered persuasion are tactics which elevate the persuader above the message.

## Prestige and Legitimation

Within every subgroup of society, there are a few leaders who have the power to give an aura of legitimacy to the causes they endorse. Their presence may add a sense of success or importance to a gathering, such as when a president chooses a local forum for an appearance. These high-ethos figures may be politicians, business leaders, entertainers, artists, clergy, or local civic leaders. Their names may be as recent and familiar as basketball's Michael Jordan, CBS's Dan Rather, or Microsoft's Bill Gates, or as seemingly distant as the folk heroes Charles Lindburgh and Edward R. Morrow. What all of these figures have exhibited is the power to gain acceptance for a point of view because of who they are.

The relationship between political figures and sports or film stars is especially interesting. Each, to some extent, feeds on the legitimacy of the other. One reason actors get involved in political campaigns, Robert Redford has noted, is sheer guilt. A lot of actors feel they are in a "shallow profession. Other people are out there digging trenches and working in dangerous jobs . . . That guilt produces some desire for credibility, so they go into campaigns." What political figures receive in return is more obvious. Whether it is Bill Clinton accepting the praise of Barbra Streisand or former Senator Bill Bradley accepting a large campaign

*Proponents of controversial issues should be aware that qualities which make a source believable vary depending on the audience. Here a senator, an actress and children (potent symbols for voting parents) combine to win approval from a broad spectrum of viewers.*

*Tribune* photo by Ernie Cox, Jr.

contribution from the Disney Studio's Michael Eisner, the fact remains that Hollywood's stars have the power to confer on others a special aura of glamour and celebrity.[37]

In advertising, the counterpart of political legitimation is the product endorsement in which an attractive figure appears as a contented user of a product. As early as the 1880s, tobacco companies sought to identify their products with athletes and actors.[38] Endorsements by celebrities reached their peak on network television in the late 1950s when many stars, program hosts, and even some news reporters were expected to sell their sponsors' products. As the recent troubles of Michael Jackson and O. J. Simpson attest, celebrity endorsements represent a sometimes risky advertising strategy.

# Mystification

In the strategy of legitimation, a high-ethos figure is used to shore up support for a person, product, or point of view. Imagine this pattern reversed. There are times when persuasive language is used to protect what may be the already considerable influence of a persuader. An impressive display of language can become a way to persuade or to ward off challenges from opponents. Such mystification is a common, fascinating, and troubling form of influence. Ironically, mystifications are perhaps the only forms of communication that succeed because the persuadee does not fully understand what is being expressed.

In its simplest form as a communication strategy, mystification is the use of special symbols and technical jargon (see discussion in chapter 3) to imply that the persuader has special authority and expertise to which others should defer. Mystification is a way of pulling rank because its use produces acquiescence to the apparent authority of the advocate. Those who acquire formal or legal authority usually inherit verbal and symbolic references that serve as emblems of prestige. Special status comes with its own set of ideas and terms. As Hugh Duncan explains:

> Fathers teach us that if we disobey them the family will suffer, not simply that father will be "unhappy." School principals convince us (more or less) that our disobedience hinders group activities and that we spoil the fun of being together. Christian priests teach that a sin against the church is a sin against God, and since God upholds order (in nature as well as society), sin threatens the very foundation of the world.[39]

## Mystification and the Professions

Typically, challenges to individuals are treated (and renamed) as challenges to authorities or institutions. A persuader may not employ mystifications in a calculated attempt to suppress opposition, but the result may be the same. Our contacts with others are normally within a framework of hierarchies which either suggest expertise and authority or indicate the lack of it.

Consider Thurman Arnold's classic analysis of the confusing mysteries of "jurisprudence," the impressive term used to designate the study of legal philosophy. "Here is a subject," he notes, "which not even lawyers read. Its content is vague; its literature is abstruse and difficult. Nevertheless there is a general feeling that under this title are hidden the most sacred mysteries of the law."[40] He notes that the confusing and jargon-laden language of the legal profession "performs its social task most effectively for those who encourage it, praise it, but do not read it."[41] For most of us, legal jargon remains a mysterious but impressive set of codes which provide a reason for placing our faith in highly trained specialists.

Assuming that the easiest persuasion involves the course of least resistance, nearly every advocate will occasionally look for ways to use symbols of authority to lessen audience opposition. Mystifications, then, are appeals to the legitimacy of authority based on symbols which indicate expertise. An advocate is unlikely to impress us by simply stating,

> Too many cooks spoil the broth.

But even this cliché can be easily whipped into a tall verbal concoction that overflows with the imagery of expertise.

> Undue multiplicity of personnel assigned either concurrently or consecutively to a single function involves deterioration of quality in the resultant product as compared with the product of the labor of an exact sufficiency of personnel.[42]

### The Unique Role of the Placebo Effect

One of the most fascinating forms of mystification is the "placebo effect." A placebo is a harmless, neutral agent that a shaman or doctor presents to a patient as treatment for an illness. The most common form of a placebo is a sugar pill, but it may also include impressive machines, bundles of herbs, or virtually any object invested by an authority figure with special powers. The remarkable fact about placebos is that they sometimes work. When administered by medical authorities, placebos can have very real therapeutic benefits that defy explanation in terms of their chemistry. Patients who are led to believe that they are receiving help for a medical problem—even when taking only placebos—often report improvements. This is because the mere suggestion of receiving a therapeutic treatment is often sufficient for healing to begin. The power of suggestion based on both expectations and faith in authority produces its own physical and mental changes. "Physicians have always known that their ability to inspire expectant trust in a patient partly determines the success of treatment," notes Jerome Frank.[43] The patient's inability to understand the medical terminology, complicated apparatus, medicines, and equipment may actually enhance the possibilities for cure. There is irony in the fact that a more thorough understanding of the limitations of treatments might only serve to take away the mystery that is the basis of the "cure." As Frank notes, "a patient's expectations have been shown to affect his physiological responses so powerfully that they can reverse the pharmacological action of a drug."[44]

None of us are immune from benefits of the placebo effect. Expectations have a powerful persuasive function. When we remark that an aspirin helped end a headache, or that a new prescription "seemed to work," we naturally assume the drug's chemistry did the trick. But, as many health professionals concede, doctors and drugs often help us by functioning as symbolic agents which give us a clear reason to feel better.

## The Charismatic Persuader

Sociologist Edward Shils described charismatic leaders as "persistent, effectively expressive personalities who impose themselves on their environment by their exceptional courage . . . self-confidence, fluency, [and] insight. . . ."[45] Although, charisma is not an easy concept to apply to leaders and persuaders, it remains a unique—if somewhat diminished—form of authority. We begin with a classic case of such leadership before turning to a brief discussion of the limitations and advantages of the charismatic label.

### Kennedy in Berlin

Many United States presidents have visited Berlin, but none have recreated the rhetorical fireworks of John Kennedy in 1963.[46] After his visit to the concrete and barbed-wire barricade erected by the Soviet Union, Kennedy planned to make a few brief remarks at Rudolf Wilde Platz. Historian Arthur Schlesinger, Jr. recalls that no one anticipated the passionate speech Kennedy delivered or the reaction from the audience. Over half of the city's population filled the streets "clapping, waving, crying, cheering, as if it were the second coming."[47] People had packed themselves into the plaza, "compressed into a single excited, impassioned mass." Kennedy, routinely dubbed "the leader of the free world" by journalists, came to pay homage to the most powerful symbol of Soviet repression, but the audience had come to pay homage to him. Visibly moved by the sight of a city and its people, Kennedy put aside most of his planned text to direct a dramatic challenge to the secrecy and suspicion of the Kremlin. He spoke from a few scribbled key phrases:

> There are some who say that communism is the wave of the future.
> Let them come to Berlin!

> And there are some who say in Europe and elsewhere we can work with the communists.
>
> Let them come to Berlin!
>
> And there are even a few who say that it is true that communism is an evil system, but it permits us to make economic progress.
>
> Lass sie nach Berlin Kommen! Let them come to Berlin![48]

Schlesinger's description of the event perfectly captures the essence of a charismatic leader's effect on an audience.

> The crowd shook itself and rose and roared like an animal. Absorbed in his short remarks, Kennedy hurried on. In a moment he concluded: "All free men, wherever they may live, are citizens of Berlin, and therefore, as a free man, I take pride in the words 'Ich bein ein Berliner.' [I am a Berliner.] The hysteria spread almost visibly through the square. Kennedy was first exhilarated, then disturbed; he felt, as he remarked on his return, that if he had said, "March to the wall—tear it down," his listeners would have marched.[49]

### Traits of Charismatic Leadership

In its modern usage, the term charisma comes from the turn-of-the-century work of sociologist Max Weber. Weber was fascinated by the fact that some public figures gain respect and power from their followers which dramatically exceed whatever legal authority they may have. He knew that social movements and persuasive campaigns have often been headed by individuals with limited formal power but enormous personal support. In different ways, figures as diverse as Mohandas Gandhi in India, Nelson Mandela when he was still a prisoner in South Africa, and Martin Luther King in the United States were sometimes as powerful as the legal "legitimate" authorities they confronted in their quests for independence and civil liberties. As Edward Sills has noted, "According to Weber's usage, charismatic quality may be attributed to religious prophets and reformers, to dominating political leaders, to daring military heroes, and to sages who by example and command indicate a way of life to their disciples. . . . "[50] John Kennedy garnered an enormous following even on foreign soil. He followed a number of leaders from recent world history who owed part of their effectiveness to the force of their public images and personalities—among them, Adolph Hitler, Theodore Roosevelt, Franklin Roosevelt, Louisiana's Huey Long, France's Charles de Gaulle, and Cuba's Fidel Castro.

The single most important dimension of charismatic leadership seems to be a leader's ability to make others feel like they are participants in his or her victories and defeats. Charismatic figures are able to mobilize resentments, anxieties, and fears, such that personal attacks on them are taken as attacks on their followers as well. "I do not know how to describe the emotions that swept over me as I heard this man," recalls one of Hitler's followers. "His words were like a scourge. When he spoke of the disgrace of Germany, I felt ready to spring on any enemy.''[51]

The popular leader often becomes the symbol of a ''just'' and moral cause. Almost every aspect of his or her life is seen as illustrating a vital moral issue. It was not surprising, for example, that the young and photogenic Kennedy came off so well as an anticommunist cold warrior. Kennedy was a naval hero, so there was credibility to his dangerous showdown with Soviet ships carrying missiles to Cuba. He talked like a man who was prepared to back up his words with actions when faced with Soviet threats to ''free'' West Berlin from the control of France, Britain, and the United States. Kennedy is still remembered for how he ''stood up to the Russians.'' In contrast to the older and overweight Soviet leader, Nikita Khrushchev, he personified a nation that was certain about its place and aggressive in its desire to control the growth of Soviet power.

### The Decline of a Model?

The fact that all of our examples of charismatic leadership are at least twenty years old points toward several interesting questions. Is charisma now little more than a label applied to figures who are safely frozen in the past? Is any sort of leadership based on an unquestioning idolatry possible in an age that prizes journalistic skepticism and the intrusive presence of the television camera? Does the very concept of charisma lead us to overestimate persuaders at the expense of willing and supportive persuadees?

To the last question, Andrew King answers with a qualified yes. ''The power of the great speaker,'' he notes, ''is an illusion. The speaker's power is granted by the audience.'' By focusing on single personalities, we may overlook the fact that audiences empower certain individuals to carry their messages for them. In a nation as suspect of official authority as the United States, King believes, no leader can act without being given a mandate to act as a mouthpiece for a group.[52]

In addition, the technology of communication has made it more difficult to view figures as separate and special. Television, especially, makes many leaders seem ordinary. The pervasiveness of personalized journalism has made it all but impossible for one individual to retain the mixture of public support and private remoteness that gave many earlier leaders some of their stature. As Joshua Meyorwitz has noted, public figures today are now subject to intense coverage; gossip about their private lives and sometimes very human failings can easily undermine their power.[53]

For example, reports of varying accuracy in the late 1980s suggested that Martin Luther King was an unfaithful husband and was guilty of plagiarism in his doctoral dissertation.[54] These claims from acquaintances and researchers will probably not affect his reputation as the single most potent force for civil rights in the 1960s. They do, however, point to a process of erosion of the perceptions of specialness

**CALVIN AND HOBBES**

Calvin and Hobbes © Watterson. Reprinted with the permission of Universal Press Syndicate.

we previously had about important national leaders. That process involves increased media attention to the mundane details or private failings of important figures.

Such has been the fate of Bill Clinton, who—even as president—is defined by the questionable choices he made as a teenager (avoided the draft) and husband (possibly had an affair). The majestic presidency of the early 1900s (of Teddy or Franklin Roosevelt) has now shriveled under the weight of an increasingly inward-looking culture in which every person's experience is reducible to the same dimensions of ambition and dysfunction. Leaders who in the past might have been known for their moral leadership are now covered not just in terms of their achievements but also in terms of their traits of imperfect character. As Richard Sennett has noted, the trivia that flows from the celebrity-making machinery of the mass media increasingly eclipse a person's genuine accomplishments. It may now be easier to be a celebrity—to be well known—than to sustain public attention on an agenda for social action.[55] Being an "interesting personality" may now be more important than having something to say.

## Authoritarianism and Acquiescence

History is filled with examples of strong leaders who have been able to use threats and persuasion to reshape the attitudes and actions of compliant people. During World War II Hitler, Mussolini, and Japan's Tojo were widely portrayed in the United States as having hypnotic control over their followers. Many thought that they could persuade their supporters to do almost anything. Like Jim Jones or David Koresh, their powers seemed strong enough at times to justify mass suicides. The popular press often portrays such persuasion in overly simple but familiar terms. A group of "gullible" people are taken in by a "cult" and "brainwashed" by a clever and demonic figure. These terms are reassuring, even if mass movements arise for reasons other than the presence of one strong leader. Yet the problem of excessive deference to authority remains. In describing the "true believer," for example, Eric Hoffer summarized in the 1960s what seems to be an immutable feature of everyday life. For millions of people who see themselves as society's victims rather than beneficiaries, social causes espoused by strong leaders are especially seductive. In Hoffer's words:

> People whose lives are barren and insecure seem to show a greater willingness to obey than people who are self-sufficient and self-confident. To the frustrated, freedom from responsibility is more attractive than freedom from restraint. . . . They willingly abdicate the directing of their lives to those who want to plan, command and shoulder all responsibility.[56]

### The Concept of the Authoritarian Personality

In the 1930s Sigmund Freud wrote about the manipulation and "re-infantilization of the masses" in prewar Europe.[57] Since the 1950s considerable research in the social sciences has focused on the social conditions and personality traits that give rise to obedience to authority. The first major English language analysis of enslavement to mass movements was *The Authoritarian Personality* by T. W. Adorno, Else Frankel-Brunswik, and their associates.[58] The 1950 study is considered a classic, although serious questions have been raised about its complex attitude-research methodology.[59] The authors—some of whom had escaped from Austria in advance of Nazi attacks on Jews—sought to trace the origins of a multitude of personality traits, including antisemitism, "susceptibility to antidemocratic propaganda," ethnocentrism (judging others by one's own cultural values), and predispositions toward fascism. Their efforts to determine how patterns of upbringing instilled such traits is less important here than the fascinating questions their study brought into focus. Are certain kinds of listeners overly susceptible to appeals based on authority, especially "official" sources? Are some types of audiences too willing to look past the natural ambiguities of everyday life for the rigid ideological certainties of a demagogue (i.e., Hitler's stereotypes of Jewish "failings")? What psychological needs are satisfied when total allegiance is promised to a leader?

The F (antidemocratic) Scale questionnaire which Adorno, Frankel-Brunswik, and their associates used to locate the "authoritarian type" consisted of several agree-disagree claims. They sought to discover the signs of "authoritarian submission" and evidence of an "uncritical attitude toward idealized moral authorities." Among some of the typical statements in the questionnaire used to measure authoritarianism were the following:

- Obedience and respect for authority are the most important virtues children should learn.

- Every person should have complete faith in some supernatural power whose decisions will be obeyed without question.
- What this country needs most, more than laws and political programs, are a few courageous, tireless, devoted leaders in whom the people can put their faith.[60]

In analyzing scores of responses to questions like these, the authors discovered what they expected. Antisemitism, rigidity, ethnocentrism, undue respect for power, and many other traits tend to cluster within many of the same people and are probably tied to certain styles of family life. They learned that authoritarianism can be identified and recognized in segments of almost any population. What remains unanswered, however, is whether such people represent a unique persuadable type.

### The Dilemma of Obedience to Authority

There is a significant irony in the whole issue of how individuals respond to threats or appeals from officials with formal power. Every society has an important stake in the rule of law. We generally regard the loss of respect for authority as a problem when people ignore laws or established social customs. We equally regret, however, the failure of ordinary people to challenge the appeals or coercion of leaders who may seek support for unjust laws or twisted values. There have been times (in colonial America, for example) when disorder arguably brings about a better order and when an illegal act can be justified as obedience to a higher moral code.

From the perspective of the present, order and obedience almost always seem preferable to their opposites. The advantage of hindsight, however, helps gauge when the price of obedience has been too costly. For instance, it is now easy to criticize the average German soldier's obedience to Hitler and his lieutenants during World War II. Nearly every discussion of that conflict includes a query about how it could have happened that so many "decent" people in Germany could have initially accepted the blatant xenophobia and racism implicit in the Third Reich.

Even the inhabitants of the newly united Germany must still ponder this question, which is one reason they have been reluctant to redevelop their own military forces. Others have similarly questioned why many Americans were so acquiescent to the official decision to jail thousands of Japanese Americans in the same period. Why was the nation silent when it became federal policy to detain 117,000 American citizens of Japanese ancestry in prison camps on the West Coast?[61] What made the official propaganda line that a San Francisco "Jap" could be as dangerous as a Tokyo "Jap" acceptable? The rhetoric of our leaders and slick Hollywood war films played their parts.[62] A more complete answer must include the fact that governments, businesses, and institutions have enormous interests in protecting their own authority. Obviously, a stable society needs clearly defined codes of conduct as well as leaders who are respected by their followers. Unfortunately, there are no guarantees that "legal," "expert," or "official" authorities will use their persuasive powers wisely.

### The Milgram Studies

Evidence of how "decent" people can be made to obey oppressive authority has been strikingly illustrated in the research of psychologist Stanley Milgram. His well-known and controversial work in the 1960s measured the degree to which ordinary people would follow problematic orders from a responsible official. His research design was ingenious and quite simple. Milgram advertised for volunteers to help conduct what he falsely described to them as a learning experiment. Those whom he selected were asked to assist him in the teaching of a "learner" who was, in reality, a Milgram confederate. Every time the learner incorrectly answered a question, the white-coated researcher explained, the volunteer would be instructed to act as the "teacher" and administer an electrical shock. This scheme of reward and punishment was ostensibly designed to help improve the skills of the learner.

No shock was actually administered. The real purpose of the study was to chart the extent to which the volunteer would follow an authority figure's orders to inflict pain on the learner. In *Obedience to Authority*, Milgram explained how the teachers were introduced to the setting.

> After watching the learner being strapped into place, he is taken into the main experimental room and seated before an impressive shock generator. Its main feature is a horizontal line of thirty switches, ranging from 15 volts to 450 volts, in 15 volt increments. There are also verbal designations which range from slight shock to danger-severe shock. The teacher is told that he is to administer the learning test to the man in the other room.
>
> *   *   *   *
>
> The learner, or victim, is an actor who actually receives no shock at all. The point of the experiment is to see how far a person will proceed in a concrete and measurable situation in which he is ordered to inflict increasing pain on a protesting victim.[63]

The dilemma the "teacher" faced was one of traumatic obedience. At what point should the commands of the experimenter to "keep going" be rejected?

> For the subject, the situation is not a game; conflict is intense and obvious. On one hand, the manifest suffering of the learner presses him to quit. On the other hand, the experimenter, a legitimate authority to whom the subject feels some commitment, enjoins him to continue.[64]

Many did continue, even when the "learner" cried out in agonizing pain. Had the learners actually been wired to the shock box as the volunteers were led to believe, many would have died a slow and painful death.

To witnesses of this research, the volunteers who continued to obey Milgram appeared to be incredibly sadistic. However, Milgram concludes otherwise, citing the very human tendency to shift responsibility to a higher and seemingly legitimate authority. He notes that "relatively few people have the resources needed to resist authority. A variety of inhibitions against disobeying authority come into play and successfully keep the person in his place."[65]

Admittedly, there are differences between a setting in which a volunteer agrees to carry out the orders of a researcher and a persuasive situation in which a popular advocate elicits support from an autonomous collection of individuals. The volunteer's desire to be helpful is probably greater than the average listener's motivations to accept the views of many persuaders. We doubt that most people in open societies are the "servile flock . . . incapable of ever doing without a master" that Gustave Le Bon described in his famous study of social movements.[66] Even so, any casual observer of the workplace, the classroom, and scores of other hierarchical settings will readily see how references to authority function as effective legitimizing appeals.

## Summary

In human communication, the content of a message must always be understood in terms of the quality and acceptability of a source. As we noted at the beginning of this chapter, there are many questions about the nature of authority that still need answers, and there are many ways to describe how credibility enables persuaders to succeed. Three forms of credibility were outlined. Audiences expect that those seeking their support will demonstrate positive traits of character, common sense, and goodwill. Persuasion theorists from Aristotle onward have described such traits of *good character* as essential to all individuals who would call themselves worthy advocates. In settings such as the courtroom and the laboratory where audiences are prepared to weigh evidence to determine truth, sources are best measured by reference to their abilities to observe events accurately and objectively. We called this second form of credibility the *rational/legal* model of credibility. A third type involves the idea that specific personal attributes of persuaders are likely to be attractive or unattractive to particular types of people. This *believability* standard has less to do with the search for truth or good character than with the recognition of audience attitudes as they are rather than, perhaps, as they should be.

However inconclusive our present understanding of credibility is, it remains central to the study of persuasion. An audience's awareness of the personal biography of an advocate is often the first important moment in the communication process. In addition, for public figures and persuaders reaching large audiences, the presence of charisma or a mystifying expertise may double or redouble the impact of a message. The sheer force of a dominating public character can generate an intensely loyal following—sometimes because of the extraordinary nature of an advocate's leadership, at other times because individuals may have a strong and sometimes dangerous desire to relinquish responsibility to others.

## Questions and Projects for Further Study

1. Recall a doctor's office that you have visited recently. Analyze that space in terms of the subtle technical symbols and mystifying messages it communicates. Be sure to consider specific categories such as patterns of dress, use of technical jargon, and the presence of scientific equipment. What are some of the common effects these elements have on patients? How would demystifying some of these elements change some of the effects you have cited?

2. Observe some of the experts or spokespersons who appear in a network news program (i.e., CNN's *Larry King Live*, ABC's *Nightline*, etc.). They may be seen making observations about the day's events from their vantage points in government, business, the arts, and so on. Using the rational/legal model as well as their own explanations, assess the credibility of one or two experts.

3. Locate several magazine ads which use prestige and legitimation as a persuasive strategy. Describe the verbal and visual symbols that help sell the product.

4. Attend a portion of a criminal trial in your area. Study the way the prosecution and defense attorneys attempt to establish or discredit the credibility of specific witnesses.

5. From films or television programs you have seen recently, locate a character who seems to exhibit some of the characteristics of the authoritarian personality.

6. Using textbooks, self-help manuals, news or magazine articles, locate some examples of persuasion by mystification. Explain what it is about your samples that qualifies them as good instances.

7. You may have noticed that this chapter poses a dilemma. Persuasion requires deference to many types of experts and authorities. Yet we concluded with a caution about the dangers of persuasion which exploit the symbols of expertise and authority (as illustrated by Milgram). Attempt to explain the differences between persuasion based on genuine credibility and persuasion that abuses an audience's faith in authority. Cite a real or hypothetical example.

8. Choosing from the list below, identify and defend eight credibility traits that would most help (1) a male member of a persuasion course

advocating a compulsory year of government service for all American eighteen-year-olds or (2) a senator from your state urging a cross section of citizens to support a 15 percent pay increase for all members of Congress. The traits include the following:

| | | |
|---|---|---|
| fair | good speaker | respectful |
| good | right | honest |
| trustworthy | loyal to listeners | admirable |
| patient | correct | sincere |
| straightforward | reliable | valuable |
| unselfish | nice | virtuous |
| displays goodwill | calm | moral |
| frank | friendly | professional |
| experienced | authoritative | energetic |
| aggressive | active | bold |
| decisive | proud | open-minded |
| objective | impartial | forward-thinking |

# Notes

[1] Daniel Webster described by John Kennedy in *Profiles in Courage, Memorial Edition*. New York: Harper and Row, 1964, p. 56.

[2] Andrew King, *Power and Communication*. Prospect Heights, IL: Waveland Press, 1987, p. 138.

[3] Aristotle, *The Rhetoric in The Basic Works of Aristotle*, ed. by Richard McKeon. New York: Random House, 1941, p. 1379.

[4] *Ibid*, p. 1380.

[5] Robert M. Pirsig, *Zen and the Art of Motorcycle Maintenance: An Inquiry Into Values*. New York: William Morrow, 1974, p. 32.

[6] *Ibid*, pp. 33–34.

[7] These are high credibility indicators cited by Jack L. Whitehead, Jr. in "Factors of Sources Credibility," *Quarterly Journal of Speech*, February 1968, p. 61.

[8] Jack Germond and Jules Witcover, *Mad as Hell, Revolt at the Ballot Box*. New York: Warner Books, 1993, p. 283.

[9] Ronald Reagan, "Encroaching Control," *Vital Speeches*, September 1, 1961, p. 677.

[10] *Ibid*.

[11] Robert P. Newman and Dale R. Newman, *Evidence*. Boston: Houghton Mifflin, 1969, p. viii. We are indebted to the authors of this book for the general scheme developed in this section.

[12] Harper Lee, *To Kill A Mockingbird*. New York: Popular Library, 1962, p. 208.

[13] *Ibid*, p. 244.

[14] William Robbins, "Watching and Waiting for a Quake to Happen," *New York Times*, December 4, 1990, p. A22.

[15] Newman and Newman, p. 79.

[16] Jane Gross, "203 Rape Cases Reopened in Oakland as the Police Chief Admits Mistakes," *New York Times*, September 20, 1990, p. A14.

[17] Exxon Corporation, *The Lamp*, Summer, 1990, p. 6.

[18] Keith Schneider, "In Aftermath of Oil Spill, Alaska Waters Lanquish," *New York Times*, July 7, 1994, p. A16.

[19] Carl Hovland, Irving L. Janis, and Harold Kelley, *Communication and Persuasion*. New Haven, CT: Yale, 1953.

[20] Carolyn W. Sherif, Muzafer Sherif, and Roger E. Nebergall, *Attitude and Attitude Change*. Philadelphia: W. B. Saunders, 1965, p. 201.

[21] Carl Hovland and Walter Weiss, "The Influence of Source Credibility on Communication Effectiveness," *Public Opinion Quarterly* 15, 1951, pp. 535–60.

[22] For a critique and review of this study see Philip G. Zimbardo, Ebbe B. Ebbesen and Christina Maslach, *Influencing Attitudes and Changing Behavior*, Second Edition. Reading, MA: Addison-Wesley, 1977, pp. 94–98, 125–27.

[23] *Ibid*, p. 126.

[24] For more detailed analyses of experimental research on source credibility see: Kenneth Andersen and Theodore Clevenger, Jr., "A Summary of Experimental Research in Ethos," in *The Rhetoric of Our Times*, ed. by J. Jeffrey Auer, New York: Appleton-Century-Crofts, 1969, pp. 127–51; Jesse G. Delia, "A Constructivist Analysis of the Concept of Credibility," *Quarterly Journal of Speech*, December 1976, pp. 361–75; Icek Ajzen and Martin Fishbein, *Understanding Attitudes and Predicting Social Behavior*, Englewood Cliffs, NJ: Prentice Hall, 1980, pp. 13–27, 218–28; and Dominick A. Infante, Kenneth R. Parker, Christoper H. Clarke, Laverne Wilson, and Indrani A. Nathu, "A Comparison of Factor and Functional Approaches to Source Credibility," *Communication Quarterly*, Winter 1983, pp. 43–48.

[25] Arthur R. Cohen, *Attitude Change and Social Influence*. New York: Basic Books, 1964, p. 26.

[26] Andersen and Clevenger, p. 132.

[27] Don A. Schweitzer, "The Effect of Presentation on Source Evaluation," *Quarterly Journal of Speech*, February 1970, pp. 33–39.

[28] Herbert W. Simons, Nancy N. Berkowitz, and John Moyer, "Similarity, Credibility, and Attitude Change: A Review and Theory," *Psychological Bulletin*, January 1970, pp. 2–4.

[29] Michael Sunnafrank, "Attitude Similarity and Interpersonal Attraction in Communication Processes: In Pursuit of an Ephemeral Influence," *Communication Monographs*, December 1983, pp. 273–84.

[30] For general discussions of these findings see: Mark L. Knapp, *Nonverbal Communication and Human Behavior*, New York: Holt, Rinehart, and Winston, 1972, pp. 63–90; and Raymond S. Ross, *Understanding Persuasion*, Fourth Edition, Englewood Cliffs, NJ: Prentice Hall, 1994, pp. 99–100.

[31] Wayne N. Thompson, *Quantitative Research in Public Address and Communication*. New York: Random House, 1967, pp. 54–55.

[32] *Ibid*, p. 59.

[33] Thomas E. Patterson and Robert D. McClure, *The Unseeing Eye: The Myth of Television Power in Politics*. New York: G.P. Putnams, 1976, pp. 22–23.

[34] Charles Kiesler, Barry E. Collins, Norman Miller, *Attitude Change: A Critical Analysis of Theoretical Approaches*. New York: John Wiley and Sons, 1969, p. 108.

[35] Burns W. Roper, *America's Watching: Public Attitudes Toward Television*. New York: Television Information Office, 1987, p. 5.

[36] Gary Cronkhite and Jo Liska, "The Judgment of Communicant Acceptability," in *Persuasion: New Directions in theory and Research*, ed. by Michael Roloff and Gerald Miller, Beverly Hills, Sage, 1980, p. 104. See also Daniel J. O'Keefe, *Persuasion: Theory and Research*. Newbury Park, CA: Sage, 1990, pp. 130–57.

37 Ronald Brownstein, "Hollywood's Hot Love: Politics," *New York Times*, January 6, 1991, pp. 13, 16, 17.

38 Daniel Pope, *The Making of Modern Advertising*. New York: Basic Books, 1983, p. 228.

39 Hugh Dalziel Duncan, *Communication and Social Order*. New York: Oxford, 1962, pp. 285–86.

40 Thurman Arnold, *The Symbols of Government*. New York: Harcourt, Brace and World, 1962, p. 46.

41 *Ibid*, p. 70.

42 Quoted in Richard Weaver, *The Ethics of Rhetoric*. Chicago: Henry Regnery, 1953, p. 200.

43 Jerome D. Frank, *Persuasion and Healing*. New York: Schrocken, 1974, p. 137.

44 *Ibid*, p. 139.

45 Quoted in J. Louis Campbell II, "Jimmy Carter and the Rhetoric of Charisma," *Central States Speech Journal*, Summer 1979, p. 175.

46 President Bill Clinton spoke in Berlin in July of 1994. See John Tagliabue, "Clinton at the Brandenburg Gate: Mixed Reviews," *New York Times*, July 14, 1994, p. A4.

47 Arthur M. Schlesinger, Jr. *A Thousand Days: John F. Kennedy in the White House*. Boston: Houghton Mifflin, 1965, p. 884.

48 *Ibid*, pp. 884–85.

49 *Ibid*, p. 885.

50 Edward Shils, "Charisma," in The Encyclopedia of the Social Sciences, Vol 2, ed. by David Sills. New York: Macmillan, 1968, p. 387.

51 Quoted in Doris A. Graber, *Verbal Behavior and Politics*. Urbana: University of Illinois, 1976, p. 182.

52 King, pp. 21–23.

53 Joshua Meyrowitz, *No Sense of Place: The Impact of Electronic Media on Social Behavior*. New York: Oxford, 1985, pp. 268–304.

54 See, for example, Ralph Abernathy, And the Walls Came Tumbling Down: An Autobiography. New York: Harper and Row, 1989.

55 Richard Sennett, *The Fall of Public Man*. New York: Vintage, 1978, pp. 282–87.

56 Eric Hoffer, *The True Believer: Thoughts on the Nature of Mass Movements*. New York: Harper and Row, 1966, p. 109.

57 Richard Sennett, *Authority*. New York: Alfred A. Knoph, 1980, p. 24.

58 T. W. Adorno, Else Frankel-Brunswik, Daniel J. Levinson, and R. Nevitt Sanford, *The Authoritarian Personality*. New York: Harper and Brothers, 1950.

59 See for example, Roger Brown, *Social Psychology*. New York: Free Press, 1965, pp. 509–26.

60 Adorno, et al., p. 248.

61 Charles Goodell, *Political Prisoners in America*. New York: Random House, 1973, p. 87.

62 David Hwang, "Are Movies Ready for Real Orientals?" *New York Times*, August 11, 1985, Sec. 2, pp. 1, 21.

63 Stanley Milgram, *Obedience to Authority: An Experimental View*. New York: Harper & Row, 1974, pp. 3–4.

64 *Ibid*, p. 4.

65 *Ibid*, p. 6.

66 Gustave Le Bon, *The Crowd*. New York: Viking, 1960, p. 118.

## Additional Reading

T. W. Adorno, Else Frankel-Brunswik, Daniel J. Levinson, and R. Nevitt Sanford, *The Authoritarian Personality*. New York: Harper and Brothers, 1950.

Gary Cronkhite and Jo R. Liska, "The Judgment of Communicant Acceptability," in *Persuasion: New Directions in Theory and Research*, ed. by Michael Roloff and Gerald Miller. Beverly Hills: Sage, 1980, pp. 101–39.

Carl Hovland, Irving L. Janis, and Harold Kelley, *Communication and Persuasion*. New Haven, CT: Yale, 1953.

Charles A. Kiesler, Barry E. Collins, Norman Miller, *Attitude Change: A Critical Analysis of Theoretical Approaches*. New York: John Wiley and Sons, 1969.

Andrew King, *Power and Communication*. Prospect Heights, IL: Waveland Press, 1987.

Stanley Milgram, *Obedience to Authority: An Experimental View*. New York: Harper & Row, 1974.

Robert P. Newman and Dale R. Newman, *Evidence*. Boston, MA: Houghton Mifflin, 1969.

Daniel J. O'Keefe, *Persuasion: Theory and Research*. Newbury Park, CA: Sage, 1990.

Carolyn W. Sherif, Muzafer Sherif, and Roger E. Nebergall, *Attitudes and Attitude Change*. Philadelphia: W. B. Saunders, 1965.

Edward Shils, "Charisma," in *The Encyclopedia of the Social Sciences*, Vol. 2. ed. by David Sills. New York: Macmillan, 1968, pp. 386–90.

Jack L. Whitehead, "Factors in Source Credibility," *Quarterly Journal of Speech*, February 1968, pp. 59–63.

# 6

# The Psychology of
# Persuasion

## OVERVIEW

> The most serious offense many of the depth manipulators commit, it seems to me, is that they try to invade the privacy of our minds. It is this right to privacy in our minds—privacy to be either rational or irrational—that I believe we must strive to protect.[1]
>
> —Vance Packard

In the quotation above, Vance Packard warns against precisely what persuasion scholars have attempted for years to discover. Much of the research on persuasion has tried to pinpoint the processes individuals go through in deciding whether to accept or reject a particular message. Think about the decisions you make daily. How many people try to convince you to behave one way or another? From your parents to your friends to your teachers to your boss to the advertisers in countless media, the attempts to influence are pervasive. If someone were to discover a failsafe method to dissect the private deliberations of individuals, that ability would give them awesome power to influence others. Fortunately, fears about a Svengali mastermind can be put to rest, since most theories of persuasion address tendencies of certain people in certain contexts. As such, they provide useful information about numerous processes, but no single theory can predict with absolute certainly how one person will behave at all times.

In this chapter we will investigate various behavioral theories of persuasion. The persuader who is thinking like a psychologist attempts to determine what happens "inside" individuals when they are confronted with appeals urging change. Specifically, we will consider various theories that attempt to account for internal changes that occur when we feel compelled to alter our beliefs, attitudes, and values. Also, we will discuss several persuasive strategies correlated with behavioral theories.

## Logic and Rationality

If you were to ask people how they make decisions, most would reply that they think about possible alternatives and choose the one that makes the most sense. While they might not use the terms rational and logical, they would be describing the exercise of reason—the ability to think, infer, and comprehend in an orderly, intelligent fashion. Yet, if most of us believe we are rational beings, how do we explain seemingly irrational behavior? Why do people continue to smoke when the evidence clearly indicates that smoking is a health risk? Why do people with children keep loaded guns in their homes when evidence warns that firearm accidents often occur? Why do people take "recreational" drugs routinely when such usage is socially and personally harmful? Logic would dictate that we should avoid smoking, storing loaded firearms in our homes, and consuming drugs. How can large numbers of people ignore the seemingly obvious?

Mr. Spock, on the original television show *Star Trek*, was a totally logical person. He functioned as a computer devoid of human emotion and motivation. In contrast, Dr. McCoy on the show was highly emotional, responding to situations based on feelings and instinct. Captain Kirk, the hero of *Star Trek*, was a combination of the two. When confronted with choices, he used both logic and instinct, reason and compassion. In the spirit of the original, the subsequent show *Star Trek: The Next Generation* incorporated the same characterizations. This time the crew had an officer named Data, an android, who was even more logical than Spock. In addition, Deanna Troi was an empath whose psychic awareness of the feelings and emotions of others served Captain Picard in times of crisis. As in the original series, however, Captain Picard balanced the extremes in decision making. These characterizations continue in the new series, *Voyager*. Again, pure logic is represented by the Vulcan, Tuvok, and emotion and empathy by the medical assistant, Kes. Captain Janeway in her role as decision maker must balance her emotions and intuition with what seems logically best for her ship and crew. These characters embody the processes all of us go through—in varying degrees—when confronting possible behavior choices.

Human logic is a complex and sometimes subjective notion comprised of more than mere "facts." How we interpret pieces of information and assign meaning and significance to them depends on which process we decide to use in categorizing inputs received. Interaction between speaker and listener affects both the information retained and the assessment process. A teenager with a sense of immortality and a strong desire to belong can easily find enough evidence to maintain that cigarettes are emblems of adulthood. "Logical" alternatives are not obvious; rather, they must be discussed, argued, and debated. Persuasion is more than an exercise in formal logic, because humans are more than machines. There can never be absolute predictable behavior as long as there are choices and human motives. There are too many situations, emotions, and differences among people for there to be singular solutions or arguments. Persuasion is a bridge across these differences. Persuasion is not something one does *to* someone; rather, it is a cooperative venture *with* another person.

# Attitudes, Beliefs, and Values

In chapter 1, we defined persuasion as the process of preparing messages to alter or strengthen the attitudes, beliefs, or behaviors of the intended autonomous audience. Attitudes, beliefs and values all contribute to how we view the world and how we behave. The clearest evidence of successful persuasion is some form of overt behavior. The ultimate goal of most persuasive endeavors is to get someone to do something. That action usually only follows after important internal changes. Traditional persuasion theory argues that behavior change or modification is predicated on attitude change. Consequently, attitude change is the core concept to nearly all theories of persuasion.

Attitudes, beliefs, and values are theoretical or hypothetical constructs. You cannot point to them as you can to a tree, a car, or a house. As a result, they are difficult to define, difficult to measure, and difficult to manage or even to be cognizant of as individuals. Yet, the concepts provide the basis for all social scientific investigations of human persuasion. Therefore, before we can discuss behavioral theories of persuasion, we need to explore the concepts of attitudes, beliefs, and values. We separate the three terms and note some distinguishing features, but it is important to remember that the three work together. Not everyone agrees on how to define these elements or even whether we can distinguish one from the other. Attempting to delineate differences does, however, help us sort out human tendencies and focuses our attention on the myriad influences on our behavior.

## Attitudes

Attitudes are the "evaluative dimension of a concept."[2] They comprise our likes and dislikes of people, places, or things; they influence our responses to stimuli and ultimately our behavior. Thus, when we evaluate some symbol in the world as desirable or undesirable, we are forming an attitude. If we say "abortion is bad," we are expressing an attitude. Attitudes are learned predispositions—tendencies to react favorably or unfavorably. They are learned patterns of response based on past personal experiences or the experiences of trusted others. Attitudes result from an accumulation of information; therefore, they can change based on new information. While we have numerous attitudes, they differ greatly in terms of their importance or *salience* to us.

The formation, changing, and maintenance of attitudes are ongoing and lifelong processes. Crime, for example, may not be viewed as a major problem until one becomes a victim. It is very easy to see how our attitudes on the emotional issue of abortion may result from our experience and environment at home and among friends. We also form many attitudes based on vicarious or symbolic experience. Much of what we know is based on what we read, are told, or see on television. This is why it is important that the sources of our information be accurate and fair. Otherwise, the very basis for our attitudes may be questionable. Finally, we form many of our attitudes based on stereotypes—assumptions resulting from limited and largely inaccurate information. Attitudes of this nature abound. Statements of sexism and racism reflect attitudes based on stereotypes.

## Beliefs

Martin Fishbein characterizes beliefs as informational statements that link a specific attribute to an object.[3] For example, the belief that humans are special beings with the ability to communicate symbolically as opposed to other animals links the attribute of "uniqueness" to the object of humans. A belief is what we personally "know" to be true—our convictions—even if others disagree. Beliefs are our perceptions of how two or more things are related. In terms of persuasion, beliefs are our perceptions about the consequences of a suggested course of action.[4]

Beliefs, like attitudes, may vary in terms of the degrees of certainty we assign to them. Attitudes are correlated with beliefs. Several beliefs may contribute to the formation of an attitude, some more strongly than others. A successful persuasive message may challenge the certainty of particular beliefs in an effort to change our attitudes.

Mary John Smith identifies four factors that determine the "potency" of any specific attitude: the number of beliefs an individual has regarding some area of experience, the extent to which one's beliefs are hierarchically arranged in an interrelated, supportive structure, the

---

### Figure 6.1
### Belief Structure of an Attitude

**Attitude:**                    I don't like "rap" music.

| **Beliefs:** | rap music is atonal | rap lyrics are often violent and profane | rap glorifies gang lifestyle | rap degrades; it does not inspire |
|---|---|---|---|---|

**Values:**                conservative, respect

degree to which individuals judge their beliefs to be "true," and the intensity of one's affective evaluation of each belief.[5]

Consider, for example, some potential beliefs that may contribute to one's attitude about abortion.

1. The purpose of sexual intercourse is procreation.
2. Children should be raised in a family environment, not in a single-parent environment.
3. Life begins at conception.
4. To have a child or father a child outside of marriage would greatly embarrass my family.
5. A woman should decide what happens to her body.
6. Human life does not begin until the fetus can survive outside the womb.
7. Our regard for the human fetus is a test of our own compassion for all humans.
8. People who care so much for unborn fetuses should show at least as much compassion for children who are now on this earth.
9. Some religious beliefs view abortion as the murder of innocent life.

There are undoubtedly many other beliefs that one could identify. The important point is that one individual would rank some of these as more important than others. Another person might rank them in exactly the opposite order. The ranking would be based on each individual's particular experience and knowledge which would affect the depth of feeling and the confidence to evaluate the issues.

It follows that the more information we have or know about an issue or topic, the more certain our beliefs (which lead to the formation of a strongly held attitude on the issue or topic) will be. While one new bit of information may not have much effect, multiple inputs may cause us to question some of the beliefs which contributed to an attitude. With the issue of abortion, one strategy to alter attitudes would be to present information that addresses the issue of "when life begins." To confirm or challenge an individual's belief about the beginning of life will strengthen or weaken an individual's attitude on the issue. For some, however, the issue of freedom of choice may be more salient than the conception of life, hence the need for multiple persuasive messages to address a number of the audience's beliefs.

## Values

Values are our central, core ideals about how to conduct our lives. They represent what we consider intrinsically right or wrong. As a result, values are far more stable than attitudes and beliefs. In general, we learn our value system in childhood, and it remains essentially unchanged throughout our lives. As we will see in chapter 7, many values are a product of our culture. American values of democracy, liberty, freedom, and equality are culturally based. Another source of values is intense lifetime experiences. Strong religious values, for example, may result from early training and church attendance, or perhaps from a special "conversion" experience. A strong work ethic may be a product of early poverty. Although our values rarely change, they may assume more or less importance at different stages in our lives. At one point, social awareness of others may be the predominant focus; at other times we might value solitude. One may become more "conservative" as one grows older because of work and social experiences and an increased desire to protect what one has accumulated.

Now that we have sketched some distinctive features of attitudes, beliefs, and values, let's return to the concept that the three interact. As mentioned at the beginning of this section, the goal of persuasion is to stimulate a preferred action.

The likelihood that we will accept or reject a message and act accordingly depends on three dimensions. The "affective" dimension focuses on our attitude—how we feel about the object. The "cognitive" dimension focuses on our beliefs—what we know about the object. The

Figure 6.2

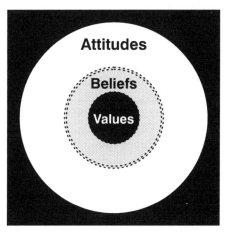

Attitudes are learned predispositions—how we feel about something. Beliefs are our convictions about what is true—our perceptions about how two or more things are related. New information may alter our attitudes or beliefs or both. Our core values rarely change. Persuasion is primarily concerned with the possibility that our behavior will be affected by changes in our attitudes and beliefs.

"behavioral" dimension reveals the probability of our acting in accordance with our attitudes and beliefs. For example, supporters of more stringent gun laws attempt to tap into strong feelings and memories of tragedies resulting from handgun violence. Handgun Control Inc. sponsors campaigns that link handguns with deaths. Their ultimate goal, of course, is to combine negative feelings about guns with specific information that will encourage individuals to act on their attitudes and beliefs. The behavioral outcome of the "right" attitudes is to give money to counteract the legislative clout of the powerful National Rifle Association. The NRA uses much the same attitude-belief-behavior linkage. Editorials in *The American Rifleman* tap into existing views that gun control threatens basic freedoms. Members are encouraged to vote for political candidates who support the NRA. The motivating language is both graphic and masculine: "It means a total commitment to safeguarding your firearm freedoms on every front with a square jaw and an iron fist."

As already mentioned, the link between attitudes and overt behavior is a tenuous one. There has been a great deal of debate about the relationship between attitudes and behavior. Historically, some have argued that attitudes produce behavior, while others argue behavior formulates attitudes.[6] Scholars have also discovered strong individual differences among people in terms of attitudes and behavior. Some people exhibit a high degree of consistency between attitudes and behavior. For others there is very little consistency.[7] For our purposes, there is no urgency in resolving the debate about the direction of influence. We can draw important conclusions without that resolution. It is easier to alter attitudes than beliefs. We have far more attitudes than beliefs and values. Many of them are the result of "unexamined inheritances." As rational beings, it is likely that we can be persuaded to take a look at the underpinnings of certain attitudes and to reassess our opinions. We also have a number of beliefs that may have been formed without a sufficient amount of information. These, too, are subject to change. Both attitudes and beliefs are relatively easy to ascertain. We express them daily in conversations. Values are much more elusive. We don't as frequently discuss them—perhaps we could not even name some of the principles guiding our actions. Thus, values are the least likely candidates for change through persuasion.

Let's review the functions our attitude-belief-value systems play in our daily decision making. The first is a utilitarian function—influencing our behavior. As we attempt to cope with people, ideas, and situations, our attitudes incline us toward or against certain actions and responses to daily social life.[8] The crush of information, requests, and solicitations we receive daily would overwhelm and paralyze us if we had to assess the consequences of each proposal without any shortcuts. Attitudes provide familiar scripts—a pattern of response which has been effective in the past. Scripts provide a shorthand method of response which allows

*This message uses a mixture of communication forms including information, expression, and persuasion in its appeal for support.*

—Mrs. James S. Brady—

# "Help me fight the National Rifle Association."

"[On March 30, 1981], John Hinckley pulled a $29 revolver from his pocket and opened fire on a Washington street. He shot the President. He also shot my husband.

I'm not asking for your sympathy. I'm asking for your help.

I've learned from my own experience that, alone, there's only so much you can do to stop handgun violence. But that together, we can confront the mightiest gun lobby—the N.R.A.—and win.

I've only to look at my husband Jim to remember that awful day...the unending TV coverage of the handgun firing over and over... the nightmare panic and fear.

It's an absolute miracle nobody was killed. After all, twenty thousand Americans are killed by handguns every year. Thousands more—men, women, even children—are maimed for life.

Like me, I know you support *stronger* handgun control laws. So does the vast majority of Americans. But the National Rifle Association can spend so much in elections that Congress is afraid to pass an effective national handgun law.

It's time to change that. Before it's too late for another family like mine... a family like yours.

I joined Handgun Control, Inc. because they're willing to take on the N.R.A. Right now we're campaigning for a national waiting period and background check on handgun purchases.

If such simple, basic measures had been on the books [fifteen] years ago, John Hinckley would never have walked out of that Texas pawnshop with the handgun which came within an inch of killing Ronald Reagan. He lied on his purchase application. Given time, the police could have caught the lie and put him in jail.

Of course, John Hinckley's not the only one. Police report that thousands of known criminals buy handguns right over the counter in this country. We have to stop them.

So, please, pick up a pen. Fill out the coupon. Add a check for as much as you can afford, and mail it to me today.

It's time we kept handguns out of the wrong hands. It's time to break the National Rifle Association's grip on Congress and start making our cities and neighborhoods safe again.

Thank you and God bless you."

## "Together we can win."

**Dear Sarah,**

It's time to break the N.R.A.'s grip on Congress once and for all. Here's my contribution to Handgun Control, Inc., the million-strong nonprofit citizens' group you help direct:

☐ $15  ☐ $25  ☐ $35  ☐ $50  ☐ $100 or $_____.
☐ Tell me more about how I can help.

NAME _____

ADDRESS _____

CITY _____ STATE _____ ZIP _____

**HANDGUN CONTROL**

1400 K Street, N.W., Washington, D.C. 20005, (202) 898-0792

Reprinted by permission of Handgun Control

us to follow a "cognitive course of least resistance."[9] We simply don't have the time, energy, or capacity to analyze everything exhaustively.

Attitudes also serve an ego-defense function by helping us know who we are and what we stand for; thus, they reduce internal, mental conflict.[10] They help mask truths known to us which we prefer that others not see, and they protect us from unpleasant realities. We can infer now, for example, that the class bullies of our youth lacked self-confidence and self-esteem. The tough attitudes displayed masked the true feelings of low self-worth and abilities.

Third, there is a knowledge function. Our values system gives meaning to the world around us by providing frames of reference and cues for accepted behavior.[11] Attitudes help us form the "dos" and the "don'ts" of our daily life. The danger is, of course, that some attitudes and beliefs are comprised of stereotypes or misinformation. In times of war, sentiments about protecting one's country and dislike of those threatening the security of a nation may be helpful in uniting people against a common enemy. Even then, such beliefs can be dangerously unfair, as was the incarceration of United States *citizens* of Japanese descent during World World II. In times of peace, such attitudes and beliefs are harmful since they reflect only negative feelings—fear, dislike, hatred—which do nothing to address or correct the underlying causes of resentment. Today, Japanese purchases of American companies and properties have created some anti-Japanese attitudes in the United States.

Finally, there is a value-expressive function[12]—a vehicle for expressing our core feelings, beliefs, and values about self, society, and others. We display our attitudes and beliefs proudly. Patriotism was manifested in the proliferation of flags and yellow ribbons during the Persian Gulf War of 1991. Such displays demonstrated more than support for the troops. They served to reinforce our feelings about America, our support for freedom, and our heroic conflicts of the past. By understanding the functions of attitudes, beliefs and values, a persuader may formulate more appropriate strategies for attitude change.

## Behavioral Theories of Persuasion

The study of persuasion from a behavioral perspective began as early as World War I. The focus of much of this research was on propaganda. Specifically, the research identified elements of the persuasive process. The researchers investigated predictable patterns of response predicated on various elements of information and misinformation. This very early research laid the structural foundation for studies to follow. World War II stimulated additional studies in the area. This time, however, the research was more exploratory and experimental rather than historical and focused on the relatively new concept of attitudes. The "Yale Studies" directed by Carl Hovland had a profound impact on persuasion theory. Hovland and his colleagues perceived persuasion "as a process of teaching persuadees to learn new attitudes or modify old ones, in much the same way that animals in a learning laboratory are trained to traverse a maze or to modify past maze-crossing habits."[13] Behavioral theories of persuasion are grounded in social psychology and are characterized by experimental, laboratory research concerned with how beliefs, attitudes, and values impact human behavior. While we cannot be exhaustive, we will review some of the more important behavioral theories of persuasion.

## Stimulus-Response Theory

A simplistic behavioral model for persuasion is the stimulus-response model of learning theory. The most famous example of this theory is Pavlov's dog. Each time the dog was fed, a bell was rung. Soon, upon only hearing the bell, the animal began to salivate. Learning theories center on the relationship between stimuli and responses. Infants enter the world with a "clean slate." They *learn* what behavior is acceptable, what is right, and what not to do. Most learning theories assume reinforcement is necessary to induce learning.[14] Throughout life we learn to seek favorable rewards and to avoid unfavorable ones. Positive rewards reinforce certain attitudes and behavior. If we are told enough that we are good, beautiful, or smart, we then begin to believe it and act accordingly. We tend to give more credence to attitudes and behaviors that occur in the presence of positive reinforcements. The stimulus of a teacher's praise for a student is obviously designed to reinforce the motivation of doing good work. To the extent this linkage works, a *conditioned response* is a predictable outcome. When there are concrete, positive reinforcements, we tend to give more credence to the attitudes and behavior.

Learning theory is important in persuasion. The persuader wants the audience to associate particular feelings with a proposal. "Persuasion, then, involves conditioning new affect (feelings) to the proposal and allowing previous (unwanted) associations to weaken. The goal is to extinguish the relationship between the proposal and previous associations."[15] Advertising uses this concept daily. What do we think of when we think of Michelob—friends, good times, women or men? Why does that trademark create these associations? Because the ads keep giving us messages that cause us to identify certain things with Michelob. This is a form of stimulus-response. If you were to exchange an expensive wine and a cheap wine in the bottles, which do you think would win a taste contest among your friends? Would the stimulus of an expensive label predispose them to favor that bottle? If you were to purchase two

*We* learn *what behavior is acceptable, what is right, and what not to do.*

*Tribune* photo by Bob Langer

paintings from a local artist and sign one Smith and the other Picasso, which do you think would receive more money at an auction? The same process is used when advertisers use a famous spokesperson for ads. They hope we will suspend judgement and attach our good feelings about the celebrity (the stimulus) to their product. As a result, we respond to the person and not to the attributes of the product. The key is the power of association between objects and images.

Although the structure of the stimulus-response model is rather simple, its variables can become complex. Focusing on the nature of the stimulus highlights factors of human motivation and conditioning. For example, what makes us recognize and value a Picasso painting more than one by Smith? Focusing on the nature of the response evaluates factors of choice and reasonableness. What rationale would we provide for a preference for the Picasso painting? And finally, focusing on the organism of response emphasizes factors of background, beliefs, and values. What motivates an interest in paintings, impressionism, etc.? In many ways, the stimulus-response model provides the basic premises for all the other behavioral theories of persuasion.

## Attribution Theory

Attribution theory attempts to explain how people account for the actions of others. It is human nature to try to make sense of the world and the behavior of others. We receive messages, decode them, and interpret them. By analyzing the broad situation or context of an action, we attribute a motive, cause, or reason for a behavior. It is important to remember that an ever-present feature of all communication is the identification of a source's or person's motives. Even though they are often left unspoken, attributions of motives are a part of the "subtext" of all messages. For example, suppose you are a car salesperson and you begin a conversation with a potential customer by complimenting his or her clothing. How will the customer interpret the compliment? It could be read as a sincere gesture, as a ploy to gain rapport, or as an invitation to start a social relationship. The entire communication that follows is

---

*Because no two people process information the same way, attributions of intent can vary within an audience exposed to the same persuasion.*

CATHY © Cathy Guisewite. Reprinted with permission of Universal Press Syndicate.

understood in terms of the customer's perception of the persuader's intent. Similarly, a fascinating feature of most films, plays, and novels is the way authors weave cues about the intentions of particular characters into the script. Part of the pleasure we derive from fiction is in learning whether we were right in judging that a character had evil or honorable intentions. Every James Bond story, for example, features at least one or two women whose loyalty to Bond is in doubt. In Bond films, love scenes can quickly turn into murder scenes, confirming our suspicions about the motives behind the association.

The task for the persuader is to figure out how certain messages or behaviors will be interpreted. What makes the process complex is that human perception plays a major role in interpreting the messages of others. Perception is comprised of a multitude of variables that function differently in separate individuals. Because no two people process information the same way, attributions of intent can vary within an audience exposed to the same persuasion. One person may praise a president for making a courageous defense of policy; another may condemn the very same effort as a collection of cleverly worded half-truths.

There are two classifications of attributions: situational and dispositional.[16] Situational identifies factors in the environment that are believed to cause people to act in certain ways. A classic example is attributing criminal behavior to environmental factors such as poverty, broken homes, or ineffective schools. In chapter 7, we will see that an important source of attitudes is the peer group and the varied audiences they represent. For example, one of the authors of this text comes from the Appalachian region of North Carolina. In that region, there is a great deal of sensitivity towards issues of poverty, hunger, education and the role of government in addressing those issues. Thus, the coauthor tends to favor governmental involvement in financing educational programs and scholarships as well as social welfare programs. For most observers, this would appear to be a rather "liberal" political position.

Dispositional attributions identify internal, personal factors that are believed to cause people to behave in certain ways. Such reasons for behavior lie at the core of individual beliefs or values. For example, elements of religion or philosophy may influence behavior. A privileged individual with inherited wealth may favor a social role of government in addressing poverty because of a strong belief in a high standard of life for all Americans. In chapter 5 we noted that certain personality traits (authoritarianism, for example) may correlate with predictable attitudes, such as excessive faith in the judgments of authority figures. To relate to the previous example, the coauthor from the mountains of North Carolina tends to be rather "conservative" on social issues such as abortion because of the social values and Baptist upbringing of his youth.

An important consideration based on attribution theory is that we actively infer reasons for our own behavior as well as for the behavior of others. Examining how we analyze ourselves provides insight into developing arguments for persuading people to act in a certain way. A persuader can provide reasons to justify desired behavior. Listing positive consequences of desired behavior can increase commitment to that particular behavior.

There are, however, problems with this approach. There is no certainty of correct or precise interpretation of individual motives, and such an approach encourages oversimplification of human behavior. Each day our actions are influenced by the roles we play. The authors at various times assume the roles of teacher, parent, husband, and citizen—all of which impact behavior. We may show compassion as a parent and husband but show little sympathy for poor performance as a teacher or citizen. In the example above, it would be just as easy for a privileged person not to favor a social role of government because of the belief that poor people are lazy and undeserving of governmental financial help.

It is important to remember that although attribution theory appears to be less than precise, the fact is that we must account for the behaviors of others so that we can assess our own behavior.

## Consistency Theories

One of the most important and powerful groups of all psychological theories are consistency theories. Some persuasion theorists focus on the mind as the intermediary between stimulus-response.[17] The mind organizes incoming, often unrelated stimuli into useful patterns. *Balance theories* assume individuals are uncomfortable with inconsistency and will work to reduce any discrepancies between new information and their attitudes and beliefs. For example, if you overheard a friend whose honesty you never questioned telling a lie, how would you feel? If you felt uneasy, would you change your beliefs about honesty? Would you change your attitude about your friend? Would you rationalize about the situation in which the lie was told? Persuasive strategies, according to balance theory, should highlight inconsistencies while providing more acceptable (consistent) alternatives for behavior.

To imagine how imbalance produces change, consider that—for any attitude—there is at least one related attitude that should be consistent. If the related attitude is inconsistent, calling attention to that inconsistency may produce change. For example, if you have a high regard for the president but a low regard for the military service, your attitude toward the president's decision to support a policy reinstituting the military draft will be in a state of imbalance.

How does a person resolve the discrepancy created when a respected person takes on a disliked idea? Balance theory predicts that the disparity will be resolved by altering one or both of the two original attitudes. If respect for the president is roughly equal to dislike for the draft, we would expect a process of change that would bring the two elements in consonance. That is, the person's enthusiasm for the president will *moderate*, and/or his dislike of the draft will be less intense. In short, the balance is restored by changing attitudes to create consistency and may be revealed in comments like, "I still think he's a pretty good president" or "I don't like the idea of the draft, but there may be times when it is necessary." Such comments reveal that there has been a change that reduces the inconsistency between the two elements.

The concept of cognitive dissonance was introduced by Leon Festinger in 1957.[18] The theory has been refined and modified by many since it was first proposed, but it is sufficient for our purposes to outline only its basic assertions. Revealed inconsistency produces dissonance or mental stress. The removal of the stress may take the form of changing an attitude or behavior to reduce the inconsistency. Roger Brown has offered a concise summary of dissonance theory.

> A state of cognitive dissonance is said to be a state of psychological discomfort or tension which motivates efforts to achieve consonance. *Dissonance* is the name for a disequilibrium and consonance the name for an equilibrium. Two cognitive elements, A and B, are dissonant if one *implies* the negation of the other; i.e., if A implies not-B. Two cognitive elements are consonant when one implies not the negation of the other element but the other element itself; i.e., A implies B. Finally, two elements, A and B, are irrelevant when neither implies anything about the other. Dissonance is comparable to imbalance; consonance to balance . . .[19]

The basic assumptions of Festinger's theory—that dissonance causes tension and that inconsistency will motivate people to do something to reduce the uncomfortable imbalance—are similar to other consistency theories. The difference is that the theory of cognitive dissonance emphasizes the activities people employ to justify changes in attitudes and/or behaviors *after* they have been convinced to do something.[20] Stephen Littlejohn lists the situations where dissonance is likely: decision making, forced compliance, initiation, effort, and social support.[21]

The more important or critical the decision, the more dissonance one experiences. The pressure of making the "right decision" increases the relative importance of each element of consideration.

Also, the magnitude of difference between elements of the decision increases the potential of experiencing dissonance. The choice between purchasing toothpaste versus purchasing a car heightens careful consideration. In contrast, however, the more similar the choices, the less potential for dissonance. For example, deciding between two televisions will create less dissonance than choosing between purchasing a television or a new video camera. In addition to the importance of the decision and the similarity between two alternatives, Littlejohn states that two other variables affect the amount of dissonance experienced. The attractiveness of the choice we made will either alleviate or increase the dissonance, and the perceived attractiveness of the alternative *not* chosen will similarly affect how we feel about a decision.[22] For example, if your parents decided to replace the wiring in their house instead of taking a trip to Hawaii, the level of dissonance would depend on which option had more attraction for them.

When a person is forced to do something contrary to his or her beliefs, the resulting dissonance may lead to attitude change. Being forced to do something we do not want to do (in the military, in school, by parents, by employers, etc.) is sometimes called enforced discrepant behavior by psychologists. We naturally want to lessen the discrepancy between the enforced behavior and the inconsistent attitude. The outcome may be that we may like a person more if we are forced to say nice things to them in public, or we may come to share the belief that military discipline is good training for later life. These changes in attitude give meaning and consistency to behaviors that we have publicly undertaken.

Interestingly, the stronger the threat of punishment or the higher the reward, the less dissonance an individual may experience. As Littlejohn states, the less external justification (such as reward or punishment), the more prominence internal inconsistency assumes.[23] Initiation ceremonies can be linked both to strong rewards/threats and to effort. Robert Cialdini relates a number of incidents from tribal coming-of-age ordeals to hell week campus activities to military boot camps and freshman hazing at West Point to illustrate the concept that the severity of an initiation ceremony heightens commitment to the group.[24] Despite experiencing pain, exposure to the elements, hunger, thirst, and embarrassment, there is less dissonance about the group which inflicted the torment than milder initiation activities would cause. Cialdini quotes William Styron on his Marine boot camp experience: ". . . who does not view the training as a crucible out of which he emerged in some way more resilient, simply braver and better for the wear."[25]

Researchers have tested the theory that people who exert great effort or go through pain and hardship to gain something will value the results more highly than those who achieve the same thing with minimal

*There is no internal inconsistency if two concepts are not related or if a person's attitudes toward two concepts are similar.*

Will your

heart pound any

less because

it's safe?

Will your

goose bumps care that it's practical?

Find your own road.

9000 CS Turbo

Will that giddy feeling deep in your stomach diminish because the 9000 is ranked the safest car in production?* Will your exhilaration be dampened by the turbo's fuel efficiency? Will the guilty pleasure of driving it be compromised by its large interior and 56 cubic feet of cargo space? We don't think so. Experience turbo rush in the Saab 9000 CS. **For a free Saab Excursion Kit, call 1-800-582-SAAB, Ext. 230.** www.saabusa.com

**SAAB**

effort.[26] Personal effort or investment plays a role in the amount of dissonance one may experience. The greater the personal effort, the more likely we will rationalize our behavior or attitude as correct. For example, although we may not like selling Bibles to poor people, the higher the profit and success rate of sales we receive from such people, the less personal dissonance we experience. The personal pride of success erodes the guilt. Finally, social acceptance of behavior drastically lessens dissonance. As the parents of older children frequently lament, strong peer pressure can virtually eliminate a lifetime of value training.

Two important qualifications are important to remember when applying consistency theories to the study of particular messages. First, there is no internal inconsistency if two concepts are not related or if a person's attitudes toward two concepts are similar. For example, if a president we did *not* like proposed a policy we also feared, there would be no psychological need for change.

As the model suggests, both attitudes are already aligned. The model provides a simple guide to whether a communication situation is balanced. An odd number of negative signs indicates imbalance; a positive number of negative signs (or zero) indicates balance.[27]

The second caution is that the human mind, when confronted with an inconsistency, provides many different options, not all of which call for adjusted attitudes. An individual may discount the source of the inconsistency, rationalize his or her behavior, or seek new supporting information to negate the inconsistency. The various cognitive elements (bits of information) that comprise the attitude become critical. For example, Philip Zimbardo and his colleagues analyzed the issue of smoking.[28] There is now undeniable evidence that smoking causes cancer. Other elements can, however, mitigate the threat of cancer. A smoker may only consume low tar cigarettes or may believe that smoking is good for relaxation or weight control. The smoker may also espouse the old adage that you've got to die of something; the relationship between smoking and cancer thus becomes less important.

Researchers are attempting to discover the reasons for attempting to achieve consistency. Factors such as self-concept and the potential for rewards and punishments are among the most important reasons for people maintaining consistency among their beliefs, attitudes, and values. However, it is important to remember that there is no direct relationship between attitudes and behavior. Seldom is there one attitude that dictates behavior. There are many attitudes that influence us. For this reason, it is difficult for anyone to achieve consistency at all times for all beliefs, attitudes, and values.

## Social Judgment Theory

Social judgment theory grew out of the work of psychologist Muzafer Sherif.[29] The theory predicts the effects of a persuasive message based on how the message relates to current beliefs.[30] Sherif's insights were drawn from physiological psychology where research indicated that people use "anchors" in judging certain attributes of an object. For example, if an experimenter turned on a light in a darkened room and said the wattage was 100, that brightness would become the anchor, the reference point. If you were asked to judge the brightness of four other lights, you would probably see the ones closest in intensity to the anchor as even more similar than they really are; this is the assimilation effect. Thus, you might judge a 75 watt light as the same as the 100. You would probably judge dimmer lights as even less similar than they actually are; this is the contrast effect.

Sherif applied these principles to how we judge messages, with current beliefs serving as the anchor point. He added one more critical ingredient—ego involvement. This theory treats attitudes and beliefs as a continuum in which there is a range of acceptable positions, a range of neutral feelings and a range of unacceptable positions. Individuals judge messages based on both internal anchors and ego involvement. The more relevant an issue is to one's self-image, the stronger the anchoring opinion.

In understanding how our internal anchors or reference points function in terms of attitude change, there are three important concepts to consider: latitudes of acceptance, rejection, and noncommitment. The *latitude of acceptance* is the cluster or range of attitudinal positions around the anchor that is acceptable. On most issues, there is a range of positions or statements that people could accept. Even those who are generally against abortion may favor exceptions in cases of rape or incest. Persuasive messages that fall within the audience's latitude of acceptance are more likely to be successful.

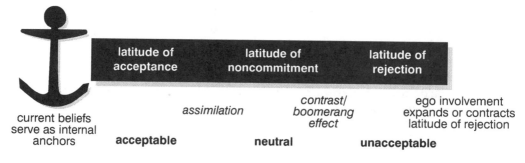

Messages which fall into the *latitude of noncommitment* are interesting. Because of the assimilation effect, certain messages in this range may be perceived as similar to the anchor point, while those farther along the continuum may be pushed into the unacceptable range by the contrast effect. Again, ego involvement will determine the width of each band. Low ego involvement with a message results in a wide attitude of noncommitment and the possibility of persuasion.

In contrast, the *latitude of rejection* is the cluster of positions which are absolutely unacceptable. Obviously, messages that fall within this category will not encourage attitude change. In fact, just the opposite often occurs. Messages that fall within this region tend to reinforce existing attitudes or positions—the boomerang effect. Therefore, it is important to know where the latitude of acceptance ends and the latitude of rejection begins. For example, when does one person's free speech become another person's obscene language? When does one advocate's plea for equal opportunity become the receiver's perception of discriminatory preferences? When one is highly ego-involved, the latitude of rejection is quite large and the latitude of noncommitment is small. Highly ego-involved people are difficult to persuade.[31]

The theory's implications for persuasion are many. Assimilation constitutes persuasion; contrast effect represents failure to persuade.[32] If our audience is known to favor an idea similar to ours or is at least noncommittal, it may take only one or two attempts to have our messages be assimilated into the latitude of acceptance. If the audience is highly ego-involved and opposed to our position, a single message will probably be contrasted and rejected. "Persuasion would require many messages over a long period of time, each gradually expanding the latitude of acceptance and slowly moving the favorite position (another belief)."[33]

## Long-Term Attitude Change

Kathleen Reardon argues that there are three main steps in achieving long-term change.[34] First is receiver motivation. A listener must have some predisposition to change. If not, the persuader must create an environment for change. This may take several efforts, creating a sense of trust, support, etc. It is not enough, for example, to explain the medical benefits of losing weight to overweight people. Supportive family and friends are essential to successful weight loss. To influence motivation "involves finding out what matters to the persuadee and shaping one's initial message(s) to address those concerns and needs.[35] Simply saying that smoking is unhealthy does not address concerns about weight gain, nicotine addiction, psychological dependency, etc.

The second step is participation. The receiver must be able to participate in the elements of change. We know that people are more accepting of a decision if they participate in the decision-making process. Sometimes, calling for small changes first may lead to larger, long-term changes in attitudes and behavior. A call for action is an important part of the attitude change process.

The final step is reward. There must be some positive reward for a changed behavior, belief, or attitude. Since most of us do not feel comfortable with uncertainty, we usually do not seek change and prefer the status-quo—a known quantity. If there is to be long-term change, there must be some visible or noticeable reward for the changed attitude or behavior. The greater the reward, the greater the potential magnitude of change.

## Elaboration Likelihood Theory

Earlier in the chapter, we discussed the tendency to rely on shortcuts or "scripts"—patterns of response that have been successful in previous experiences. As Robert Cialdini states,

> You and I exist in an extraordinarily complicated environment, easily the most rapidly moving and complex that has ever existed on this planet. To deal with it, we *need* shortcuts. We can't be expected to recognize and analyze all the aspects in each person, event, and situation we encounter in even one day. We haven't the time, energy, or capacity for it. Instead, we must very often use our stereotypes, our rules of thumb, to classify things according to a few key features and then to respond without thinking when one or another of these trigger features is present.[36]

Richard Petty and John Cacioppo developed elaboration likelihood theory to explain the different processing methods individuals use for persuasive messages. The shortcut method described above fits the *peripheral* processing route. The *central* processing route involves thoughtful analysis using critical thinking to assess the arguments presented in the message. The focus of the central route is the message. In the peripheral route, characteristics of the speaker or the context are more influential. Rather than testing whether the ideas presented in the argument make sense (central route), we are influenced by affective factors such as whether the source is likeable or attractive.

Two key elements affect the probability of choosing one route over the other: ability and motivation. Ability includes not only the capacity to apply reason but our knowledge about the subject matter presented in the persuasive message, the ease of understanding the message as presented, and the number of distractions at the time the message is received.[37]

Motivation is affected by our involvement with the issues presented—how important we believe the consequences of accepting the message will be to us. The number and variety of arguments presented also affect motivation. If we hear a number of competing views, the central route may be the only means available to process and organize the information. One other factor influencing motivation is personality. Some people thrive on analyzing issues and weighing possibilities; others find the process stressful. The higher one's ability and motivation, the more likely the central route will be employed. If an issue is important enough to us to activate our powers of reasoning to understand it, we use the central route. If the issue is important but we don't feel qualified to assess the argument, our emotions will seek cues from the situation.

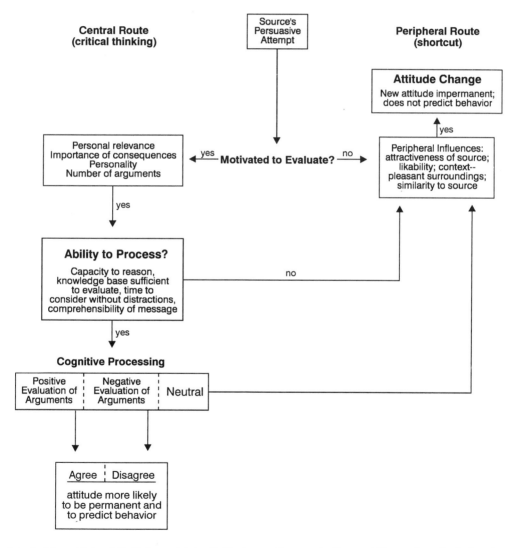

Adapted from Richard E. Petty and John T. Cacioppo, *Communication and Persuasion: Central and Peripheral Routes to Attitude Change.*

Since the probability of elaboration depends on a number of factors, individuals will differ in how they react to messages. As was true with social judgment theory, there is a "likelihood continuum" for individuals. Some issues will fall squarely in the central route while others will almost certainly be peripheral. For issues between those two extremes, persuasion may involve cues associated with both the central and peripheral routes.[38] For example, a doctor who has seen that marijuana is an effective pain reliever for glaucoma patients would have both the ability and the motivation to process messages relating to the legalization of marijuana via the central route. A parent who believes any drug use will lead to addiction will reject such a proposition without listening to the arguments, possibly by labelling the source irresponsible. A college student without strong feelings about the subject could be persuaded by both the arguments presented and by feelings about the source.

The theory raises interesting issues for persuaders. Is their message more likely to be processed centrally or peripherally? What constitutes an understandable message for what audience? Messages processed through the central route seem to result in longer-lasting attitude change. If a persuader judges that the peripheral route is more likely for a particular message, what is the best strategy to enhance the chances for central processing? While the peripheral route may not lead to long-term attitude change, is it easier to trigger acceptance, even if short-term? For some messages, that strategy could be useful.

## Summary

In this chapter, we discussed how the concepts of attitudes, beliefs, and values provide the basis for our behavior. In addition, we highlighted the importance of perception and social situations in influencing our actions. Human nature basically seeks rewards and attempts to avoid punishment. Stimulus-response theory explores this tendency. A number of other theories build from this one. Attribution theory explains the desire to make sense of the behavior of others and ourselves. We attribute motives for actions taken. Our belief that attitudes and behavior should be consistent is explored in consistency theories. What happens when we confront an inconsistency? How do we learn what behaviors are acceptable, and how do we decide how to judge the behavior of others? Social judgment theory alerts us to the anchors and reference points we use for analyzing messages. Elaboration likelihood theory recognizes that we sometimes apply full reasoning powers to messages and sometimes we rely on "tried and true," automatic responses that have worked in the past. All of these theories help us make sense of the world and the behavior of ourselves and others. If we take the time to reflect on the processes revealed by the theories, we will be much more likely to recognize—and to construct—effective persuasive encounters.

## Questions and Projects for Further Study

1. Select a television advertisement and see how many specific techniques and behavioral theories of persuasion you can find.

2. Select a magazine advertisement and see how many specific techniques and behavioral theories of persuasion you can find.

3. Select a contemporary controversial political issue and identify the underlying attitudes, beliefs, and values on each side of the issue. Attempt to construct a belief structure of the attitudes identified as illustrated in figure 2 of the chapter.

4. Select a contemporary controversial political issue and identify the positive or negative attitudes about the various factors of the issue. Attempt to isolate the source or formation of each attitude, i.e., direct experience, symbolic experience, and/or stereotypes. How do these attitudes compare with those of a friend?

5. How would your persuasive strategies differ if you were to advocate mandatory military service when speaking before an audience comprised of veterans, women, or college students? Would socioeconomic status make a difference? Why?

## Notes

[1] Vance Packard, *The Hidden Persuaders*. New York: Pocket Books, 1957, p. 229.

[2] Martin Fishbein and B. Raven, "The AB Scale: An Operational Definition of Belief and Attitude." *Human Relations*, 15 (February 1962), p. 42.

[3] Martin Fishbein and Icek Ajzen, *Belief Attitude, Intention, and Behavior*. Reading, MA: Addison-Wesley, 1975, pp. 222–28.

[4] Infante, et al., *Building Communication Theory*, Second Edition. Prospect Heights, IL: Waveland Press, 1993, p. 175.

[5] Mary John Smith, *Persuasion and Human Action*. Belmont, CA: Wadsworth, 1982, p. 39.

[6] Smith, pp. 45–46.

[7] Richard Perloff, *The Dynamics of Persuasion*. Hillsdale, NJ: Lawrence Rebaum Associates, 1993, p. 85.

[8] Gerald Miller, Michael Burgoon and Judee Burgoon, "The Functions of Human Communication in Changing Attitudes and Gaining Compliance" in *Handbook of Rhetorical and Communication Theory*, ed. by Carroll Arnold and John W. Bowers. Boston: Allyn and Bacon, 1984, pp. 442–44.

[9] Infante, et al., p. 178.

[10] Miller, et al., pp. 442–44.

[11] *Ibid*.

[12] *Ibid*.

[13] Herbert W. Simons, *Persuasion: Understanding, Practice and Analysis*, Second Edition. New York: Random House, 1986, p. 29.

[14] Burgoon, Hunsaker, and Dawson, *Human Communication*, Third Edition. Thousand Oaks, CA: Sage, 1994, p. 188.

[15] Infante, et al., p. 144.

[16] Philip Zimbardo, Ebbe Ebbesen, and Christina Maslach, *Influencing Attitudes and Changing Behavior*. Reading. MA: Addison-Wesley Publishing Co., 1977.

[17] Burgoon, et al., p. 192.

[18] L. Festinger, *A Theory of Cognitive Dissonance*. Evanston. IL: Row, Peterson, 1957.

[19] Roger Brown, *Social Psychology*. New York: Free Press, 1965, p. 584.

[20] Burgoon, et al., p. 200.

[21] Stephen W. Littlejohn, *Theories of Human Communication*, Fifth Edition. Belmont CA: Wadsworth, 1996, p. 142.

[22] *Ibid.*

[23] *Ibid.*

[24] Robert B. Cialdini, *Influence*, Third Edition. New York: Harper Collins, 1993, pp. 70–76.

[25] *Ibid.*, p. 75.

[26] *Ibid.*, p. 74.

[27] Burgoon, et al., p. 196.

[28] Zimbardo, et al., p. 66–67.

[29] See Muzafer Sherif and Carl Hovland, *Social Judgment: Assimilation and Contrast Effects in Communication and Attitude Change*. New Haven: Yale University Press, 1961: Carolyn Sherif, Muzafer Sherif, and Roger Nebergall, *Attitude and Attitude Change: The Social Judgment-Involvement Approach*. Philadelphia: W. B. Saunders Co., 1963: Smith, pp. 264–74; Littlejohn, pp. 152–54.

[30] Infante, et al., p. 194.

[31] Littlejohn, p. 153.

[32] Infante, et al., p. 194–95.

[33] *Ibid.*, p. 197

[34] Kathleen Reardon, *Persuasion in Practice*, Newbury Park, CA: Sage, 1991, pp. 10–11.

[35] *Ibid.*

[36] Cialdini, p. 8.

[37] Infante, et al., p. 202.

[38] *Ibid.*, p. 203.

## Additional Reading

Robert B. Cialdini, *Influences*, Third Edition. New York: Harper Collins, 1993.

Leon Festinger, A Theory of Cognitive Dissonance. Evanston, IL: Row, Peterson, 1957.

Martin Fishbein and Icek Ajzen, *Belief Attitude, Intention, and Behavior*. Reading, MA: Addison-Wesley, 1975.

Gerald Miller, et al., "The Functions of Human Communication in Changing Attitudes and Gaining Compliance" in *Handbook of Rhetorical and Communication Theory*, ed. by Carroll Arnold and John W. Bowers. Boston: Allyn and Bacon, 1984.

Daniel J. O'Keefe, *Persuasion: Theory and Research*. Newbury Park. CA: Sage, 1990.

Richard Perloff, The Dynamics of Persuasion. Hillside, NJ: Lawrence Erlbaum, 1993.

Richard Petty and John Cacioppo, *Attitudes and Persuasion: Classic and Contemporary Approaches.* Dubuque, IA: William C. Brown, 1981.

Kathleen Reardon, *Persuasion in Practice.* Newbury Park, CA: Sage, 1991.

Milton Rokeach, *Beliefs, Attitudes, and Values.* San Francisco: Jossey-Bass, 1968.

Milton Rokeach, *The Open and Closed Mind.* New York: Basic Books, 1960.

Phillip Zimbardo, et al., *Influencing Attitudes and Changing Behavior.* Reading, MA: Addison-Wesley, 1977.

# 7

# Social Bases of Persuasion

## OVERVIEW

■ Social and Psychological Perspectives Contrasted
Social Proof
Authority

■ The Audience Analysis Process
Auditioning Messages, Hollywood Style
The Principle of Identification
Commonplaces and Norms
Universal Commonplaces
Tracking Durable Commonplaces
Audience-Specific Norms
Norms and Political Correctness
Traditional Methods For Judging Audience Attitudes and Beliefs
Inferring Audience Attitudes
Surveying Audience Attitudes

■ An Audience-Based Model for Auditioning Ideas
Believing in Our Words
High Credibility/High Agreement Persuasion
High Credibility/Low Agreement Persuasion
Low Credibility/High Agreement Persuasion
Low Credibility/Low Agreement Persuasion

■ The Wildcard of Unintended Audiences

■ Summary

■ Questions and Projects for Further Study

■ Notes

■ Additional Reading

[A] man's opinions depend not so much on his own character, as on his social environment, on the people he associates with and lives among.[1]

—Chaim Perelman

Explanations of persuasion generally operate along two perspectives. The psychological perspective is concerned with the internal processes within the individual that accompany persuasive attempts. The social perspective focuses primarily on how group beliefs and values affect the construction of messages. After exploring the differences between these two approaches, we will look at the social view, with special emphasis on how public opinion affects the ways we act and think.

## Social and Psychological Perspectives Contrasted

Psychological explanations of persuasion (discussed in the preceding chapter) generally account for the internal processes activated when individuals are confronted with messages that reinforce or challenge existing attitudes. For the psychologist, the ultimate subject is the individual, and the primary medium of study is the individual's behavior. Targets of psychological research can range over a diverse spectrum. For example, how do people react to a persuasive message that uses fear as a motivation to change? Will charting a magazine reader's eye movement reveal the success or failure of the graphics layout and text in a print ad? What attitudes do children develop as a result of watching hundreds of hours of television news shows portraying the social chaos of crime, corruption, and cruelty?

By contrast, theories of persuasion which have their roots in social explanations assume that the personalities of specific individuals are reflections of the society in which they live. Social theorists look at the power of culture to shape values and beliefs. They start with the premise that we are largely what our contact with others has made us. As soon as we enter the world, we begin to acquire attitudes from a maze of contacts which give our lives meaning and purpose. This socialization process begins with the family, but it is soon shaped by a variety of forces: school, work, church, and the casual associations of daily life. Our world becomes governed by networks of obligations and memberships through which we acquire and share common attitudes.

A complete understanding of persuasion requires a combination of perspectives. Successful persuasion involves some degree of internal transformation of attitudes, beliefs, opinions, and behaviors.[2] At the same time, it must address our socially determined inclinations.[3] The presence of formal and informal groups within a culture accounts for how we acquire and hold attitudes. We may exercise our choices on many decisions, but we first acquire an awareness of our choices through the dominating presence of our associations. As Émile Durkheim (one of the early founders of sociology) described:

> Sentiments born and developed in the group have a greater energy than purely individual sentiments. A man who experiences such sentiments feels himself dominated by outside forces that lead him and pervade his milieu. He feels himself in a world quite distinct from his own private existence. . . . Following the collectivity, the individual forgets himself for the common end and his conduct is oriented in terms of a standard outside himself.[4]

The familiar claim that we are "social" animals is thus basic to the study of persuasion. By nature we are learners and imitators. For persuasion theorists, these patterns are analyzed in audiences made up of people with similar beliefs or characteristics, and with access to the same persuasive messages.

## Social Proof

Robert Cialdini discusses "triggers of influence" used by persuaders to reach their audiences, among them: social proof. Cialdini defines this principle as the tendency to decide what is correct by finding out what other people think is correct—particularly when deciding what behavior is appropriate.[5] Whether we are deciding the appropriate topics of conversation in a restaurant, if we should laugh out loud in a movie theatre, or if we should voice our opinion about a politician, we often look for cues from others present.

> The tendency to see an action as appropriate when others are doing it works quite well normally. As a rule, we will make fewer mistakes by acting in accord with social evidence than by acting contrary to it. Usually, when a lot of people are doing something, it is the right thing to do. This feature of the principle of social proof is simultaneously its major strength and its major weakness. Like the other weapons of influence, it provides a convenient shortcut for determining the way to behave but, at the same time, makes one who uses the shortcut vulnerable to the attacks of profiteers who lie in wait along its path.[6]

Cialdini also alerts us to two important factors which help determine our dependence on what others do. When we feel uncertain, we are even more likely to accept the behavior of people we perceive as similar to us. Cialdini uses these two factors to offer a fascinating assessment of the tragedy in Guyana (outlined in chapter 1). Those who followed Jim Jones found themselves totally isolated in an environment completely alien to anything in their previous experience. In such a state of uncertainty, they were particularly susceptible to following the example of others—not just the charismatic Jones, but all the similar others who were in Jonestown. Cialdini astutely notes that Jones' real genius as a leader was to recognize the power of social influence.[7] No leader can be totally persuasive for all members of a group all the time—but he or she can rely on social tendencies which operate when similar others are present.

# Authority

A corollary to social proof is the tendency to rely on authority. Society benefits greatly from such reliance. It facilitates legal, military and political systems and is the basis for social control at all levels—family, school, work, and society. As children, we learned how the world operates from parents, teachers and other adults. Cialdini points out that we followed such advice partly because it was useful and partly because authority figures controlled rewards and punishments. As adults, we often find ourselves in similar situations. Certain positions represent information and power. The pattern has been established, and we follow the directions of authorities. Cialdini warns that the pattern has become so ingrained that we often follow it when it makes no sense at all.

> The strength of this tendency to obey legitimate authorities comes from systematic socialization practices designed to instill in members of society the perception that such obedience constitutes correct conduct. In addition, it is frequently adaptive to obey the dictates of genuine authorities because such individuals possess high levels of knowledge, wisdom, and power. For these reasons, deference to authorities can occur in a mindless fashion as a kind of decision-making shortcut.[8]

The danger of the tendency to defer to authority is that it often bypasses critical thinking. If we respond to the symbols of authority—for example, titles or status symbols (jewelry, clothing, automobiles, addresses)—without analyzing whether the symbols have any relevance to the specific issue being proposed, we can find ourselves "obeying" empty commands. Someone wearing an Armani suit, a Rolex, and driving a Mercedes could tell you that everyone living in Palm Beach believes private schools are far superior to public schools. None of the symbols mentioned have any "authority" in the evaluation of education, but we can become so accustomed to deferring to authority that we stop analyzing the accuracy of statements and the qualifications of those making them. The use of celebrities to endorse products plays on the human tendency to defer to authority.

These brief descriptions of social tendencies sketched some of the vulnerabilities we have to accepting persuasive messages on "automatic pilot." The tendencies sometimes provide valuable shortcuts to making decisions; other times unconscious adherence to established patterns can be a mistake. Unethical persuaders can play on these vulnerabilities. The remainder of the chapter explores issues that persuaders who hope to reach an audience must consider in order to gain a fair hearing for their messages.

# The Audience Analysis Process

The test of the practical effectiveness of persuasion rests in determining whether specific messages will produce desired responses from audiences. Experienced persuaders usually "try out" their messages prior to their presentation. This auditioning may be informal, such as when we attempt to gauge the probable reactions that friends may have to a statement prior to actually expressing it. Alternatively, it may be formal, as in the elaborate and expensive audience analysis studies that are used by broadcasters and advertisers. In either case, the goal is the same: to locate points of identification that will bridge whatever gulf exists between persuaders and those they want to influence.

## Auditioning Messages, Hollywood Style

Preview House is a four-hundred-seat theater in Hollywood that has been used by advertisers and the television industry to audition new programs and commercials.[9] A wide range of ordinary people are given free tickets to screenings. The participants begin their roles as audience members by completing questionnaires about their television-viewing and product-purchasing habits. They are then seated in the comfortable theater where each chair contains a control knob which can be turned to settings reflecting their opinions about the action unfolding on the screen in front of them (very good, good, normal, dull, and very dull). These controls are connected to a computer which registers the audience's collective reaction to whatever is on the screen. An upbeat host guides the audience through the evening's viewing. One participant recalls his experiences:

> He shows us an ancient Mr. Magoo cartoon so we can practice rating what we see.

> On comes the [television] pilot for "Owl and the Pussycat." My pointer settles into the dull range. Upstairs in the control booth, computers are recording all our responses and logging them for later analysis.

\*   \*   \*   \*

On comes a series of dreadful spot commercials. . . . There's one for a mouthwash, a pain reliever, a savings and loan, etc. Our pointers are busy.

Once the commercials are over, we fill out more papers. They want to know what we remember about the commercials. Translation: Did they brand the brand name into our brains?

Then comes Preview House White Lie No. 1: They're sorry, but one of the sheets we filled out was missing a product category. Would we mind filling it out again. This is a phony ploy to see if we like Excedrin better after seeing the commercial than we did before. Most everybody falls for it.

\* \* \* \*

Finally they want us to see a short animated film. . . . The film turns out to be the award-winning Ernest Pintoff-Mel Brooks short subject, *The Critic*, a guaranteed laugh riot. This is the control study: If we won't laugh at this, we have no sense of humor and our group attitude toward *Owl and the Pussycat* is invalid.[10]

Preview House is an elaborate method of auditioning, but it follows patterns common to every form of persuasive communication. Perhaps advertisers and the networks are more anxious than other persuaders to follow rather than to lead opinion. Like all of us, however, they know that finding a way to anticipate audience reactions is important.

## The Principle of Identification

Not all communicators are persuaders, because some communication is not intended to win over audiences. For example, some writers and musicians may work to please only themselves or to achieve a private aesthetic goal. For them the act of self-expression may be its own reward. Even though most art is rhetorical (that is, artists usually seek receptive audiences) it is at least plausible to imagine the creator of an art form saying "I like it, and that is all that's important." Persuaders, however, must always go further; they must construct messages which narrow the gap between their attitudes and those of their audiences. In ways not demanded of other manipulators of words and images, they must reconcile their differences with those whom they seek to influence. "You persuade a man," notes theorist Kenneth Burke, "only insofar as you can talk his language by speech, gesture, tonality, order, image, attitude, idea, identifying your ways with his."[11]

The principle of identification may be the most universal of all the rules of persuasion. Reaching an audience is rooted in an advocate's ability to understand the collective beliefs of the members of the audience: what they like and dislike, what they take for granted, and what they are likely to challenge. St. Augustine noted that a person is persuaded if he

*Persuaders must construct messages which invite the audience to identify with the images presented.*

**DR. RON LEE** *is director of emergency medical services at Loyola University Medical Center. He has taken off and landed in a flying ambulance nearly 50 times, and has helped design Loyola's new emergency room. Today, he leads the team that is saving lives there.*

**PROFESSOR JOYCE WEXLER** *teaches English at Loyola University Chicago. She enjoys two challenges: an empty sheet of paper and a student with an open mind. She knows what to do with both. She won the Illinois Arts Council Essay Award and was honored by her students for teaching excellence.*

# National recognition and a focus on the individual
## **bring them** together. And set *Loyola* apart.

At Loyola University Chicago, we're concerned with the whole person, whether patient or student. Call it an unbending belief in human potential, if you will. It's a belief that permeates every department of the university, from emergency medical services to undergraduate English, and influences everything we do.

For example, we passionately believe knowledge is only of value when put into action that will make a positive difference for others. That's why we make a point of actively recruiting people who are not only the best in their chosen fields, but also the best at applying what they know. As a result, our people make up a stimulating, intellectually diverse community—a community of professionals who collaborate to best serve the individual. That's been a hallmark of our Jesuit tradition for over four hundred years.

With patients, we're concerned with the individual as a whole human being, treating not just the body but the spirit, as well. With students, we maximize their potential for rich, full, productive lives. In fact, the most striking point of difference between Loyola and all other institutions of health care and higher education may be an unwavering faith in human potential—patient or student. Please call **1-800-7-LOYOLA** for more information regarding Loyola University Chicago or Loyola University Medical Center. **NATIONALLY RECOGNIZED. INDIVIDUALLY FOCUSED.**

*Loyola University Chicago is an institution of higher education and health care founded in the Jesuit philosophy, which values diversity and nurtures individuals through superior programs and the collaboration of its outstanding professionals.*

LOYOLA
UNIVERSITY
CHICAGO

"embraces what you commend, regrets whatever you build up as regrettable, rejoices at what you say is cause for rejoicing"—in short, when the person thinks as you do.[12] Persuasion may be described as a process that uses the familiar to gain acceptance for the unfamiliar.

We can establish identification on many different levels. Our manner of dress and style of delivery can communicate physical similarity, while the expressions and examples we use can reassure an audience that we share similar experiences. This method can be seen in the work of Tony Schwartz, who has created many successful radio and television commercials. Schwartz believes that the most effective persuasion acts to trigger beliefs and feelings that already exist within a person. Effective advocacy depends as much on calling forth what individuals presently believe or "know" as on putting forth new or foreign ideas. A persuader, he notes, "must deeply understand the kinds of information and experiences stored in his audience, the patterning of this information, and the interactive . . . process whereby stimuli evoke this stored information."[13] Identification is the sharing of experiences and values; it is achieved when listeners and readers sense that what is being said expresses their own attitudes. Schwartz's presidential campaign commercials for George McGovern in 1972 thus openly dealt with the private doubts that many Americans had about the Democratic senator from South Dakota. In the still widely studied 30-second classic "Voting Booth," an obviously undecided voter stands with his hand poised between the separate levers for Richard Nixon and McGovern. The narrative device of an interior monologue lets us eavesdrop on his indecision, an attitude that Schwartz knew was common in the United States at the time:

| **Video** | **Audio** |
|---|---|
| Camera close-up of voting machine panel in booth—"Nixon" and "McGovern" labels on voting levers. Male voter enters, stands with back to camera. He makes face, fidgets. | Voice-over (obviously thoughts of voter in booth): "Either way it won't be a disaster. What am I looking for? I mean, so I'll vote for Nixon. Why rock the boat? I'm not crazy about him, never was. I got to decide though, got to make up my mind. I'm not crazy about McGovern. I don't have that much time, I can't keep people waiting. The fellas are voting for Nixon. They expect me to vote for him too. Me vote for Nixon! My father would roll over in his grave. The fellas say they are. Maybe they're not. Crime? I don't feel safe. |

| | Prices up. I got a gut feeling: Don't vote for Nixon. Why am I confused? Who am I measuring McGovern against? My gut feeling, my gut feeling—McGovern. |
| --- | --- |
| He looks at his hand | This hand voted for [John F.] Kennedy. I mean, it's just possible McGovern's straight. Maybe he can— |
| Cut to slide, white letters on black: "Democrats for McGovern."[14] | That's the way!'' |

The spot cleverly invited viewers to identify with the voter's quandary, while subtly attempting to allay fears about McGovern.

## Commonplaces and Norms

The word communicate has its origins in the Latin word *communicare*, meaning ''to make common to many.'' The Latin definition is a perfect reminder that communication is fundamentally about the process of locating ideas that audiences can recognize as their own.

### Universal Commonplaces

Commonplaces are widely shared cultural beliefs. They represent the core values and beliefs that characterize a particular society. As basic expressions of shared values, commonplaces are frequently unstated but important assumptions behind everyday thought. According to the French social theorist Jacques Ellul, a commonplace may be taken for granted as part of the fabric of ideas governing everyday life. ''It serves everyone as a touchstone,'' he notes, ''an instrument of recognition. It is rarely quoted, but it is constantly present; it is behind thought and speech; it is behind conversation. It is the common standard that enables people to understand one another. . . .''[15]

Some of the most faithful compilers of commonplaces have been anthropologists and sociologists determined to map the ideological landscape of a tribe, nation, or culture. W. Lloyd Warner's classic five-volume ''Yankee City'' series, for example, studied a ''typical'' American city (allegedly Newburyport, Massachusetts) with the same intensity and objectivity that a visiting team of anthropologists might employ in looking at an unknown tribe on a Pacific island. Warner examined political speeches, advertisements, sermons, cemetery markers, and even floats in a Memorial Day parade to discover what they revealed about the beliefs and values of the city's social life.[16] In 1935 researchers Robert and Helen Lynd studied an American city dubbed ''Middletown''

*Commonplaces are expressions of shared values—frequently unstated but important assumptions guiding everyday thought. They serve as common standards enabling people to understand one another.*

with a similar interest in discovering the attitudes large sections of the community held in common. They catalogued the essential commonplaces of the city, "the things that one does and feels and says so naturally that mentioning them in Middletown implies an 'of course.'"[17] A sampling from their list of attitudes on the general subject of "the proper roles for government" points out the durability of many American commonplaces.

> That the American democratic form of government is the final and ideal form of government.
> That the Constitution should not be fundamentally changed.
> That Americans are the freest people in the world.
> That America will always be the land of opportunity and the greatest and richest country in the world.
> That England is the finest country in Europe.
> That Washington and Lincoln were the greatest Americans. . . .
> That the voters, in the main, really control the operation of the American government.
> That the two-party system is the "American way."
> That it does not pay to throw away one's vote on a minority party.
> That government ownership is inefficient and more costly than private ownership.
> "More business in government and less government in business."
> That the government should leave things to private initiative.
> That people should have community spirit.
> [That it is good to be against] centralized government, bureaucracy, large scale planning by government.
> That in a real emergency anyone with any human feeling will "share his shirt with an unfortunate who needs it."[18]

Not every individual would accept all of these fundamental starting points, nor do they always remain unchanged from generation to generation.[19] They are characterized as universal because they reflect mainstream public opinion at a specific time. We can isolate them as the building blocks of persuasion because they are readily accepted by so many within a culture. Awareness of key commonplaces makes it easier to initiate a sequence of persuasive appeals.

### Tracking Durable Commonplaces

Almost any persuasive message can be shown to have broad-based commonplaces as key starting points. Presidents, for example, frequently employ many of the items from the above list.

In his 1992 inaugural address, Bill Clinton used a condensed form of the last three commonplaces, emphasizing the limits of government and the virtues of helping for the good of the community. "We must do what America does best," he noted, "offer more opportunity to all and demand more responsibility from all."

> It is time to break the bad habit of expecting something for nothing from our government or from each other. Let us all take more responsibility, not only for ourselves and our families, but for our communities and our country.[20]

These statements reflected the general view of the Clinton administration toward welfare reform, but they also built on long-standing American suspicions about the ability of governments to perform efficiently.

Consider an additional example involving the highly effective use of these commonplaces in the 1988 presidential campaign of George Bush. One traditional benchmark of the campaign is the acceptance address given immediately after the selection of the presidential candidate. Behind in most public opinion polls to Democratic nominee Michael Dukakis, Bush struck out at his opponent with a stinging set of declarations that separated him—often misleadingly—from the Massachusetts governor. Speechwriter Peggy Noonan helped Bush define himself—and not Dukakis—as part of the American mainstream.

> I am one who knows that it is only the United States that can strongly stand up for freedom and democracy around the world.
>
> I am one who understands the limits of Federal Government and understands the power of the private sector—churches, families, local governments—one who understands the power of the individual to help his fellow man. . . .
>
> I am one who will work with Congress, but understands that one party domination of Congress by big spenders there resulted in huge deficits.[21]

The speech concluded with what would become its rhetorical signature—a syrupy expression of the ideal of community service.

> I am guided by certain traditions. One is that there is a God and He is good. . .
>
> And there is another tradition. And that is the idea of community—a beautiful word with a given meaning, though liberal Democrats have an odd view of it. They see community as a limited cluster of interest groups, locked in odd conformity. . . . But that's not what community means—not to me. For we are a nation of communities, of thousands of ethnic, religious, social, business, labor union, neighborhood, regional and other organizations, all of them varied, voluntary and unique.
>
> This is America: the Knights of Columbus, the Grange, Hadassah, the Disabled American Veterans, the Order of Ahepa, the Business and Professional Women of America, the union hall, the Bible study group, LULAC, Holy Name—a brilliant diversity spread like the stars, like a thousand points of light in a broad and peaceful sky.[22]

"A thousand points of light"—it was Noonan's favorite phrase in the address and her ticket to national fame. She loved it, she said, "because its power is born in the fact that it sounds like what it is describing."[23] She had found a potent phrase to express deeply held commonplaces about the diversity of American communities and the obligations they share in providing support for Americans in trouble.

### Audience-Specific Norms

Some topics require persuasion that uses more specific and sometimes more controversial starting points. Audience-specific norms differ from universal commonplaces by appealing to a limited number of groups within a society. Divisive subjects such as abortion rights for women, controls on the sale of firearms, the death penalty, and farm subsidies for tobacco growers evoke passionate responses from both sides. As issues become more specific, individuals become more selective in the values and attitudes they accept. American society consists of numerous organizations and coalitions, some formal and some informal. All of us are in the mainstream of opinion on some topics and in the minority on others. Our membership in a complex society inevitably means that we will be moving with the tide of public opinion sometimes and swimming against it at other times.

As public discussion of controversial issues becomes more specific, differences emerge that cannot be resolved by persuasion based on universal commonplaces. The presence of controversy makes audience-specific norms important. These "in-group" ideas are not universally accepted by a society but are sustained by specific groups within it. Most controversies displayed in headlines encourage persuasion directed to various constituencies with specialized priorities or norms (for example, Handgun Control Incorporated, the National Rifle Association, the National Association of Chiefs of Police, and Mothers Against Drunk Driving). It is obvious but vital to remember that some groups have very different ideas about what is "good," "just," "fair," and "important."

Consider the diverse audiences that American corporations must address—stockholders, customers, wholesalers, and critics, to name a few. Maxell, for example, sells its premium videotape to customers with claims about its "superior" performance. In trade magazines directed only to retailers, the same products are described as "how to get rich tapes" which yield "higher dollar per unit return" than less expensive and more competitively priced "standard grade" tapes.[24] Obviously, such a message is far more acceptable to Maxell's dealers than to its consumers, who might resent the implication that the "premium" line is designed in part to increase the profits of retailers.

### Norms and Political Correctness

It is interesting to note how audience-specific norms are frequently at the root of discussions about the "political correctness" of certain expressions or attitudes. When members of one group within society are accused of misnaming the members or actions of another, what is frequently in question are specific terms that either offend or affirm certain in-group sensibilities. The critic Robert Hughes has noted that "there are certainly worse things in American society than the ongoing vogue for politically correct language," but he notes that there are few actions that are more futile than attempting to create "a sort of linguistic Lourdes, where evil and misfortune are dispelled by a dip in the waters of euphemism."[25] Phrases such as "physically challenged" or "gay rights" acknowledge clusters of norms important to advocates for American disabilities rights and homosexuals. "Non-PC" phrases— references to "handicapped" or "sexual deviates," for example—imply the user's denial of norms important to specific groups.

Norms vary significantly from individual to individual, let alone from group to group. However, even if they are difficult to pin down precisely, persuaders ignore in-group norms at their peril. The question of what constitutes "modern feminism," for example, will inevitably involve the discussion of norms *reflected in language* that some will accept and others reject. Political consultant Mary Matalin, for example, offers her own view of why "the feminist movement has a problem," citing group norms that she is confident will be rejected by most of her readers.

> Ask any woman why she's not a feminist and she's likely to say: "I don't want to emulate men to succeed—I like being a woman; I respect the right of women to stay home; I don't hate men."[26]

Matalin uses these short declarations to characterize what she sees as the negative norms of the movement. Other writers engaged in these issues, such as Susan Faludi and Gail Dines, defend feminist concerns in language that invokes different cultural norms that perpetuate oppression and victimage: women as *victims of sexual violence*[27] or what Dines calls *the white-male patriarchy*.[28] They are obviously not endorsing these norms but identifying them as part of a gender-biased power structure.

To some extent, all of these views illustrate what writer Naomi Wolf has described as the very different traditions that feminists must deal with in the 1990s. The older tradition of "victim feminism," she argues, is giving way to a newer "power feminism" that defines women as free agents capable of setting their own agendas. Unlike an older feminism that was sometimes "antisexual" and preached a doctrine that asked women to "identify with powerlessness," "power feminism" defines different norms, among them:

> Is unapologetically sexual . . .
> Hates sexism without hating men . . .
> Seeks power and uses it responsibly, both for women as individuals
>     and to make the world more fair to others . . . [and]
> Encourages a woman to claim her individual voice . . .[29]

# Traditional Methods for Judging Audience
# Attitudes and Beliefs

The thoughtful persuader can discern many of the attitudes of an audi-ence without much difficulty. It takes no extensive study to predict that an advocate for higher tuition is going to meet opposition on a college campus. The process of audience analysis is not always so predictable, however. Generalizations about what a collection of people "think" are reliable only if individuals in the group are similar in basic and important ways.

There are two ways to learn about audience characteristics. One is to make generalizations about what the audience thinks based on group attributes. Certain attributes such as age, occupation, and religious affiliation can predict attitudes. The second method is to test for attitudes by systematically polling a representative sample of the audience. In actual practice, both of these methods are used together, but it is useful to consider their differences.

## Inferring Audience Attitudes

Every audience can be profiled by certain traditional measures: age, sex, income level, education, geographical location, and membership in formal associations. These are standard demographic categories. Demographics literally means "measurement of the people." Since most groups show greater similarities than differences in at least some of these traits, it is possible to make cautious generalizations about group attitudes. Radio stations and their advertisers, for example, typically find that preferences for musical formats correlate with age, gender, and geographic location (teens, older adults, suburban adults, men, and so on). Similarly, television networks attempt to show prospective advertisers that their programs reach commercially lucrative segments of the population such as adult women who make a high percentage of all household purchases. Consumer magazines such as Time-Warner's successful *Money* also exist in part to capture audiences with income levels that will attract potential advertisers.

Inference making is partly a matter of guesswork. It involves using known facts to arrive at conclusions about unknown facts. Although such inferences are inexact, it is advantageous to make estimations about the attitudes of people based on what is known about their personal and social situations. Audiences with heavy concentrations of farmers should be treated differently than audiences of bankers, retirees, union members, or college seniors. Persuaders addressing these groups would work backwards from general traits to an estimate of probable attitudes and values each group could be expected to endorse or condemn.

Jury selection in trials remains one of the most visible forms of inference making about audiences. In criminal trials lawyers and judges

Figure 7.1

**A Note on the Concept of ''Audience''**

How real is the idea of the audience? Scholars and professionals in most areas of communication assume that *communication is addressed to audiences who can be identified by their common features and attitudes.* Our intellectual life—as well as the study of persuasion—would be unmanageable without the convenient idea of the audience.

Even so, the concept rarely works as well in fact as it does in theory. Although we are sometimes slow to acknowledge it, audiences rarely turn out to be as uniform or homogeneous as we assume. The problems of characterizing audiences in the 1990s are diverse:

1. The concept of audience was born in a simpler period. Aristotle wrote his text, *The Rhetoric*, with an eye on a few hundred citizens of a small city meeting in the same place at the same time. Even American participatory democracy in the late 1700s was intended for a very restricted citizenry of white male landowners. Today, by contrast, presidents speak to a much more diverse constituency.

2. The largest of our mass media—especially the commercial television networks—have made diverse audiences a given. Who is the audience for television's *CBS Evening News, 60 Minutes,* or *Roseanne?* In the jargon of the media, the ''demographics'' for these programs are ''mixed.'' Indeed, they are designed to cast their nets broadly, catching as many viewers for their lucrative commercials as possible.

3. As citizens of a large nation, we seem to have growing doubts about the beliefs and values that we actually have in common. In contrast to our old rhetorical tradition embracing the idea of inclusion (i.e.: ''All men are created equal . . .''), the United States—like many other complex cultures—has fostered racial and class distinctions. Since at least the 1940s a number of writers have documented the frayed edges of our national community in efforts to explore the question, do we still share a common culture?[1] As some social theorists have noted, we are less a ''melting pot'' that blends away our differences, than a culture that more or less accommodates them.

For all of these reasons, persuaders must be cautious about making simple or glib judgments about the features that audiences allegedly have in common.

[1] See, for example, Nathan Glazer and Daniel P. Moynihan, *Beyond the Melting Pot*, Second Revised Edition, Boston: MIT, 1970; Robert N. Bellah et al., *The Good Society*, New York: Knopf, 1991, esp. ch. 4; and David Zarefsky, ''The Postmodern Public,'' *SPECTRA*, March, 1994, p. 9.

# BOYS

watch MTV's Spring Break. They

watch it with pleasure, devotion, and unbridled gratitude. So do

# GIRLS

, who watch it with

passion, eagerness, and awestruck thankfulness.

Why is this so? Because only MTV can satisfy the

craving for the kind of programming that young people

want, demand, and deserve. In fact, we've never had any

# TROUBLE

getting a nice mix of viewers. Maybe that's because

we have so many (last year, Spring Break attracted

34 million).* The best thing about the boys and girls who watch

MTV? They're men and women: 65% are over 18 years old.**

**Read between the lines.**

*Audience demographics are not always easily predictable, as this promotion cleverly illustrates.*

Reprinted by permission of MTV

have the right to reject prospective jurors. In the age of the televised "mega-trial," the attempts by defense attorneys to seat twelve sympathetic individuals on the jury are highly visible. In selecting members of the panel to hear evidence against O. J. Simpson a number of jury consultants were paid for their expertise. According to several prominent defense attorneys and jury consultants the ideal panel to return a "not guilty" verdict for Simpson should have included men rather than women (the prosecutor was female, as was one of the victims), older rather than younger members (in the same generation as Simpson), African Americans (a match of the defendant's race), and "football buffs rather than football widows" (in keeping with Simpson's reputation as a former star of the game).[30]

These hunches may seem crude and inexact. Yet when the stakes are high, most persuaders are willing to second-guess outcomes based on broad demographic categories.

### Surveying Audience Attitudes

Inference making is useful but risky. Concluding that "older Americans" think in a certain way just because they are older involves a good deal of simplistic stereotyping. Age (or sex, income level, education level, and so on) is no *guarantee* that someone will think or act in a certain way. In addition, large and demographically diverse audiences cannot be easily targeted for specific and unique sets of attitudes.

Directly measuring attitudes usually gives more reliable information about an audience than an inferred assessment. Survey research is more expensive and time-consuming than simple demographic analysis, but it will reveal more than who the audience is; it will measure what they think. Access to a representative sample of a target group in face-to-face interviews (or in settings such as Preview House) makes it possible to determine the values and beliefs that may present opportunities for or obstacles to persuasion.

Persuaders such as advertisers and political campaigners use many different survey research techniques. Among them are "in-depth" interviews with sample audience members and questionnaires that use scales to measure responses to key concepts or evocative words. As the attitude scale in figure 7.2 demonstrates, it is relatively easy to determine specific attitudes individuals may have toward one concept, such as the proposal that television advertising of beer and wine be banned. Knowledge gained from understanding negative and positive feelings triggered by certain words can help determine how a controversial subject might best be approached. Regardless of the system used, the goal of attitude surveys is to learn as much as possible about the priorities, feelings, and judgments of those who will be the focus of appeals. Although survey research is now common for professional persuaders, it is prohibitively expensive. Most of us must analyze an unfamiliar audience by generalizing from who they are to what they think.

Figure 7.2

For the past several years, Congress has been considering whether television advertising for beer and wine produces harmful effects. The following Attitude Rating Scale might be used by advocates on this issue (the wine and beer industry, and other groups) to determine audience attitudes. Respondents are asked to mark a place on the scale that comes closest to their feelings about a specific topic. In this case:

**Television and Radio Commercials for Beer and Wine**
(Mark the scale at the point closest to your own feelings.)

| | | |
|---|---|---|
| Helpful | _____ | Useless |
| Unwise | _____ | Wise |
| Fun | _____ | Dangerous |
| Silly | _____ | Clever |
| Exciting | _____ | Dull |
| Truthful | _____ | Untruthful |
| Useless | _____ | Useful |
| Informative | _____ | False |
| Safe | _____ | Dangerous |

# An Audience-Based Model for Auditioning Ideas

At its simplest, persuasion can be reduced to three important variables. For persuasion to occur, there must be an advocate (someone or a group with a viewpoint to express), a message (the point of view the advocate wants listeners to accept), and an audience (listeners, viewers, or readers). Removing any variable makes communication impossible. Our three-sided model of this process (presented in figure 7.3) is based on the work of researchers attempting to look at how people maintain and change their attitudes.[31] In the remainder of this chapter, we will discuss what the model reveals about six possible types of persuasive encounters.

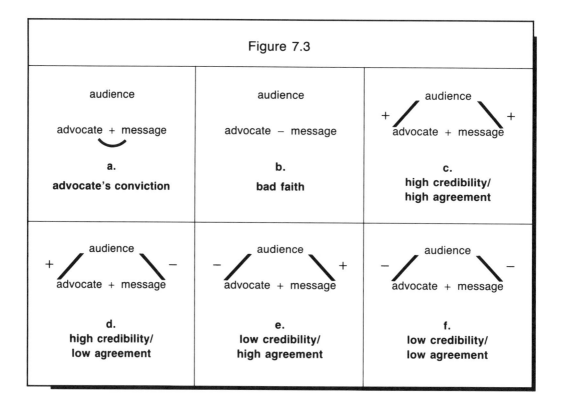

Figure 7.3

This simple guide illustrates the fact that advocates, audiences, and messages directly interact with each other in six different configurations. It implies that two key questions should be asked about any persuasive encounter: Does the audience like the advocate? and Does the audience share the advocate's point of view?

Here is how these important questions are answered. Imagine that for any persuasive setting it is reasonable to estimate relationships between the three variables as positive (+) or negative (−). A positive sign indicates approval, a negative sign indicates disapproval. For example, the most difficult form of persuasion is diagrammed in 7.3.f. This is a case where—as we would expect—the persuader has a positive regard for the ideas in the message; but it is also a setting where the audience has negative feelings not only toward the persuader but also toward the ideas. Before turning to this and other variations, however, we begin our analysis with a look at the only relationship that should be (but is not always) constant: the advocate's positive faith in the rightness of the ideas presented.

## Believing in Our Words

Figure 7.3.a diagrams a normal expectation built into all communication. Although what an audience thinks about a topic may range from approval to disapproval, the audience rightly assumes that our expressions of support for an idea are sincere. Assuming we are not coerced, we are unlikely to argue for what we do not believe. An ethical presumption underlying all forms of persuasion is that advocates believe in what they want others to accept.

If someone deceptively supports a position that he or she privately dislikes, we may feel used. Such "bad faith" communication is diagrammed in figure 7.3.b, suggesting that the speaker may lack the courage of his or her convictions by saying one thing but believing another. To be sure, there are times when people are required to "front" for someone else's viewpoints. "Fronting" for an individual or agency is required when individuals must represent the views of organizations or clients, as when a governmental press aide defends an official policy with which she or he privately disagrees. In the remainder of this section, we will assume that a positive relationship between advocate and idea remains relatively fixed and invariable.

## High Credibility/High Agreement Persuasion

The ideal communication environment is one in which the audience is positive about both the message and its presenter. In this case, they agree with the persuader's message and have a positive attitude about the persuader's character. Figure 7.3.c represents situations in which enthusiastic supporters gather to hear a popular leader recite esteemed beliefs. Democratic campaign speeches given to Democratic audiences and Methodist sermons given to Methodist congregations are two examples of "preaching to the converted." Audiences attentive to a candidate appearing on television or face-to-face are heavily populated by people who already appreciate the source and the message.[32] Basic persuasion research suggests that "people pay attention primarily to content that already interests them and that is congenial to their point of view."[33]

High credibility/high agreement persuasion may seem unnecessary, but it is a mistake to overlook the need for "reinforcing" communication. Rhetoric that resonates with an existing attitude is extremely satisfying; it fulfills our need for membership in associations and it involves practically no risk. It is obviously more rewarding and less threatening than the reverse, which would involve facing an audience whose members have doubts about us and our message. Such reinforcement may seem empty and ritualistic, but organizations and movements must periodically remind believers of the tenets basic to their faith. Speeches,

*The ideal communication environment is one in which the audience is positive about both the message and its presenter.*

*Tribune* photo by James Crump

messages, rallies, and leaflets prolong the enthusiasm of members who need occasional renewal.[34]

Persuasion for reinforcement obtains additional benefits from mass media exposure, which allows it to reach secondary audiences who are not so unified. In some instances, a message seemingly intended for people who are already true believers may actually be designed to use the enthusiasm of supporters to infect a larger and previously indifferent mass media audience. The primary audience's support becomes part of the persuasive message, generating enthusiasm that may impress others who see the event secondhand (involving the tendency to be influenced by others mentioned earlier in the chapter). The planners of political conventions exploit this dual audience arrangement. They know that potential voters viewing televised proceedings may be influenced by the zeal of the convention floor. The familiar sight of a presidential candidate addressing like-minded party members offering unbridled support can draw us in. The activity of the supporters is a perfect backdrop against which to address the undecided 5 or 6 percent who could make the difference between electoral success and failure.

## High Credibility/Low Agreement Persuasion

One of the most fascinating political events at the close of the 1980s was the rise of Vaclav Havel from obscure playwright to president of Czechoslovakia. The remarkable transformation of one of the most repressive Communist regimes to an innovative democracy had captured the attention of the world. Havel was at the center of this Cinderella story. He had been jailed by the old government for criticizing its actions in his plays and essays. In 1989 he was chosen as its head of state. A hero's welcome in Washington and an invitation to address Congress made him the symbol of the tide of democracy sweeping through the old Eastern bloc. Not everything Havel said, however, added to the gloss of his new image. In July 1990 he told an international gathering of journalists who were meeting in Prague that journalism must honor the right of governments to keep their secrets and that press freedoms were not necessarily absolute.[35] He expressed concern about the social unrest that a truly free press can create, leading some writers at the meeting to wonder if Havel had conveniently set aside the memory of his own repression.

Although he remains a strong democrat, Havel seemed to be uncharacteristically at war with one of democracy's strongest principles. Americans saw the soft-spoken playwright as a Czech version of Thomas Jefferson. He reminded us that ideas matter and that sometimes the pen can be mightier than the sword. His new message of caution was at odds with this image. This high credibility/low agreement setting—diagrammed in figure 7.3.d—is a classic persuasion case. Typically, an advocate has earned the goodwill of the audience but uses that goodwill to argue the merits of an unpopular idea.

Two very different strategies seem well suited to the high credibility/ low agreement setting. One is to intensify audience identification with the favorable public image of the advocate ("If such a terrific person believes this, maybe my own view is wrong"). With this approach, time is spent intensifying the advocate's association with the proposal but downplaying the ideas associated with it. Most celebrity endorsements of products function this way. In advertisements very little is said on behalf of the product other than the fact that it is associated with a person we admire. A second strategy—and one which has far greater merit—is to make the best case possible in defense of the idea to which the audience is indifferent or hostile. The advocate's reputation is sufficient to guarantee that an audience will listen to a reasoned presentation. Havel and his supporters had no choice but to explore the second high credibility/low agreement strategy, pointing out that it takes time to establish an open society where citizens must assume more independence and personal responsibility. American society has had over two hundred years to refine its freedoms. It is not unreasonable, they noted, to expect that former totalitarian states will need more than a few years to evolve into liberal democracies with similar guarantees.

A high credibility/low agreement setting is not without risks. Since a well-liked person is affirming a position that many do not accept, it is possible that the personal prestige of the advocate will suffer. In 1968 Robert Kennedy toured college campuses arguing in behalf of his pro-civil rights and anti-Vietnam War attitudes. Kennedy had decided to challenge his party's Vietnam policy; later he went even further by opposing President Johnson's hand-picked successor, Vice President Hubert Humphrey. On campuses the youthful Kennedy drew enormous crowds, but he was also party to the most bitter presidential primary campaign in modern American history.

Robert Kennedy was a microcosm of the ironies and dilemmas of the age. He denounced the Vietnam War, but he also stunned his draft-age audiences by urging that the draft deferments which kept many college students out of the war should be ended. Facing both friendly and hostile Indiana medical students, for example, Kennedy pushed his message for equality uncomfortably close to home.

> Part of civilized society is to let people go to medical schools who come from ghettos. I don't see many black faces who will become doctors. . . . You are the privileged ones here. It's easy to sit back and say it's the fault of the Federal Government. But it's our responsibility, too. It's our society too, not our government, that spends twice as much on pets as on the poverty program. It's the poor who carry the major burden of the struggle in Vietnam. You sit here as white medical students, while black people carry the burden of the fighting in Vietnam.[36]

Kennedy's views cost him some supporters, but his political courage also won at least a willingness to consider his political agenda. The positive support an audience has for a persuader can be the basis for urging consideration of an unpopular idea. Tragically, Kennedy never finished the campaign. He was assassinated in a hotel hallway minutes after giving a victory speech to supporters who had helped him win the California Primary.

## Low Credibility/High Agreement Persuasion

The situation represented in figure 7.3.e represents an arrangement that is just the reverse of the previous discussion. Unlike the well-liked persuader outlining what an audience does not want to hear, the audience in this situation fundamentally agrees with the ideas being expressed but has low regard for the advocate.

A persuader might analyze this situation and conclude, "Why bother? I'm content if the audience agrees with me. There's no need to attempt to persuade if my presence may be counterproductive, risking a loss of support for the very attitude that I want them to hold." Fear of alienating an audience in this way is based on what is called the *boomerang effect*. A persuasive attempt "boomerangs" when receivers of a message respond in ways that are just the reverse of what we seek. In television's classic situation comedy *All in the Family*, the reactionary Archie Bunker often attempted to reshape the liberal political views of his daughter Gloria and son-in-law ("Meathead") Mike. But Archie's outlandish stereotypes of women and African-Americans inevitably alienated Gloria and Mike even further.

The clever advocate can find at least one major reason for using low credibility/high agreement persuasion: the opportunity to increase personal credibility. By exploiting the audience's agreement on an issue, he or she may be able to reverse any negative feelings toward the persuader. Like the chameleon that blends in with the colors of a landscape, the advocate may gain protection against an audience's hostility by carefully cultivating shared ideas as a vindication of his or her own suspect character. The mythical Senator Claghorn of modern political folklore thus clothes himself in whatever he thinks his constituents want to hear.[37] As a windbag constantly in search of votes for the next election, he represents the politician we love to stereotype: supporting farm subsidies in agricultural communities, tax breaks for homeowners in the suburbs, free food for the inner-city poor, and "less government" for audiences who are ineligible for federal handouts. It does not matter that the combined proposals of countless speeches would be contradictory. Each individual speech before a distinct audience serves as a way to reduce suspicions about his competence; he uses ideas as membership cards to groups.

Undoubtedly, one of the most difficult speeches Bill Clinton ever gave was a 1993 Memorial Day address at Washington's Vietnam Veterans Memorial. To many of the veterans and military leaders who had gathered, Clinton did not have the required credentials to be a Veterans Day speaker. Notwithstanding his position as commander in chief, the perception among many that he was a "draft dodger" had endured beyond the bitter 1992 campaign. Like many other college students of his day, Clinton avoided service in Vietnam and protested against the continuance of the war. Not surprisingly, he was greeted with both applause and boos. However, he persisted with ideas stressing unification. Clinton was eloquent in identifying common ground with his audience, and in making a plea to put the divisive war behind the nation:

Let us continue to disagree, if we must, about the war, but let us not let it divide us as a people any longer. No one has come here today to disagree about the heroism of those whom we honor, but the only way we can really honor their memory is to resolve to live and serve today and tomorrow as best we can. . . . Surely that is what we owe to all those whose names are etched in this beautiful memorial.[38]

The primary strategy of a persuader confronting audience perceptions of low credibility is to identify shared values, experiences, and ideas—commonplaces that can function as bridges between a suspicious audience and the persuader. For example, when humorist Garrison Keillor parodies the "proper" etiquette for "meeting famous people," he reminds us of the importance of the ways we act as evidence of who we really are. The advice may be humorous, but it carries the unmistakable form of the unwritten rules of conduct that we honor all of the time in order to meet the expectations of those around us:

1. Never grab or paw the famous. They will instantly recoil and you will never win their respect. Stand at least thirty-two inches away. If your words of admiration move him or her to pat your shoulder, then of course you can pat back, but don't initiate contact and don't hang on. Be cool.

2. Don't gush, don't babble, don't grovel or fawn. Never snivel. Be tall. Bootlicking builds a wall you'll never break through. A simple pleasantry is enough—e.g., "Like your work!" If you need to say more than that (I think you're the most wonderful lyric poet in America today), try to modify your praise slightly (but your critical essays really suck). Or cough hard, about five times. That relieves the famous person of having to fawn back. . . . Be cool. Famous people much prefer a chummy insult to lavish nonsense: a little dig about the exorbitant price of tickets to the star's show, perhaps, or the cheesiness of the posters.[39]

In sum, we are not only spokespersons for positions but advocates attempting to cultivate our personal credibility as well. As we noted in more detail in chapter 5, the question of what makes a source "credible" has produced many different and sometimes conflicting answers. It is evident here that credibility can be sought by taking public positions that will be embraced by an approving audience.

## Low Credibility/Low Agreement Persuasion

Figure 7.3.f represents the persuasive situation which carries the heaviest burdens. It indicates a lack of audience support for both the persuader and his or her ideas. Not unexpectedly, most people do not joyfully tackle such an arrangement. Indeed, more than a few students have suggested that a persuader should come to this setting only with bodyguards and a familiarity with possible escape routes! Reality is usually less ominous.

Films and novels occasionally portray a single-minded persuader who reverses the hostility built into the low credibility/low agreement double dilemma. Sidney Lumet explored this theme in several courtroom dramas (*Twelve Angry Men* with Henry Fonda and *The Verdict* with Paul Newman). Actual results are less dramatic than either our imaginations or Hollywood suggest. Audiences are rarely won over by such attempts, but they are also usually less hostile than the model implies.

Senator Ted Kennedy has often addressed audiences sharply at odds with his generally liberal political views and somewhat flamboyant public persona. In one of his most famous appearances, he accepted an invitation by Jerry Falwell to visit Liberty Baptist College, which was then the center of the religious right's crusade against the "godless" politics represented by Kennedy and others. He emerged successfully from that encounter, even if his audience's attitudes on abortion, school prayer, and the Equal Rights Amendment remained unchanged.[40] While many observers might view such efforts as exercises in futility, there is often considerable value in making listeners a little less comfortable with their own beliefs.

In a milder vein, former First Lady Barbara Bush faced an audience with some of the features of the low credibility/low agreement model. In 1990 Bush was invited to give the commencement address at Wellesley College. However, as news of the invitation spread, so did objections that she was not the kind of model most of the women students could look up to. Their reasoning was that her identity was created largely by her husband's position. Students made it known that Bush was the school's second choice, after author Alice Walker declined. A full quarter of the senior class signed a petition asking for another choice. Other speakers might have gracefully declined to attend in response to the comparatively graceless criticism of her planned visit. However, Bush persisted, and won the day with a heartfelt speech celebrating the freer choices available to women today, but also embracing the connections to family that men and women need to make.

> For several years you've had impressed upon you the importance to your career of dedication and hard work, and of course that's true. But as important as your obligations as a doctor, a lawyer, a business leader will be, you are a human being first and those human connections with spouses, with children, with friends are the most important investment you will ever make.[41]

## The Wildcard of Unintended Audiences

Persuasion theory usually presupposes that messages will be targeted to specific audiences and ignored by nearly all others. Often this is precisely what happens, especially when communication takes place in relatively private settings. Even so, actual events and the realities of the communication age have a way of working against perfect isolation of messages.

Many forms of communication are now easily carried to others beyond their primary audiences, often with unintended effects. The results may be humorous, as in the 1988 farce *The Naked Gun*, where a forgetful public official concludes a speech to a large gathering, only to discover later that he did not remove his cordless public address microphone before visiting the restroom. A seemingly "dead" microphone, or comments narrowly intended for one group but reported to another, can easily create unwanted audiences. Ronald Reagan prepared for a "fireside chat" in 1984 by warming up with the jocular observation that he would begin bombing the Soviet Union "in five minutes." He did not know that journalists were already listening in and gleefully jotting down his comments.[42] At the other extreme, unintentional revelations may cast doubts over the reputation of an entire government. During the early months of the Persian Gulf crisis, Secretary of Defense Dick Cheney fired the Air Force's chief of staff because of widely reported remarks about military contingency plans. In comments to *The Washington Post*, the chief had endorsed a proposal to kill Iraq's leader and family and heavily bomb the city of Baghdad.[43] Although the bombing of Iraq started a short time later, the premature discussion of war plans embarrassed the Bush administration at a time when it was still attempting to explore diplomatic solutions with its nervous Middle Eastern allies.

In various ways, the mass media generally make it harder to identify only one audience for a message. Difficulties arise when a message intended for one group is reported via the mass media to a second group with different expectations. Sociologist Orrin Klapp has noted that this is one of the "ailments" of leaders and celebrities who must conduct much of their work in public.[44] It can be extremely difficult for persuaders to construct and maintain a consistent public image as they move through various settings with notably different communication requirements.

Columnist and commentator Andy Rooney was in just such a bind in 1990 when he made comments that violated the expectation that television heroes should stay away from controversy. Rooney's publications and his commentaries on CBS's *60 Minutes* are generally constructed as good-humored attacks on some of the absurdities of daily life: bigger boxes that hold less cereal, the difficulties of fixing household gadgets, the silly names that people call their pets. He generally stays away from using his populist style to tackle issues that seriously divide Americans. On one program, he remarked that too many things were killing us, including "too much alcohol, too much food, drugs, homosexual unions, and cigarettes. They're all known to lead quite often to premature death." When pressed by a gay newspaper to explain what he meant, Rooney wrote a letter noting that he found homosexuality "repugnant." The paper also quoted a slur against African Americans that Rooney had allegedly made.[45] Whether or not he was accurately quoted, Rooney experienced the problem of conflicting images. In an attempt to manage the variety of messages—some at odds with his benign television persona—CBS temporarily removed him from the air. Regular television personalities cannot be heroes one week and villains the next. The medium allows its best-known celebrities to poke fun at many things, but it usually does not give them the freedom to express the same variety of convictions and prejudices found in its audience members.

## Summary

The central theme of this chapter has been that successful persuasion must be measured against the necessity to adapt to specific audiences. We assess our strengths and weaknesses depending on the people we want to influence. Sometimes our strengths lie in who we are; in many instances they reside in the specific ideas we intend to communicate. Commonplaces and group-specific norms establish important points of identification between persuaders and receivers. In its most elemental form, persuasion is the strategy of building acceptance by communicating in the common currency of shared experience and attitude.

Built into this theme is what many consider the troubling question of when adaptation goes too far. Plato called excessive adaptation to audience beliefs "pandering" and claimed that it was a common feature of persuasion. "Isn't it highly likely," modern counterparts to Plato might argue, "that audience-based persuasion encourages a persuader to sacrifice personal beliefs as the price for winning audience approval? Doesn't the presence of the audience and its norms put enormous pressure on a persuader when his or her personal vision differs from the demands of the group whose support is sought?"

These are evocative questions, but they pose several false dilemmas. They presuppose that many forms of communication are not audience based—that somehow in other settings we are truer to our authentic selves. In truth, the reactions of others are factors in almost every context. The admonishments to "be ourselves" and "not to worry about what others think" sound good but are almost impossible to obey. Unless we are entirely self-sufficient, economically and socially, we must confront and accommodate both audience demands and private convictions everyday. Moreover, the process of considering how our words affect others does not preclude asserting ourselves as we wish. There is ample room for us to learn how to be rhetorically accommodating without "selling out." Much of the activity of daily life is a constant process of mediation between our own and other people's beliefs. We are fit company for others largely because of our willingness to engage in this accommodation. We heap a great deal of praise on personalities who show the courage to "do and say what they think without regard for what others may say." Clint Eastwood, Susan Sarandon and Tom Cruise have played their share of independent-thinking role models, perhaps serving as surrogates for the rest of us who like the fantasy of the defiant "outsider" better than reality. There is very little evidence to suggest that people are happier and better adjusted when they are able to ignore the ideological constraints around them. For better or worse, the wards of mental hospitals are filled with people who are unable or incapable of adjusting their attitudes to the differing views of others. To be sure, not all attempts to "fit in" are necessarily healthy, but successful accommodation to audiences is not by itself an intellectual crime.

The ethical line is crossed when adaptation extends beyond the natural process of mediation and reaches into denying authentic convictions. The persuader who deliberately ignores beliefs for the sake of performance has violated the acceptable threshold of accommodation. It is reasonable and shrewd to determine and to laud audience values that also support a deeply held personal belief, but it is unethical to sacrifice personal feelings for the sake of simply winning over others. A former presidential press secretary, Jerry terHorst, faced this ethical issue squarely when he was asked to "front" for a decision he abhorred. The action was President Ford's sudden and total pardon of Richard Nixon in September of 1974, granting the former chief executive immunity from all prosecution for covering up information during the Watergate Affair. The newsman-turned-presidential-spokesman served only thirteen days before realizing that he could not be an advocate for policies with which he strongly disagreed.[46]

Finally, it is important to remember that the audience is asked to do most of the "giving" in many persuasive situations. The persuader's intention to transform the attitudes or actions of a group of people implicitly says "give me both your attention and the benefit of your agreement." We often readily accept the premise that audiences rather than persuaders are the ones who are expected to take the risk of giving up old attitudes for new ones. However, it also seems reasonable to expect that audience adaptation should be a "dialogue" between the advocate and audience. The persuader who seeks change from a group of people but is at the same time unwilling to reciprocate in giving their ideas serious consideration is possibly more unreasonable than the person who is accused of "pandering" too much.

## Questions and Projects for Further Study

1. How do commonplaces differ from audience-specific norms? Look for key commonplaces within an article in a mass-market magazine such as *Reader's Digest*. Locate more specialized norms in a magazine with a narrower audience such as *Rolling Stone* or *Soldier of Fortune*.

2. *Broadcasting* magazine and *Advertising Age* are two trade magazines that are filled with discussions of audiences and their characteristics. *Broadcasting*, for example, contains numerous ads for syndicated programs that stations may rent, programs which already attract certain kinds of desirable audiences. *Advertising Age* contains articles describing the plans of companies for reaching certain audiences. Prepare a written or oral summary of the audience that one advertiser or program producer wants to reach.

3. In spite of the fact that we believe that we are responsible for our own commitments, a major theme in this chapter is that we acquire most of our attitudes through our associations with others. What contacts or associations can you identify that have influenced your beliefs and attitudes?

4. At one point in the chapter, the authors note that "an ethical presumption that goes with all forms of persuasion is that persuaders should believe in what they want others to accept." Publicly arguing for a position in which one does not personally believe is sometimes called "fronting." Cite an instance of fronting that involved you, or cite some situations where fronting is common and perhaps necessary. Do any of these situations suggest that fronting may be ethical?

5. Using examples from television, films, or recent news events, illustrate what is meant by the following terms:

   Boomerang Effect
   Low Credibility/Low Agreement Persuasion
   Norms
   Pandering
   Secondary Audience

6. Most libraries have copies of *Vital Speeches of the Day*, which reprints speeches given in a wide variety of fields and indicates the nature of the audiences. Using the scheme presented in figure 7.3, look through several recent issues and diagram three different kinds of communication settings (such as 7.3.c, d, and e).

7. Pick an issue or position on which you hold strong views. Given your position on the particular issue chosen (i.e., defending a politician,

a controversial policy, or group), identify an organization that would hold contrary or different attitudes. Imagine that you were invited by this organization to explain your convictions. After giving your "invitation" some thought, explain your case to a friend. Describe the norms and commonplaces you think the hypothetical audience holds and how you would "build bridges" to increase their support or understanding of your point of view. Ask your partner how his or her approach to this audience might be similar or different.

8. In this chapter we suggest that the process of persuasion is complicated by the "wildcard" of extensive media coverage of a public figure out of character. Andy Rooney and others are cited as examples of this process. Using a different example, describe a similar instance of a message that reached an unintended audience. What effect did it have on the persuader's overall effectiveness or public image?

# Notes

[1] Chaim Perelman and L. Olbrechts-Tyteca, *The New Rhetoric: A Treatise on Argumentation*, trans. by John Wilkinson and Purcell Weaver. Notre Dame, IN: Notre Dame, 1969, p. 20.

[2] In this chapter we use these terms interchangeably, although other analysts have attempted to differentiate between them. See chaper 6 for a more detailed discussion.

[3] This provocative thesis has been at the heart of the Sociology of Knowledge, which informs persuasion studies by linking what we say with what we know. See, for example, Peter L. Berger and Thomas Luchmann, *The Social Construction of Reality*, New York: Anchor, 1969, pp. 1–17; and Karl Mannheim, *Ideology and Utopia*, New York: Harvest, 1936, pp. 1–5.

[4] Émile Durkheim quoted in Hugh Dalziel Duncan, *Symbols and Social Theory*. New York: Oxford, 1969, pp. 152–53.

[5] Robert B. Cialdini, *Influence: Science and Practice*, Third Edition. New York: HarperCollins, 1993, p. 95.

[6] *Ibid.*, p. 96.

[7] *Ibid.*, p. 126.

[8] *Ibid.*, p. 192.

[9] This summary is drawn from Todd Gitlin, *Inside Prime Time*. New York: Pantheon, 1983, pp. 36–40; and Ron Miller, "At Preview House, Viewers are the Guinea Pigs," *Philadelphia Inquirer*, August 16, 1983, p. 6E.

[10] Miller, p. 6E.

[11] Kenneth Burke, *A Rhetoric of Motives*. Berkeley, CA: University of California, 1969, p. 55.

[12] Augustine quoted in Burke, p. 50.

[13] Tony Schwartz, *The Responsive Chord*. New York: Anchor, 1974, p. 25.

[14] Quoted from Edwin Diamond and Stephen Bates, *The Spot: The Rise of Political Advertising on Television*, Revised Edition. Cambridge, MA: MIT, 1988, pp. 211–12.

[15] Jacques Ellul, *A Critique of the New Commonplaces*, trans. by Helen Weaver. New York: Knopf, 1968, p. 13.

[16] W. Lloyd Warner, *The Living and the Dead: A Study in the Symbolic Life of Americans*. New Haven, CT: Yale University, 1959, Parts 1–1:11.

[17] Robert S. Lynd and Helen Merrell Lynd, *Middletown in Transition: A Study in Cultural Conflicts*. New York: Harvest, 1937, p. 402.

[18] *Ibid.*, pp. 413–15, 418.

[19] Some commonplaces in the Lynds' study have become antiques, for example, "a married woman's place is first of all in the home and any other activities should be secondary to 'making a good home for her husband and children'" and "married people owe it to society to have children." p. 410.

[20] Bill Clinton, Inaugural Address, in Michael Osborn and Suzanne Osborn, *Public Speaking*, Third Edition. Boston: Houghton Mifflin, 1994, p. B24.

[21] Bush quoted in Peggy Noonan, *What I Saw at the Revolution*. New York: Random House, 1990, p. 301.

[22] *Ibid.*, p. 311.

[23] *Ibid.*, p. 312.

[24] "Videotapes," *Consumer Reports*, September 1990, p. 584.

[25] Robert Hughes, *The Culture of Complaint*. New York: Oxford, 1993. p. 18.

[26] Mary Matalin, "Stop Whining!," *Newsweek*, October 25, 1993, p. 62.

[27] Susan Faludi, "Who's Hype?" in *Ibid.*, p. 61.

[28] Quoted in Sarah Crichton, "Sexual Correctness: Has It Gone Too Far?" in *Ibid.*, p. 55.

[29] Naomi Wolf, *Fire With Fire*. New York: Random House, 1993, pp. 135–137.

[30] David Margolick, "Ideal Juror for O.J. Simpson: Football Fan Who Can Listen," *New York Times*, September 23, 1994, p. A1.

[31] This model is adapted from one originally proposed by psychologist Fritz Heider. For a review of his model and other variations on it see Charles A. Kiesler, Barry E. Collins, and Norman Miller, *Attitude Change: A Critical Analysis of Theoretical Approaches*. New York: John Wiley, 1968, pp. 155–78. Also see chapter 6.

[32] Thomas Patterson and Robert D. McClure, *The Unseeing Eye: The Myth of Television Power in National Politics*. New York: G. P. Putnams, 1976, p. 121.

[33] Kurt Lang and Gladys Engle Lang, *Politics and Television*. New York: Quadrangle, 1968, p. 16.

[34] To cite studies of just two types of messages, see Arthur M. Schlesinger, Jr., "Annual Messages of the Presidents: Major Themes of American History," in *The State of the Union Messages, Volume 1, 1790–1860*, ed. by Fred L Israel, New York: Chelsea House/Robert Hector, 1966, pp. xiii–xvi; and Donald Wolfarth, "John F. Kennedy in the Tradition of Inaugural Speeches," *Quarterly Journal of Speech*, April 1961, pp. 124–32.

[35] Bill Kovach and Tom Winship, "Havel: Prison for Journalists?" *New York Times*, July 15, 1990, p. E19.

[36] Quoted in Jack Newfield, *Robert Kennedy: A Memoir*. New York: E.P. Dutton, 1969, p. 256.

[37] Senator Beauregard Claghorn was a character created with some affection by radio humorist Fred Allen. See Arthur Frank Wertheim, *Radio Comedy*. New York: Oxford, 1979, pp. 335–42.

[38] Bill Clinton, Memorial Day Address, 1993, C-SPAN (Purdue University Video Archives).

[39] Garrison Keillor, *We Are Still Married*. New York: Viking/Penguin, 1989, p. 297.

[40] See Gary Woodward, *Persuasive Encounters: Case Studies in Constructive Confrontation*. New York: Praeger, 1990, pp. 53–75.

[41] Barbara Bush, "Commencement Address at Wellesley College," June 1, 1990, C-SPAN (Purdue University Video Archives).

[42] Larry Speakes, *Speaking Out*. New York: Avon, 1988, p. 312.

[43] Eric Schmitt, "Air Force Chief Dismissed for Remarks on Gulf Plan," *New York Times*, September 18, 1990, pp. A1, A12.

[44] Orrin E. Klapp, *Symbolic Leaders*. Chicago: Aldine, 1964, pp. 101–75.

[45] Walter Goodman, "Why Andy Rooney Had to Go, Guilty or Not," *New York Times*, February 13, 1990, p. C18.

[46] Robert T. Hartmann, *Palace Politics: An Inside Account of the Ford Years*. New York: McGraw-Hill, 1980, p. 265.

# Additional Reading

George Gordon, *Persuasion: The Theory and Practice of Manipulative Communication*. New York: Hastings House, 1971.

Charles Kiesler, Barry E. Collins, and Norman Miller, *Attitude Change: A Critical Analysis of Theoretical Approaches*. New York: John Wiley, 1968.

Robert S. Lynd and Helen Merrell Lynd, *Middletown in Transition: A Study in Cultural Conflicts*. New York: Harvest, 1937.

Peggy Noonan, *What I Saw at the Revolution*. New York: Random House, 1990.

Chaim Perelman and L. Olbrechts-Tyteca, *The New Rhetoric: A Treatise on Argumentation*, trans. by John Wilkinson and Purcell Weaver. Notre Dame, IN: Notre Dame, 1969.

William Safire, "The All Purpose Political Speech," in *The Rhetoric of our Times*, ed. by J. Jeffrey Auer. New York: Meredith, 1969.

Tony Schwartz, *The Responsive Chord*. New York: Anchor, 1974.

W. Lloyd Warner, The Living and the Dead: A Study of the Symbolic Life of Americans. New Haven: Yale University, 1959.

# The Contexts of Persuasion

# III

We have described persuasion as primarily a *process*, offering a number of observations about its general nature. Sooner or later, most communication must finally be understood with reference to the unique attributes and requirements of specific contexts. This section contains four chapters that focus on familiar but very different settings for persuasion.

Chapter 8 considers the special verbal and nonverbal patterns of communication that exist in the environments where only a limited number of participants are observers to each other's persuasion. Chapter 9 looks at persuasive efforts to reach larger audiences and explores the special features of persuasive campaigns as structured by specific organizations and social movements. In Chapter 10 we look at advertising messages designed to encourage the consumption of products or services. The primary goal of advertisers is to create favorable attitudes toward products and the companies that provide them. In Chapter 11 we explore the efforts of political activists (as seekers of public office, as elected leaders, and as agents for change using the political and the "nonpolitical" media) to shape our attitudes toward themselves and their ideas.

# 8

## Interpersonal Persuasion

## OVERVIEW

> We have the capacity for controlling and choosing among alternative patterns of communication behaviors. By understanding the interactive, ongoing, process nature of interpersonal communication, it becomes possible to alter elements within the process with more predictable results.[1]
>
> —Bobby Patton and Kim Griffin

We experience the process of communication and persuasion in a wide variety of contexts ranging from sitting alone thinking to participating in a mass demonstration. There are three basic levels of persuasion: intrapersonal, interpersonal, and public. Although the essential processes of persuasion are alike for each level, there are noticeable differences in appeals, strategies, and tactics. Intrapersonal persuasion is communication with oneself. This form of communication provides cues about self—feelings, sensations, and images of "who we are." Self-reflection reveals our inner being and motives for our behavior. Interpersonal persuasion, the topic of this chapter, focuses on face-to-face interaction with others. We address public persuasion in the next chapter.

We spend a great deal of time interacting face-to-face with others. Much of this interaction, whether among family, friends, or strangers, is purposeful and persuasive. It may be as simple as requesting someone to bring you a book, as important as asking someone to hire you, or as emotional as asking someone to marry you. Within the interpersonal context, persuasive efforts may be characterized as:

1. dynamic—participants are both sending and receiving signals continually and simultaneously; the situation is not static.

2. interactive—there is mutual influence and interdependence between the participants. Each person is constantly aware of the other and assumes the roles of both sender and receiver, which involves constant adaptation and adjustment.

3. proactive—it involves the total person. Beliefs, attitudes, values, social background and previous transactions all influence the nature of the interaction.

4. contextual—environmental and situational factors influence the interaction.

5. intense—content of the interactions are most often personal, intimate, and revealing thus producing the risks of rejection, withdrawal, exposure, and even weakness.

In this chapter, we are going to investigate interpersonal persuasion. After reviewing in greater detail those elements of persuasion most related to interpersonal interaction, we will focus on the specialized contexts of organizations, interviews, and sales. The persuasive potential of interpersonal persuasion is particularly apparent in these three areas.

# Interpersonal Persuasion

The various theories, strategies, and tactics of persuasion are applicable to any level or context of human communication. They may differ, however, in terms of degree and effectiveness. The forms of dyadic (two-person) communication range from the most social (intimate), to the most formal (interview), to the most stressful (interrogation). Within these areas, persuasive strategies and tactics may range from the subtle to the overt, the rational to the psychological, and the verbal to the nonverbal.

Kathleen Reardon defines interpersonal persuasion as "when two or a few people interact in a way that involves verbal and nonverbal behaviors, personal feedback, coherence of behaviors (relevance or fit of remarks and actions), and the purpose (on the part of at least one interactant) of changing the attitudes and/or behaviors of the others."[2] As one can imagine, interpersonal persuasion is challenging, difficult, and complex. In addition to the material already presented in previous chapters, we wish to highlight some information specific to interpersonal persuasion.

## Levels of Interpersonal Communication

Dan Rothwell and James Costigan recognize three distinct levels of interpersonal communication: instrumental, manipulative, and expressive.[3] Persuasion plays a role on each level. The instrumental level of interpersonal communication is directive in nature. The communication is primarily one-way. It is on this level that much business is conducted. The manager conveys information, establishes goals, and assigns tasks. The communication is task oriented requiring little or no sustained interaction. The question of compliance is not an issue. Discussion focuses on methods of task completion. On the instrumental level, most of the persuasive activities rely upon the elements of power, credibility, authority, information, rational argument, and negotiation.

The manipulative level attempts to elicit favors, action, or consensus from other individuals. Persuasive activities, while also encompassing those of the instrumental level, include more subtle and psychological appeals. From the receiver's standpoint, the motives of the persuader may be hidden. For example, in a business setting individuals may lobby for project support, extra help, or pay raises. This perspective implies that many of our actions are self-motivated rather than other-motivated.

On the expressive level, individuals share their thoughts, ideas, and feelings through more creative and artistic forms of communication. The purpose is neither directive nor manipulative. Rather, expressive communication seeks an airing, testing, and sharing of impressions. However, literary and artistic works may also project a social critique, perspective, or ideology. In such cases, the art is not purely expressive but contains elements from the manipulative level as well. Of course, we daily engage in all levels of interpersonal communication. Although it may be difficult to distinguish between the levels, the manipulative is the most strategic and involves the most overt persuasive endeavors.

*Expressive communication seeks a sharing of impressions. Artistic works may also project a perspective or social critique that invites a particular response.*

*Tribune* photo by Charles Osgood

# Dimensions of Interpersonal Communication

There are two basic dimensions of the interpersonal communication process that persuasion can address. The first deals with cognitive or rational processes. These are planned, inherent persuasive strategies to be executed. Elements of these strategies include language choice, attitudes, logic, and credibility. Most interactions are purposeful; the parties have a goal or business to accomplish. During the encounter, information, opinion, and action will be exchanged. Information shared may be incomplete, inaccurate, or biased. Opinions expressed may be unwarranted based on the information presented. The actions or behavior desired may reveal the persuader's motives.

To illustrate the cognitive or rational dimension of the interpersonal communication process, suppose you wanted to sell your old car. How much information should you share in the sales pitch—mileage, motor size, oil usage, miles per gallon, prior accidents, etc.? What type of opinions will you offer about the car's condition, treatment, value, etc.? Will you attempt to sell the car by placing an ad in the paper or by offering it to your friends or acquaintances? As the example reveals, on the rational level there are many decisions one must make that influence the degree of persuasiveness of the message.

The second persuasive dimension of interpersonal communication deals with relational processes. William Schultz argues there are three primary human needs that interpersonal communication can help fulfill.[4] The first is the need for inclusion. As social animals, we need to belong, to be accepted, and to be recognized. Through interaction we establish friends and relationships, prestige and status, commitment and group participation. A well-adjusted person is usually characterized as one who has self-confidence, is well liked by others, and who is comfortable in a wide variety of social settings. Social inclusion is important for acceptance, compliance, and task performance.

Control is the second basic human need; it implies more than just power over others. It includes knowing when to defer to others as well as when and how to assert one's self-interests. The military is primarily organized by control. Roles are very clearly defined. In most other organizations, control is a process of give and take, negotiating different opinions, experiences, skills, and knowledge. We will have more to say about the role of control in interpersonal persuasion later in the chapter.

The third need is for affection. This need progresses beyond the emotional support and relationships associated with the notion of inclusion. All humans need affection, to be able to love and to be loved. Through interpersonal communication, we grow in relationships from first introductions or greetings to personal intimacy. We know, for example, that it is easier to persuade someone if they know us, trust us, and like us.

*On the interpersonal level, persuasion addresses either cognitive/rational issues or relational processes—or both.*

*Tribune* photo by Jose More

Our car example might not seem the best illustration of relational processes. However, even if you sell the car to a stranger, the first part of the interaction would be to establish trust and identification. You must persuade the person that you are honest and have nothing to hide; the potential buyer must convince you that he or she intends to buy the car and has the funds to pay for it. You might emphasize similarities and commonalities such as mutual friends, places, or experiences between you and the potential buyer to establish a mini-relationship during the transaction.

## Variables of Interpersonal Persuasion

With this overview in mind, it is useful to investigate more fully several variables of interpersonal persuasion. As we have already noted, some would argue that all persuasion is interpersonal in the sense that some source creates and sends a message received by another person who renders judgment and responds to the message. We will discuss elements introduced in previous chapters in greater detail, as they apply to face-to-face interactions.

# Symbols, Language, and Environments

In chapter 3, we discussed the nature of symbols and language in creating the reality within which we act. Human communication is a purposeful process of selection, interpretation, and symbolism. Through interaction with others, we come to know who we are, how we fit in, and what we are supposed to do. We noted how language can be used to control us, confuse us, and to hide information from us. Our purpose here is to identify some of the unique strategies or uses of language within an interpersonal context.

## Verbal Characteristics

We select our verbal behaviors largely based on interactions that were successful in the past. That is, verbal behaviors that created satisfying exchanges will be repeated. Those that were ineffective will be dropped from our repertoire of possible behaviors.

Interpersonal communication is a very complex process. Joe DeVito has identified several characteristics of effective interpersonal communication which have strategic implications for persuasive interpersonal interactions.[5] He derived his list of characteristics from three rather distinct perspectives: humanism, pragmatism, and social exchange.

The humanistic perspective stresses honest and satisfying relationships. The interpersonal communication of this perspective reflects the qualities of openness, empathy, supportiveness, positiveness, and equality. These qualities stimulate the perceptions of honesty, trust, and accessibility which are valuable in situations of negotiation and persuasion.

How do you enhance humanistic qualities in interpersonal conversation? Be willing to reveal information not commonly known about yourself. Respond spontaneously to the communication and feedback of others. Be sensitive to the desires and feelings of others. Be less judgmental and evaluative of others. Be pleasant and engage in "stroking" behavior that acknowledges the presence and importance of others.

The pragmatic approach to interpersonal effectiveness focuses on communicative behaviors that help the speaker or listener accomplish desired goals or outcomes. Qualities from this approach include: confidence, immediacy, interaction management, expressiveness, and communication that is other-oriented. In each case, the language and approach is strategic and planned. The qualities of confidence and expressiveness are stylistic endeavors to generate trust, self-control, and involvement. Immediacy of direct response and interaction management qualities apply pressure and maintain the proper pacing of interaction toward a decision or issue resolution. Other-oriented communication generates attentiveness and interest; it also demonstrates consideration and respect for the interaction participant.

A pragmatic approach to interpersonal effectiveness incorporates a sense of control, status, and power. Link yourself to others in the conversation by using such terms as "we," "our," or "us." Echo the feelings expressed by others by relating similar stories or experiences. Reinforce the comments of others with head nods, smiles, and physical touches of friendship (nonverbal behaviors, which are discussed below).

The social exchange approach to interpersonal effectiveness recognizes a costs/benefits dimension of relationship involvement. We tend to develop and maintain relationships that provide more rewards than costs. Obviously, the most satisfying relationships are those where the rewards and costs are equal to those of our partner. At the heart of this approach to interpersonal communication is the conscious effort of providing positive rewards in our daily interactions. Some examples are simple behaviors such as saying "thank you," inquiring how people are feeling, or acknowledging their efforts.

Both the structure and content of an interpersonal interaction help establish a relationship that will provide a context for future compliance and receiver behavior. One needs to recognize that a conversation today impacts future conversations. For example, in a job where you depend on others for task completion, the quality of your interpersonal interactions will certainly affect your job performance and evaluations.

### Nonverbal Characteristics

Nonverbal codes and symbols have many of the same characteristics as verbal codes and symbols. Nonverbal behaviors acquire distinct meanings within a culture or society. As with verbal systems, meanings of nonverbal behavior are arbitrary and are formed as a result of social interactions.

Nonverbal communication is very important. Some scholars argue that the meaning we get from interactions comes primarily from the nonverbal dimensions of message exchange.[6] There are several ways nonverbal messages relate to verbal messages. Nonverbal messages may emphasize or accent a particular part of a verbal message. A certain look, gesture, or increase in volume may provide an interpretation of attitude or emotion. Nonverbal messages may complement or contradict what is stated verbally. In addition to reinforcing what is stated, nonverbal messages may also regulate the flow of interactions. From certain nonverbal cues, we learn when it is our turn to speak or when someone wishes to interrupt. Of course, nonverbal messages may substitute for verbal messages. A simple nod of the head or shaking of a finger is all

*Some scholars argue that the meaning we get from interactions comes primarily from the nonverbal dimensions of message exchanges.*

"You wanna have some fun, Fred? Watch. . . . Growling and bristling, I'm gonna stand in front of the closet door and just stare."

the reply one may need to a question. Nonverbal communication is an essential part of all human communication.

There are numerous nonverbal codes or systems in our culture.[7] Body communication refers to the various messages sent by our physical presence such as gestures, posture, movements, and appearance. Facial and eye communication involves all facial expressions including smiles or frowns and eye movements such as eye contact and pupil dilation. Artifactual communication includes all the material objects associated with ourselves and others such as clothing, cars, pens, etc. Such artifacts may communicate social class, status, and success. There are often expectations of style and dress, for example, associated with many professions. Spatial communication deals with human use of personal space and territory. Tactile communication focuses on touch and physical contact between and among people. Paralanguage is defined as the sounds and the meanings associated with how words are spoken. Vocal rate, pitch, volume, and pauses all affect the meaning communicated in our verbal messages. Smell, as a code system, deals with how odor communicates. Besides natural scents and perfumes, there are

*Human use of time (temporal communication) is one of the nonverbal codes in our culture.*

*Tribune* photo by Carl Wagner

cultural differences in reactions to smell. Finally, temporal communication focuses on human uses of time. This list of the many types of nonverbal codes emphasizes how pervasive and important the role of nonverbal communication is in everyday conversation.

There are three aspects of nonverbal behaviors that affect persuasion. First, the level of animation, expression, or enthusiasm shown during an interaction enhances persuasion and the effectiveness of our message. Vocal variety, affirming nods and gestures, and maintaining eye contact are a few behaviors that enliven our contact with others. Second, nonverbal behaviors that express liking and attraction also enhance message reception. Increased proximity, smiling, and touching are obvious ways to show attraction. Finally, the level of relaxation displayed during interaction is important in gaining trust and the appearance of truthfulness. A relaxed posture and the absence of vocal anxiety are important elements in establishing our credibility. Thus, general persuasiveness increases when nonverbal behaviors communicate enthusiasm, attraction or similarity and a related attitude.

Scholars have reported other findings about body movements, eye contact, distance, touching, and vocal delivery that link persuasiveness and nonverbal behaviors.[8] In general, these studies reinforce the concept that more dynamic speakers are more persuasive. Specific examples of dynamic behavior include frequent gesturing, hand movements, head nodding, smiling, and high levels of energy. Of course, these activities must appear natural, genuine, and sincere or the issue of credibility will outweigh any persuasive gains from dynamic presentation.

Studies show that direct eye contact between 60 to 90 percent of the time is most effective. While touching tends to stimulate feelings of liking, trust and interpersonal involvement, there are cultural norms and limitations to such behavior. In making a request, a slight touch on the arm may increase compliance. However, a sustained touch may increase anxiety and stress. How well you know the participant in the interaction is crucial in deciding how and when to touch someone.

Speech fluency is another important factor to consider. Speech pauses, "uhs," and vocal repetitions decrease speaker credibility and perceived competence, thus reducing the persuasiveness of a message. A conversational style of delivery is perceived as more reasonable, knowledgeable, sincere, and trustworthy. A more passionate presentation tends to be perceived as emotional. Of course, the purpose and context of the event would dictate the style of presentation. At the very least, a confident speaker will be more successful than a tentative, hesitant one.

## Power and Control

In the process of negotiating meaning through verbal and nonverbal codes, the need for control is often the agenda hidden in our interactions with others. We tend to react negatively to overt displays of power and control. Yet, we generally admire those whom we perceive as having "clout" and influence. Space does not permit a detailed discussion of the concepts of interpersonal power and control. However, they are important elements of influence and persuasion.

Power should not be confused with authority and responsibility. Authority is a legal or managerial right to make decisions, assign tasks, and ensure satisfactory performance. In this sense, authority is delegated. Responsibility is an obligation or duty to meet established goals or task performance. Power is a force that when used properly enhances authority. Therefore, authority is the *right* to do something, power is the *ability* to do something. Power is a form of control or influence over others.

John French and Bertram Raven identify five sources of power.[9] *Coercive power* is based primarily upon the use of punishments or threats to induce desired behavior. Obviously, coercive power is not an enduring form of influence and may cause resentment and a lack of trust among acquaintances. *Reward power* is the ability to give something of value to others in exchange for desired behavior. Rewards can range from a simple "thank you" to more tangible items such as money or a larger office, etc. The use of rewards to stimulate compliance can enhance cooperation and motivation. *Legitimate power* is based on the authority of a position. Naturally, commanding a task solely on the basis of one's position as "the boss" may be legitimate, but it will be far less satisfying and effective for the employee than other forms of power. *Expert power* is based on the skills and general competence of a person. Compliance results from mutual trust and respect. In effect, one earns power as a result of expertise. This form of power is positive and long lasting. Finally, French and Raven identify *referent power* that results from feelings of admiration, affection, and loyalty. People comply with requests out of respect and a willingness to return favors for past actions. This form of power takes a long time to develop.

There may be times and situations when all the types of power are necessary and successful. Generally, however, the most useful forms for persuasion are those based on personal qualities of individuals rather than those based on the authority of position or coercion.

Julia Wood argues that all relationships are organized in terms of power and the degree of interdependence.[10] She identifies three rather distinct types of organizing structures for interpersonal relationships.

---

### Figure 8.1
### Forms of Relationships

| Relationship Type | Power | Dependence |
|---|---|---|
| Complementary | Unequal | Highly Interdependent |
| Parallel | Distributed | Moderately Interdependent |
| Symmetrical | Equal | Highly Independent |

---

Complementary relationships involve unequal power and high interdependence. From a social perspective, males historically enjoyed greater power in terms of social positions and jobs. The traditional role of the male being the "bread winner" tended to contribute to unequal power and a mutual interdependence and reliance of one party on the other. The female needed economic security and shelter. The male needed comfort, support, and someone to nurture the family. Within such relationships, roles were clearly defined, as were rules of interaction and behavior expectations. While there was a similarity in needs, males enjoyed more social power and status. Problems due to such discrepancies are obvious. Ironically, if fully complementary, such relationships may be very stable. Studies also show they may be quite satisfying for those who desire distinct role expectations within relationships. Many relationships are predicated on complementary structures: teacher-student; parent-child; supervisor-employee. These relationships emphasize differences. If based on expert, legitimate or reward power, they can be efficient and harmonious. In other instances, these relationships stagnate and prohibit personal growth.

In symmetrical relationship structures, each person strives for the same amount of power and status and has an equal share of responsibilities. Individuals in these relationships are very independent. Emotional and social links are shared values, life philosophies, and common experiences. Studies show that satisfaction tends to be lower for couples in such relationships, and the couples tend to have fewer children. Symmetrical relationships, however, are the structure of most friendships. Differences are minimized in symmetrical relationships, but they can become very competitive when equality is constantly negotiated. As a result, they are often less stable and are prone to hostility and stress.

Parallel structures provide moderate interdependence and distributed power in the relationships. Partners define themselves as equal, but each has differing amounts of power and authority in certain realms based on each party's area of competence. Parallel relationships are actually a blend of complementary and symmetrical. In certain subjects, one partner will assume the role of expert while the other willingly takes the role of subordinate. On a different question, the roles may be reversed. Alternatively, some issues will be resolved by each person taking symmetrical roles. Parallel relationships are thus marked by flexibility and a focus on understanding what each person's expectations are in particular situations. Blending expert and referent power usually characterizes parallel relationships.

Of course, most relationships are a blend of the three structures. Relationships are not static, they evolve over time and structures may change. For instance, sometimes a relationship may begin as complementary but evolve into parallel. Power is frequently discussed, but the concept is very complex. How we communicate plays an important role in enhancing interpersonal power and control.

## Compliance-Seeking Messages

There are numerous studies investigating interpersonal persuasion strategies. Rudolph and Kathleen Verderber reviewed the literature and found more than 50 different techniques of compliance gaining.[11] Some are very obvious, while others are more subtle. Some scholars would argue that all compliance-gaining strategies are persuasive—that is, intentional verbal and nonverbal attempts to influence the beliefs, attitudes, values, or behaviors of others. All the strategies are grounded in some form of interpersonal power as discussed above.

Erwin Bettinghaus and Michael Cody have developed a useful typology of strategies for persuading people to comply with one's wishes.[12] There are seven general categories in their typology. *Direct requests* are the most common method of getting others to do what we want them to do. What makes direct requests powerful in gaining compliance is the context and social dynamics of the situation. Responding to a friend or boss is different than responding to a total stranger. In addition, the size or magnitude of the request naturally impacts compliance.

*Rationality* is the category of strategies that involves providing reasons and evidence to support one's request. The supporting data legitimize the request as well as provide motivation for compliance. This general strategy works well when making requests of strangers or those in a work environment. It is well worth the extra time necessary to provide more details and information to support a request. Such an approach develops trust, rapport, and does not "cost" the requester future favors.

*Exchange* strategies seek some mutual benefit in exchange for compliance to a request. These strategies may be as simple as trading favors ("I'll drive today if you drive tomorrow") or as elaborate as negotiating the exchange of money or more tangible items. The key to such strategies is the benefit to both parties through compliance to a request.

*Manipulation* strategies are more varied and complex. They seek compliance through emotional appeals. The most common, of course, is to "butter up" the individual prior to making a request. The use of high praise and flattery may enhance compliance. This strategy can fail, however, if the praise and flattery are viewed as shallow or insincere. Another tactic, especially in the workplace, is to demonstrate competence, worth, and likability that produce trust and confidence in one's judgment. A strong and favorable image provides motivation and justification for others to comply with various requests. There are also many negative emotional appeals that will gain compliance. Displays of anger, disappointment, and hurt will often force compliance. Guilt is another strong negative motivator. Negative appeals are very effective in the short-run but may hinder future compliance.

*Coercive* strategies employ the use of negative sanctions and threats for noncompliance. These are the most extreme and harsh tactics. While certainly effective, they do not enhance future compliance and may decrease motivation for cooperation involving even simple requests.

*Indirect* strategies involve dropping hints of a desired behavior or action without actually making a direct request. For example, by stating how important it is to have the phones answered exactly when the store opens or mentioning how the phones start ringing before the store even opens may motivate an employee to arrive to work and be at their desk a few minutes early every day. The key is to provide enough information, needs, or desires so that the target will recognize the desired behavior.

The final category of compliance strategies identified by Bettinghaus and Cody is *emotional appeals*, involving love and affection. These appeals are more intimate and are based on personal commitments. An example would be appealing to your parents to take better care of themselves or to get regular physical examinations because of your love for them or personal desire for their well-being.

Situational factors influence compliance.[13] The degree of intimacy is a powerful factor that influences our willingness to comply with requests. The more intimate the relationship, the more we tend to rely on emotional appeals, threats of personal rejection, or more prosocial messages. The degree of dominance also impacts our choice of persuasive strategies. In superior-subordinate relationships, people tend to use nonconfrontational strategies with rational appeals and demands. Finally, in situations where an individual is resistant to persuasive efforts, we tend to rely on threats of negative sanctions and appeals.

The context of a request is also an important consideration as well as prior interactions with the individual and our own personal motives. We comply with requests for a multitude of reasons. We may respond to a superior's request not out of fear of sanctions but out of respect. We may respond to a friend's request out of a sense of loyalty and value rather than out of an anticipated exchange of future favors. The strategic dimensions of a request or compliance may not be apparent from the verbal statement.

It is important to remember that one-shot persuasive attempts are not very successful. It generally takes several attempts. Studies show that a succession of influence tactics are best.[14] These tactics are called "sequential influence techniques." One such technique is the "foot-in-the-door" tactic. This tactic assumes that people will comply with a second, larger request if they first agree with a smaller initial request. However, if the first request is too large, the tactic is less successful. Another technique is the "door-in-the-face" tactic. Here, the first request is so large that it is certain to be declined. The second, smaller request is granted, which is what the person wanted in the first place. The basis of this tactic is to start high and scale down. Another example of multiple attempts at compliance is called "low balling." With this tactic, compliance is obtained resulting from starting low and then scaling up or adding to the original requests. The difference among all these examples is the magnitude of the initial request.

Interpersonal persuasion is challenging, difficult, and complex. It is also a daily occurrence. The nature of the relationship is the key to strategy selection.

# Conflict

Resistance to persuasion can lead to open conflict just as open conflict can lead to attempts at persuasion. The process of persuasion assumes differences of attitudes, beliefs, values, and behavior among people. Therein lie the seeds of conflict. Persuasion also often assumes that there will be winners and losers, elements of compromise and acquiescence. The fact of the matter is that conflict is not an external reality but an increased perception of incompatible differences, the loss of perceptions of credibility and the dissolution of perceived similarity.[15]

Today it is increasingly difficult to have disagreements without anger or hostility. Talk shows and the evening news are full of stories of international conflict, hate, and anger. Since most of us feel uncomfortable in conflict situations, we often blindly adopt the postures we have seen at home, with friends, or displayed by the media. In an increasingly strident society, that behavior can be disastrous for relationships. There is, however, a difference between disagreement and conflict. Disagreements are rather common, but they do not need to escalate into conflict. The communication strategies one chooses often determine whether disagreements are resolved or conflict erupts. As James McCroskey and Virginia Richmond point out, "Communication is the means for structuring conflict in our interpersonal relationships. Whether the results will be constructive or destructive depends on our skills."[16] Tolerance for disagreement differs among people. In addition, the degree of friendship and likability between individuals affects the likelihood of disagreement growing into conflict. Communication plays a dual role in conflict and conflict management. Communication—the particular verbal and nonverbal symbols chosen—probably created the original conflict. Improperly managed, more communication may worsen the conflict. On the other hand, skillful communication may also be the only path to ending or lessening the problem.

There are several different kinds of conflict. Pseudoconflicts are those where people believe their differing goals cannot be achieved simultaneously. In such instances, solutions to the conflicts seldom require compromise; they normally provide "win-win" opportunities for the individuals when the perceived discrepancy is satisfactorily demonstrated not to exist. Content conflicts are most common, involving disagreement over facts, definitions, goals, or interpretation of information. More interaction between the parties is critical in solving content conflicts. More interaction often results in more mutual understanding and the realization that the differences are not as great as originally believed to be. Ego conflicts can become the most harmful. Such conflicts are based on the personalities of the participants. In a sense, each side gets pleasure out of disagreeing with the other side. Participants view themselves as equals in power, knowledge, and expertise. The participants feel compelled to advocate and even defend specific views or

*Conflict and disagreement are not synonymous. Disagreements do not need to escalate into conflict; the communication strategies we choose determine the outcome.*

Calvin and Hobbes © Watterson. Reprinted with the permission of Universal Press Syndicate. All rights reserved.

arguments. More interaction alone will have little impact on resolving ego conflicts. Value conflicts are the most difficult to solve. Depending on the values in conflict, they can also be the most intense or violent.

There are many different ways people cope with adversity and conflict. Some people are very passive. They become reluctant to state their opinions or feelings. They may even submit to demands regardless of the consequences.

More specifically, some individuals withdraw physically or psychologically, thus removing themselves from the situation. This strategy, of course, does not address or solve the conflict. Others surrender or give in to the opposition in order to avoid further conflict or spare emotional turmoil. While this may seem sensitive to the feelings of others, it is really being dishonest. It is better to deal with conflict in the proper way than to hold feelings of hurt and anger inside. Other people become more aggressive in confrontational situations. They lash out with highly charged, emotional responses. Aggressive behavior tends to be judgmental, dogmatic, and coercive. Outright displays of aggression are likely to result in lose-lose situations. Such behaviors are not in the best interest of a relationship and may escalate the degree of hostility. Finally, some people adopt assertive behavior. Here the person stands up for him- or herself expressing opinions and feelings while keeping the potential impact on and possible response of the receiver in mind. In short, assertive people employ persuasive techniques, including discussion and negotiation.

The essence of interpersonal persuasion involves strategies of bargaining and negotiation. Craig Johnson and Michael Hackman distinguish between the two concepts.[17] For them, bargaining is a "win-lose" situation. Bargaining often involves an adversarial relationship—one or more parties taking rather extreme positions. The bargaining process also involves clashes of wills, demands for concessions, the use of threats, and sometimes even deception. Negotiation, according to Johnson and Hackman, is a process of "problem solving" more often resulting in a "win-win" situation. The focus is on a common goal, not emotional clashes or a test of wills. Objectivity and fairness are important characteristics of the negotiation process.

There are some people who naturally tend to be very resistant to any persuasive effort. Those who are highly ego-involved in an issue or those who possess an extreme conviction or position on an issue will not be open to opposing views. In addition, those who are rigid, authoritarian, and older tend to be less open to persuasive attempts. Persuasion is also difficult when listeners have been rewarded for their positions in the past and are unfamiliar with the speaker's background and opinions.

In terms of your own persuasive efforts, there are specific communication styles or behaviors that encourage conflict and thus should be avoided. The use of value statements makes an audience defensive about their own opinions rather than open to your arguments. Avoid labeling actions of opponents as bad, silly, crazy, etc. Second, avoid presenting "all or none" distinctions or alternatives. It is best to make suggestions and offer solutions without implicit threats. Third, avoid name calling and personal attacks. Although you may be angry, you want to keep the lines of communication open as well as the minds of people who have not firmly committed to one action or position. Insulting friends or acquaintances will surely lose allies. Fourth, avoid speaking in broad generalities. Always provide specific facts and examples to support arguments. Fifth, avoid speaking from an authoritarian perspective. Remember, the best "logic" is that which is created jointly between the speaker and the audience. Position the discussion as an exploration of alternative perspectives, not a debate on values. Finally, avoid emotional verbal and nonverbal communications. Emotional outbursts dilute arguments by redirecting attention to the outbursts rather than to the arguments. Aggression, hostility, tension, or rivalry seldom help in accomplishing long-term goals and objectives.

There are numerous suggestions for managing conflict. They generally revolve around good practices of persuasion and human communication. For example, it is important to accept the other party as a person. This recognizes that all parties involved have opinions to be respected and are operating under similar stress. This basic understanding helps us look for commonalities rather than differences. Therein lies the basis for compromise. Indeed, we want to keep our focus on the actual problem by being descriptive and not judgmental, and making sure that our words match reality. As good persuaders, we should check frequently for validity to confirm that our message is being understood and interpreted as we intended. Finally, by projecting a positive attitude, persuadees will more likely grant a fair hearing. Depending on the degree of conflict, one may seek help from outside the relationship. In extreme cases an arbitrator or facilitator may be necessary to negotiate elements of the conflict.

Solving a conflict is not unlike solving any other communication problem. First, you must analyze the conflict. Second, assess the causes of conflict. Third, develop possible solutions and course of action. Fourth, select the best solution. Fifth, implement the course of action or solution.

It would be a mistake to view all conflict as bad. Conflict can be most positive. The difference between helpful and nonhelpful conflict is "the extent to which it dominates interaction and the degree to which it is or is not balanced by more positive communication."[18] Conflict can establish social interactional boundaries; reduce tensions; clarify roles, objectives, or differences; and provide the basis for negotiation and continued interaction. Gerald Miller finds conflict desirable because humans are creative through conflict, and it causes some form of human relationship or contact.[19] Conflict, according to Saul Alinski, is an essential element of life. He asserts, "Life is conflict and in conflict you're alive."[20] From this brief overview, we can characterize conflict as: inevitable, based on communication, both harmful and beneficial, varying in degree based on communication style, and sometimes incapable of resolution.

## Gender Differences

There is a growing interest in the issue of communication differences between the sexes. Differences in communication behavior develop because of cultural and societal influences plus individual backgrounds and experiences. As previously emphasized, society establishes norms and expectations for behavior. Social roles influence the content of communication. As more women enter the workplace and advance to positions of technological and social leadership, issues of communication styles and techniques become very important to organizations and management personnel. Problems may arise when individuals use different styles within the workplace. Deborah Tannen urges that recognizing the differences between men and women means seeking understanding—not placing blame or rendering judgment. As Tannen observes, "recognizing gender differences frees individuals from the burden of individual pathology. . . . If we can sort out differences based on conversational style, we will be in a better position to confront real conflicts of interest—and to find a shared language in which to negotiate them."[21]

The research literature describes masculine and feminine styles of communication. One style is not superior to another, nor do they necessarily correlate with specific sexes. Some women may be socialized in the masculine style while some men may show more characteristics of a feminine style of communication. The styles identify specific communication behaviors, goals, and rules. Essentially, men and women differ in frequency of talk; with whom they talk; amount of disclosure; and use, purpose, and content of talk.

From a social perspective, women speak and hear a language of connection and intimacy. Men speak and hear a language of status and independence. For women, the language of conversation is one of rapport, a way to develop and maintain relationships. For men, talk is more "report talk," a means to preserve independence and to maintain status in the social hierarchy.[22]

The masculine style is characterized as competitive, assertive, and task oriented. Communication tends to be more individualistic, instrumental, and reserved. In contrast, the feminine style is characterized as cooperative, supportive, and relational. Communication tends to be more expressive and focused on interpersonal relationships.[23]

There are several specific behaviors associated with the different styles of communication. Men tend to interrupt others more frequently, to talk for longer periods of time, to be less self-disclosive, and to control the situation by offering opinions, suggestions, and information. Women tend to disclose more information about themselves, use more euphemisms and emotional terms, provide greater frequency and longer duration of eye contact, and are more likely to respond, offering agreement or disagreement.[24]

To improve the interpersonal communication between the sexes, Tannen recommends taking "each other on their own terms rather than applying the standards of one group to the behavior of the other."[25] Perhaps, "women could learn from men to accept some conflict and difference without seeing it as a threat to intimacy, and many men could learn from women to accept interdependence without seeing it as a threat

CATHY © Cathy Guisewite. Reprinted with permission of Universal Press Syndicate.

to their freedom.''[26] Tannen concludes her best-selling book with the notion that ''understanding the other's ways of talking is a giant leap across the communication gap between women and men, and a giant step toward opening lines of communication.''[27]

# Leadership

Although the concept of leadership is difficult to define, we agree with Michael Hackman and Craig Johnson that ''leadership shares all of the features of human communication.''[28] Leaders certainly use symbols to create reality, communicate about the past/present/future, and use persuasion to accomplish goals. Leadership may be viewed as a special form of human communication. At the core of nearly all definitions of the term is the notion of influence. Hackman and Johnson define leadership as ''human (symbolic) communication which modifies the attitudes and behaviors of others in order to meet shared group goals and needs.''[29]

Research identifies traits of leaders that relate to ability, sociability, motivation, and communication skills. In terms of ability, leaders exceed other group members in the areas of intelligence, scholarship, insight, and verbal facility. In terms of sociability, leaders are more dependable, active, cooperative, and popular. In areas of motivation, leaders exceed others in terms of initiative, persistence, and enthusiam.[30]

From a communication perspective, there are specific communication skills that enhance leadership effectiveness. According to Hackman and Johnson, they include being able to: develop perceptions of credibility, build and use power bases effectively, empower followers, make effective use of verbal and nonverbal influence cues, develop positive expectations for others, foster creativity, manage change, gain compliance, negotiate productive solutions, develop argumentative competence, and adapt to cultural differences.[31] We discuss many of these activities in describing the leaders of social movements.

In addition to specific communication skills associated with leadership, there are also styles of leadership that impact overall effectiveness and popularity.[32] An authoritarian style of leadership often exhibits group control, direction, and conflict. Although such a style may result in increased productivity and task performance, it may also result in less satisfaction and more aggression among followers. A more democratic style of leadership attempts to involve followers in setting goals and encourages group interaction and teamwork. This leadership style tends to foster better follower morale, participation, innovation, and commitment. Communication skills and abilities are essential in developing and maintaining a democratic leadership style. Such a style demands supportive communication endeavors that facilitate interaction among group members.

Do you want to be the leader of a group? Rudolph and Kathleen Verderber suggest to be knowledgeable about the particular group tasks, work harder than anyone else in the group, be personally committed to group goals and needs, be willing to be decisive at key moments in the discussion, interact freely with others in the group, and develop skill in maintenance functions as well as in task functions.[33]

Legal authority or responsibility is no guarantee of leadership status. Ultimately, the role of leader is granted by the follower; as a result, leadership is a special circumstance of interpersonal communication. Although certain aspects of leadership are more suited to group, organizational, or mass contexts, the foundation is the relationship between each leader and follower.

## Contexts of Interpersonal Persuasion

Every interaction takes place within a specific situation or environment. We conclude the chapter with three rather specialized situations that involve interpersonal persuasion: organizations, interviews, and sales.

## Organizations

Organizations are usually defined as collectivities of individuals organized to achieve some purpose or goal. In some cases, the purpose may be economic—to produce some product or to provide a particular service. In other cases, the purpose of the group may be more social—people brought together because of common beliefs, ideology, or community function.

Because all organizations are purposeful and structured, they impact the nature of human communication in very specific ways. The notion of organization involves concepts such as rules, roles, power, specialization, hierarchy, and control, to name only a few. The structure of organizations often masks the fact that a majority of the communication interactions that take place are interpersonal. The nature of the relationships is often affected by the hierarchical nature of superior/subordinate roles and by the culture of the organizational enviornment, but the theories and approaches to interpersonal persuasion still apply.

Communication activities within organizations can be formal or informal. Formal communication activities are those officially sanctioned by the organization and are usually task oriented. These include items like memos, policy statements, and newsletters. Informal communication activities are those among the individuals of an organization.

---

*Collectivities of individuals may organize for a social, humanitarian purpose. They may form a community based on common beliefs and a particular goal. The Names Project AIDS Memorial Quilt involved the creation of a work of art by a number of dedicated participants to celebrate the memories of those lost to a gruesome disease.*

*Tribune* photo by James Mayo

Informal communication activities are just as important, and some would argue perhaps more important, than the routine formal organizational communication activities.

The flow of communication is usually characterized by the direction from which it originates. Upward communication consists of messages sent from lower levels of the organization to upper levels of the hierarchy. Such messages are important in terms of worker morale, job satisfaction, and problem solving. In fact, most large organizations spend a great deal of time nurturing and encouraging messages from the people involved with activities on a daily basis. For managers, upward communication is the primary source of information about worker problems and issues, thus providing an informed basis for decision making. As a process, upward communication encourages employee participation and provides an outlet for conflict and tension. Upward communication, however, is difficult. Workers are usually reluctant to share negative messages with superiors. Mid-level supervisors may actively discourage upward messages because they feel threatened. They may view upward communication as intruding on their power and as jeopardizing their job security. Thus, how one communicates dissatisfaction or general problems becomes a serious dilemma for employees at all levels of an organization.

Downward communication is the most obvious and prevalent within organizations. These messages are from higher levels to lower levels within organizations. They range from direct verbal orders to more formal activities such as employee performance evaluations. Downward communication provides the primary means for sharing job-related information and organizational goals and philosophies. The challenge, of course, is for downward communication to be respectful of employees and to enhance their job performance.

Lateral communication describes messages shared between equals (those at the same level in the hierarchy) within an organization such as manager to manager or worker to worker. This form of communication is also very important. In addition to improving teamwork and worker morale, it also facilitates task coordination and completion. It provides an informal network of employee support and information. Nevertheless, even lateral communication endeavors can be problematic. A lack of cooperation and trust among colleagues, as well as power-hungry peers, may sour the work environment.

Phillip Tompkins summarizes some of the research findings related to the flow of communication:[34]

1. Those higher in an organization communicate more while performing their jobs than do those lower in the organization.

2. Job responsibilities significantly impact the quantity and direction of communication activities.

3. Communication within organizations is usually initiated by the person of higher status.

4. Those of the same level or status within an organization are more likely to discuss problems and solutions than those of differing status.

5. Message content influences who will transmit it, who receives it, and message accuracy.

6. Job satisfaction, trust in superiors, and mobility aspirations influence willingness to engage in upward communication.

7. Physical proximity results in more interaction.

8. The number of interactions a person initiates within an organization is related to the number the person receives.

9. Most employees do not have the opportunity to send a great amount of information upward in their organizations.

10. Most employees receive their information through interpersonal, informal channels of communication.

Kathleen Reardon talks about three models of organization-employee interaction.[35] The first is called the "exchange model." Employee motivation for productivity is by organizational incentives and rewards. In essence, the organization exchanges money, benefits, and social outlets in return for work performed. As you can imagine, employee participation is limited and rules are seldom challenged. Because employee motivation is "externally" motivated, there is little corporate loyalty.

The second model Reardon refers to is the "socialization model." The organization actively persuades employees of the value of organizational goals and objectives. Corporate culture, peer pressure, and leadership by example are key factors of employee acquiescence and cooperation. While there is more individual autonomy, there is still little direct employee participation in the life of the organization.

The final approach to organization-employee interaction is the "accommodation model." Employees actively participate in shaping organizational rules as well as production goals. The structure of the organization attempts to maximize the skills, abilities, and unique characteristics of each employee. They become partners involved in problem-solving and decision-making activities of the organization.

Note that interpersonal interactions and relationships are important to the overall productivity of an organization. Dan O'Hair and Gustav Friedrich suggest several guidelines to help form positive "shared-task relationships": ignore personal idiosyncrasies as much as possible, stay focused on mutual task goals, know your responsibilities, be accountable for your performance, share credit for success with co-workers, and take your share of the blame for failure.[36]

Today, scholars are approaching organizational communication from a cultural perspective. From this perspective, organizational communication is important in establishing the corporate climate, socializing employees, and establishing expectations of behavior. Communication skills are an important element of survival and success within every organization.

## Interviews

It is possible to argue that nearly all dyadic communication is a form of interviewing. Even in social conversation with another person, there is the rotation of roles and the exchange of information that provides the basis for future transactions and behavior. However, here we are referring to a more formal, prescribed form of dyadic communication. Charles Stewart and William Cash define interviewing as "a process of dyadic, relational communication, with a predetermined and serious purpose designed to interchange behavior, and involving the asking and answering of questions."[37] The key concepts to this definition lie in the words "predetermined and serious purpose." Thus, according to Stewart and Cash, an interview is a formal communication transaction where one or both of the parties have specific behavioral objectives in mind (i.e., altering a belief, attitude, or action). Even "mini-interviews"—those that seek to elicit the opinions of colleagues, etc.—may mask a persuasive intent. The questioner may appear to have an open mind but may, in reality, have no intention of accepting the interviewee's position.

In an interview situation, there are the dual roles of interviewer and interviewee. These roles, however, are interchangeable. In fact, a really good interview is one where the participants freely rotate between the roles. Without such an exchange, participants sacrifice power, control, and personal motives. This perspective recognizes that each participant in an interview has a purpose and thus needs to prepare for the encounter. The rest of the discussion is directed to the roles of both the interviewer and the interviewee.

There are many types of interviews: informational, persuasive, employment, appraisal, or counseling, to name only a few. The differences distinguishing each type are the general purposes and contexts of the interviews. Most interviews employ strategies and tactics found in other persuasive contexts, such as public speaking and advertising. Before entering an interview, you should analyze all the elements thoroughly. What should be accomplished? What can be expected? How can you best present yourself? Many of the suggestions provided in this book relating to other persuasive topics can be used in your analysis (especially chapter 13).

Minimally, you should consider the persuadee, situation, and topic and then carefully develop appropriate strategies and tactics. In terms of the persuadee, you should analyze the person's values and background in order to gain insight into possible motivation. The goal is to understand better how the receiver will perceive the situation. You will then be able

*Productive interviews are those in which both participants are prepared and freely exchange roles.*

to develop strong arguments and appeals. Attention to the situation of the interview is also important. When and where the interview takes place will impact such persuasive elements as attention, control, and length of interview. Finally, you should spend as much time preparing the content of the interview as you would a public presentation. You should structure your argument carefully by identifying key appeals and supporting your ideas with examples and evidence.

Stewart and Cash suggest a basic structure to follow for a persuasive interview.[38] In the opening, it is important to establish rapport with the other party. The goal is to establish an open climate where there can be free exchange of dialogue and information. A feeling of trust and mutual goodwill between the participants is important. This is accomplished by briefly explaining the purpose and nature of the interview.

In the body of the interview, Stewart and Cash recommend preparing a clear and concise statement of the need or problem being confronted. This should be followed by a point-by-point development of the reasons and causes of the problem or need. It is important to present more than one reason or cause for the problem discussed. You should begin with your strongest point. As with a public or written presentation, specific information and evidence should be provided to support arguments. Throughout this portion of the interview, it is useful to obtain agreement periodically from the interviewee about the problem, causes, and information presented. Finally, you should present solutions and evaluate each one by providing advantages and disadvantages. Obviously the goal is to get agreement on the best or preferred solution.

In the closing portion of the interview, it is important to summarize what has been discussed and to review agreements reached. The closing usually occurs in three stages. When appropriate, you begin to focus on the solution and ask "yes-response" questions to verify positions. The agreement stage of the closing is the most dangerous period. At this point, you should obtain a final agreement and commitment from the interviewee to the course of action. While being pleasant and reassuring, you want to eliminate doubt as to the desired action to follow. Finally, it is a good idea to arrange for a follow-up interview. This is useful to establish rapport once again and to check the status of commitment expressed throughout the interview. Your leave-taking should be relaxed and positive. Do not bring up any new issues or items to discuss; take some time for small talk if possible.

Rudolph and Kathleen Verderber provide ten tips for interviewing successfully.[39]

1. Be aware of your own presentation.
2. Do not waste time.
3. Avoid trick or loaded questions.
4. Avoid questions that violate fair employment practice.

 5. Give the applicant an opportunity to ask questions.
 6. Do your homework and background investigation.
 7. Be prompt.
 8. Be alert and look at the interviewer.
 9. Give yourself time to think before responding.
10. Show enthusiasm.

Interviewing is a good example of how persuasion resembles other forms of communication. The key ingredients for all forms of communication are planning and preparation.

# Sales

Selling can be viewed as a special form of interpersonal communication. In a sense, we are all salespeople whether advocating a specific position, idea, service, or product. Regardless of occupation, anyone who is successful is an effective salesperson. As with interviewing, the basic appeals, strategies, and tactics of persuasion are essential to successful sales.

The key element in sales, as with all persuasion, is the potential customer. Spencer Johnson and Larry Wilson, authors of *The One Minute Sales Person*, state that one must not forget that "behind every sale is a person," and the sole purpose of selling anything is "to help people get the good feelings they want about what they bought and about themselves."[40] They describe the "wonderful paradox" of selling where "you will have more fun and enjoy more financial success when you stop trying to get what *you* want and start helping other people get what *they* want."[41] For them, salespeople are problem solvers attempting to meet other people's needs, wants, and desires.

Every sales transaction is based on some form of interpersonal relationship between customer and salesperson. The higher the risk or costs, the more involved the relationship. Dan O'Hair and Gustav Friedrich offer five basic rules of conduct for successful customer relationships:[42]

1. Know the customer.
2. Take responsibility for customer satisfaction.
3. Avoid unresponsive behavior.
4. Employ effective communication skills.
5. Treat customers with respect.

An interesting approach to sales is provided by Theodore Levitt in *The Marketing Imagination*.[43] He argues that expectations are what people buy—not things. These expectations encompass aspects of trust, service,

## Figure 8.2
## Characteristics of Relationship Management
### A. Stages and Objects of the Sale

| Stage of Sale | The Seller | The Buyer |
|---|---|---|
| 1. Before | Real hope | Vague need |
| 2. Romance | Hot & heavy | Testing & hopeful |
| 3. Purchase | Fantasy—bed | Fantasy—board |
| 4. After | Looks for next sale | "You don't care." |
| 5. Long after | Indifferent | "Can't quality be better?" |
| 6. Next sale | "How about a new one?" | "Why?" |

### B. When the First Sale Is Made

| The Seller | The Buyer |
|---|---|
| Objective achieved | Judgment postponed, applies test of time |
| Selling stops | Shopping continues |
| Focus goes elswhere | Focus on purchase, wants affirmation of expectations |
| Tension released | Tension increased |
| Relationship reduced or ended | Relationship intensified because of commitment to sale |

### C. Two Approaches to Sales

| Positive | Negative |
|---|---|
| Initiate positive phone calls | Make only callbacks |
| Make recommendations | Make justifications |
| Candor in language | Accommodative language |
| Use phone | Use correspondence |
| Show appreciation | Wait for misunderstandings |
| Make service suggestions | Wait for service requests |
| Use "we" problem-solving language | Use "owe-us" legal language |
| Get to problems | Only respond to problems |
| Use jargon/shorthand | Use long-winded communications |
| Personality problems aired | Personality problems hidden |
| Talk of "our future together" | Talk about making good on the past |
| Routinize responses | Fire drill/emergency responsiveness |
| Accept responsibility | Shift blame |
| Plan the future | Rehash the past |

It is useful to remember that motives, emotions, and attitudes differ between buyers and sellers throughout a transaction.

and satisfaction. The "act" of buying changes the buyer. Although the active, intense aspects of the purchase end for the seller, the process just begins for the buyer.

Before the sale, the seller has high expectations and real hope of completing the sale, whereas the buyer may be unaware of the product or impending sale or may have a vague or general interest in the product. Levitt argues that the most intense stage of the sale for the seller is convincing the prospect to buy. During this stage, the buyer is testing arguments and confirming desire. The culmination of the sale reduces tension for the seller but increases tension for the buyer. Upon the sale, the seller has met the objective and begins to refocus on the next opportunity, virtually ending the personal relationship. The buyer, however, seeks commitment and affirmation of expectations and promises made. For Levitt, relationship selling means understanding the process from the viewpoint of the buyer and consciously spending time after the sale to confirm and reassure the buyer that the right decision was made.

In sales, therefore, the goal is to meet a need of the buyer. This is done in two ways. First, the product or service must be couched in human motivational terms. Edwin Greif provides eight classifications of buyer motivations: profit and thrift, safety and protection, ease and convenience, pride and prestige, sex and romance, love and affection, adventure and excitement, and performance and durability.[44] Thus, whatever the product or service, the task is to rationalize the purchase based on one of the motives listed. The second way to address the needs of buyers is to discuss product benefits. Each product feature has a corresponding benefit. For example, if a car has a larger engine that generates more power, the benefits to be discussed are greater passing safety, less strain from driving, longer-lasting engine, fewer repair costs, etc. In short, benefits—not features—sell products.

Finally, the steps and preparation for a sales presentation are very similar to other persuasive endeavors.

1. *Pre-approach*—The buyer becomes familiar with product features and benefits and the seller learns about target customers. Sales questions and statements for an automobile would probably include specific features of the car, buyer budget, buyer auto usage, and exploration of buyer motives for purchasing a new car.

2. *Approach*—In this step, the seller designs sale messages based on customer types and needs. The assumption here is that different arguments and benefit emphases are needed for different customers who have varying needs, desires, or problems. If a middle-aged business executive were buying a car, the salesperson would emphasize such factors as auto luxury, comfort, status, design, and style. If the buyer was seeking a second family car, the salesperson would probably emphasize cost, reliability, gas mileage, and quality.

3. *Presentation*—This step refers to the face-to-face interaction with the buyer. The presentation must have the appropriate introduction to build rapport and uncover customer needs, the body which argues product benefits, and the conclusion to address objections and close the sale. Presentation is the most spontaneous and reactive phase of the sales pitch; it is critical to the success of any salesperson.

4. *Follow-up*—Depending on the size of the purchase, this phase refers to showing appreciation and providing reassurance or confirmation of the buyer's decision. Here the salesperson acknowledges the wisdom of both the selection and the value of the product and projects a vision of customer usage and satisfaction.

In sales situations, you may encounter a difficult customer—one who is unsatisfied with a product or service or who may even be hostile. You have a responsibility not only to address the issue at hand, but also to properly represent your organization. There are several things you can do in such difficult situations: let customers talk, reassure them that their concerns will be heard, do not personalize the issue (the anger is not aimed at you), acknowledge instances where the customer is correct, apologize and provide immediate corrective action when the company or yourself is at fault, and be sure to ask the customer to suggest how the problem or issue could be avoided in the future.[45]

We would be remiss if we did not highlight some of the problematic areas of sales in relationship to traditional persuasive theory. Especially in a democratic society, persuasion is based on the concept of informed choice. Despite the phrase *caveat emptor* (let the buyer beware), the ethical burden is on the persuader to ensure that products are fairly presented. There are also other issues to consider. Does the seller really *believe* in the product? Are the products offered to solve real needs or transparent needs? Does the buyer really need the product or service? These are but a few of the issues that sellers should address. In terms of persuasion there is little difference between the selling of ideas and the selling of products. Both are important to our society and utilize the same tools of persuasion.

## Summary

The foundation for all persuasion is preparation and a thorough understanding of audience—whether it is an audience of one or millions. Informally, we engage in interpersonal persuasion much more frequently than we recognize.

The amount and type of persuasion we use (or are exposed to) depends on the nature of particular interpersonal encounters. We may seek the approval of others to satisfy the relational needs of acceptance, affection and respect. We frequently seek compliance to accomplish specific tasks: to finish a project, to sell a product, or to be hired. Many interpersonal encounters involve both cognitive and relational processes. The verbal and nonverbal symbols we choose to communicate our intentions affect the outcome. Compliance depends on the strategies we select, the situation or context, and the nature of the relationship.

Conflict often results from prolonged, intense efforts of interpersonal persuasion. Frequently, a negative reaction results not from the actual facts of the disagreement but from the quality of the communication exchanged. The most important aspect to remember about conflict is that it must be managed. If we apply the knowledge we have gained about how to communicate effectively, we should be able to conduct our participation in interpersonal exchanges—including conflict—successfully.

The overlay of organizational structure houses a great deal of interpersonal interaction. While interpersonal communication within the organizational context ranges on a continuum from formal to informal, much of the work accomplished depends on effective interpersonal communication. We investigated the more formal forms of interpersonal persuasion in the discussions of interviews and sales. These forms of interpersonal persuasion are more similar than different. They rely on all the principles previously identified and discussed throughout this book.

## Questions and Projects for Further Study

1. In terms of the three types of relationship structures, how would you categorize your relationship with your father? mother? teacher? employer? girlfriend? boyfriend? classmates?

2. Can you think of a time when you and an intimate friend had an argument? What happened? Analyze the conversation and argument in terms of gender differences discussed in this chapter.

3. You have a 1990 Toyota Celica automobile you wish to sell. Develop the sales appeals and arguments for persuading a friend, a stranger, a middle-aged man or woman to purchase the car. How do the appeals differ and why?

4. For the above automobile, prepare a specific appeal that would address buyer motivations of profit and thrift, safety and protection, ease and convenience, pride and prestige, sex and romance, love and affection, adventure and excitement, performance and durability.

5. Describe the leadership qualities you like best. Why? Describe the leadership qualities you do not like. Why?

6. You are the manager of a department at a large clothing store. Prepare questions for a job interview, a work appraisal interview for a problem employee, and an employee termination interview. How do these interviews differ in strategies and appeals?

7. From your own experience, provide an example of a pseudoconflict, a content conflict, and an ego-conflict.

8. You have been working in a furniture store for one year. Prepare arguments you would use in asking for a raise.

9. Discuss the ethical issues, dimensions, and implications of:

   a. attempts to sell a $50 Bible to a family of six with an income of $10,000 a year.

   b. attempts to sell a used car that had been in a major accident and recently repaired.

10. Describe the nonverbal behaviors associated with interactions with friends, acquaintances, and employers.

11. If you work for an organization or company, how would you describe its values and climate? Whom do you interact with the most on the job? Do you feel free to make suggestions for job improvement to superiors?

# Notes

[1] Bobby Patton and Kim Giffin, *Interpersonal Communication*. New York: Harper & Row, 1974, p. 45.

[2] Kathleen Reardon, *Persuasion in Practice*. Newbury Park, CA: Sage, 1991, p. 112.

[3] Dan Rothwell and James Costigan, *Interpersonal Communication*. Columbus, OH: Charles Merrill Publishing Co., 1975, pp. 20–23.

[4] See William Schultz, *Firo: A Three-Dimensional Theory of Interpersonal Behavior*, New York: Holt, Rinehart and Winston, 1958; and "The Postulate of Interpersonal Needs" in *Messages*, ed. by Jean Civikly. New York: Random House, 1977, pp. 174–84.

[5] Joseph A. DeVito, *The Interpersonal Communication Book*, Sixth Edition. New York: HarperCollins, 1992, pp. 90–105.

[6] Joseph A. DeVito and Michael L. Hecht, *The Nonverbal Communication Reader*. Prospect Heights, IL: Waveland Press, 1990, p. 4.

[7] *Ibid.*, pp. 11–13.

[8] Erwin Bettinghaus and Michael Cody, *Persuasive Communication*, Fourth Edition. New York: Holt, Rinehart and Winston, 1987, pp. 123–31.

[9] The work of French and Raven are widely cited. See John French and Bertram Raven, "The Bases of Social Power" in *Studies in Social Power*, ed. by D. Cartwright. Ann Arbor, MI: Institute for Social Research, 1959, pp. 150–67.

[10] Julia T. Wood, *Relational Communication*. Belmont, CA: Wadsworth, 1995, pp. 160–63.

[11] Rudolph Verderber and Kathleen Verderber, *Inter-Act*, Seventh Edition. Belmont, CA: Wadsworth, 1995, pp. 265–67.

[12] Bettinghaus and Cody, pp. 185–88.

[13] Richard Perloff, *The Dynamics of Persuasion*. Hillsdale, NJ: Lawrence Erbaum Associates, 1993, p. 271.

[14] *Ibid.*, pp. 283–90.

[15] James McCroskey and Virginia Richmond, *Fundamentals of Human Communication: An Interpersonal Perspective*. Prospect Heights, IL: Waveland, 1996, p. 261.

[16] McCroskey and Richmond, p. 260.

[17] Craig Johnson and Michael Hackman, *Creative Communication: Principles and Applications*. Prospect Heights, IL: Waveland Press, 1995, pp.214–22.

[18] Wood, p. 263.

[19] Gerald Miller, "Introduction: Conflict Resolution through Communication" in *Conflict Resolution through Communication*, ed. by Fred Jandt. New York: Harper & Row, 1973, p. 3.

[20] Saul Alinski, *Rules for Radicals*. New York: Vintage Books, 1969, p. vii.

[21] Deborah Tannen, *You Just Don't Understand*. New York: Ballantyne Books, 1990, p. 17, 18.

[22] *Ibid.*, p. 77.

[23] Wood, p.134.

[24] McCroskey and Richmond, pp. 301–306; Wood, p. 135; and Tannen, p. 129.

[25] Tannen, p. 121.

[26] *Ibid.*, p. 294.

[27] *Ibid.*, p.298.

[28] Michael Hackman and Craig Johnson, *Leadership: A Communication Perspective*, Second Edition. Prospect Heights, IL: Waveland Press, 1996, p. 7.

[29] *Ibid.*, p. 14.

[30] Verderber and Verderber, p. 378.

[31] Hackman and Johnson, p. 22.

[32] For a very good discussion and summary of research, see Hackman and Johnson, chapter 2.

[33] Verderber and Verderber, p. 382.

[34] See Phillip K. Tompkins, "The Functions of Human Communication in Organization" in *Handbook of Rhetorical and Communication Theory*, ed. by Carroll Arnold and John Bowers. Boston: Allyn and Bacon, 1984, pp. 683–98 and DeVito, *Human Communication*, Fifth Edition, 1991, pp. 697–98.

[35] Reardon, pp. 143–46.

[36] Dan O'Hair and Gustav Friedrich, *Strategic Communication in Business and the Professions*. Boston: Houghton Mifflin, 1992, p. 183.

[37] Charles Stewart and William Cash, *Interviewing: Principles and Practices*, Seventh Edition. Dubuque, IA: Wm. C. Brown, 1988, p. 1.

[38] *Ibid.*, p. 241–74.

[39] Verderber and Verderber.

[40] Spencer Johnson and Larry Wilson, *The One Minute Sales Person*. New York: William Morrow & Co., 1984, pp. 17, 25.

[41] *Ibid.*, p. 21.

[42] O'Hair and Friedrich, p.186.

[43] Theodore Levitt, *The Marketing Imagination*. New York: The Free Press, 1983, pp. 111–26.

[44] Edwin Greif, *Personal Salesmanship*. Reston, VA: Reston Publishing Co., 1974, p. 32.

[45] O'Hair and Friedrich, p. 190–92.

## Additional Reading

Joseph A. DeVito, *The Interpersonal Communication Book*, Seventh Edition. New York: HarperCollins, 1995.

Joseph A. DeVito and Michael Hecht, *The Nonverbal Communication Reader*. Prospect Heights, IL: Waveland Press, 1990.

Michael Hackman and Craig Johnson, *Leadership: A Communication Perspective*, Second Edition. Prospect Heights, IL: Waveland Press, 1996.

Fred Jandt, *Conflict Resolution Through Communication*. New York: Harper & Row, 1973.

Joyce Hocker, and William Wilmot, *Interpersonal Conflict*, Fourth Edition. Dubuque, IA: W.C. Brown, 1995.

Mark Knapp and Gerald Miller, eds., *Handbook of Interpersonal Communication*. Beverly Hills: Sage, 1985.

Gerald Miller, ed., *Explorations in Interpersonal Communication*. Beverly Hills: Sage, 1976.

Gerald Miller and Herbert Simons, *Perspectives on Communication in Social Conflict*. Englewood Cliffs, NJ: Prentice Hall, 1974.

Charles Stewart and William Cash, *Interviewing: Principles and Practices*, Seventh Edition, Dubuque, IA: Wm. C. Brown, 1988.

Julia T. Wood, *Relational Communication*. Belmont, CA: Wadsworth, 1995.

# 9

# Public and Mass Persuasion

## OVERVIEW

■ Public Communication and Persuasion
    Characteristics of Public Communication
    Public Opinion and Persuasion

■ Persuasive Campaigns
    Product or Commercial Campaigns
    Political Campaigns
    Issue Campaigns
      Grassroots Lobbying
      Corporate Advocacy/Issues Management
    Social Movements
      Characteristics
      Persuasive Functions
      Life Cycle
      Leadership
      Resistance to Social Movements

■ Campaign Implementation

■ Summary

■ Questions and Projects for Further Study

■ Notes

■ Additional Reading

We feel ourselves at the mercy of language and its manipulators, the slick professionals—advertisers, politicians, televangelists—who use it with cynical skill to entice us, innocent amateurs, into their web of words. . . . In communicating, no matter what the level or function, we all have the same basic needs, which we try to meet through our linguistic interaction.[1]

—Robin Lakoff

Public persuasion involves interactions on a societal scale. Through public communication, we discuss issues, formulate and debate policy, campaign for public office, and implement societal reform and changes. As our society becomes more complex, individual and independent actions are no longer sufficient to guarantee success or survival. Group efforts impact us daily, and we join forces with others to insure that our views are heard and our needs are met.

Shearon Lowery and Melvin DeFleur argue that America has become a "mass society." For them, a mass society means more than a large number of citizens. It refers to "a distinctive pattern of social organization . . . a process of changing social organization that occurs when industrialization, urbanization, and modernization increasingly modify the social order."[2]

Especially since World War II, Americans have progressively identified their interests with the goals of formal organizations such as unions, interest groups, professional associations, and political alliances. Contacts with formal organizations help establish our sense of social power and also help us recognize our potential.

In this chapter, we are going to investigate the nature of public communication and persuasion. Our focus is on the variety of types and strategies of public persuasive campaigns.

## Public Communication and Persuasion

Early in human history, public communication was oral and face to face. As we noted in chapter 2, ancient texts reveal a rather sophisticated approach to public persuasion. Over 2,000 years ago, Aristotle's *Rhetoric* detailed the art of persuasive communication. Verbal skills were highly valued and necessary for public life. The master of public discourse was eloquent, ethical, and civic minded. The Greeks trusted and preferred oral, face-to-face interaction to the written word. With the advent of the printing press, literacy was no longer a privilege of the aristocracy. With the printed word, public communication and persuasion extended beyond immediate audiences. Electronic communication further extended the power and impact of human communication and persuasion. In our modern world, oral, written, and electronic communication are an essential and pervasive part of our lives. However, more public communication has not necessarily improved the human condition. Some argue that the increase of public communication and technologies have increased public deception, confusion, and the complexity of modern life.

## Characteristics of Public Communication

Public communication may be defined as intentional efforts to change or modify the beliefs, attitudes, values, and behaviors of an audience through the use of symbols in a public forum. Americans engage in more public communication and oratory today than ever before in our nation's history. Media technology and the communications industry have increased the quantity and the quality of public communication. They have also changed the form and content of public discourse.

This rather broad definition of public communication identifies persuasion as its goal, the use of symbols as its means of meeting its objective, and the public arena as its context of interaction.

*Tribune* photo by Jose More.

Public communication possesses several characteristics that are different from other forms of communication. Although these distinctions have been identified in other chapters, it is useful to review them briefly again.

1. Public communication is simply more "public." The interactions are not private, and intimacy is sacrificed. The communication settings become less relevant. Although Barbara Walters, a television journalist for ABC, frequently interviews celebrities within the seemingly comfortable security of their homes, their responses will be heard by millions of people—people who can directly impact the personality's future popularity and income. The comments of politicians, for example, are no longer limited to their immediate audiences. Comments made in Iowa are broadcast throughout the nation.

2. The audience is larger, more diverse, heterogeneous, and anonymous. This makes audience analysis more difficult. One message must suffice for many different people with varying backgrounds, beliefs, and values. Adapting to a diverse audience becomes nearly impossible. Appeals are more general and often devoid of commitment. In addition, language tends to be more restricted and less precise. As noted above, politicians campaigning in Iowa must be careful in making promises to farmers that may upset urban voters in another region.

3. The media affects the form and content of interactions. Presentation of messages depends on the medium used. Television is naturally better suited for movement, action, and drama than is radio. Newspapers and magazines offer expanded space for written messages allowing for more examples, details, and argumentation. The use of mass media restricts audience feedback, and the interpretation of the message is thus vulnerable to misunderstanding. The 20-second television sound bite for the evening news has become the mainstay of contemporary political discourse. Such statements can be taken out of context and may result in misleading impressions.

4. Public communication allows the possibility for greater impact and potential change. People, groups, and opinions can be mobilized quickly and behavior can be converted immediately. Mass persuasion is best at linking ideas and potential audiences for some common action rather than individual conversion or attitude change.

Public communication provides several social functions: information, persuasion, entertainment, and culture dissemination, for example. Public communication shares information needed to conduct business and to regulate social life. It has a persuasive function that provides opportunities for various viewpoints or ideas to be presented, discussed, and debated. The entertainment function often blends several purposes. For example, in the academy award-winning film *Philadelphia*, Tom Hanks portrayed the struggles of a successful lawyer who contracted AIDS. Although entertaining, the film was also informative about the dilemmas and issues associated with the illness. It was also persuasive in presenting different arguments and positions about the treatment and prevention of the disease. Finally, public communication preserves and disseminates all the rituals and ceremonies of our culture. Films, speeches, lectures, television programs, and other similar events weave a cultural fabric that unites people, groups, and ideas. Through public communication, humans give cultural meaning to a bewildering variety of daily events.

## Public Opinion and Persuasion

Public opinion, revealed through countless polls, has emerged as a critical factor in public campaigns and persuasion today. Opinion polls guide nearly every phase and decision of all campaigns. We tend to think of public opinion as a monolithic entity (review figure 7.1). Leaders espouse views and positions based on the "public's opinion" with great certainty. However, the truth is that public opinion is not static and polls are just another tool of persuasion. In order to understand the persuasive potential and impact of polls and public opinion, we need to look briefly at the nature of public opinion.

Few issues inspire opinions or feelings from the entire citizenry. At the heart of any opinion is the issue of salience or self-interest. We may offer opinions on many issues, but there are few that motivate us to take some action, such as writing a letter, going to a public rally, or sending money to an organization. A small group of individuals may gain media attention that stimulates national exposure, but public opinion is usually splintered in several directions, no matter what the issue. From this perspective, public opinion may be thought of as "the collective expression of opinion of many individuals bound into a group by common aims, aspirations, needs and ideals."[3] Persuasive appeals and messages focus on the commonality of the group.

Events are critical to the concept of public opinion. Public opinion does not anticipate events; it only reacts to them. For example, the Exxon oil spill in Alaska generated a great deal of public attention and support for environmental actions. Memberships in environmental groups increased, and regulatory legislation was drafted at state and federal levels. The tragic bombing of the federal building in Oklahoma City in 1995 focused a great deal of attention and debate about civilian paramilitary groups and organizations across America. Specific events may thus create a social issue that had languished for lack of attention until dramatized by an event. Awareness and discussion may lead to crystallizing of opinions and attitudes. However, even dramatic events rarely sway public opinion for an extended length of time.

Finally, the more abstract the goal or objective, the greater the consensus of opinion. For example, nearly everyone wants to curb the increase in crime. There is much less agreement about *how* to lower crime. The more specific a claim, the less consensus one will find among the public. Thus, many politicians are very general in their pronouncements and calls to action. There is more risk in being specific.

Despite these cautions, polls are valuable because they provide information about a specific audience. Gary Selnow argues that at the heart of polls is the ancient and simple wisdom that "information is power, power to preempt what other people are likely to do, power to manipulate how they behave."[4]

Public opinion polls, audience analysis techniques, and computer technologies have become the primary data-gathering tools and lifeblood of public persuasion campaigns. Historically, mass public persuasive campaigns were based on reaching the largest number of people with the broadest message. Perhaps in recognition of the fragmentation discussed above, the consensus about polls today is different. The more targeted the message, the better. Polls, computers, and specific databases allow greater flexibility in segmenting audiences and targeting messages.

## Persuasive Campaigns

Herbert Simons defines persuasive campaigns as "organized, sustained attempts at influencing groups or masses of people through a series of messages."[5] This definition of persuasive campaigns emphasizes three key characteristics. First, campaigns are generally well-organized events; they are not spontaneous public events. There is an identifiable organizational structure with leaders, goals, and established routines. Campaigns most often have beginning and ending dates. The second major characteristic of a campaign is the audience size of the persuasive endeavor. Persuasive messages are designed to appeal to groups and to large numbers of people. As already discussed, this factor influences greatly the form and content of messages. Finally, this definition of persuasive campaigns argues that there are multiple messages and attempts to alter the beliefs, attitudes, values, or behaviors of a segment of the general public. Single messages or persuasive attempts are only parts of a larger systematic plan of persuasion.

Broadly speaking, there are four types of campaigns that warrant discussion. While specific strategies and tactics of persuasion may overlap, these types of campaigns contain unique elements and specific processes of persuasion.

## Product or Commercial Campaigns

Product or commercial advertising campaigns are the focus of chapter 10. The purpose of such campaigns is to sell specific ideas, products, or services of identifiable commercial organizations. Advertising is the most pervasive form of persuasion in America. It is both a creative and a scientific process. Advertising campaigns are intricate and complex, utilizing psychological strategies and tactics to move consumers along a continuum from awareness to knowledge, to liking, to preference, to conviction, and to purchase. They fulfill social as well as economic functions. Because of their scope and impact, advertising campaigns are significant elements of public communication.

## Political Campaigns

Political campaigns will be discussed in chapter 11. Michael Pfau and Roxanne Parrott identify three unique features of political campaigns.[6] First, political campaigns are more person oriented rather than product, goods, or services oriented. Thus, the message will focus on a person running for office or appeals to voters. Second, political campaigns are more restricted in terms of time frame. With political campaigns, there are more specific beginning and ending points. The very specific time frame impacts strategies and media outlets, as well as various appeals. Finally, political campaigns tend to use more diverse media than other types of campaigns—speeches, debates, news media, paid advertising, brochures, posters, and bumper stickers, to name a few.

Political campaigns do more than elect public officials. They reinforce voter attitudes and help change voter preferences. They also motivate specific action, such as casting ballots on election day and volunteering to help with campaigns. By discussing issues, campaigns may stimulate awareness about vital national concerns. Political campaigns help to legitimize our brand of democracy by facilitating new leadership. Campaign-created, metapolitical images and social psychological associations provide the glue that holds our political system together. Political campaigns offer personal involvement in many forms, including direct participation, self-reflection and definition, social interaction and discussion, and aesthetic experiences of public drama and group life. Political campaigns, then, communicate and influence, motivate and inform, reinforce and convert.

## Issue Campaigns

Although related to political campaigns, issue campaigns attempt to get audiences to support a certain course of action or belief independent of official political structure, system, or procedures. Units generating such

*Advertising campaigns are significant elements of public communication.*

At AT&T, BLACK HISTORY wasn't born yesterday.

*Ruby Dee, on the job at Western Electric, 1942*

AT&T and the African American community go way back. These days, we're proud that acclaimed actress Ruby Dee is the voice of one of our key advertising campaigns. But we're even prouder that back in 1942, an unknown Ruby Dee could find employment at our Western Electric company.

That's not surprising when you consider that Alexander Graham Bell called on an African American, Lewis Latimer, to draft the plans for the very first telephone. Or that the benefits we've reaped by offering opportunity to African American employees can be measured in decades, not years.

During Black History Month, AT&T salutes the scores of talented African Americans who have helped the world discover what we've known all along. Given the opportunity, Black Americans make history every day.

**AT&T**

campaigns include political action committees, religious organizations, schools, and hospitals, to name only a few. Campaigns range from specific lobbying efforts to general public awareness campaigns.

It is interesting to note that because of the perceptions of the term *public relations*, the federal government and most state agencies only allow "public affairs" or "public information" activities. Such activities, however, are persuasive and most effective. Consider the nearly 50-year-old Smokey Bear forest-fire prevention campaign. In surveys, 98 percent of the people know who Smokey Bear is and his purpose. In addition, most people are familiar with his adage, "Only you can prevent forest fires." The Smokey Bear campaign is credited with reducing forest fires by 50 percent since 1944. Smokey is so popular and receives so much mail, he even has his own zip code (20252).[7]

There is an increasing trend toward the "organized dissemination of government information." According to Dennis Wilcox and his colleagues, the factors of increasing urban population, social mobility, societal complexity, citizen demands, and public scrutiny have all contributed to increasing volume, variety, and frequency of informative communication endeavors. News releases, press conferences, posters, reports, bulletins, special events, exhibits, broadcast public service announcements, brochures, and paid advertising are rather routine governmental communication endeavors. In fact, the federal government spends nearly $3 billion a year on "public-affairs" and "public affairs-related activities" and employs an estimated 12,000 communication specialists.[8] Because the government does not publish its own newspaper or operate radio or television stations, it must rely on communication professionals to transmit vital information to the general public. Today, it is not unusual to see local, state, or federal governments launch campaigns using press releases, press conferences, media events, and advertising. In the mid-1980s, for example, the U.S. Army was spending nearly *$70 million* a year for recruitment advertising. Recent campaigns include such diverse topics as antismoking, AIDS, drunk driving, and seat-belt safety, to name a few.

### Grassroots Lobbying

Information technology has transformed American culture and politics. One result is that corporations and trade associations are building public constituencies for their issues. The number of national citizen action groups has grown from just a handful to well over 5,000.[9] All such groups have a particular issue or larger organization to protect, define, and/or promote. Although citizen action groups have existed since the beginning of our nation's history, political action committees (PACs) are a more recent phenomenon. Beyond serving as an essential source of political campaign funding, organizational PACs often run their own issue campaigns. According to Ron Faucheux, "in the modern world,

# YOU'RE IN CHARGE.

As an Army Military Policeman you'll set the standard for
excellence. When you're required to make split second decisions of
critical importance entirely on your own, you develop something
invaluable: self-confidence and discipline. With those qualities, you'll
always be one step ahead, whether you go into civilian law enforce-
ment or any other field.

You will also be eligible for the Montgomery G.I. Bill, which
helps pay for your continuing education.

It's your decision. The U.S. Army Military Police Corps—
Assist, Protect, Defend. If you want to get an
edge on life, call 1-800-USA-ARMY today.

**ARMY M.P.
BE ALL YOU CAN BE.**

few major issues are merely lobbied anymore. Most of them are now managed, using a triad of public relations, grassroots mobilization, and lobbyists."[10] Many large public affairs firms are now organized by the divisions servicing governmental relations, public relations, and grassroots lobbying.

Citizen action groups must make four strategic decisions concerning issues and tactics: (1) whether to encourage member input; in many large citizen action groups, member participation is limited to financial contributions to the organization; (2) whether to lobby on highly visible issues with extensive media attention and to reject compromises or to work behind the scenes and bargain with opposition groups, (3) whether to use direct lobbying by the organization's staff or rely on grassroots efforts; and (4) whether to join coalitions with other groups or lobby alone.[11]

Modern grassroots lobbying is one of the hottest trends in politics today. Interest groups expand and quickly become professional; the news media can spotlight group activities, and technology makes building volunteer organizations as simple as soliciting financial support and creating/maintaining a computer database. Corporations such as tobacco giants Philip Morris and R. J. Reynolds and the waste firm WBX Technologies use proactive, grassroots mobilization for more controversial issues. Single-issue organizations such as the National Rifle Association and the American Association of Retired Persons are most sophisticated in mobilizing grassroots support.

Grassroots lobbying is the "process by which an interest group identifies, recruits, and activates citizens to contact public officials, usually legislators, on behalf of their shared public policy views."[12] Citizens targeted for mobilization usually have some affiliation with the organization and are predisposed to support the cause advocated.

There are several approaches, strategies, and tactics to grassroots lobbying. Mass or volume grassroots programs involve getting sympathizers to sign petitions, preprinted postcards or form letters, or to send mailgrams to public officials. Member mobilization is the process by which individuals are organized to demonstrate a show of strength to a public official on a certain issue. The term "astroturf" refers to a mass grassroots program that involves the instant manufacture of public support for a point of view and plays on the emotional reactions of the public to a specific event or news story. An action alert is a letter, newsletter, mailgram, phone call, fax, e-mail, or other communication from an interest group to supporters, designed to activate a response. In order to generate a response, most direct-mail solicitation stresses conflict and extremism rather than compromise or moderation. Negativism and emotional appeals characterize the vast majority of messages.[13] A "grasstops" action by an interest group involves the identification, recruitment, and activation of a small number of opinion

*Grassroots originally described the basic level of society—particularly as viewed from centralized positions of power. The voices of "ordinary" citizens are now prized targets. Techniques of mobilizing and recruiting those "grassroots" opinions are highly sophisticated and technologically advanced—and big business.*

# Real Issues
# Real People
# Real Victories
# Real Grass Roots

(Not Astroturf)

leaders and influential citizens to contact public officials through personalized letters, phone calls, or visits.

More specific tactics include telephone patch-throughs, bounce-backs, satellite conferencing, and interactive kiosks. A telephone patch-through is when an organization calls members and, if the reaction is suitable, immediately forwards the calls to an elected official so the members can deliver a personal message or view. Bounce-backs are direct-mail response vehicles signed by members and forwarded to officials to register a specific message or opinion. Satellite conferencing is an electronic meeting in which group constituents in a targeted legislator's district can discuss a specific issue or pending legislation. Interactive kiosks are exhibit booths at conventions or related conferences where interested citizens or group members may forward phone calls, faxes, or messages to elected officials.[14]

Just how do grassroots campaigns work? Let's examine a couple of examples of advocacy. The National Federation of Independent Business (NFIB) is one of the largest and most sophisticated associations in America. It has over 600,000 members. The association built a state-of-the-art information system that contains a database on members which includes names, addresses, phone and fax numbers, geographic region, legislative districts, number of employees, type of business, issue positions, and political backgrounds. The computer network is connected to fax machines that make instant communication possible. The association has 50 state directors and employs 600 field representatives whose jobs include membership growth and some lobbying activities. The membership list of NFIB is divided into several categories. The "A" list identifies 400,000 members who responded to at least one direct mail solicitation. The 200,000 "AA" list contains members who responded to more than one direct mail solicitation. The 40,000 "guardian" list contains the most active members. Finally, the most valued list is the 3,000 "key contact" members, who have close relationships with public officials and decision makers.

While direct mail is the mainstay of their communication efforts, NFIB uses extensive "telelobbying" efforts to connect members to elected officials. They report a response rate among members of 66 percent. Another technique is "rolling" of mail. This involves timing mailings among congressional districts in order to maximize the flow of member response to legislative officials.

The American Association of Retired Persons (AARP) also uses a variety of methods to mobilize their more than 33 million members. They carry a great deal of influence, especially on issues related to health care and social security. They rely on direct mail, monthly publications, and telephone trees to mobilize their most active members. In addition, they use paid ads, video teleconferencing, and community meetings to reach members. AARP employs a 10-member grassroots lobbying staff in Washington, plus another 9 field offices across the country. According

*The American Association of Retired Persons (AARP) has access to 33 million members to influence legislation.*

to John Rother, AARP's chief lobbyist, "we beefed up our grassroots efforts for health care reform [of 1994], but will keep them beefed up because of other looming issues such as entitlements and threats to Medicare."[15]

The goal of grassroots lobbying is to create massive pressure to move a legislator toward the desired position of an organization and to convince him or her to cast a key vote. The more individualized or personalized the appeal, the better. The most effective grassroots programs are those that allow constituents to communicate in their own words to legislators. Sometimes, to supplement the various contacts of voters, organizations must use the paid media to broadcast its point of view or to educate the public on the specific legislation or issue. For example, the Health Insurance Industry of America spent $15 million on television advertising during the health care debate of 1994. The now-famous television spots of "Harry and Louise" generated over 350,000 phone calls to the toll-free number resulting in over 40,000 active volunteers for the cause. The spots were targeted in specific congressional districts where members served on key legislative committees. In addition, the ads were placed on news and public affairs programs whose audiences are more likely to follow and to get involved in the debate. Overall, the total campaign generated over 200,000 contacts with members of Congress.[16]

Like most campaigns, grassroots lobbying efforts follow seven distinct phases (see figure 9.1). The first phase is research, when public attitudes as well as legislative voting records are reviewed. During this phase, the basic strategy and campaign plan is prepared. The targeting phase is when the organization determines which public officials need to hear from constituents and which constituents should be mobilized. Sensitizing is a phase unique to grassroots campaigns. The goal of this phase is to create the right political climate for the message by using public relations events, press conferences, ad campaigns, editorial board meetings, and other similar strategies. Recruitment is another unique

*Tribune* photo by John Bartley

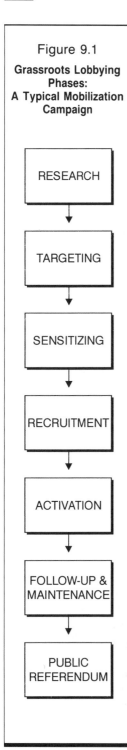

Figure 9.1

**Grassroots Lobbying Phases: A Typical Mobilization Campaign**

RESEARCH

↓

TARGETING

↓

SENSITIZING

↓

RECRUITMENT

↓

ACTIVATION

↓

FOLLOW-UP & MAINTENANCE

↓

PUBLIC REFERENDUM

and important phase to grassroots lobbying campaigns. During this phase, direct mail, phone banks, and other methods are used to recruit volunteer activists. Activation is the phase of getting volunteers to write, fax, call, or visit elected officials. During legislative battles, this phase usually occurs while legislatures are in session and focuses on key votes or issue debates. Because the ultimate success of grassroots campaigns depends on volunteers, the follow-up/maintenance phase is important for successive mobilization attempts. Organizations express appreciation to volunteers and regularly communicate with them through direct mail, newsletters, or local meetings. While listed as a discrete phase in our diagram, communication with activists is really an on-going and fundamental task of any interest group. Finally, if an issue goes to ballot or a public referendum, a political campaign must be organized and orchestrated. This requires, in many ways, a new and distinct campaign initiative.[17]

Orchestrated grassroots activities alarm many political observers. Some view grassroots lobbying as a weapon of powerful and rich corporations and special interest groups. Others, however, view such efforts as ways to reinvigorate and educate the public on issues of great importance to our nation. The orchestration of public opinion is nothing new and is certainly within our democratic tradition. The trend toward grassroots lobbying will probably increase in both level of activity and intensity in the future.

## Corporate Advocacy/Issues Management

Within recent years, corporate advocacy and issue campaigns have increased in prominence and thus merit special consideration. Corporations have expanded their public communication activities well beyond product marketing, merchandising, and advertising. Other traditional forms of corporate communication activities include:[18]

press agentry — the planning and staging of events that will attract attention to a person, product, or institution.

publicity — the placing of information in a news medium.

## Figure 9.2

### Planning an Event for News Coverage

An important part of the process of designing persuasive campaigns involves planning public events that may be covered as part of the day's news. Press conferences, open meetings, rallies, and protests can become powerful forums for the communication of a group's social or political agenda. Many now routinely employ guidelines developed by political campaigners, who have always needed to reach potential supporters via the "free" news media. Here is a list of common rules for promoting the coverage of an event by the broadcast and print media:

- Schedule events early in the day, at times convenient for the media from whom you want coverage. If you want to make a noon newscast, plan a 9:30 to 10:00 A.M. starting time.
- Organize the event around one basic theme. Determine the "lead" you want the press to write, then organize the event to achieve it.
- Make sure your primary spokesperson is well briefed with accurate information and knowledge of the questions he or she may be asked.
- Call assignment editors and ask for coverage. In the unsubtle publicity arts, shyness is not a virtue.
- Make your event as visual as possible. The announcement of a lawsuit against a local polluter will be more interesting to television if it is made at the site of the pollution rather than in an organization's office.
- Prepare packets of information to back up your basic message. Make it as easy as possible for reporters to get the necessary facts.
- Consider the convenience of the reporters from whom you want coverage. Will they need telephones, suitable background and lighting for video, a common audio feed from the public address system, a place to sit, etc.?
- If the goal is television and radio coverage, break up your statement into short, quotable segments. In a perfect world the average television news story would run longer than 40 seconds. Because short stories are the rule, your advocate will probably receive a 15-second "sound bite." Make it count.
- If members of the press fail to attend, send them coverage of the event anyway: press releases with relevant quotes to the print media; your own videotape with sound bites and interesting shots to the television media.

> promotion—the garnering of support and endorsement for a person, product, or institution.
>
> public affairs—the working with public officials, legislative bodies, or interest groups in local communities promoting organizational citizenship.

In the early 1970s, corporations were suffering from a variety of social and economic problems: recession, inflation, oil crises, decline of public trust, increase of public hostility toward large companies, and increased legislative restrictions and controls upon corporate America. In this social and political environment, corporations developed extensive public relations staffs whose jobs were to present the companies' policies to the public through the distribution of information. Today, most corporate communication endeavors are mainly persuasive activities. Practitioners must possess the skills necessary for developing and executing strategic communication campaigns and activities. They require the skills of anticipation, interpretation of public opinion, research, campaign implementation, and evaluation. Most corporate communication professionals argue that public relations is a social science utilizing the latest communication skills, theories, and technologies.

Public relations campaigns are designed to address an issue, to solve a problem, or to improve a situation. Doug Newsom, Alan Scott, and Judy Turk identify five types of public relations campaigns.[19] A "public awareness" campaign is designed simply to make people aware of something. This type of campaign ranges from something as simple as the date of a school opening to a local civic event. A "public information" campaign goes beyond citizen awareness of an event and also shares some vital information. For example, in addition to publicizing the emergency 911 phone number, there is usually some explanation of its use. A "public education" campaign goes an additional step beyond awareness and information to explanation of the material to the extent that the public can apply the information to daily behavior. Some of the contemporary campaigns on drugs, smoking, and drunk driving, for example, may attempt to "reinforce existing attitudes and behavior," or to "change or modify existing attitudes and behavior." Finally, "behavior modification" campaigns are the most difficult and complex. As you can see, the defining focus of the various types of public relations campaigns is on the desired outcome or behavior of the targeted audience.

Corporations, for many years, have been concerned with their overall image in the general public. They recognized the value of maintaining an image and public "goodwill." Today, however, corporations are more aggressive in their public communication endeavors and are more willing to engage in open debate about a variety of social issues. They compete for public attitudes and/or behavior that will influence legislators, product purchases, and stock decisions. In exercising their First Amendment right of freedom of speech, companies are increasingly asserting their own social, political, and economic agendas. The participation in the formation of public opinion is now an essential element of corporate public relations. Such activities are part of a genre of advertising known as corporate advocacy and issue management.

Prakash Sethi defines advocacy advertising as "the propagation of ideas and elucidation of controversial social issues of public importance in a manner that supports the position and interests of the sponsor while expressly denying the accuracy of facts and downgrading the sponsor's opponents."[20] The goals of advocacy advertising are to counteract public hostility to corporate activities, to counter the spread of misleading information by critics of the organization, to educate the public on complex issues of importance to an organization, to counteract inadequate access to and bias in the news media, and to promote the values of free enterprise.[21]

*Issues management includes advocacy advertising and proactive public relations. When AT&T announced that it would begin laying off 40,000 workers, public sentiment—already sensitized to downsizing trends—was highly negative toward the company. AT&T took out full-page advertisements in major newspapers in March 1996 to demonstrate their efforts to help those who lost their jobs. As mentioned in chapter 1, cigarette companies also devote considerable efforts to inform the public about positions taken and efforts expended.*

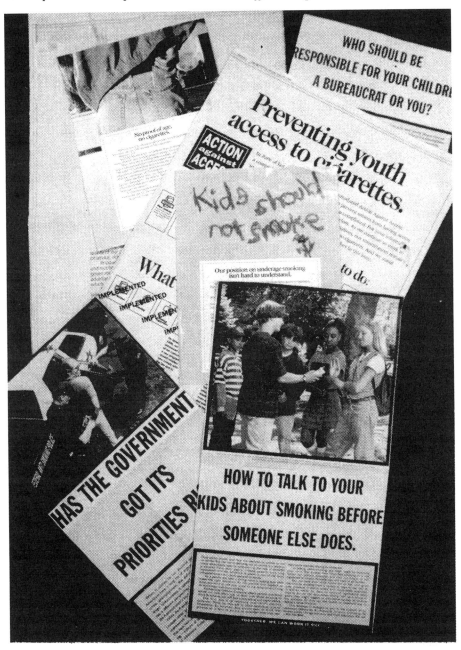

Issues management encompasses more strategic activities than does advocacy advertising. Issues management includes proactive public relations activities designed to head off problems between corporations and their publics. According to Robert Heath and Kenneth Cousino, the process involves the functions of involvement of public policy experts in strategic business planning and management, issue communication, issue monitoring and analysis, and efforts to meet changing standards of corporate social responsibility.[22]

One of the earliest and most successful advocacy campaigns has been the Mobil op-ed advertising program. Since 1970, Mobil has provided "editorial ads" placed in newspapers, news magazines, and service-club magazines like *Rotarian, Kiwanian,* and *Elks.* The goal, according to Mobil's public affairs director Herb Schmertz, was for the company to inject "into the debate, and to make sure [our] viewpoint [was] heard by the intellectual establishment."[23] The approach was to "take the offensive without being offensive."[24] "In political terms," according to Schmertz, "the ads constitute the platform on which we run. Each week, in effect, we add another plank or reinforce a previous one. To continue the analogy, we are continually seeking new supporters among the undecided, and one way we do this is by a continuing series of position papers on the important issues of the day."[25]

When Mobil began the campaign in 1970, three major issues faced the oil industry: oil cutoffs from foreign nations, environmental concerns from the public over oil drilling and excavation, and low public confidence in the credibility of corporations. The first op-ed piece appeared on October 19, 1970, with the headline: "America has the world's best highways and the world's worst mass transit. We hope this ad moves people . . ." The ad was not self-serving but actually addressed the need for more and better mass transit systems to reduce oil consumption. Ultimately, Mobil wants to portray itself as a credible champion of public interest. Based on content analyses of Mobil Oil's op-ed ads from 1982–86, Gerri Smith and Robert Heath found both moral and expertise appeals.[26] The moral appeals involved traditional values and sought to enhance the company's image and to convince the audience that it was morally wrong not to agree or comply with the message. The use of expertise appeals attempted to enhance the company's credibility. From the beginning, Mobil accepted the long-term perspective, realizing that it would take years for the campaign to yield results.

The broad issues of primary concern to corporations tend to revolve around the environment, public health and safety, and specific governmental regulations. For example, oil and chemical companies usually address environmental issues of conservation and pollution. Tobacco companies address freedom of choice and smokers' rights. Insurance companies actively support seat belts and airbags for automobiles.

# Electric vehicles: a promise too far

While the road to cleaner air may be paved with good intentions, it's also littered with broken promises. Take the promise of cleaner air—a promise some states have used to mandate the sale of electric vehicles (EVs).

According to a recent U.S. General Accounting Office (GAO) report, when the impact of electricity generation is included, new EVs use more energy and generate more air pollution than the average new gasoline-powered car. Other roadblocks to widespread use of EVs include battery technology, cost, safety and convenience. Efforts to overcome these barriers the GAO noted, "are inherently risky and will require substantial time, money and attention."

The biggest push for EVs has come from the states, though federal support exists as well. Without waiting for evidence that EVs can deliver, California, Massachusetts and New York have mandated market shares for EVs—2 percent of new car sales in 1998, rising to 10 percent by 2003. Other states have said they'll keep an EV option open.

After nearly two years of research, the GAO basically concluded EVs aren't ready. Nor are they likely to become so even in the rosiest of scenarios. Here are some key findings:

■ Battery technology just cannot compete with internal combustion engines today or in the foreseeable future in terms of driving range, power and recharging capability. Today's commercially available EVs have a driving range of 30–50 miles under city driving conditions. Even advanced technology batteries only have a range of 80–100 miles.

■ Electric vehicles are expensive—costing two to three times more than conventional autos. Even at mass production volumes, EVs with lead-based batteries are likely to be priced 20 percent higher, while those using more advanced battery technologies will cost substantially more.

■ EVs present some potential safety hazards. Some batteries use toxic, corrosive and explosive chemicals; some use higher voltage, which poses a potentially lethal shock hazard. Battery weight may affect a vehicle's maneuverability; and questions on their "crashworthiness" remain unanswered.

■ The environmental benefits of EVs are dubious—particularly if one considers the impact of generating the required electricity, which state regulators should be doing. If they did they'd know that when EVs are substituted for gasoline-powered autos, primary energy consumption increases by some 30 percent, greenhouse gas emissions rise by 5 percent and sulfur dioxide emissions climb over 700 percent.

It's time to take another approach. Mandates won't make "promises" come true. And putting EVs on the road before they can produce on those promises is the wrong thing to do to consumers and the nation's clean air effort. It's a price tag that gives no value for the money we'll pay.

Brad Hainsworth argues that corporate issues evolve in a rather predictable manner.[27] The process is composed of four stages: origin, mediation and amplification, organization, and resolution. In the origin stage, "an issue arises when an organization or public attaches significance to a perceived problem that is a consequence of a developing political, economic, or social trend."[28] Issues already defined and being addressed are more a problem of crisis management than issue management. Awareness and concern are expressed by identifiable publics or social groups. Conflict begins to emerge over the perceived problem, and there are calls to do something about the issue. Corporations must constantly survey the social and political environment for such issues. The process of mediation and amplification occurs when multiple publics (i.e., interest groups, professions, and industries) expand the discussion of the issue through specialized media and begin to address policy implications. Regulations may be drafted or legislation proposed. Theorists argue it is at this stage of issue development that an organization may have the greatest influence on further development and resolution of the issue. The organizational stage of issue emergence is when publics unite around the issue and support specific actions of resolution. Public visibility is heightened, and the issue is propelled into public debate and policy process. Opinion leaders and public officials rally around the issue and seek a resolution to the conflict. The resolution stage is when the issue or conflict is addressed through legislation or regulatory policies. Thus, within this process, corporate advocacy and issue management efforts first attempt early identification of potential issues and follow up with efforts to influence the policy-making process.

Corporations use a variety of media to address various issues of image and public policy. For example, Dow Chemical Company has generated a series of television ads that portray young college graduates excited about the opportunity to solve farming and world food crises by working for Dow Chemical. Their musical tag line is, "Dow lets you do great things!" Dow Chemical may also be remembered for its chemical warfare products used in Vietnam and more recently as the parent company of Dow Corning which filed for chapter 11 bankruptcy to stave off product-liability claims over the manufacture of breast implants. Obviously, to attract bright young people, Dow must present an image of a good place to work and a humanitarian corporation.

Several years ago Dow distributed a publication entitled "Life is in the Balance" to college deans and professors.[29] The purpose of the brochure was "to explain how a 'balance' in life can be achieved when risks and the benefits derived from activities are understood." They suggested "it could be used as reference or extra reading material for the courses you offer." Additional copies were available for the asking.

The attractive brochure argued that risk taking is a normal part of everyday life. While risk can be reduced, it can never be totally

*The issue of informed choice is often the foundation of many issues campaigns. The emphasis may change from alcohol to tobacco to red meat to the use of chemicals in the environment, but the theme is to weigh risks versus benefits.*

 DOW CHEMICAL U.S.A.

MIDLAND, MICHIGAN 48674

**"LIFE IS IN THE BALANCE" BROCHURE**

Dear College Dean, Department Head or Professor,

Enclosed is a copy of the brochure "Life is in the Balance." The brochure discusses risk assessment in layman's terms and cites numerous examples from industry and everyday life in which risk analysis is important. The brochure also helps to explain how a "balance" in life can be achieved when risks, and the benefits derived from activities are understood.

You have been sent a copy of the brochure because of your influence in education in the United States and around the world. As you read the brochure please consider keeping it, or giving it to someone in your institution or department that could put it to the best use. For instance, it could be used as reference or extra reading material for the courses you offer.

National distribution of the brochure has begun, with the objective being to inform educators, opinion leaders, policy-makers, and citizens about the importance of taking risks and benefits into account when making decisions that influence the future of our society.

More free copies of the brochure can be obtained by calling Dow Literature Services at 517-636-1834 and requesting Form #233-34.

Thank you for using the brochure to communicate the importance of risk analysis to your colleagues and the students that are taught at your institution.

Sincerely,

*J. E. LeBeau*

J. E. LeBeau
R&D Director, Health and Environmental Sciences

Enclosure

AN OPERATING UNIT OF THE DOW CHEMICAL COMPANY

eliminated. The brochure provides the example, "Our risk is diminished when we cross the ocean in an oceanliner rather than a rowboat, but the crossing never becomes risk free—as passengers on the *Titanic* found out. The only way to eliminate the risk is to eliminate the ocean, which we cannot do" (page 8 of brochure). As the argument develops, risk reduction is a matter of cost. "Many of the costs of risk reduction are obvious, but some are not . . . the consumer may think government risk reduction measures are free, when in reality they are not. . . . If overly stringent environmental or risk reduction measures are forced on industry, products may become so costly that American products will be priced right out of world markets. . . . Lost jobs and a lesser share of the international market are very expensive hidden costs" (page 9 of brochure).

The brochure corrects the myth that nature is somehow "the good guy." After all, the bubonic plague "wiped out 25 million Europeans in the 14th Century, and today, six million children in the Third World die yearly of diarrhea" (page 13 of brochure).

Another issue addressed in the brochure through the argument of risk management is cancer. While certainly a problem, "we should keep all cancer-causing factors in perspective" (page 16 of brochure).

The brochure concludes by advising that we should prioritize risks in a rational and reasonable way. "For we must, as a national society, and as members of a global community, decide where to put our time, energy, and resources of both people and money" (page 18 of brochure). Above all, we must not view "technology as the bad guy." "Some people blame technology for today's problems, while forgetting that it has cured many. . . . Living is, and always has been, a risky business" (page 20 of brochure). Our children "should have some choice in their own tomorrow—a choice to risk sorrow and learn from it, and above all, the right to risk failure for success and joy!" (page 20 of brochure).

Needless to say, the brochure is a persuasive document, not merely an informative one. Through the concept of risk management, the document attempts to reduce our fears of environmental contamination, warns against cancer, warns against excessive governmental regulation and celebrates the values of technology. It is important to Dow Chemical Company that the public understand and appreciate the role and value of chemicals in contemporary life. What better way to disseminate the message than to have it presented in a college classroom?

An aggressive corporate advocacy and issue management perspective allows large companies to become active players in the political process. There are some legitimate causes for concern. Large corporations have access to media and multimillion-dollar budgets, unlike most citizens and civic groups. How will opposing viewpoints or legitimate challenges to corporate claims and information be disseminated? Should corporations pay for such ads from after-tax profits, or are these campaigns general business expenses and thus tax deductible?

# Social Movements

There have been times in our nation's history when large groups of citizens mobilized to express anger, support, or ideas about a wide variety of issues and topics. Groups were organized by race, sex, age, and social or political beliefs. Actions ranged from advocacy to violent demonstrations. From the American Revolution to the Moral Majority, Americans have always joined together to exercise, and sometimes even stretch, the principles of democracy. Such social collective actions are called social movements and are a special form or type of persuasive campaign. Charles Stewart, Craig Smith, and Robert Denton argue that social movements are unique, with special characteristics that distinguish them from other forms and functions of mass persuasion.[30]

## Characteristics

Social movements must have a *minimal organization*. This means that there are identifiable leaders and proclaimed followers. Some movements are more organized than others. During the 1960s, the civil rights movement was well organized, with Martin Luther King recognized as the major leader; the American Indian movement was less visible and much smaller in scope. It should be noted that there may be many organizations within the same basic movement. For example, within the prolife movement there are various religious and secular organizations that seek legislation limiting abortions.

Social movements are *uninstitutionalized collectivities* because they operate outside the established social order. This means that access to institutional channels of power, communication, and funding are not available. The activities of most unions, PACs, and certainly legislative committees are not social movements. Such groups, however, may have been part of a movement. For example, the United Auto Workers was at one time a movement organization but today is part of the established order.

Movements must be *significantly large in scope*. Movements must be large enough in terms of geographic area, time, and participants to accomplish specified programs and tasks. The larger the movement, the greater the visibility and funding possibilities. Movements grow from the ground up rather than some institutional, downward formation.

Movements *propose or oppose programs for change in societal norms, values, or both*. Innovative social movements, for example, may seek a limited replacement or reform of existing norms or values with totally new ones. Examples of innovative movements include women's rights, black civil rights, or gay liberation movements. Revivalistic movements seek replacement or reform of existing norms or values with ones from an idealized past. The Native American and the Back to Africa movements are examples of revivalistic movements. Finally, resistance movements are those that seek to block changes in the existing norms or values. Often, such movements favor the status quo and arise in opposition to newly formed movements. Classification of movements is difficult because perceptions of members and audiences vary. A movement may seem just and moderate to some members but radical to many citizens.

A movement's rhetoric is *moral in tone.* Movement leaders and followers view their actions as a moral imperative, a mission to correct social injustice or evil. While their goals and objectives may be concrete, such as a specific piece of legislation, their philosophy is elaborate, righteous, and principled.

Social movements are *countered by an institution.* The established order is more than just governmental officials. It includes various organizations such as universities, churches, businesses, regulatory bodies, and so on. Sooner or later, challenges to social norms and the status quo will generate opposition. The established order has many resources and avenues available to confront and to stall movement actions.

Finally, *persuasion is pervasive* in social movements. As Stewart, Smith, and Denton argue, "persuasion is a communication process by which a social movement seeks through the use of verbal and nonverbal symbols to affect audience perceptions and thus to bring about changes in ways of thinking, feeling, and/or acting."[31] Violence associated with social movements is incidental and used primarily for symbolic purposes. Persuasion is the primary means for satisfying the major functions and requirements of social movements.

### Persuasive Functions

Social movements must fulfill a number of roles if they hope to contribute significantly to change. Stewart, Smith, and Denton identify four basic persuasive functions: transform perceptions of reality, prescribe and sell courses of action, mobilize the disaffected, and sustain the social movement.[32] Transforming perceptions of reality include altering over time perceptions of the past, present, and future. Movements must challenge accepted ways of viewing historical events and people in order to emphasize the severity of a problem and the need for drastic action. While most Americans initially viewed our involvement in Vietnam as support for a free, democratic country against communist aggression, some claimed that our actions were aggressive, intrusive, and provided aid for a dictator and repressive government. The women's movement had to confront the established view that the woman's place was in the home caring for the children while a husband established a career and provided for the family.

There are several ways movements alter the perceptions of the present. For example, renaming or redefining an event or object provides an opportunity for people to view the circumstance differently. Within the prolife movement, language referring to the fetus as a baby and abortion as murder has a strong impact upon a listener. Movements create "god terms" and "devil terms" to create clear images of good and bad behavior or thought. For most Americans "god terms" include democracy, freedom, liberty, equality, and justice, to name only a few. "Devil terms" would be opposite notions such as communism, slavery, or prejudice. Another common way to alter perceptions of the present is to provide information that counters or demonstrates inconsistencies with the information provided by the established order.

Social movement leaders, like political candidates, must provide a utopian vision of the future that is full of hope and optimism. At the same time, the vision of a utopian future is tempered by bleak images if the goals of the movement are not met.

In transforming perceptions of society, movements must alter not only perceptions of the opposition but also current perceptions of the movement and its members. The opposition must be portrayed as bad with selfish motives and no redeeming value. The opposition are grand conspirators who have secretly committed a crime against the people. They are, according to the movement, the sole cause of the problem at hand. The opposition is subjected to name calling, ridicule, and cruel associations. The movement is simply at war with the opposition.

Social movements must transform self-perceptions of members to believe in the righteousness of their cause and in their power to accomplish the goals of the movement. For example, the women's liberation movement conducted "consciousness-raising" groups to enhance self-concept, dignity, and worth. Through this transformation, women could recognize their potential and gain strength to compete in a "man's world." In the 1960s, blacks selected the word *black* to replace the word *Negro*, which had been selected by whites. "Black power" became the symbol for independence, power, and dignity.

In prescribing courses of action, social movements must first explain what should be done. Movements must not only develop a program of change with specific demands, actions, and solutions to problems, but they must also sell, defend, and justify the program to the people. In addition, movements must prescribe who ought to do the job. They provide rationales for why their organization, leaders, and members are best to bring about the desired change. Finally, movements must articulate how the changes should be brought about. This may be one of the more critical persuasive tasks. Movement members differ in terms of intensity of feeling, identification with the cause, social abuse, and patience. Thus, the more radical factions or members may prefer ultimatums, confrontation, or terrorism to bring about the desired change. Others may prefer nonviolent resistance tactics such as sit-ins, boycotts, or strikes. Others may simply wish to petition the establishment for a fair hearing, preferring to work within the legislative structure to bring about the desired change.

The most difficult persuasive task for any movement leader is to inspire people to believe, join, and participate in the movement. Movements encounter opposition; available channels of communication are restricted. Leaders must continually attempt to disseminate the movement's message in order to attract new members and to maintain old ones. Leaders must unify, organize, and energize a diverse membership while simultaneously pressuring the opposition and never losing sight of the ultimate goal.

Social movements often last for years; sustaining a movement is a major persuasive task. It is easier to start a movement than to sustain one. Leaders must justify setbacks and remain optimistic about accomplishing movement goals. For the movement to be successful, it must remain visible and viable. As a movement becomes older, these tasks become more difficult.

### Life Cycle

Although it is nearly impossible to divide movements into separate phases, there are recognizable patterns of development. Stewart, Smith, and Denton identify five stages of social movements: genesis, social unrest, enthusiastic mobilization, maintenance, and termination.[33] As a movement matures, the persuasive requirements evolve and change among the various stages.

The genesis stage consists primarily of intellectuals or prophets articulating some imperfection in society through essays, editorials, songs, poems, pamphlets, lectures, or books. They identify a problem and visualize a bleak future if the problem is not solved. Bob Dylan and others addressed the Vietnam War in folk songs nearly a year before the Gulf of Tonkin incident that escalated American involvement in the conflict. Betty Friedan's book entitled *The Feminine Mystique* initiated the women's movement by addressing status and the need for change. Such works provide a source for public discussion about key issues. Sometimes a special event will trigger attention to an issue or cause. The Supreme Court decision of 1973 allowing abortion in all the states provided the impetus for creating the prolife movement.

In the social unrest stage, prophets and intellectuals become agitators, and the purpose and goals of the movement develop. Concerned citizens alerted to the problems become active members. The movement produces its own literature, often including a manifesto or declaration presented at a convention or conference. The ideology clearly identifies the "devils" responsible for the problem and the "gods" who will forge solutions. In attempting to transform perceptions of society, such we-they distinctions are extremely important. Most rhetorical energies during this stage involve petitioning the groups perceived to be responsibile for the status quo. When such institutions frustrate the movement's efforts, members become disaffected and enter the enthusiastic mobilization stage.

The enthusiastic mobilization period of a social movement is exciting. The charismatic leader emerges and captures a great deal of attention for the movement and its issues. Membership expands to include sympathizers from both the general public and the establishment. All available channels and means of communication are utilized to advance the cause. The movement must now confront serious opposition, and the strategies must extend beyond legislative petition and discursive measures. Mass rallies and demonstrations are used to disseminate the movement's message and to pressure the opposition. The persuasive goal of the movement during this phase is to raise the consciousness level of the public and to force the establishment to comply with movement demands.

It is difficult to maintain the energy and enthusiasm of the earlier stages. As defeats mount and goals are not immediately realized, the members become impatient and the public becomes bored. In the maintenance stage, persuasive tactics focus on legislative measures, membership retention, and fund raising. The leadership changes from agitators to statesmen. The primary channels of communication are newsletters, journals, and the occasional television talk show. Sweeping demands are compromised and the rhetoric is moderated. As noted earlier, movement visibility and viability are primary concerns.

In the termination stage, the social movement ceases to be a social movement. The movement may have accomplished its goal (as did the antislavery movement of 1865 with the passage of the Thirteenth Amendment to the Constitution) or it may be transformed into part of the establishment (as was the Nazi movement in Germany). Some movements die while others become pressure groups, such as the American Indian movement or the consumer rights movement. Few social movements are totally successful in their efforts. Some members become disaffected with the movement and drop out or join a splinter group while others simply become part of "the system."

Each stage requires specific persuasive skills, personalities, and tactics. In open societies, social movements are often the primary initiators of social change. Thus, although all social movements end, they do impact society in a variety of ways, such as new laws, social awareness, or new social groups, to name only a few.

*Leadership*

As already noted, the type of leadership skills and qualities needed change as a social movement grows and develops. Social movement leaders do not come from the marginal areas or "lunatic fringe" of society but from the higher-strata groups and subcultures—teachers, students, business, clergy, and so on.[34] While they are decision makers, they lack the powers of reward and punishment usually associated with more traditional views of leadership. Movement leaders are confronted with a variety of tasks, pressures, and audiences. Most leaders must be capable of handling diverse and often conflicting roles on a daily basis. They must be presentable to media and establishment members as well as acceptable to the "true believers" of the movement. Perhaps the most important function of social movement leaders is as the symbol of their movement. They are identified with its mission and cause and are responsible for the members' actions.

Movement leaders obtain their positions by being perceived as charismatic, prophetic, or pragmatic. While charisma is a public presence that instills pride and confidence, prophecy relates to the leader's ideology and the ability to articulate movement principles, values, and beliefs. Of course, a leader must ultimately get something done. A mere ideologue will not last long.

Movement leadership is a difficult and challenging task. Without question, most movement leaders are admired by some and hated by others. They must be able to handle diverse and conflicting roles, change as the movement changes, adapt to events, and lead without getting too far ahead or behind their movements.

### Resistance to Social Movements

Because establishments have a strong commitment to maintain "law and order," it is not surprising—in fact, it should be expected—that they will respond to disruptions and challenges to the social order.[35] In a democratic society, just how strong should the response be? While the First Amendment protects freedom of speech, there are certainly limits of expression. When does a shout become disruptive? When does a gesture become obscene? In essence, how does the establishment balance its legal obligations and the rights of society against the rights of individuals, minorities, and/or unpopular ideas or opinions?

There are four general strategies employed by the established order to confront and resist social movements.[36] The strategy of avoidance attempts to counter challenges with persuasive efforts that discredit a movement's goals and leaders. Leaders may claim that the movement threatens democracy and promotes anarchy. Movement leaders are characterized as extremists or fanatics. Such rhetoric will often generate fear among the "silent majority." From a bureaucratic perspective, government agencies can postpone action upon movement requests or deny permits for meetings or parades.

A more aggressive approach is the strategy of suppression which involves tactics ranging from general harassment to prosecution of social movement leaders and members. Covert means of harassment include such activities as police arrests and creation of secret files. More overt forms include tax audits, military reclassifications, challenges to government funding or loans—to name only a few. Such tactics send a powerful message to movement leaders and followers. They may create fear and hesitation among movement members as well as portray movement leaders as criminal and dangerous citizens.

The strategy of adjustment gives the appearance of working with the movement, providing some concessions without accepting movement demands or goals. Symbolic gestures may include appointing special committees or commissions to study proposals, firing or replacing mid-level personnel who were targets of attacks, or incorporating movement leaders and sympathizers within the institutional structure.

The strategy of capitulation is the total acceptance of a movement's goals, beliefs, and ideology. This rarely occurs because the established order has too many resources and controls communication channels. However, over a period of time, many movement goals and objectives find their way into mainstream American life.

Because social movements are such a unique phenomenon and an important part of American history, we have provided a detailed perspective of movement campaigns and persuasion.

# Campaign Implementation

The key to the execution of any successful campaign is systematic planning. The basic steps in developing a campaign are the same regardless of its size, scope, or focus. While many schemes are available, we prefer to focus on six basic considerations that would be appropriate for nearly all types of campaigns. The considerations are: situation analysis, objectives and/or positioning, strategies, budget, implementation, and evaluation.[37]

1. A careful *situation analysis* provides an assessment of the social environment, potential audiences or market, and product or idea strengths and weaknesses. From an advertising perspective, the situation analysis includes investigations of the consumer, the product, and the competition. Research becomes vital to this phase of campaign planning. There are two basic ways to gather information: secondary and primary research. Secondary research is finding relevant information that is already produced and collected by others. The major source of secondary research is the local library. Such research can provide a general orientation and guide for campaign planning. Primary research is original research conducted to gather specific information. For example, although secondary research efforts may reveal a national trend toward more healthy food and drink, a specific survey may be needed to isolate probable successful appeals and which categories of food items to target.

In terms of the audience, there are three descriptive variables that should be investigated. Demographic characteristics are derived from statistical studies of the population. Such characteristics include age, sex, income, education, family size, and occupation. Geographic characteristics focus on differences among urban, suburban, and rural areas of the country as well as regional differences. Finally, psychographic analysis attempts to describe markets based on lifestyle issues, activities, interests, and opinions. From this brief overview of the situation analysis step of campaign planning, we can see that the primary purpose is to gather needed information that will become the basis for designing the persuasive message, strategies, and execution.

2. After research has been conducted and analyzed, *objectives* should be determined. Objectives are clear, specific, and measurable statements of desired outcomes of the campaign. Clear objectives help reduce uncertainty, direct message formation, and provide standards for evaluation. Some objectives may be stated in terms of unit or dollar sales. Others may be set in terms of some type of behavioral activity by the audience. For example, the targeted audience of the campaign may be asked to purchase a product, call a number, return a reply card, seek more information, contribute to a cause, vote for a specific candidate, or attend an event. Sometimes the objectives focus on communication effects such as general awareness, message recall, product knowledge and preference, or issue-position conviction. Campaign organizers must know what the campaign seeks to accomplish. Different objectives will influence how the campaign is developed.

3. If objectives are concerned with *what* needs to be done, then *strategies* are concerned with *how* to do it. Strategic areas of concern include message construction, media selection, tactics, publicity, and promotions. The goal of the message strategy, according to Michael Rothschild, is "to develop a message or a series of messages that will be informative and persuasive in their compelling presentation of relevant issues to the target audience."[38] The key to most successful strategies is to isolate the appeals, promises, solutions, or benefits that will have the greatest impact upon the target audience. Good research provides the clues to message creation and tactic selection. (Message construction strategies are discussed in detail in chapters 4, 6, and 13.)

4. Whether conducting a commercial advertising campaign or a political campaign, *budget* impacts all other elements of campaign design and development. For some campaigns, budgets are of little concern; for others, funds may be limited. Today with the cost of media, labor, and material, the campaign budget becomes a vital consideration in the formation of a campaign.

5. After the previous steps have been conducted, the chosen plan of action must be *implemented*. Timing is important and follow-up both reinforces impressions made and provides the foundation for the final step.

6. Finally, the campaign should be *evaluated*. A systematic evaluation of the campaign not only reveals what worked and what did not work but also allows for the fine-tuning of various campaign elements in order to maximize effectiveness. Commercial advertising campaign evaluation is a form of research that attempts to determine what actually happened in the marketplace and why. There are many things to measure other than a win-lose situation. Elements of awareness (knowledge, recall, or recognition), attitude (perceptions, feelings, or preferences), and behavior (purchase, vote, or support) are examples of areas to assess and evaluate. Many of the same research techniques used in analyzing the situation can be used in evaluating the persuasive campaign.

Figure 9.3

**Campaign Implementation Overview**

| *Stage* | *Components* |
|---|---|
| 1. Situation analysis | target audience |
| | product/issue/idea |
| | competition or opponent |
| 2. Objectives | mission |
| | goals |
| | outcomes |
| 3. Strategies | messages |
| | media |
| | presentation activities |
| 4. Budget | labor |
| | material |
| | media |
| | talent |
| | production |
| 5. Implementation | timing |
| | follow-up |
| 6. Evaluation | what people say |
| | what people think |
| | what people do |

# Summary

Public persuasion differs from interpersonal persuasion in size and scope. The larger the audience, the more elements of persuasion that are needed to alter beliefs, attitudes, and values. Mass persuasion requires numerous messages, numerous appeals, and numerous communication channels. Persuasive campaigns, therefore, are a highly organized and constructed series of messages designed to meet all these criteria. The messages must appeal to large numbers of people.

The systematic execution of a campaign includes analyzing the situation, developing objectives, planning strategies, preparing budgets, implementing the campaign, and evaluating its success. These processes are true for all types of campaigns: product advertising, political, and issue, which includes grassroots and corporate advocacy/issue management.

Although a form of public persuasion, social movements are unique collective phenomena that are more complex than the other types of campaigns. Persuasion is the essence of social movements. It is the key ingredient needed to transform conceptions of history, alter current perceptions, prescribe courses of action, mobilize for action, and sustain the movement. Across the various stages of a movement—genesis, social unrest, enthusiastic mobilization, maintenance, and termination— persuasion requirements evolve and change.

Social movements have played an important role in our society. They have stimulated argument and debate about human rights, war, and peace. They have provided the catalyst for social change and legislative action. Public persuasion is a vital part of a democratic society influencing what we want, what we buy, what we think, and how we interact with others.

## Questions and Projects for Further Study

1. Select a product and find ads for the item in 8 to 10 different magazines. How are the ads similar? How do they differ?

2. Select an example of the following types of campaigns: commercial advertising, political, governmental, corporate advocacy and issue management. How are they similar? How do they differ?

3. Formulate a hypothetical product and develop a campaign according to the steps presented in the chapter.

4. Construct a national public relations campaign on the issue of alcohol abuse using awareness, information, education, reinforcement, and behavior modification approaches. How are they similar? How do they differ?

5. According to the criteria presented in the chapter, which of the following is a social movement? Why?

    survivalists
    consumer rights
    ecology
    American Indian
    Nazi
    Gray Panthers
    tax reform
    Greenpeace

6. Select a social movement and demonstrate how the movement fulfills the persuasive functions identified in the chapter.

# Notes

[1] Robin Lakoff, *Talking Power: The Language of Politics*. NY: Basic Books, 1990, p. 1.

[2] Shearon Lowery and Melvin DeFleur, *Milestones in Mass Communication Research*, Third Edition. New York: Longman, 1995, p. 11.

[3] Dennis Wilcox, Phillip Ault, and Warren Agee, *Public Relations: Strategies and Tactics*, Fourth Edition. New York: HarperCollins, 1995, p. 258.

[4] Gary Selnow, *High-tech Campaigns: Computer Technology in Political Communication*. Westport, CT: Praeger, 1994.

[5] Herbert Simons, *Persuasion*, Second Edition. New York: Random House, 1986, p. 227.

[6] Michael Pfau and Roxanne Parrott, *Persuasive Communication Campaigns*. Boston: Allyn & Bacon, 1993, pp. 332–33.

[7] Doug Newsom, Alan Scott, and Judy Turk, *This is PR: The Realities of Public Relations*, Fourth Edition. Belmont, CA: Wadsworth, 1989, p. 315.

[8] Wilcox, et al., p. 389.

[9] Stephen Frantzich, *Political Parties in the Technological Age*. New York: Longman, 1989, p. 195.

[10] Ron Faucheux, "The Grassroots Explosion," *Campaigns & Elections*, December/January 1995, p. 20.

[11] Kenneth Godwin, *One Billion Dollars of Influence*. Chatham, NJ: Chatham House, 1988, p. 74.

[12] Faucheux, p. 22.

[13] Godwin, p. 94.

[14] Faucheux, p. 22.

[15] *Ibid.*, p. 23.

[16] *Ibid.*, p. 25, 53.

[17] *Ibid.*, p. 23.

[18] These forms of corporate communication are common to most introductory texts. For example, see Newsom, Scott, and Turk, pp. 6–10.

[19] *Ibid.*, pp. 294–96.

[20] S. Prakash Sethi, *Advocacy Advertising and Large Corporations*. Lexington, MA: Lexington Books, 1977, p. 7.

[21] *Ibid.*, p. 57.

[22] Robert Heath and Kenneth Cousino, "Issues Management: End of First Decade Progress Report," *Public Relations Review*, Vol. XVI, No. 1, Spring 1990, p .10.

[23] Herb Schmertz, *Good-bye to the Low Profile: The Art of Creative Confrontation*. Boston: Little, Brown & Co., 1986, p. 133.

[24] *Ibid.*, p 138.

[25] *Ibid.*, p. 134.

[26] Gerri Smith and Robert Heath, "Moral Appeals in Mobil Oil's Op-Ed Campaign," *Public Relations Review*, Vol. XVI, No. 4, Winter 1990, pp. 48–54.

[27] Brad E. Hainsworth, "The Distribution of Advantages and Disadvantages," *Public Relations Review*, Vol. XVI, No. 1, Spring 1990, pp. 34–36.

[28] *Ibid.*, p. 34.

[29] Elyse Rogers, "Life Is In the Balance," Dow Chemical USA, 1991, Midland, Michigan.

[30] See Charles Stewart, Craig Smith, and Robert E. Denton, Jr., *Persuasion and Social Movements*, Third Edition. Prospect Heights, IL: Waveland Press, 1994, pp. 3–13.

[31] *Ibid.*, p. 14.

[32] *Ibid.*, see Chapter 3, pp. 43–69.

[33] *Ibid.*, see Chapter 4, pp. 71–87.

[34] *Ibid.*, see Chapter 5, pp. 89–109.

[35] *Ibid.*, see Chapter 8, pp. 145–57.

[36] John Bowers, Donovan Ochs, and Richard Jenson, *The Rhetoric of Agitation and Control*, Second Edition. Prospect Heights, IL: Waveland Press, 1993, pp. 49–64.

[37] There are numerous classifications of campaign planning and execution. The one used here is found in Michael Rothschild, *Advertising*. Lexington, MA: D.C. Heath & Co., 1987, pp. 10–14.

[38] *Ibid.*, p. 180.

# Additional Reading

Edward Brody, *Managing Communication Processes*. New York: Praeger, 1991.

James Combs and Dan Nimmo, *The New Propaganda*. New York: Longman, 1993.

Robert E. Denton, Jr., and Gary Woodward, *Political Communication in America*, Second Edition. New York: Praeger, 1990.

Robert Jackall, *Propaganda*. New York: MacMillan, 1995.

Doug Newsom, Judy Turk, and Dean Kruckeberg, *This is PR: The Realities of Public Relations*, Sixth Edition. Belmont, CA: Wadsworth, 1996.

Michael Pfau and Roxanne Parrott, *Persuasive Communication Campaigns*. Boston: Allyn & Bacon, 1993.

Gary Selnow, *High-Tech Campaigns*, Westport, CT: Praeger, 1994.

Don Schultz, Dennis Martin, and William Brown, *Strategic Advertising Campaigns*. Chicago: Crain Books, 1984.

Fraser P. Seitel, *The Practice of Public Relations*, Sixth Edition. Englewood Cliffs, NJ: Prentice-Hall, 1996.

Charles Stewart, Craig Smith, and Robert E. Denton, Jr., *Persuasion and Social Movements*, Third Edition. Prospect Heights, IL: Waveland Press, 1994.

Judith Trent and Robert Friedenberg, *Political Campaign Communication*, Third Edition. New York: Praeger, 1995.

# 10

# Advertising as Persuasion

## OVERVIEW

> Advertising depends upon the simple precepts of human persuasion. And these have to do, for the most part, with treating the other party as a unique, important individual, letting him recognize your distinct positive identity and starting off by getting him nodding in agreement.
>
> —John O'Toole

Advertising is undoubtedly the most pervasive form of persuasion in our society. Studies estimate that Americans are exposed to 16,000 ads, logos, and announcements every day. In just a 24-hour period, for example, we will see approximately 100 television ads, or nearly 38,000 television ads in one year. In fact, Americans will spend over three years of their lives just watching television commercials.[1] Advertising continues to expand and invade our daily lives. Monthly bills are full of ads; clothing has become billboards for products like Coca-Cola; movies and home videos now offer a series of commercials prior to the main feature. Today, there are over 35 firms that specialize in product placement in movies and television shows. The 1991 top grossing film, *Home Alone*, contained 31 brand-name products with over 42 verbal mentions of the products in the movie.[2] There are several advertising firms that sell space on the inside of public restrooms.

In 1994 advertisers spent over $150 billion to persuade Americans to buy their products and services. This amount represents a 50 percent increase since 1981 and reflects 2 percent of our gross national product. That amount also exceeds what our entire nation spent on higher education in 1990.[3] Experts predict that advertising expenditures will reach $1 *trillion* by the year 2000.[4]

Many commercials, produced and directed by the best of the entertainment industry, rival the network shows. As consumers, we pay dearly for those commercials. According to Donna Cross, 20 percent to 40 percent of a product's price represents the production costs of commercials.[5] In her opinion, this amounts to ''double shafting.'' Manufacturers convince us to purchase their products and then charge us for their advertising expenses.

Commercials are not only a fact of daily life, but many Americans seemingly enjoy them. We can easily identify our favorite commercial characters, slogans, and songs. Thus, in some way, we are all experts on advertising. We know what we like, what is in good taste, what is clearly right or wrong. Ironically, according to Stewart Alter, we do not believe advertising influences our buying decisions.[6] In a telephone survey, only 14 percent of the respondents said they were influenced by advertising. Interestingly, however, respondents believed that women, young people, and people in low-income groups are more affected by advertising than other groups. Individuals from those groups disagreed. As a society we endure, remember, and enjoy advertising messages but are quick to dismiss their value or impact.

The more pervasive and persuasive, the more invisible advertising becomes in terms of influence and impact. Its presence and images become natural, expected, and even desired for the entertainment value. The irony is that the less we notice, the more open we are to the persuasive message.

In this chapter, we investigate the persuasive dimensions of advertising. By identifying the tactics and techniques of persuasion, we can become better critics of advertising and more knowledgeable consumers.

# What Is Advertising?

There are several ways to discuss the essential nature and characteristics of advertising. In the traditional sense, advertising is a function or tool of marketing. Most definitions from this perspective emphasize four major characteristics.

1. Advertising is a *paid* form of communication. The message is shared as a result of financial payment.

2. Advertising is a *nonpersonal, presentational* form of communication. Advertising is distinct from face-to-face sales presentations.

3. Advertising messages are concerned with the presentation of *ideas, products, and services*. All too often, we associate advertising only with products. Increasingly, advertising addresses political, social, and philosophical ideas. Because of the drastic increase in service occupations and employment, much advertising espouses the virtues of the various service industries.

4. Sponsors of advertising messages are *identified*. Sponsorship identification contributes to message accountability and financial responsibility.

Another perspective is to define advertising in informational and persuasive dimensions. This perspective tells what advertising *does* rather than what advertising *is*. In the early 1900s, N.W. Ayer, who later founded the first advertising agency in America, defined advertising as "keeping your name before the public."[7] Later, the sales function was combined with information and awareness. Most commercial messages contain a great deal of information about product purpose, usage, price, or availability, but they also do more than inform. The messages are highly controlled. Great care is given to message content, direction, and length. Persuasion is now an essential element of advertising.

Advertising does not pretend to present both sides of a purchasing decision, nor is it required to do so. By design, advertising is perhaps the strongest form of advocacy. Finally, a communication definition of advertising recognizes the importance of the mass media in carrying the messages. The various media impact the style, content, and presentation of any message.

Still another way to gain insight into the nature of advertising is to review methods of classifying advertising. One classification scheme is by audience. Some ads are aimed at large, general audiences while others are aimed at small, perhaps regional audiences. Some are designed for audiences with specific demographic characteristics (age, sex, income, or occupational status), while other ads appeal to specific lifestyles or psychographic variables based on audience beliefs, attitudes, or values. Advertising is also classified according to the types of advertisers: national (general) or local (retail), business (industrial, trade, professional) or noncommercial (government, civic groups, religious groups), product (service, goods) or corporate (image, ideas), primary (create a demand for generic product for entire industry) or selective (create demand for a specific brand of product).

Finally, social scientists tend to investigate advertising from a more theoretical and social perspective. From this orientation, advertising is viewed as the most influential institution of socialization in modern society. Sut Jhally, for example, provides an interesting approach to advertising. He argues that advertising plays an important role in the modern mediation of the person-object relationship. Jhally defines advertising as a "discourse through and about objects."[8] The content of the discourse is about the relationship between people and objects. As you will see, most of this chapter is concerned with the social implications of advertising.

To define advertising, therefore, is not a simple task. It is a vital force in our economy as well as a powerful means of communication. It influences who we are, how we live, and how we judge others. For our purposes, advertising is defined as *one-to-one communication by a specific group or industry utilizing mass media for purposes of selling a product, service, or idea*. This definition has several advantages. First, it recognizes that the most effective form of persuasion is that which is created with a *specific audience* in mind. An effective commercial is one that speaks to a specific group — to its wants, desires, problems. It is one that gains attention, addresses needs, and solves problems. The definition also recognizes the importance of media adaptation. Today's technology is more than just a conduit for the transmission of symbols. Its role is as important to the reception and understanding of the message as is the package in enticing us to select a product.

Finally, advertising, as with most persuasion, is both an art and a science. As a science, advertising must observe, measure and analyze individuals, groups, and institutional behavior. It must seek to establish

*The most effective persuasion is created with a specific audience in mind.*

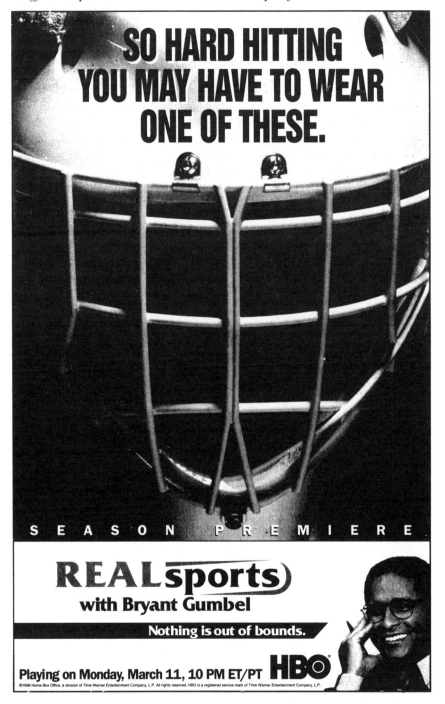

cause-and-effect relationships and to provide a rationale and evidence for conclusions reached. Advertising is also an art; it embraces intuitive judgment, encourages creative application of symbols (both verbal and nonverbal), and harnesses subjectivity to connect with the audience it works to persuade.

Advertising not only informs us about products but, more importantly, informs us about ourselves, society, social values, and behavior. We learn from the roles and models presented in ads. The functions of advertising, then, go beyond increasing sales and corporate profits. We must not only be aware of the world presented but also of the tactics and techniques of presentation. Decades ago, Vance Packard recognized the potential impact of advertising and warned, "the result is that many of us are being influenced and manipulated far more than we realize, in the patterns of our everyday lives."[9]

# The Evolution of Advertising from a Communication Perspective

As mentioned earlier, the focus of advertising has changed since 1900.[10] Early advertising focused on product benefits and attributes. Ads provided general product information, stressed the unique qualities of the product, and stated the price. By 1930, advertising messages moved away from describing the product to focusing on the user of the product. Attributes of the product were associated with the user. Testimonials became the primary structure of most ads. Durable goods, food, and tobacco were advertised heavily, and the advertising played upon themes of family, status, health, and social authority.

By the mid-1950s, advertising shifted focus from the user of the product toward a defined image associated with the product. Instead of certain people using certain products, the products promised a transformation of the user. Although subtle, this is an important shift of emphasis. Such an approach to advertising encourages an internalization of product values. Personal gratification and narcissism become goals of product usage. Happiness, romance, and glamor will be ours if only we use the prescribed product. This image era of advertising is attributed to David Ogilvy, whose primary concerns were product image, long-term brand identification, and loyalty.

Finally, by the early 1970s there had been another major shift of emphasis in American advertising. Products became emblems for group identification. From an advertiser's perspective, the strategy was to utilize behavioral and social science research techniques. According to William Myers, "advertisers found that the only way to create successful advertising was to address consumers' psychological needs and help solve their personal problems."[11] Thus, designer jeans become status symbols and special brands of cologne guarantee romance and sexiness. To be "in," "rich," or "enlightened" demands the use of certain products.

CATHY © Cathy Guisewite. Reprinted with permission of Universal Press Syndicate.

William Leiss, Stephen Kline, and Sut Jhally have provided a detailed analysis of the evolution of the "cultural frames" for goods.[12] They view advertising as social communication. They argue that individuals become acquainted with meanings of objects through society's culture and customs. Today, advertising and marketing are the primary means of imparting the meaning of objects to people. Leiss and his colleagues have identified four cultural frames for goods that incorporate distinct time periods, advertising and marketing strategies, and themes. (See figure 10.1.)

The period from 1890 to 1920 is the "idolatry phase," where the focus was on the product and the approach was rational, descriptive, and informative. Products were devices to meet utilitarian needs of consumers. The "iconistic phase" of advertising, 1920 to 1950, shifted attention away from attributes of products to what the product represents. A brand of soap did more than get you clean; it also demonstrated caring. Products developed social meaning through symbolic attributes. In the "narcissistic phase," 1950 to 1970, advertising explained how products would meet personal, individual needs. Products were less symbolic and more transformative. They became the vehicles for personal change and satisfaction. The insight of psychology provided the emotional strategies for ad development and execution. The final phase, "totemic," 1970 to 1990, reflects a synthesis of the other three phases. Products are portrayed as emblems of group membership. Product usage defines self within a larger context or social group. Thus, the advertising is more specific and targeted to lifestyle variables.

Advertising messages, then, have evolved from what a product *does* to what a product *says*. Clothes are worn for fashion rather than warmth,

Figure 10.1
**Evolution of Cultural Frames for Goods**

| | Newspapers/<br>Magazines | Radio | Television | |
|---|---|---|---|---|
| **Media for Advertising** | | | | |
| **Marketing Strategy** | Rational | Non-Rational | Behaviorist | Segmentation |
| **Advertising Strategy** | Utility | Product Symbols | Personalization | Lifestyle |
| **Period** | 1890 1900 1910 | 1920 1930 1940 | 1950    1960 | 1970    1980 |
| **Elements in Ads** | product qualities<br>price<br>use | symbolic<br>attributes of<br>products | products meet<br>personal needs | people in<br>specific<br>activities,<br>settings |
| **Themes in Ads** | quality<br>useful<br>descriptive | status<br>family<br>health<br>social authority | glamor<br>romance<br>sensuality<br>self-transformation | leisure<br>health<br>groups<br>friendship |
| **Cultural Frames** | **Idolatry**<br>products meet<br>utilitarian needs | **Iconology**<br>products embody<br>attributes<br>approved by<br>society | **Narcissism**<br>products<br>transform<br>self; personal<br>satisfaction | **Totemism**<br>membership<br>products signal<br>group<br>membership |

for social status rather than durability, for personal style rather than utility. Even the appeal of toilet paper is not based on its function but rather on its range of colors, designs, or softness. Does pastel toilet paper really work better than white? The absurdity of the question demonstrates the potential problems with the focus of today's advertising messages. Products have unique personalities, emotions, and significance beyond their chemical and physical characteristics. Recall the American public's outcry against Coca-Cola changing the flavor of its product in 1985. The emotional attachment to the product went beyond preference of taste. Since 1886 we were told that ''Things go better with Coke,'' ''It's the real thing,'' ''Have a Coke and a smile,'' ''Coke adds life,'' ''Coke is it,'' and ''Can't beat the feeling.'' The product represents a significant emblem in American culture.

The structure and nature of advertising is directly related to the political and social structure of society. In countries where tradition and the status quo are valued and there is little technological innovation, advertising is not needed and thus has little social impact. In authoritarian countries, advertising is tightly controlled and is used to promote national goals and specific consumption patterns. In America, which values the ideas of self-interest, individualism, rationality, competition, and the freedom of choice, advertising is less restrictive. Capitalistic society encourages consumerism. For many immigrants, America was presented as a "land of milk and honey" where they might find an abundance of goods. The wage system of labor encouraged consumption. Advertising is vital to advanced capitalistic societies, where it is necessary to motivate people to work hard so they can accumulate money which can then be used to buy products.[13]

From this brief overview of the evolution of advertising, we can make several assumptions about its practice in America. Advertising must be considered within the cultural context of a nation. Advertising messages are extremely complex, utilizing rational, emotional, and social elements. Thus, the messages are open to various interpretations and actual effects are not clearly known. What does the practice of advertising today say about human nature? According to Vance Packard, humans are "simply reactors to stimulus from the environment" and are "creatures of almost limitless plasticity."[14] This skepticism stems from the heavy reliance on modern techniques and theories of psychology in advertising.

## The Role of Psychology in Advertising

As early as 1954, several professional publications began devoting more and more attention to what they called "motivation research."[15] Advertisers began looking for those "extra-psychological values" related to products in order to give them a more potent appeal. The concern is not with specific psychological strategies or tactics but with a general orientation to product definition that plays on individual strengths, weaknesses, hopes, and fears. In the advertising industry, such an orientation is known as product positioning.[16] From this perspective, the advertiser does not begin with the product but with the *mind of the consumer.* That is, advertising does not try to change minds but links product attributes to the existing beliefs, ideas, goals, and desires of the consumer. Our minds accept attitudes or behaviors that match prior knowledge and experience. To say that a cookie tastes "homemade" or "like mother used to make" does not tell whether the cookie is good or bad, hard or soft, sweet or bland. Rather, the statement elicits the aroma of fresh-baked cookies and fond memories of mother's baking. Advertisers are more successful if they position a product to capitalize on established beliefs or expectations of the consumer.

A positioning approach to advertising is a response to an "overcommunicated" society. Today, communication itself is a problem. Over

35,000 new books are introduced in America each year. It would take 17 years of reading 24 hours a day to finish that many books. Even an 8-ounce box of Total cereal has over 1,268 words of copy. Each year over 5,000 new products are introduced to the American public.[17] In addition, during a year, the average American will view 1,550 hours of television, listen to 1,160 hours of radio, and spend 180 hours reading newspapers and 110 hours reading magazines.[18] There is a great deal of competition for our attention. Product positioning provides a way to cut through the clutter and to take a shortcut to the brain. Simplified messages based on consumer experience and knowledge do not require logic, debate, or lengthy explanations. The most effective ads are those that work on a "stimulus-response" motivation. How can Bill Cosby be so effective pitching Jello products? Is it because he is an expert on children and nutrition? Probably not. Since he is funny and likeable, people are attuned to his message because of his public persona. The use of children and small animals in commercials aids in gaining viewers' attention. However, beyond the celebrity status of Bill Cosby and the "cute" commercials is the fact that on his television show he played the warm, funny, insightful pediatrician, Dr. Cliff Huxtable. Crosby's credibility profits from his character on the television show. The same is true for Karl Malden, who for many years warned people never to leave home without their American Express Cards. Again, he was perceived as an expert on crime based on his television character, police lieutenant Mike Stone on the hit series, *The Streets of San Francisco*.[19]

There is another important reason why psychology invaded the advertising community. By the early 1970s, the age of affluence was over for most Americans. The purchasing power of the dollar decreased by 60 percent, and many households required two paychecks to survive.[20] As inflation grew, the "Woodstock generation" became cynical. Bigger was not better. Change for the sake of "progress" was suspect. The advertising industry needed to stimulate the public to buy. The solution to the problem was image transformation. Advertisers sought to increase the perceived value and worth of mass-produced products. The primary strategy was to offer an *emotional* reward for using a product. In short, brand "personality" became more important than brand "performance." Sexy jeans have a stronger appeal than long-lasting jeans. A stylish, designer watch is favored over an accurate one.

Product brand selection or loyalty says more about "who we wish to be" than "who we are." John Jones, who spent over 25 years in the advertising business, argues that "in product design, in packaging, in promotion, in direct-response materials—in short, in every piece of communication directed to consumers—there is a speaker, someone who is making assumptions about the reader. And there is a mock reader, the person you and I are supposed to become."[21]

Today, staff psychologists are an essential part of campaign development. For example, Carol Moog is a clinical psychologist who is president of an advertising consulting firm, Creative Focus, that specializes in helping advertisers and agencies focus on and understand the psychological effects of their ads.[22] Psychographic variables (lifestyle, likes, dislikes, perceptions, etc.) rather than demographic variables (age, sex, income, occupation) have become the core of marketing endeavors. Psychographic variables tend to be better motivators and predictors of purchasing behavior.

## How Advertising Works

There are four basic models of buyer behavior.[23] Psychological models are based on the notions of stimulus-response. Humans respond to external stimuli in the environment. Such models become predictive and focus on the various forms of stimuli that can be created to ensure mass response. Economic models assume that people are rational and make reasoned purchasing decisions based on price, quality, pleasure, or esteem. The difference between psychological and economic models is the underlying assumption concerning human behavior. The psychological model views humans as robots; buying decisions are automatic as long as the right stimulus is used. In contrast, the economic model assumes that people process available information and have reasons for decisions. The model does not judge the quality of the reasons—only that we can identify and/or justify reasons for decisions.

Sociological models of buying behavior argue that specific social groups directly influence consumer desires, preferences, and purchases. Thus, such variables as status, lifestyle, and reference groups dictate buying habits. Finally, statistical models of buying behavior focus on the purchasing patterns of groups or types of consumers. For example, a certain type of individual buys items from direct mail or catalogs (demographics include higher-income, well-educated, professional). If individuals buy from one catalog, they will buy from *many* catalogs. The frequency of catalog purchase is directly related to recency of purchase. The more recent the last purchase, the greater the likelihood that individuals will make another purchase from a catalog when given the opportunity.[24] For a retailer, this means that a family purchasing from catalogs can receive several a month and not decrease the likelihood of purchase.

Each of these models provides insight into why people buy when they do. Basically, all advertising attempts to move a consumer along a continuum from awareness, to knowledge, to "liking," to preference, to conviction, and finally to purchase—in short, to persuade.

At each stage of the continuum, ads attack different behavioral dimensions and use different types of appeals and techniques. From awareness to knowledge, ads attempt to provide the consumer with

*Advertisements must first capture attention and then provide sufficient information to move the consumer along a continuum from awareness to knowledge to preference to purchase.*

Reprinted by permission of Hewlett Packard

product information and facts. Creatively, the ads use descriptive copy and slogans or jingles to capture attention. To move the consumer from liking to product preference, the ads play upon emotions and feelings. The ads use image, status, and glamour appeals. To reinforce conviction and repeat purchases, ads attempt to stimulate and to direct consumer desires. Price appeals and testimonials are useful techniques at these stages of consumer reactions.

From this rather simple continuum of consumer reaction, we can see four distinct levels of persuasion.[25] The most simple and basic level is what Kim Rotzoll and her colleagues call "precipitation." Here the

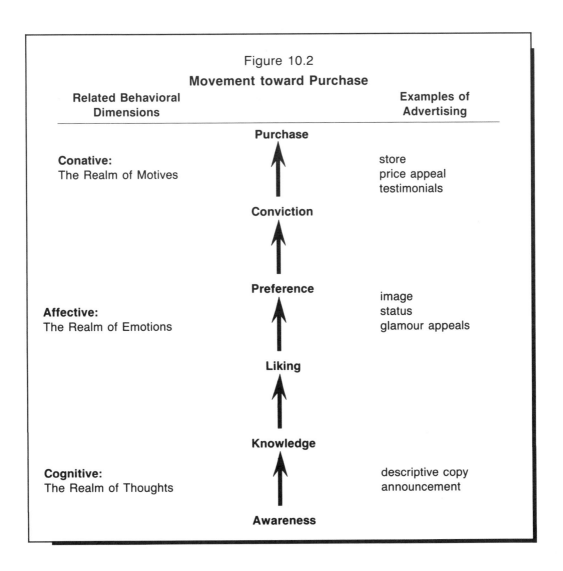

Figure 10.2
**Movement toward Purchase**

| **Related Behavioral Dimensions** | | **Examples of Advertising** |
|---|---|---|
| | **Purchase** | |
| **Conative:** The Realm of Motives | ↑ | store price appeal testimonials |
| | **Conviction** | |
| | ↑ | |
| | **Preference** | |
| **Affective:** The Realm of Emotions | ↑ | image status glamour appeals |
| | **Liking** | |
| | ↑ | |
| | **Knowledge** | |
| **Cognitive:** The Realm of Thoughts | ↑ | descriptive copy announcement |
| | **Awareness** | |

persuasive goals are brand awareness and knowledge. The advertising messages must fight clutter and penetrate the mind of the consumer. The second level they simply call "persuasion." At this level, the messages appeal to human feelings and emotions and attempt to induce purchase. This level is the most powerful and perhaps the most subtle. The third level of persuasion is "reinforcement." Here the goal is to legitimize existing purchases and to validate previous purchasing decisions. "Reminder" is the final level of persuasion identified in advertising. The nature of persuasive efforts at this level is to reinforce brand loyalty. Many ads are designed to counter the competition in order to insulate the consumer. Most of the McDonald's ads are designed to keep "top-of-mind" awareness rather than to describe product attributes.

According to William Leiss, Stephen Kline, and Sut Jhally, advertising creates demand in three ways.[26] First, through "technological manipulation," advertising utilizes the latest in psychographic and demographic research to identify tactics and techniques of mass appeal. The production techniques and drama available with the various media heighten impact and response to creative advertising messages. The second way advertising creates demand is through "false symbolism." The concern here is how products become symbols for desired attributes. Why do specific articles of clothing represent status or group identification; why do certain perfumes promise sex? The third way advertising creates demand is through "false claims." Leiss and his colleagues argue many ads simply promise more than they can deliver and are deceptive in nature.

Another interesting explanation of how advertising works is provided by the advertising agency of Foote, Cone & Belding.[27] Their model suggests that purchasing decisions are based upon the degree of "involvement" in the decision and the degree to which thinking or feeling provides the basis for making a decision. These elements can be visualized as two continuums which cross to form a matrix. One has high and low involvement as its endpoints; the other has thinking and feeling (see figure 10.3).

Each quadrant of the matrix suggests a different "learn-do-feel" orientation in making a purchasing decision. In other words, we buy something ("do") based upon product information provided ("learn") or based on some feeling or emotion about use of the product ("feel"). In order to illustrate these orientations, let's consider each quadrant separately.

### High Involvement—Thinking

According to the model, purchasing major expensive items such as houses, cars, or major furnishings requires high consumer involvement and careful thinking. Consumers seek product information to insure product value and quality. The consumer is reflective, seeks the best deal, and bases the decision on product information and demonstration.

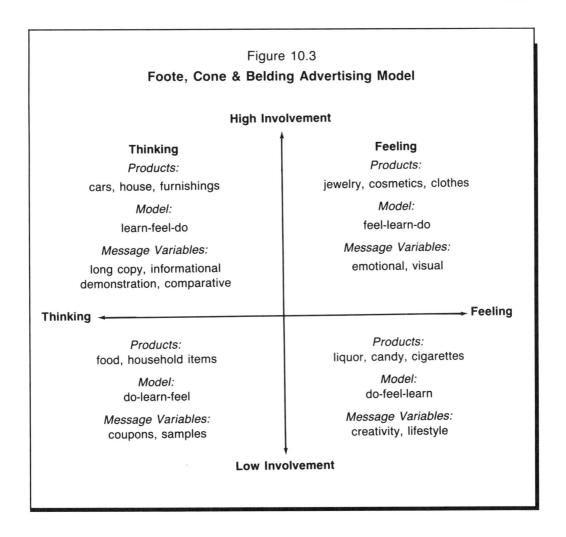

Figure 10.3
**Foote, Cone & Belding Advertising Model**

**High Involvement**

**Thinking**
*Products:*
cars, house, furnishings

*Model:*
learn-feel-do

*Message Variables:*
long copy, informational
demonstration, comparative

**Feeling**
*Products:*
jewelry, cosmetics, clothes

*Model:*
feel-learn-do

*Message Variables:*
emotional, visual

**Thinking** ←――――――――――――――――――→ **Feeling**

*Products:*
food, household items

*Model:*
do-learn-feel

*Message Variables:*
coupons, samples

*Products:*
liquor, candy, cigarettes

*Model:*
do-feel-learn

*Message Variables:*
creativity, lifestyle

**Low Involvement**

From this perspective, consumers follow the "learn-feel-do" sequence in making a purchasing decision. Note too that this sequence provides insight into how to create the advertising. Advertising for products in this category would require much information, long copy, comparative product analyses, and visual demonstration.

*High Involvement—Feeling*

Some products (such as jewelry, cosmetics, clothing, or other fashion products) are based primarily on subjective, emotional reactions while also demanding a great deal of consumer time and involvement. The products often have more expressive, symbolic meaning than functional usage; thus, purchase decisions are rather personal. Because product information is less important than consumer attitudes, the purchasing sequence is "feel-learn-do." Advertising for products in this category must rely on emotional and visual elements as well as the psychological needs of the consumer. The products are selected to tell others how we want to be perceived and understood.

### Low Involvement — Thinking

Food and household items comprise this category of products. Just how excited can we get over toothpaste or washing detergent? For most consumers, brand loyalty is strong for these products, and purchasing is based on habit rather than major product differentiation. Developing brand loyalty does involve some rational thinking. We ultimately decide to use a product because it is cheaper or better. The buying sequence here is "do-learn-feel." Most of the advertising for this category is to provide top-of-mind awareness and to counter the "invasion" of other product ads. You also find a great number of free sample offers, coupons, and quantity pricing for such products to encourage loyalty and to provide a concrete reason for purchase.

### Low Involvement — Feeling

In many ways, this category is a "catch-all" for a variety of products ranging from candy, cigarettes, and liquor to movies. The key is that these products are highly subjective and depend on personal taste. They are low involvement primarily because they are inexpensive and consumed quickly. They involve feelings because preferences are personal and many of the items are promoted using imagery. The sequence for this category is "do-feel-learn." Quick self-satisfaction and gratification is the primary goal of much of the advertising. The messages stress creativity and self-indulgence. Some products in this category (liquors and drinks, for example) also stress lifestyles.

Although the model is rather challenging, it is useful in many ways. It recognizes that there are many reasons and variables in making a decision to purchase an item. The model also attempts to link products to the process of consumer decision making. The model suggests appropriate approaches to creating effective advertising messages based on the sequence of buying decisions. Perhaps most importantly, the model demonstrates the complexity of consumer buying decisions ranging from what type of gum to buy to what type of house to purchase. This is also part of the reason why advertising is so persuasive.

It is important to recognize that advertising, in many ways, counters traditional ideas about how we learn and how we acquire attitudes. Many scholars argue that the learning process is linear and consistent. Information is transmitted; once the information is understood, attitudes may change or some reorganization of belief structure will occur. Once an attitude alters, then a corresponding behavior follows. The FCB model counters this notion. We purchase some products simply because we recall the ads from television and just want to try them. We may then like the product and will form a favorable attitude. In other cases, the advertising causes an attitude to form without ever experiencing the product—as in the belief that Mercedes are superior automobiles. We attach emotional significance to the products (status or prestige, for example) before any purchase takes place. In this sequence, we start with an attitude change, develop emotional ties, and then, if circumstances allow, purchase the car.

Perhaps the most questionable practice in the advertising industry is the use of subliminal messages. Such messages are aimed to reach the consumer below the threshold of consciousness. Wilson Bryan Keys, in his books *Subliminal Seduction* and *Media Sexploitation*, provides numerous examples of sexual symbols, words, and pictures embedded in ads.[28] According to Keys, such messages succeed on two levels: people remember the ads, and the targeted behavior is stimulated. The notion of subliminal advertising originated in the famous study which projected messages of "eat popcorn" and "drink Coca-Cola" on movie screens for 1/3,000 of a second.[29] The messages increased sales of popcorn by 57 percent and of Coke by 10 percent.

There are several problems with the notion of subliminal advertising. First, the original study was conducted during the movie *Picnic* that contained several scenes of people eating and drinking during hot summer weather. Was the audience responding to the subliminal advertisement or simply mimicking the behavior in the movie? In addition, the study has never been replicated with the same dramatic results. In fact, scholars Anthony Pratkanis and Elliot Aronson reviewed over 150 academic articles and more than 200 professional papers on subliminal advertising. They concluded that "in none of the papers is there clear evidence that supports the proposition that subliminal messages influence behavior."[30] Also, industry professionals continue to deny widespread use of subliminal techniques because they simply do not work. John O'Toole, former chairman of the advertising agency of Foote, Cone & Belding, emphatically states, "I don't like to destroy cherished illusions, but I must state unequivocally that there is no such thing as subliminal advertising. I have never seen an example of it, nor have I ever heard it seriously discussed as a technique by advertising people."[31]

Of course, as we have already argued, the appeals are very subtle. Subliminal advertising may be in the eyes of the beholder, because many of the appeals are a matter of perception. For example, a product that uses a movie star as a spokesperson might appeal to one consumer because the star has successfully portrayed practical, down-to-earth characters. Another consumer might focus on the celebrity's fame and wealth. Another may be driven by the star's physical attractiveness. The appeal is emotional and depends on the receiver's perception of the star.

# WALNUT COVE

*Do subliminal suggestions work in advertising? Do many of the implied linkages in advertisements function below the threshold of consciousness?*

Even the most subtle actions may generate a strong appeal. When the loveable alien in Steven Spielberg's film, *E.T.* was shown to love to eat Reese's Pieces, national sales of the candy increased 66 percent.[32] Other products, such as perfume or cologne, may explicitly show an attractive couple in bed. One appeal is the person, the other is sex. One approach is subtle, the other is more direct and plays on our human interest in sex. Advertising utilizes deeply ingrained desires and motives of human nature.

The advertising industry relies on the subtle and the obvious, the rational and the absurd, the everyday and the novel in order to lead us from awareness to ultimate purchase. Keeping that in mind, we will now consider some of the more common tactics and approaches to persuasion in American advertising.

## Common Advertising Appeals

Advertising attempts to motivate consumers to purchase products in countless ways. As we have already mentioned, the process is complex. Some ads hope to accomplish more than stimulating purchase of the products. Today, however, the basis of nearly all advertising is emotion. It is beyond the scope of this chapter to identify all the various techniques advertisers use. However, there are several basic emotional appeals common to most advertising messages.

### Power

There are many kinds of power—economic, physical, political and social, to name only a few. Many advertising messages offer products as a means of obtaining power. The consumer is placed in a power-seeking position. Advertisements present vignettes, images, icons, or emblems of power which can be had for a price. For example, the classic Marlboro cigarette ads offer more than image association. Few of us really want to be cowboys. We can, however, aspire to be strong and independent if we adopt this emblem of power—the cigarette. The appeal to physical power goes beyond ads for muscle building and weight machines. Many truck and car ads emphasize the power of the automobile. For many years, cars have been identified with animals: cougars, impalas, mustangs, and skyhawks, for example. Such association reflects a primitive, wild form of power. Some auto appeals are more subtle. One campaign for Jaguar avoided an overt display of aggression and power. The copy proclaimed that the Jaguar possesses "confidence born of proficiency and power" providing an "authoritative response."[33]

Power appeals abound in nearly every product category. Cologne ads for both men and women promise sexual strength and power. Some ads offer economic power with such headlines as "You can lease a BMW for only $400 per month" or "You now qualify for an additional $10,000 line of credit on your Visa or Mastercard." Of course, many political ads offer us power as members of certain groups whose views and needs will be heard in Washington if we elect the right person. Sometimes the product itself is used to epitomize power. For example, we know that Dodge trucks are "ram tough," that Sears Die-Hard batteries are "heavy duty," and that Glad's Alligator garbage bags are "puncture proof." Most products, we are told, give us some kind of additional power or strength.

### Meaning

We live in a complex world; advertising offers products that will add individual effectiveness or meaning to our complex environment. We

*This advertisement skillfully blends images of the economic and social power of potential owners with detailed information about the performance capability of the automobile.*

*Bonneville SSEi*

# RESERVED IS WHERE YOU PARK.
# NOT HOW YOU DRIVE.

The new Pontiac Bonneville SSEi," the car that looks as powerful charging down the open highway as it does unwinding in an executive parking space.

Take command of 240 supercharged horsepower. Experience the passion of one of the fastest performance sedans in the world, the car that outperformed competition like the BMW 740i.* Strengthen your connection to the road

with speed-sensitive steering, traction control and ABS. Fasten yourself into the response-oriented interior surrounded by sophisticated design. Feel power and prestige once exclusive to European performance sedans, all for thousands less.**

Choosing exactly what you want in a car is difficult. Finding it is simple. The new Bonneville SSEi, the car that knows where... and where *not* to be reserved.

For complete information, please call

1-800-2PONTIAC or check out our site

on the World Wide Web at

http://www.pontiac.com.

PONTIAC CARES with a 3-year 36,000-mile-no-deductible bumper-to-bumper limited warranty, plus free 24-hour Roadside Assistance and Courtesy Transportation. See your dealer for details. *Based on tests conducted by the United States Auto Club against 1995 BMW 530i, BMW 740i, Mercedes-Benz S420, Infiniti J30 and Lexus LS400 models. 1996 Bonneville SSEi compared to 1995 BMW 740i in 0-60 acceleration and quarter-mile tests. **Based on 1995 MSRP of BMW 530i, BMW 740i, Mercedes-Benz S420, Infiniti J30 and Lexus LS400 models. Level of equipment varies.

PONTIAC
BONNEVILLE
WE ARE DRIVING EXCITEMENT

Reprinted by permission of GM Corporation

can combat hunger by giving ten dollars per month to sponsor a child in a foreign country. We are assured: "Weekends are made for Michelob," "GE—we bring good things to life," "Coke is it," "You're in good hands with Allstate," and American Express provides "a part of a lot of interesting lives." Ads tell us what is the best, the ultimate, the chic, and so on.

Carol Moog is concerned about the product language of advertising where the specific appeals are integrated into people's searches for identity. "The trouble with the advertising mirror is that we never see ourselves reflected; we only see reflections of what advertisers want us to think their products will do for us."[34] In effect, advertisers sell definitions of who we are. Thus, all we need to do to "buy" an identity is to buy the product.

It is interesting to note the various changes in fashion which, in turn, literally changes what is "real." Moog argues that "*Glamour* is in the business of making women a bit more uncomfortable with who they are, while offering dreams, promises, or guidance that will help them become something more."[35] Several years ago, she notes, the models in the magazines were flawless in appearance and make-up. Next, they were more real and used less make-up for a more natural look. Now, sexiness and glamour are back. A woman should feel free to use make-up, stylized fashions, and a more feminine appeal. In short, the image changes and is largely initiated by advertisers.

A general review of ads in fashion magazines basically tells us that men should be powerful, rich, confident, and athletic, while women should be beautiful and thin. Unfortunately, as Michael Jacobson and Laurie Mazur observe, "personhood is defined by what we buy, never mind such traits as honesty, generosity, and loyalty."[36]

## Norms

Advertising not only purports to provide meaning for our lives, but it also tells us what is good or bad, in or out, right or wrong. Ads reveal how we should look, dress, and eat. Product usage socially defines us and can even disclose what we believe. Fashion advertising, in particular, establishes specific norms for behavior. Ask yourself, what are the characteristics of style? Where did you get such criteria? It is most likely that you received them from advertising. It is interesting to note the transformation of blue jeans from pants indicating a lower working class to a status symbol of high fashion. During the civil rights movement and anti-Vietnam years, jeans symbolized resentment, protest, and denial of high fashion. Jeans were the uniform of the counterculture. Then in 1977, Jordache used television commercials to advertise tight jeans using sexy models. Soon many designer jeans competed for the newly created market. Perhaps the most outrageous or notorious jean ads are those by Guess jeans. Sexually bold, Guess jean ads portray women as submissive, obedient, and vulnerable. The ads usually feature a seductively dressed young woman being dominated in some fashion by an older man. The ads are aimed at teenagers acknowledging their sexuality while rebelling against parental norms.[37]

Some products, rather than establishing norms, attempt to show that they meet expected norms. "Miller, made the American way" and "At Ford, quality is job 1" are examples of companies portraying themselves as meeting consumer expectations.

## Isolation

Many ads play upon the fear of individual isolation and loneliness. Product appeals provide a means of identifying with a particular crowd or protecting against an imagined faux pas. Examples include "The Pepsi generation" or Coke's "Catch the wave." Many liquor ads depict a man or woman in a party setting with friends. A well-known vodka ad proclaims "Friends are worth Smirnoff." The message not only establishes a norm, but the visual implies popularity by using or associating with those who use the product. To be liked and accepted as part of a group is a powerful appeal.

## Self-Esteem

Related to several of the other appeals, a growing number of ads play upon our fear of low self-esteem. Products promise to make us better. Most people want to look their best. The message of a Diet Center ad reads, "First I changed my body, then I changed my mind . . . I'm more confident, more in control." Researchers have found that women's magazines contain 10 times as many ads and articles promoting weight loss as men's magazines, the exact ratio of eating disorders between the sexes. In a *Glamour* magazine survey with over 33,000 women participating, 75 percent of the respondents between the ages of 13 and 35 thought they were fat, while only 25 percent of them met the medical definition of overweight. Even 45 percent of the underweight women respondents thought they were fat.[38] According to Jacobson and Mazur, "girls and teenagers are perhaps the most vulnerable to beauty-industry propaganda. For them, advertising is a window into adult life, a lesson in what it means to be a woman. And lacking the sophistication of their older sisters and mothers, girls are less likely to distinguish between fact and advertising fiction."[39] Common promises play upon our desires to improve our looks and health, to be liked, and to be happy about who we are.

# Guilt

Perhaps the most prominent appeal used in advertising is guilt. Parents must buy products to ensure the safety, health, intelligence, and social well-being of children, and they are told they must buy certain brands or spend a certain amount of money in order to show their love for spouses, friends, or parents.

Guilt, as an appeal in advertising, works in three ways. It encourages sympathy for the message or for the sender. Many of the diamond ads and commercials implicitly state that the only way to show your love for your spouse is by giving diamonds, "if you love her enough." In more direct ads, the copy suggests that you should spend no less than three months' wages on an engagement diamond. Other ways guilt works is to suggest compensation for a wrongdoing (sending flowers for missing an appointment) or to play on a desire to repair a self-image (sending a gift to "start over"). Thus, guilt provides another incentive to purchase what the marketer is trying to sell, and another norm of buying behavior is established.

# Fear

Advertising can make us fearful of many diverse circumstances—from burning in a fire to smelling bad at a party. There are many types of fears, including physical, social, and psychological. Consumers are more likely to remember ads that use fear appeals than those using positive, upbeat appeals.[40] Products will either prevent disaster, solve our problems, or at least reduce risk of embarrassment. This appeal is so basic that it is difficult to find an ad that does not play upon it in some fashion. One of the most overt appeals to fear has been utilized by Volvo for several years. Their commercials focus on safety rather than styling, gas mileage, or resale value. Some critics have suggested that American Express commercials have heightened fears about foreign travel almost as much as the threat of terrorist attacks. Since 1950, Dial soap has successfully played upon the fear of body odor with the tag "Aren't you glad you use Dial? Don't you wish everybody did?"

When advertising increases apprehensions, it may succeed in convincing us to behave according to its plan, but it leaves a residue of emotion unaddressed. Before products can solve problems, they must first convince us that we have a problem.

For more than a decade, there have been numerous ad campaigns based upon fear appeals related to smoking, drinking, and AIDS. Yet, most recent studies indicate an increase in smoking, for example, especially among the young. Too strong a fear appeal can cause a person to feel helpless and without control over the situation, thus decreasing attention and the effectiveness of the message. Fear appeals work best when they offer specific recommendations for overcoming threat, and when the recommended action is perceived as reasonable, realistic, and effective. The antidrug campaign of "Just Say No" in the 1980s was generally thought to have failed because the simple solution of "just say no" was not believable or realistic.

Recently, fear has become the main ingredient in political advertising. Doom is the promised result if an opponent is elected. Consultants have discovered that it is easier to get citizens to vote *against* a candidate than *for* a candidate.

## Sex

Today sexual appeals range from overt to subtle and appear in the majority of all advertising. Such appeals are most common in fashion and cosmetic ads. Sex is used in several ways. The most overt and provocative use of sex in ads is to gain attention. Nudity certainly gains attention, but it is less successful in aiding recall of the advertising message. Sexual innuendo in advertising abounds. One of the more celebrated attempts was a young Brooke Shields in a Calvin Klein ad where she proclaimed, "Nothing gets between me and my Calvin Klein jeans." Hennessy cognac has enjoyed a successful campaign since 1984 that utilizes a sexy sell. Although the tag simply states, "Hennessy, the civilized way to keep warm," the various scenes reveal a romantic couple in various stages of dress, coziness, and seduction. Such sexual innuendos are not just aimed at men. In a 1994 Hyundai television commercial, two women evaluate men's physical endowments based on the car they drive. They prefer the "confident" Hyundai driver who doesn't need to rely on an expensive car to make an impression and they ask, "Wonder what he's got under the hood?"

Calvin Klein's Obsession ads are among the most controversial, using nudes of both genders in various configurations, often with no text. The sexual imagery is bold. Such scenarios gain audience attention and are used for fantasy fulfillment and stimulation. In 1995, Calvin Klein once again provoked controversy by using very young models in suggestive poses. In some of the ads, the model's underwear is clearly visable. Critics of the ads charged Klein with supporting child pornography. In fact, a government investigation confirmed that all the models were over the age of eighteen. Nevertheless, within weeks, Klein canceled the ad campaign. More cynical observers noted that the company benefited from the publicity of the controversy and the brief campaign was most successful.

According to research, these usages increase the amount of time spent looking at the ad, which can translate into higher message recall and positive associations. More subliminal uses of sexual appeals are also common. Product placement, model positions, and provocative graphics

*The following copy was used in an advertisement for two fragrances. How do the adjectives chosen differ? What verbs were selected? Do the descriptions project different roles or behaviors?*

# SPACE FOR WOMEN

This alluring fragrance was created with today's woman in mind. A woman who exudes confidence yet maintains a delicate femininity. A woman who radiates beauty and draws others to her inner space.

Created by Cathy Carden, SPACE is enticing and seductive without being overbearing. Let it complement your personality and enhance your presence.

SPACE for women. As endless as space itself.

# SPACE FOR MEN

Since the beginning of time, men have marked their territory through discovery, conquests, and adventure.

Today a man must be free to determine his own space. SPACE to be himself. SPACE to share with others.

For these men, Cathy Carden has created a fragrance that embraces age-old wisdom and the true spirit of freedom . . . SPACE.

SPACE fulfills its purpose by creating an aura of tranquil confidence necessary for any man to achieve his life goals and desires.

arouse interest and, again, seek to aid recall and time spent viewing the ad.

Another important use of sexual appeals in advertising is in distinguishing and defining sex roles in society. Through ads we learn our roles and behavior in courtship, fashion, and other types of social behavior. Of major concern to many social scientists is the perpetuation of sexual stereotypes of power, dominance, and success portrayed in contemporary advertising. Not only do many of the ads using sexual appeals reinforce sexist notions about the idealized woman and man, but they also exploit human sexuality. In the former case, the ads give us unrealistic notions about our bodies, feelings, and emotions. In the latter, they encourage us to think of sex as a commodity.

## How to Critique Ads

A primary goal of this book is to provide tools of analysis for the persuasion we encounter in various contexts. Because of the extensive daily exposure to advertising, it is useful to discuss two general approaches to analyzing advertising.[41]

Judith Williamson claims advertisements are one of the most important cultural factors molding and reflecting our life today.[42] Every ad creates structures of meaning. Advertisements function to transform statements about things into statements of significance to people. For example, if a characteristic of a car is high gas mileage, then this characteristic is translated to notions of economy and rationality. The key is to transform the language of objects to the language of people. Thus, as a critic, one should look at the textual relationships between the parts of the message and the meaning created. Through ads, diamonds come to mean love—a transformation beyond mineral and rock to a purely human sign. In some ads, the objects communicate the human message such as "say it with flowers" or "gold says I love you." In other ads, people are identified with the objects that project significance such as "I'm a Pepper" or "become part of the Pepsi generation." The visual image created plays a very important part of the meaning created. In fact, the more prominent the visual in an ad, the more ambiguity created. Today, the visual implies the meaning. In a now famous television ad for Apple computers reminiscent of George Orwell's *1984*, a striking woman hurls a sledgehammer through the video screen that hundreds have been watching in a trance. The spot was a media sensation and won several creative awards. Words cannot, of course, adequately describe the visual power of the commercial. The meaning was totally implied. The new Apple MacIntosh computer would allow individual creativity and freedom, releasing us from the world of domination and "big brother" control.

Another highly visual campaign is for the Infiniti automobile. For the first two years of the television and print campaign, the car was never shown. The words were poetic and the visuals were of sweeping landscapes. The Infiniti is more than a car, the experience more than transportation. Thus, from a textual approach, we look for meanings within the ad. What are the appeals? What does the product promise in human terms? The product may promise smooth skin but imply younger looks. The product may promise a close shave but imply greater female approval. Such analysis of advertising forces us to become more critical of the claims made.

A second approach to analyzing advertising is to focus on surface meanings to detect patterns of similarities and differences. For example, how are people portrayed in print ads—as housewives or executives, smart or dumb, fat or thin? How frequently are certain roles portrayed? Surface meanings often include sex roles and modes of expected behavior. This systematic approach to viewing ads reveals cultural roles and stereotypes. First, focus on the attributes, claims, and promises of the product. Next, analyze the images, stereotypes, and placement/positions of the visuals. Finally, consider the implied audience, claims, warrants, and the evidence—the specific wording of the message. By analyzing surface and implied meanings of advertising messages, we can better recognize the persuasive appeals and assess their validity.

Below are listed several questions and considerations to use as a general guideline when reviewing an ad.

1. What does the ad promise?
2. What does the ad not say?
3. What are the claims being made?
4. What reasons are given for purchasing the product?
5. What was the first thing that caught your attention?
6. Remember, all advertising are pieces of "persuasion."
7. Remember, people often buy more than products. A Mercedes is more than transportation; we buy the world that it represents.
8. Remember, there is no relationship between the brand and its image.
9. Remember, read all the fine print.
10. Remember, we participate in our own persuasion.

## Criticisms and Social Effects of Advertising

Although we accept advertising as a daily practice, there has always been some criticism of the industry. We seem to have a "love-hate" relationship with advertising. For most businesses, advertising is a "necessary evil." For consumers, the commercial interruptions are

**DOONESBURY**

DOONESBURY © 1996. G. B. Trudeau. Reprinted with permission of Universal Press Syndicate.

sometimes pleasant, sometimes informative, but always intrusive. There are several issues of advertising that deserve our special attention.

## Deception

Most of us would agree that advertising is a business based on deception and half-truths. In reality, however, most of the factual messages presented in ads are true, and the factual statements can be verified. The problem is that there are few factual statements in most advertising messages. Consumers do not make distinctions between factual statements and value judgments. As noted in chapter 4, statements of fact are verifiable, whereas statements of value express opinions that are, to say the least, very subjective and judgmental. What does it mean when an ad claims that a restaurant has the best hamburgers? Does it mean they have the best hamburgers in terms of taste, size, toppings, or price? Certainly, several restaurant chains can claim to have the best hamburgers, but can they all claim to have the biggest? Perhaps they can. Some restaurants may have the biggest based upon weight before cooking or after cooking, or based on size by using very large buns or by using thin but large-in-circumference hamburgers.

There is a difference between false advertising and misleading advertising. False advertising means claims are explicitly and literally false. Most ads make claims that are explicitly true but generate false meanings. The implied claims are the most powerful and motivate consumers to purchase the product. Thus, most advertisers settle for the subtle "half-truth." For example, Klondike Lite ice cream bars claim to be 93 percent fat free *if* you remove the chocolate coating. With the coating, the Federal Trade Commission found that the bars actually contain 14 percent fat—twice as much as claimed in Klondike's advertising.[43]

Some ads are misleading because of the nature of the comparisons made in their presentations. Bayer aspirin claims that "All aspirin is not alike. In tests for quality, Bayer proved superior." The implication is that Bayer is better in relieving pain than other brands of aspirin. However, the tests referred to in the ad were tests for quality conducted by Bayer which showed that Bayer's tablets were "superior" because they were whiter and less breakable than other brands tested.[44] Implied superiority claims abound in product ads and are becoming even more subtle. For example, if all pain capsules take about the same amount of time to work, one brand can claim that "no pain reliever works faster!" Although the literal claim is true, consumer interpretation implies that the brand is superior to all others. Other examples include International Harvester's "Nobody builds a more productive line of farm equipment," Winston Lights cigarettes' "Nobody does it better," Selsun Blue's "No leading brand gets rid of dandruff better than Selsun Blue," or Kellogg's All-Bran's "No other cereal you can buy has more natural food fiber than Kellogg's All-Bran." Such claims state equality but imply superiority. Research has shown that consumers not only accept implied claims and puffery from ads but tend to exaggerate and expand on the claims presented.[45] Studies consistently reveal that the vast majority of assertions made in advertising are subjective rather than factual claims. We must be careful in accepting the claims made in comparative advertising.

Other ads are misleading when they imply false promises. We must always challenge the rationality of claims made in ads. Can the product really make us more beautiful, rich, young, successful, or sexy? Is there a logical relationship between the problem presented and the solution offered? For example, consider the Coast soap commercials. If you feel sleepy and sluggish in the mornings, all you have to do is shower with Coast and at once you feel alert, happy, and energetic! Solutions such as improving your nutrition or going to bed earlier would be logically connected to the problem. Showering with a particular brand of soap is not.

Visual lies and distortion also reinforce an implied claim. In a 1990 Volvo commercial, a monster truck drove across a line of cars, crushing all of them except the Volvo. Although never stated, the implied claim was that Volvo was stronger and thus safer than the other automobiles. However, the audience was not informed that the visual demonstration was false. The Volvo wagon had been reinforced with steel and wood and the other cars were weakened for the shot. Volvo paid over $600,000 in fines for the commercial.[46]

Advertising is misleading when it provides incomplete or exaggerated descriptions of products or services. An ad may state that a desk is made of "all wood" but will omit that the wood is actually compressed wood parts. The more ludicrous ads will often contain small print qualifications with caveats concerning claims made. Ads touting high-yield investments will tell you in small print that they require a large amount of money for participation; free checking requires a large minimum monthly balance; a new car for $100 a month requires a large down payment—the examples are limitless.

Most advertising also focuses on the trivial aspects of products elevating the insignificant to significant status. Minor qualities are exaggerated. In fact, differences among most brands or product categories are slight. Much of the distortion in advertising is accomplished in the visual aspects of the message. Frequently food looks better, clothes fit better, and gadgets are handier in commercials and pictures than after a purchase has been made. Ivan Preston argues that the primary cause of deceptive advertising is that "advertisers typically sell brands rather than just products. Because a brand must be presented as different from other brands although they are not, advertisers are tempted to create false differences."[47]

The consumer is deceived not only by exaggerated product differences but also by the fact that much of the competition is contrived.[48] For example, White Cloud and Charmin toilet papers are both owned by Procter & Gamble; Miracle and Parkay margarine are Kraftco brands as are Sealtest, Breyers, and Checkerboard ice creams; Maxwell House, Maxim, Sanka, and Yuban coffees are all produced by General Foods; Biz, Bold, Cheer, Duz, and Ivory belong to the Procter & Gamble stable of detergents. Such abundance of products gives us the illusion of choice, and each one tells us they are superior to their "sisters."

Perhaps the most difficult question involving deception concerns the motives of the advertiser. Many local retailers advertise a sale on low-end merchandise, hoping to sell more expensive models once the consumer gets in the store. Thus, while the ads are not deceptive, their purpose is not to offer the consumer a good value or necessarily a good product; the primary purpose is "bait-and-switch."

## Language

Advertising has a tremendous impact, and many educators are concerned that advertising debases our language. For Carol Moog, America's "second tongue" is product language.[49] The violation of rules of grammar and punctuation is commonplace. For years there was a running debate about the grammar used in the phrase, "Winston tastes good like a cigarette should." Advertising copy contains a multitude of dashes, hyphens, and sentence fragments. The United States Army receives hundreds of letters each year from teachers and students questioning the punctuation in the slogan, "Army. Be All That You Can Be."

Some scholars argue that the constant use of superlatives in ads cheapens and lessens the power of words and language. How many times can a product be "new and improved"? Words like "quick," "easy," "amazing," or "best" lose their power when used frequently.

## Children

Children are special targets for advertisers. Their purchasing power is simply staggering. In 1992 children from the ages of 4 to 12 spent over $9 million on products, and teenagers spent over $93 *billion*! In addition, research shows that children are the primary influencers of family spending on consumer goods. For example, the concept behind using Ronald McDonald is to entice young children to ask parents to take them to McDonald's. Advertisers also know if they can create brand loyalty when a child is young, they may well have a customer for the next 60 or 70 years.[50]

Marketing research shows that by the age of 6 months, babies are already forming images of corporate logos and mascots, and by the time of age 3, most children are making specific brand-name requests for products. Advertisers use bright colors, fast-paced editing, animation, and special sound effects. Most cartoons are nothing less than "program-length commercials" to sell toys and products. Commercials take advantage of children's rational capability by distorting product attributes. Toys seem larger, more exciting, and easier to operate than is actually the case. For teenagers, products are offered to solve life's problems—from unmanageable hair to the lack of friends.

Psychologists claim that children may actually suffer lower self-esteem if they do not own a popular toy, such as the Cabbage Patch doll of 1985, the Teenage Mutant Ninja Turtles of 1989, or the "right" tennis shoes, to name just a few. In 1990 there was a rash of violence associated with teenagers stealing 100-dollar gym shoes, like Nike Air Jordans, and satin starter jackets. As a result, several public school systems have proposed that students wear uniforms to school to avoid the social problems related to clothing issues.

There can be little argument that children are especially vulnerable to the persuasive impact of advertising. Many social groups are calling for more regulation and control. The nations of Belgium, Denmark, Norway, Sweden, and the Canadian province of Quebec ban all advertising to children on radio and television.

## Consumerism

The word *consumer* did not always have positive connotations. In its original French usage, consumption was viewed as an act of pillage, destruction, and waste. With industrialization, the idea of using things up became associated with prosperity. In the 1960s we became aware of wasting and destroying our natural resources. The sole purpose of advertising is to entice us to buy products. Critics argue that it makes people too materialistic. Christopher Lasch in his book *The Culture of Narcissism* argues that "advertising manufactures a product of its own: the consumer, perpetually unsatisfied, restless, anxious, and bored. Advertising serves not so much to advertise products as to promote consumption as a way of life."[51] Our happiness and success are measured by the things we possess. The race to "keep up with the Joneses" is an endless cycle. Advertising perpetuates the cycle by supplying images that may cause us to be unhappy with ourselves and our possessions.

Advertising can sell us things we do not really need or want. Did pet rocks really make us happier and healthier human beings? Admittedly, an impulse item does not cost much and is probably harmless. The item, while cute, is not an essential part of daily life. People argue that advertising can sell us things we do not need because of the huge volume of goods a capitalistic system generates. To avoid stagnation and a depressed economy, goods must be consumed. In many ways, therefore, advertising creates false needs by responding to the needs of manufacturers rather than the needs of the consumers. Advertisers do more than encourage us to buy what we do not need; they go to great lengths to make what we already have obsolete. We then have no choice but to update equipment, cars, or appliances (particularly if the manufacturers stop making replacement parts for repairs). The Huffy Corporation came out with a new 12-speed bike despite the fact that market research revealed that most people did not even use 10 speeds when riding. Why? According to then President Harry Shaw, "People don't really need the two extra speeds. The bike may not do so much for you but it should help to obsolete the 10-speeder."[52] John O'Toole, former chairman of Foote, Cone & Belding, acknowledges that advertising sells things people do not need. He claims that people only need air, food, and water. For him, the distinction is that advertising cannot sell things people *do not want*.[53]

## Social Effects

Critics are concerned about the social influence of advertising in defining who we are, our values, and our self-esteem. With the erosion of social institutions such as the family, marriage, church and schools, young people learn social skills and values from television shows and commercials. One of the problems already mentioned is that commercials tend to stereotype people. Women, old people, and minorities in particular are frequently stereotyped in terms of looks, occupations, roles, and behavior by the advertising industry.

Another problem mentioned earlier is that advertising increasingly expands our fears—fears that we are not good enough, pretty enough, smart enough, or healthy enough. Advertising feeds our hopes and desires while profiting from our insecurities. Michael Hyman and Richard Tansey caution about the ethics of what they call "psychoactive ads."[54] Psychoactive ads are those that cause "a meaningful, well-defined group of viewers to feel extremely anxious, to feel hostile toward others, or to feel a loss of self-esteem."[55] For example, a popular public service ad shows a raw egg and asks the viewer to pretend the egg is the viewer's brain. The announcer then breaks the egg and drops it into a hot skillet and says that this is what drugs do to brains. The goal of the ad is to discourage teenagers from using drugs. However, the scare appeal creates such anxiety in some drug users that they become suicidal. The fact is that emotion-arousing commercials may generate unintended, harmful influences and effects.

There is also concern about the impact of advertising upon the cultural climate of our nation. Some ads are in poor taste yet find public approval. There was mainly just public curiosity about fashion designer Perry Ellis' ad using a vulgar four-letter word that is considered among the most offensive terms of American obscenity.[56] The campaign was terminated less than a year later. Twenty years ago, advertisements for hemorrhoid treatments, contraceptives, and douche products would have shocked the public. Advertisements today are more suggestive and challenge traditional values. The pressure for AIDS education and prevention has stimulated further debate about what is acceptable for public broadcast.

## Freedom of Speech

Advertising can have a large impact on freedom of speech in America. In terms of special issues, corporate images, or political advertising, only those with money have access to the media. As mentioned in chapter 2, private interests often dictate what will be broadcast or published. Some critics suggest that influential sponsors of programs even direct the content of newscasts by threatening withdrawal of advertising support. Perhaps even more damaging is the impact on how we address each other about the social issues confronting us. Politicians compete for exposure and must speak in "sound bites" that fit a one-minute news story. It is common to hear on the radio that "the news is brought to you by . . ." Shouldn't we have access to news regardless of whether or not someone will pay for it?

Advertisers not only increasingly influence access to messages, but they also impact program content. Negative news stories jeopardize major corporate sponsorship. Product boycotts have become a major weapon for citizen groups that desire to get a program off the air. If shows, characters, or plots are too controversial, advertisers will pull support from the program. For example, Diane English, the creator of the CBS hit show *Murphy Brown*, states that abortion was not an option, even for discussion, when the main character found herself unexpectedly pregnant in 1991.[57]

## Private versus Public Interests

John Kenneth Galbraith argues that ads largely serve private rather than public interests. "Advertising operates exclusively . . . on behalf of privately produced goods and services. . . . Every corner of the public psyche is canvassed by some of the nation's most talented citizens to see if the desire for some merchantable product can be cultivated. No similar process operates on behalf of the nonmerchantable services of the state."[58] Michael Hyman and Richard Tansey argue that advertisers must be more responsible to public interests and advocate three simple practices.[59] First, advertisers should carefully target the medium as well as the market. Advertisements can have a negative impact on some groups such as AIDS victims, Vietnam combat veterans, young men and women, and gamblers, to name only a few. Thus, advertisers should use caution in some of the images used. Second, they suggest that advertisers should clearly label psychoactive ads with an introductory announcement. The point is that viewers should be warned of strong imagery or themes prior to airing, just as some news programs warn of viewer discretion. Finally, Hyman and Tansey suggest that advertisers should avoid trick endings. Shock appeals, such as showing a young child getting killed by a drunk driver, should be avoided or, at a minimum, provide a warning.

Michael Jacobson and Laurie Mazur question the value of commercialism on the practice of democracy. "Any culture that surrenders its vision and its self-sustaining human values to the narrow judgment of commerce will be neither free nor just. Commercialism does serious damage to the substance of democracy; if not to its forms. It leads to censorship or self-censorship of the media, to invisible chains that keep people from speaking out, to the indentured status of politicians, and to an overall coarseness that deprecates the humanitarian impulses and the creative drives of a culture in balance, a culture having commerce without commercialism."[60]

## Summary

Advertising is the most pervasive form of persuasion in American life. Our society is characterized by material possessions which often carry symbolic significance for the owner. The economic health of our society depends on the consumer. We are commodities to be targeted based on demographic characteristics such as age, sex, income, or lifestyle.

Our purpose in this chapter was to identify the functions, techniques, tactics, and appeals of contemporary advertising. Advertising is as powerful, subtle, and intensive as any face-to-face encounter. It is both a creative and scientific process. Advertising messages are inherently persuasive; they seek to convert the individual by playing on human emotion, hopes, and fears.

The quantity of advertising is increasing and the distinctions between advertising and other forms of communication such as news and information is becoming obfuscated. Our critical powers of analysis and understanding must provide the balance to the impact of advertising. Advertising, like all persuasive communication, is not neutral and will always involve a battle of "psychological wits." Our challenge as consumers is the constant critical understanding of advertising's messages and influence.

## Questions and Projects for Further Study

1. Using the Foote, Cone & Belding advertising model, provide a contemporary example of an ad for each quadrant of the model.

2. Select a print ad, a radio ad, and a television commercial and critique the ads following the questions and guidelines provided in the section on how to critique ads.

3. By thumbing through a monthly or weekly magazine, find examples of ads that create appeals to individual senses of:
   a. power
   b. meaning
   c. norms
   d. isolation
   e. self-esteem
   f. guilt
   g. fear

4. Select a magazine ad and perform a detailed content analysis of both the explicit and implicit meanings and promises contained in the ad.

5. Select an issue of *Gentlemen's Quarterly* and *Vogue*. How are men and women portrayed in each magazine? Do the portrayals differ? If so, how? What type of relationships, roles, and social status are the models portraying?

6. Record each ad you see in one day from all sources: television, radio, newspapers, magazines, billboards, and "point of sale" displays in stores. How does your list of the number of ads seen compare to the lists of others?

7. Think about the items you have purchased in the last two weeks. How did you learn about them? Why did you buy one particular brand rather than another?

8. Go to the library and select one product category and one major magazine (such as automobiles and *Time*) and see how the advertising for the product has changed for each decade since 1940.

9. Take one product category and see how many different appeals are used in ads for the product across various magazines.

10. Choose three ads in the same product category and identify the "positioning concept" of each.

# Notes

[1] Leslie Savan, *The Sponsored Life: Ads, TV, and American Culture*. Philadelphia: Temple University Press, 1994, p. 1.

[2] Michael Jacobson and Laurie Mazur, *Marketing Madness*. Boulder, CO: Westview Press, 1995, p. 68.

[3] *Ibid.*, p. 12.

[4] Eric Clark, *The Want Makers*. New York: Viking, 1988, p. 14.

[5] Donna Cross, *Media-Speak*. New York: Mentor Book, 1983, p. 14.

[6] Stewart Alter, "Influenced by Ads? Not Me, Most Say," *Advertising Age*, June 10, 1985, p. 15.

[7] John O'Toole. *The Trouble With Advertising*. Chelsea House, 1981, p. 15.

[8] Sut Jhally, *The Codes of Advertising*. New York: St. Martin's Press, 1987, p. 1.

[9] Vance Packard, *Hidden Persuaders*. New York: Pocket Books, 1957, p. 1.

[10] William Leiss, Stephen Kline, and Sut Jhally, *Social Communication in Advertising*. New York: Methuen, 1986, p. 229.

[11] William Meyers, *The Image-Makers*. New York: Times Books, 1984, p. 43.

[12] Leiss, et al., pp. 259-98.

[13] Arthur Gerger, *Media Analysis Techniques*. Beverly Hills: Sage Publications, 1982, p. 57.

[14] Vance Packard, *The People Shakers*. Boston: Little, Brown, and Co., 1977, p. 11.

[15] Packard, *Hidden Persuaders*, p. 21.

[16] See Al Ries and Jack Trout, *Positioning: The Battle for Your Mind*. New York: McGraw-Hill, 1981.

[17] Ries and Trout, pp. 11-14.

[18] Anthony Pratkanis and Elliot Aronson, *Age of Propaganda*. New York: W. H. Freeman and Co., 1992, p. 4.

[19] *Ibid.*, p. 89.

[20] See Meyers, *The Image-Makers*.

[21] John Jones, *Does It Pay to Advertise?* Lexington, MA: Lexington Books, 1989, p. 345.

[22] Carol Moog, *"Are They Selling Her Lips?": Advertising and Identity*. New York: William Morrow and Co., 1990, p. 216.

[23] Don E. Schultz, *Essentials of Advertising Strategy*. Chicago: Crain Books, 1981, pp. 16-17.

[24] See William Cohen, *Direct Response Marketing*. New York: John Wiley & Sons, 1984, p. 267.

[25] Kim Rotzoll and James Haefner, *Advertising in Contemporary Society*. Cincinnati, OH: South-Western, 1986, p. 87.

[26] Leiss, et al., pp. 19-23.

[27] R. Vaughn, "How Advertising Works: A Planning Model," *Journal of Advertising Research*, Vol. 20, 1980, p. 27.

[28] See Wilson Bryan Key, *Subliminal Seduction*, New York: Signet Books, 1973; and *Media Sexploitation*, New York: Signet Books, 1976.

[29] Courtland Bovee and William Arens, *Contemporary Advertising*. Homewood, IL: Irwin, 1986, p. 152.

[30] Pratkanis and Aronson, p. 201.

[31] O'Toole, p. 21.

[32] Jacobson and Mazur, p. 67.

[33] Moog, pp. 93-94.

[34] *Ibid.*, p. 35.

[35] *Ibid.*, p. 116.

[36] Jacobson and Mazur, p. 13.

[37] *Ibid.*, pp. 154-56.

[38] Jacobson and Mazur, p. 77.

[38] *Ibid.*, p. 79.

[40] Michael Hyman and Richard Tansey, "The Ethics of Psychoactive Ads," *Journal of Business Ethics*, Vol. 9, p. 108.

[41] See Leiss, et al., pp. 150-56.

[42] Judith Williamson, *Decoding Advertisements*. New York: Marion Boyars, 1983, p. 11.

[43] Jacobson and Mazur, p. 144.

[44] Cross, p. 16.

[45] See Robert Wyckham, "Implied Superiority Claims," *Journal of Advertising Research*, February/March, 1987, pp. 54-63.

[46] Ivan Preston, *The Tangled Web They Weave: Truth, Falsity, and Advertisers*. Madison: University of Wisconsin Press, 1994.

[47] Preston, p. 53.

[48] Cross, pp. 28-29.

[49] Moog, p. 89.

[50] Jacobson and Mazur, p. 21.

[51] Christopher Lasch, *The Culture of Narcissism*. New York: Warner Books, 1979, pp. 137-38.

[52] Cross, p. 21.

[53] O'Toole, p. 53.

[54] See Hyman and Tansey.

[55] *Ibid.*, p. 105.

[56] The line of controversy included, "Then I smiled my best f— you smile and walked out." See *Advertising Age*, May 12, 1986, p. 3.

[57] Jacobson and Mazur, p. 43.

[58] John Kenneth Galbraith, *The Affluent Society*, Third Edition. Boston: Houghton Mifflin, 1976, p. 198.

[59] Hyman and Tansey, pp. 111-13.

[60] Jacobson and Mazur, p. 9.

# Additional Reading

Eric Clark, *The Want Makers*. New York: Viking, 1988.

Stephen Fox, *The Mirror Makers*. New York: Morrow, 1984.

Michael Jacobson and Laurie Mazur, *Market Madness*. Boulder, CO: Westview Press, 1995.

Sut Jhally, *The Codes of Advertising*. New York: St. Martin's Press, 1987.

William Leis, Stephen Kline, and Sut Jhally, *Social Communication in Advertising*. New York: Methuen, 1986.

Matthew McAllister, *The Commercialization of American Culture*. Thousand Oaks, CA: Sage Publications, 1996.

William Meyers, *The Image-Makers*. New York: Times Books, 1984.

Carol Moog, *"Are They Selling Her Lips?": Advertising and Identity*. New York: William Morrow and Co., 1990.

David Ogilvy, *Confessions of an Advertising Man*. New York: Longmans Green, 1963.

David Ogilvy, *Ogilvy on Advertising*. New York: Crown, 1983.

Anthony Pratkanis and Elliot Aronson, *Age of Propaganda*. New York: W. H. Freeman and Co., 1992.

Ivan Preston, *The Tangled Web They Weave: Truth, Falsity, and Advertisers*. Madison: University of Wisconsin Press, 1994.

John O'Toole, *The Trouble With Advertising*. New York: Chelsea House, 1981.

Al Ries and Jack Trout, *Positioning: The Battle for Your Mind*. New York: McGraw-Hill, 1981.

Leslie Savan, *The Sponsored Life: Ads, TV, and American Culture*. Philadelphia: Temple University Press, 1994.

Judith Williamson, *Decoding Advertisings*. New York: Marion Boyars, 1983.

# 11

# Political Persuasion

## OVERVIEW

We believe that these diaries accurately reflect the mind of one of our outstanding national leaders; if the reflection seems clouded it may not be the fault of the mirror. Hacker [the bumbling cabinet leader invented by satirists Jonathan Lynn and Antony Jay] himself processed events in a variety of ways, and the readers will have to make their own judgment as to whether any given statement represents

(a) what happened

(b) what he believed happened

(c) what he would like to believe happened

(d) what he wanted others to believe happened

(e) what he wanted others to believe that he believed happened.[1]

—Jonathan Lynn and Antony Jay
introducing *The Complete Yes Minister*

Jonathan Lynn and Antony Jay's humorous account of the fictitious James Hacker and the similar caricatures of politicians in the monologues of Jay Leno, David Letterman, and others are examples of the extremes sometimes reached when we present ourselves as agents for the interests of others. For better and for worse, the processes of persuasion, negotiation, and compromise exist in all of us—the natural result of our efforts to exercise power on behalf of ideas or groups that we view as larger and more important than ourselves. Although writers love to lampoon this very human tendency in political figures, Aristotle was probably right when he said, "Man is by nature a political animal."

To be "political" is to be engaged in the process of portraying events in ways that will win the support of others and the valuable resources of organizations. These organizations may be businesses, governments, or institutions. We can talk about the politics of the National Collegiate Athletic Association or a corporate main office just as easily as we can describe the politics of tax reform in Congress. We are often more interested in the politics of sex or the workplace than in the attempts of members of Congress to justify controversial votes to constituents back home. In this sense, actor Tom Hanks' portrayal of an HIV-positive lawyer in *Philadelphia* became part of the discourse of American politics in 1994.

Presidents, governors, regulators, and legislators have been delegated a wide range of powers that touch our lives, including the abilities to tax and spend, commit us to war, define legal and illegal behavior, and determine levels of competency for students and professionals. At any single moment, it is easy to feel both the power of political institutions as well as our own powerlessness to alter many of their specific products.

Politics, free choice, and persuasion are inseparable. Open societies require political activity and the bartering that comes with it. As John Bunzel has noted, the presence of a political situation implies the absence of agreement that has created patterns of influence. "Only in a closed society, where people are accustomed to accept what the rulers are convinced is 'good' for them, can the distinctive context of politics be totally removed in favor of the art of imposition."[2]

There is probably no single set of traits that makes political communication completely unique, but we can identify many of its essential forums and features. We begin by looking at three representative cases of political persuasion. The unique problems represented by these examples are then extensively discussed in the middle of the chapter. We close with an exploration of how political issues surface in less traditional, "nonpolitical" settings.

## Three Cases of Political Persuasion

Political persuasion is usually concerned with three broad types of goals: the explanation of administrative objectives made by leaders, the election of individuals to public office, and the adoption of legislation. Consider the following representative cases.

### The Campaign for Health Care Reform

No issue better defines the first few years of the administration of Bill Clinton than health care reform. Clinton made a federally supported program of universal health care a cornerstone of his 1992 political campaign and a benchmark goal for his first term. He proposed to restructure 15 percent of the entire American economy, an enormous political risk in a society that usually favors only modest and incremental reform. The risks were also increased by his decision to put his wife in charge of developing an alternative plan. In a first in presidential politics, the first lady became the lightning rod for a controversial part of the White House's political and legislative agenda.

Throughout 1993 and the first half of 1994, Hillary Rodham Clinton was a formidable advocate for establishing federal mandates for employers and insurance providers. But "Hillarycare," as the administration's various plans came to be known, had quickly created its own opposition, especially in the private health insurance industry. Lining up supporters to lobby Congress and to sway public opinion, the insurance industry sought to alert Americans to the dangers of what one

*Hillary Clinton was a formidable advocate for universal health care.*

*Tribune* photo by Nancy Stone

of their television commercials described as "mandatory government health alliances run by tens of thousands of new bureaucrats."[3]

By the summer of 1994 both camps had employed many forums to debate the issues. In the end, the Clinton initiative failed, but not before an intense campaign had been waged on many fronts. Following are a few samples of the efforts to shape public opinion.

- In early 1993 an industry group opposed to the Clinton plan of universal health coverage began a television campaign with a multimillion-dollar budget to raise fears that new legislation would take away the health benefits Americans now already have. Polling experts working for the president, among others, found that the ads were successful in raising concerns. In the words of an ad sponsored by the American Medical Association (another opponent to segments of the Clinton plan), "Government and insurance company administrators could end up determining which types of treatment are appropriate to patients like you."[4]

- The first lady scheduled weekly visits to various locations around the country to urge support for universal health care. A typical event was held on a summer afternoon in Seattle. As Hillary Clinton took the microphone in front of thousands at an outdoor rally, she spoke of the need to make guaranteed health coverage "a human right" and a matter of "social justice." Many cheered. Others—who came out at the urging of a conservative radio station—waved signs of protest. "Hillary," said one, "Hands Off My Health Care!" Nearly all of the visits in this campaign were designed for television and widespread media coverage. At many stops victims of illness who had expended all their assets to pay hospital and doctor fees told their heartbreaking stories in open meetings.[5]

- In the quest for health care reform—and increasingly in most major efforts by presidents, governors, and other leaders—the process of shaping public opinion was governed by techniques long familiar to advertising. President Clinton's pollster, Stan Greenberg, measured the reactions of ordinary Americans through polling and focus groups—intensive interviews of eight or nine people at a time. Among other things, Greenberg advised Clinton on several occasions that support for the objectives of health care reform remained high, even while doubts among Americans grew about the workability of various proposals.[6]

- In the summer of 1994 several unions sponsored a bus tour for reform advocates. The riders included nurses, survivors of serious injuries, and family members whose finances had been destroyed by payouts for expensive medical procedures. They were met at some stops by protesters opposing reform, in some cases bearing placards opposing "socialized health care."[7]

By midsummer 1994 it became clear that the Clinton administration and its allies would reject alternative Republican proposals, and Congress would reject the comprehensive Clinton plan. Most lawmakers realized, however, that they would eventually revisit many of the issues identified in the campaign waged by the first lady.

## Campaigns and the Politics of Attack

Most of us hold the view that presidential campaigns should be about the great issues of the day. Sometimes, though, we remember campaigns less for their attempts to deal with weighty matters of state and more for the emotional "hot buttons" they set off. In 1968 the public agonized over the United States' increasing involvement in the Vietnam War. In 1976 a faltering economy and the near-impeachment of a president dominated the news. In 1992 the most potent issues were domestic problems—health care, economic growth, the crippling national debt—

and one other concern. Few Americans wanted to repeat the 1988 presidential campaign of scare tactics. The most vivid issue in that presidential campaign was less an idea than a person, less a policy than an item from the pages of a police blotter.

In that year, George Bush clobbered Michael Dukakis by invoking the image of a murderer-turned-rapist who had fallen through the cracks of a Massachusetts prison-release program. This master stroke of "attack politics" started as a small item in a local New England paper, the *Lawrence Eagle-Tribune*, but it would eventually play itself out in television commercials and flyers. It would forever identify a black convict named Willie Horton with a "permissive" Dukakis. In the process, two of the GOP's most aggressive campaign strategists, Roger Ailes and Lee Atwater, would see their careers defined in terms of their decision to exploit the Horton case. The older Ailes became a commentator and conservative spokesman. At 38, the youthful Atwater went on to serve as chairman of the Republican party.

Dukakis never recovered from his identification as the governor of a state that permitted the weekend releases of convicts who had committed serious crimes. Although he had simply continued a penal reform program established by his Republican predecessor (which existed in other states as well), the ugly facts about Horton obliterated any such rational explanations.

In the early days of the campaign, members of Bush's staff were seeking ways to cut into Dukakis' lead. Researchers discovered that few major issues of the day—including the growth of the federal deficit, the growing American underclass, and the looming failures of thousands of banking institutions—cut as deeply as white fears about black crime.[8] Horton's weekend release from prison and his subsequent attack of a white couple in Maryland was, in the words of one media consultant, "an agenda setting battlefield nuclear weapon against Dukakis."[9] Horton represented the Bush campaign's opportunity to raise negatives about the Democratic challenger. Atwater boasted that his ads against Dukakis would "strip the bark off the little bastard" and "make Willie Horton his running mate."[10]

Horton was convicted in 1975 for the brutal murder of a 17-year-old boy in a robbery. A GOP flyer featured the brooding face of the convict and asked, "How serious is Dukakis about crime?" It went on to give an answer.

> Michael Dukakis talks about fighting crime, but there is a big gap between the rhetoric and the record. He has used his gubernatorial pardoning power to commute the sentences of 44 convicted murderers—a record for the state of Massachusetts. He has vetoed and continues to oppose the death penalty under any circumstances, even for cop-killers, drug kingpins and traitors. . . . He has also presided over and actively endorsed the most liberal prisoner furlough

programs in America, the only one in the nation releasing prisoners sentenced to life without parole.[11]

The facts were bleak. Even fellow Democrat Al Gore had noted during his own unsuccessful run in the presidential primaries that only Massachusetts gave weekend passes to murderers with life sentences.[12] As in most campaigns, what was not said is also extremely revealing. Nationally, according to Roger Simons, the average time in prison for first-degree murderers is only eight years.[13] Under Dukakis, Massachusetts had one of the lowest crime rates of any industrialized state in the United States. Many criminal justice experts continue to believe that furloughs maintain discipline by giving prisoners incentives for good behavior. The program Dukakis inherited had been started in 1972.[14]

Bush won in 1988 for reasons other than just these ads, but they became the standard for how political campaigns were run. It is obvious that such negative political commercials create more heat than light,[15] but their real damage to the political system is that they tell the public nothing about a person's qualifications to assume the responsibilities of the presidency or about policy to be pursued. The American public lost opportunities to consider the genuine issues of presidential leadership in 1988, and this void contributed to a growing unease among Americans about the basic integrity of the campaign process.

A tragic illness prompted a national focus on negative campaigns that crossed party lines. In early 1991 the forty-year-old Atwater lay dying in his Washington home, suffering from an inoperable brain tumor. To a reporter from *Life* magazine, he expressed sadness that he had become identified as one of the most ardent practitioners of negative politics and offered a public apology to Dukakis for the "naked cruelty" implied by some of his remarks.[16]

## Winning the Vote in 1920

Whether political decisions are made with great foresight and courage or made poorly, we are affected by them. How fast we can legally drive, how much tuition we pay, when we are declared legally dead, when we may marry or divorce, even how many hours we work in a day are a few examples of the local and national codes that touch our lives. Basic privileges we now take for granted such as the right to vote were won through diligent political action.

Women in the United States won the vote only in 1920 when Tennessee became the 36th state to ratify the Constitutional amendment. Congress had passed the legislation three years earlier proclaiming that "the right of citizens of the United States to vote shall not be denied or abridged . . . on account of sex . . ." The first meeting to campaign for the "social, civil, and religious rights of women" had been organized 72 years earlier by Elizabeth Cady Stanton, Lucretia Mott, and others.[17]

Like so many other causes then and now, the women's suffrage movement depended on mastery of the art of political persuasion. Virtually every technique and strategy used in the years prior to ratification are still used today. The most dramatic persuasive tactics involved pickets in front of the White House ("Mr. President, how long must women wait for liberty?"), mass parades, and rallies. Arrests of women in virtually every major city of the United States made daily headlines. Some of those given jail sentences went on hunger strikes, undergoing agonizing pain when jailers resorted to the use of stomach feeding tubes.[18]

The most effective forms of persuasion undertaken by supporters of women's suffrage were less dramatic, but no less important. The key activity involved lengthy and sustained efforts lobbying individual legislators and members of Congress. The well-organized National American Woman's Suffrage Association (NAWSA) was especially effective at securing the agreement of individual members of Congress and the state legislatures. One of the lobbyists, Maud Wood Park,

> was concerned with finding just the right woman to make a favorable impression on the member being interviewed. She always sent a woman from a man's own region if possible, recognizing the difficulty a New England woman might have, for example, with a congressman from Georgia. She thought on balance her most successful lobbyists were women from the Middle-West, middle-aged, and "rather too dressy," but "possessed of much common sense and understanding of politics in general, as well as of the men from their districts."[19]

Like most movements, the campaign for women's rights faced internal disputes about the kinds of tactics that were appropriate to produce change. Park and others in NAWSA favored quieter persuasion and less open conflict than the more confrontational Congressional Union. In the end, years of effort from many groups finally succeeded in winning the support of the men who dominated Congress and most of the state legislatures.

## The Forms of Political Persuasion

As is evident in all of the above cases, political persuasion is most directly about the negotiation of differences in a variety of contexts. In this section we turn our attention to some of the major features of administrative, legislative, and campaign persuasion.

*The techniques and strategies used to win ratification of the Nineteenth Amendment to the Constitution are still used today.*

## Administrative Persuasion

In the governmental bureaucracies that exist at all levels of public life, high-level administrators function somewhat differently than do their counterparts in large corporations. Political leaders owe their positions to those in the general population who elected them. Their responsibility for administering government involves a complex array of obligations. They may have their own agendas that include what they want to achieve, and they will have to work with legislative units and courts that must approve or interpret laws. They will also have to oversee thousands of subordinates who were in place when they took office and will probably still be present when they leave.

President Franklin Roosevelt perhaps said it best. Persuasion, even for presidents of the United States, is only a sometimes thing. The formal powers of most executives do not lend themselves to making unilateral orders that will be swiftly carried out. As Roosevelt told an amused gathering of reporters,

> The Treasury is so large and far-flung and ingrained in its practices that I find it almost impossible to get the action and results I want. . . . But the Treasury is not to be compared with the State Department. You should go through the experience of trying to get any changes in the thinking, policy, and action of the career diplomats and then you'd know what a real problem was.

And the Navy? "To change anything in the Na-a-vy," mused Roosevelt, "is like punching a feather bed."[20]

A judge in a court of law may be able to render precise decisions and exact penalties, but elected leaders know that they cannot govern only by decree. The paradox of executive leadership is that even the leaders who ostensibly "govern" from city hall or the White House must be effective persuaders to have any success at all. Most presidents have remarked on their surprise at how difficult it is to convince the agencies under their nominal control to go along with their agendas.[21] Bill Clinton compared his job to that of a captain of a not very responsive boat: "That is, I can steer it, but a storm can still come up and sink it. And the people that are supposed to be rowing can refuse to row."[22] The need to win the allegiance of their own bureaucracies, in addition to the support of members of Congress and the mass media, dictates that constant attention be paid to public opinion. The humorous observations that open this chapter are based on this fact of bureaucratic life. The fictional James Hacker proves Murphy's Law by rising to a level of complete ineptitude; he is no match for wily members of the professional civil service who actually manage the day-to-day affairs of the government. This is not to suggest that real leaders do not have considerable powers, but rather that we sometimes mistakenly equate formal authority with the ability to get things done.

For example, George Bush's decision to wage war against Iraq in January of 1991 involved both a key constitutional power and a rhetorical necessity. As commander-in-chief, a president can order American troops into short-term combat and make a case for putting American troops at risk. But no modern president has been able to sustain the use of the military in foreign combat without also carefully cultivating support in Congress and with the American people. President Lyndon Johnson chose not to run for reelection in 1968 when it was clear that many Americans had grave doubts about the wisdom of the Vietnam War. Although due to the Watergate affair rather than military involvement, Richard Nixon's unprecedented resignation from office in 1973 was guided by the same recognition that the formal powers of the presidency are nearly useless without the moral authority that comes with general public support.

Michael Novak once aptly described the president of the United States as a combination of "priest, prophet, and king."[23] All political figures have a potential range of persuasive options that come with their positions as presidents, mayors, or governors. Leaders are, by definition, individuals who are both symbols and symbol makers. We look to leaders for more than the daily management of governmental affairs. We expect that their actions and words will define the public community in terms that recognize our values and hopes. The success that any single leader enjoys is partly a function of skill in evoking a public sense of membership and participation in governmental activities. This is usually achieved in three broad ways.

### Setting the Public Agenda

One measure of any leader's success is how well he or she can focus attention on a common problem and dramatize its significance. At any given time, public attention is limited to a relatively small number of issues that dominate the headlines and command significant time on the evening news. A governor with an eye on shaping a state's agenda may repeatedly focus on a limited number of urgent issues in order to orchestrate public opinion. A recent governor of Pennsylvania, for example, sought to end the state monopoly on the sale of all liquor. He waged a highly visible, rhetorical campaign against the inefficiency and poor customer service under the state-controlled system. Richard Thornburgh intended to rally public opinion against the Pennsylvania Liquor Control Board, setting the stage for possible legislative action to permit private stores to sell beer and liquor. He failed, but not without inflicting serious wounds on an old and entrenched state bureaucracy.

### Building Productive Coalitions

A political leader is not expected to be a loner. He or she must know when to make alliances with others and when to end them. Perhaps the most admired skill of effective executives is the ability to find paths to agreement with businesses, labor groups, foreign states, or the leaders of opposing political parties. These agreements cannot appear to be "selling out" to such groups but must, instead, be seen as productive and beneficial for much of the general population. The remarkably diverse United Nations coalition against Iraq that formed in the summer of 1990, for instance, was put together by the Bush administration to isolate Iraq's leader, Saddam Hussein. While public opinion later divided in the United States and elsewhere about the wisdom of committing this coalition to war, few Americans doubted that the Bush administration had done an effective job of depriving the government of Iraq of much of its legitimacy in the West.

### Portraying the National Mood

Even before the age of television, leaders were expected to express the collective grief, anger, joy, and resolve of their constituents. Franklin Roosevelt's well-known Declaration of War address and Ronald Reagan's effective eulogy to the crew lost in the explosion of the *Challenger* space shuttle voiced what most Americans already felt. These presidents found the right expressions of national resolve and grief. At other times, a political figure advances his or her agenda by using particular examples of triumph or tragedy to represent what is "good" or "just" or "wrong" with ourselves or others. In most of his campaign and presidential speeches, Ronald Reagan identified an individual "just like the rest of us" whose experiences illustrated something important about our national character. Sometimes it was a neighbor who was frustrated with all the paperwork required before building a new house; at other times it was an ordinary person who engaged in highly visible acts of kindness, selflessness, and courage.[24] Politicians often seek examples of our national identity in isolated moments of individual lives.

## Legislative Persuasion

In the endless cycles of democratic politics, new initiatives are proposed, the problems they are intended to remedy are discussed, and decisions are made which eventually result in the enactment or defeat of legislation. The single most important function of any kind of legislative body—from local town councils to the United States Congress—is the consideration of laws. The policy under discussion may be as narrow as a town council's ruling on whether signs can be placed in front yards or as complex as a constitutional amendment prohibiting abortions.

Since policies are specific actions taken to remedy social or economic problems, their explanation and defense usually hinges on a problem-solution sequence. Successful policy proposals are based on convincing persuadees that (1) a problem is severe and (2) that a proposed course of action will alleviate either the causes of the problem or at least its worst symptoms.

In both predictable and unpredictable ways, legislatures are arenas for persuasion. The sometimes heated exchanges that occur before a key vote often present the most memorable images of legislators engaged in influencing each other, but floor debate is not where most legislative persuasion occurs. To understand how various representatives make up their minds on how they will vote on any item, we usually have to look elsewhere. Four important pressure points exist in the lengthy process of a specific bill as it moves from introduction to final passage.

### Executive Leadership

The most predictable source of leadership comes from chief executives. They regularly engineer plans for transforming issues of public concern into legislative proposals. The presidency of Lyndon Johnson is an especially interesting example. Between 1963 and 1965, Johnson introduced a number of major proposals to deal with racial discrimination, hunger, and poverty. The ambitious and widely publicized persuasive campaigns had no shortage of critics. However, Johnson was dramatically successful in following up statements of concern with specific legislative initiatives intended to provide concrete action. He persuaded members of Congress to pass the landmark Civil Rights and Voting Rights acts of 1964 and 1965, which guaranteed the right to vote, to work, and to use public facilities. Johnson's speeches on the effects of racial segregation and the need for legislative remedies were uncharacteristically effective; they provided an eloquent rationale for ending such dubious devices as poll taxes and literacy tests to restrict the rights of black citizens to vote. "We cannot, we must not, refuse to protect the right of every American to vote in every election that he may desire to participate in," he told the Congress.

> So I ask you to join me in working long hours—nights and weekends, if necessary—to pass this Bill. For from the window where I sit with the problems of our country I recognize that outside this chamber is the outraged conscience of a nation . . . and the harsh judgment of history on our acts.[25]

Johnson was a politician in the full sense of the word. He could seem petty and arrogant, but he was sometimes able to use his considerable persuasive talent to achieve the highest objective of politics: the creation of laws to assure the freedom and welfare of the weak as well as the strong.

### Lobbying

As in efforts to win the vote for women in 1920, many public laws start with the efforts of an organized group and the sympathy of a handful of legislators. Lobbyists are individuals representing businesses, unions, and political activists who fully exploit the First Amendment right of all Americans to petition their government. Many are full-time employees, working out of offices near the city, state, or federal offices of the representatives they seek to influence. Some, such as the well-financed professionals employed by the National Rifle Association, National Association of Broadcasters, and the AFL-CIO may actually draft legislation or amendments to other bills that will then be introduced by sympathetic legislators in Washington and the various states. The more routine work of lobbying involves supplying facts and arguments to legislators, usually prior to a key legislative vote.[26] The term itself comes from the fact that before legislators had private offices, they used to meet individuals seeking to influence legislation in the foyer immediately outside a legislative chamber. The noun has become a verb; to lobby

"LOBBIES"

Reprinted by permission: Tribune Media Services

is to attempt to influence a legislative or administrative decision in government.[27]

For many Americans, lobbying carries connotations of manipulative persuasion—using money, food, sex, or whatever represents a legislator's weakness—in order to win special favors for an interest group. To be sure, lobbyists have power, but their persuasion tactics are far less exotic. The most common lobbying strategies include telling a legislator what constituents back home think, making suggestions for how he or she can defend a vote, and supplying arguments about the positive or negative consequences of a certain legislative decision. Most lobbying is low-key and directed to sympathetic or undecided lawmakers.[28] Virtually all major businesses, interest groups, and unions lobby legislators—from General Electric to state student organizations, from the Catholic Church to the National Aeronautics and Space Administration. This kind of persuasion is sometimes called ''wholesale'' politics because it is directed to lawmakers and not to the general public. ''Retail'' political persuasion involves activities intended for general public consumption, such as speeches, press conferences, and television or direct-mail advertisements.

## Hearings

One of the most potent forums for the persuasion of both the American public and individual legislators is the committee hearing. This venue is where most of the real work of building support for pending proposals is done. Hearings are conducted by the members of committees who have jurisdiction over specific types of proposed legislation. In practical terms, they present the ideal setting for supporters and opponents of legislation to dramatize their concerns. Lobbyists, experts, and victims regularly appear before committees considering proposed legislation. Their testimony is often graphic and touching. They are most often selected by the committee leadership to lay the groundwork for convincing testimony that may eventually win the notice and approval of their colleagues and the general public. Sometimes they may come under hostile questioning from opposing members of the panel. In recent years, for example, Americans have watched or read about hours of hearings, ranging from the confirmation of Supreme Court Justice Clarence Thomas to testimony on health care reform by Hillary Rodham Clinton.

In legislative hearings, members often count on the presence of the press—especially television cameras—to place issues of concern before the general public. Hearings have a basic publicity function that can work well even when a proposed bill has little chance of passage. Most editors find it difficult to resist the drama of a heated exchange between a committee member and a vulnerable testifier. In 1973, to cite a notorious instance, the three major commercial networks devoted over 235 hours to the presentation of Senate hearings into the Watergate affair.[29] Millions of Americans became transfixed by the proceedings and their key players. In an important sense, the political history of the United States could be partly written in the legislative hearings that have taken place in the nation's capitol—ranging from Joseph McCarthy's attempts in 1954 to find communists in the State Department to the 1994 hearings of the House Banking Committee on "Whitewater" activities.

## Constituent and Party Pressure

Hearings are often intended as a means for legislators to influence citizens far beyond the national or state capitols. Members of legislatures are themselves subject to two sources of influence. In the oldest tradition of representative democracy, many (but by no means all) are influenced by opinions "back home." Letters, editorials, phone calls, and advice from friends and opinion leaders in the home districts can all be factors in determining votes on a pending question.[30] "Voting the constituency" works best when a clear point of view exists in the district and a member does not have a deep philosophical reason for opposing or approving a piece of legislation. It is more common among low-profile, "back bencher" legislators and in situations where there is less urgency to go along with the party position on a vote.

*Party leaders used to be able to "deliver" the votes of their members with great regularity.*

*Tribune* photo by Nancy Stone

The second source of influence is the "party line." Political parties are less dominant than they once were, but they are still important. Party leaders used to be able to "deliver" the votes of their members with great regularity. Prior to the 1950s, the act of going against one's own party was a risky business. Powerful leaders like the Senate's Lyndon Johnson and the House of Representatives' Sam Rayburn headed well-drilled teams of floor managers and whips who would regularly deliver the votes of members on questions that had been defined as party issues.

The same structure is still in place and still imposes a degree of "party discipline." Consider *Congressional Quarterly*'s description of the last few minutes on a routine budget vote in the House of Representatives in 1979. Members were in the process of voting on an amendment to cut money from the president's proposed budget, but something else was at stake. As Leon Panetta soon discovered, the possibility of embarrassing the leadership of his own party was also on the line.

> Freshman Rep. Leon E. Panetta, D-Calif., was having a tough time finishing his phone call in the House cloakroom.
>
> First, Majority Leader Jim Wright, D-Texas, interrupted. Wright was followed by several other Democrats, who took turns breaking in. Then a page brought Panetta a note saying Speaker Thomas P. O'Neill Jr., D-Mass., wanted to see him. Panetta found no escape on the House floor. As he left the cloakroom and strode down the aisle into the crowded chamber, Jim Mooney, chief aide to Majority Whip John Brademas, D-Ind., spotted him. Mooney grabbed Norman Y. Mineta, D-Calif., and steered him toward Panetta. "Can you give us a vote on this?" asked Mineta. Panetta said no, resisting his friend's plea to change the vote he had just cast in favor of an amendment by Joseph L. Fisher, D-Va., to cut about $7 billion from the first fiscal 1979 budget resolution.
>
> Undaunted by the rejection, Mineta turned to court other Democrats who had voted for the amendment—and against the wishes of the Democratic leadership.
>
> Meanwhile, Wright wove his way through a crowd of younger members in the well of the chamber, urging them to switch their votes by signing little red cards stacked on a nearby table. O'Neill and Brademas stalked up the aisle, looking like hunters in search of prey. They, too, sought vote switchers. By the time the leaders stopped stalking—10 minutes after the House scoreboard showed that time had elapsed on the roll-call vote—16 Democrats had trooped down to the well to change their votes. The amendment, which had been a sure winner when time ran out, instead was defeated, 195–203.[31]

## Campaign Persuasion

A third broad form of political persuasion occurs in the context of campaigns. By definition, a campaign is a concerted effort to influence a "targeted" group over a limited time frame. Lobbying directed toward a legislature, advertising intended for the general public, and other forms of organized persuasion have many of the features of campaigns and are discussed elsewhere in this book. (See, for example, chapter 9.) Our focus here is on the electoral campaign that is undertaken to put a person in public office. All forms of campaigns share a number of important characteristics.

### Short-Term Orientation

A campaign is always governed by a limited time frame. Political candidates must work to have public attitudes peak at just the right moment: election day. The idea of the campaign itself owes its "do or die" imagery to the battlefield. Strategies and tactics are defined, and the troops are mobilized on voting day to produce a final victory. In war as in politics, battles may not always be decisive, but on any given day there is inevitably a "winner."

### Use of Public Relations Professionals

There was a time in the United States when candidates did much of the routine work of the campaign themselves. They often hired printers, rented halls, wrote their own speeches, and depended on a close cadre of friends and associates. Even Woodrow Wilson was not beyond taking time out of his schedule to draft (in shorthand) a specific statement or campaign speech. Political parties have also carried responsibility for assisting candidates in their electoral attempts. With the exception of the most local of public offices, candidates for higher-level positions now seek the support of professional public relations specialists. They often bypass the offered assistance of leaders of the political party in favor of the expertise of specialists in electronic media and mass mail campaigns.

Scores of full-time campaign consultants operate in virtually every state with clients that include individuals, political parties, and pressure groups organized to defeat ballot questions. "Full service" consulting firms such as Washington's Matt Reese Associates or New York's Garth Associates Inc. are capable of completely managing virtually every aspect of a politician's campaign.[32] Like most complex businesses, the firms run by these consultants also subcontract more specialized work to professionals with highly prized talents. Over the last several decades the best known have included:

> Peter Hart—campaign polling, mostly for Democratic candidates.
>
> Richard Vaguerie—direct mail campaigns for conservative candidates and causes. Vaguerie is credited with refining precise direct mail campaigns for targeting voters.
>
> Tony Schwartz—radio and television commercials. As mentioned in chapter 4, Schwartz produced some of the most memorable political commercials in the 1960s and 1970s, including the "Daisy spot" that implied that presidential candidate Barry Goldwater would use nuclear weapons in Vietnam.
>
> Roger Ailes—a one-time Broadway producer, and executive at CNBC, he became the most sought-after consultant in the 1988 presidential campaign. He was considered an expert in coaching candidates in the use of the media, especially television. His clients have included Ronald Reagan and George Bush.

Ed Rollins—managed Reagan's 1984 reelection landslide; briefly joined Ross Perot's campaign in 1992. Known for his political savvy, Rollins nonetheless embarrassed himself and his client, New Jersey gubernatorial candidate Christine Todd Whitman, in 1993 by boasting that he had developed a campaign strategy to keep black voters at home on election day.

James Carville—helped manage an upset Senate victory in Pennsylvania that demonstrated the vulnerability of President Bush prior to the 1992 campaign. Carville went on to be the star political consultant to Bill Clinton, but he proved less successful in advising an incumbent who lost the hotly contested New Jersey governor's race won by the GOP's Christine Todd Whitman.

Campaign events now unfold with the professional gloss of other forms of advertising and public relations spots—and with a price tag to match. Important elements provided by professionals include speech writing, scheduling events, press relations, issues research, and the employment of frequent "tracking polls" to measure the movement of public opinion.

## Evolutionary Change

Campaigns evolve. Typically, they must progress through stages of growth that will enable them to gain new resources, such as money and workers, while continually increasing credibility and visibility. Some of the features of persuasive campaigns were discussed in chapter 9. Our attention here is on the four basic phases of electoral campaigns described by Judith Trent and Robert Friedenberg.[33]

In the first "pre-primary" stage of *surfacing*, individuals seeking public office attempt to establish their basic honesty and credibility with the American public. They try to be seen as much as possible and attempt to gain recognition as serious contenders for a particular office. In the 1992 presidential campaign, for example, the surfacing phase of Bill Clinton required months of grueling campaigning against other party hopefuls. Clinton was young, the governor of a low-profile southern state, and a novice without a national following. He successfully used the summer of 1991 to give a series of widely reported speeches defining himself as a "different kind of Democrat."[34]

The *primary stage* focuses on the elections that give individuals the right to be the official nominees of a party for an office. At the presidential level, they include the early winter contests in New Hampshire and the March "Super Tuesday" selections made by the parties in Florida, Massachusetts, and many other states. Primaries sap the energies and resources of even the most ambitious and energetic presidential candidates. Huge sums of money are spent on local television to convince sizable chunks of each state's party members. The intent is to garner the support of both pledged delegates to the summer political conventions and voters who will support the candidate in various straw polls that measure the comparative popularity of contenders in the same party. Throughout the primary process, consultants and media specialists are hired, organizations move into high gear, and messages are fine tuned. In addition, elaborate networks of fundraisers are established for the costly process of activating generally uninterested voters. Huge sums of cash are raised to buy access to the American public via television, making the primary phase a test of the contender's ability to tap the resources of organized interest groups in order to reach the less-organized masses.[35]

The third phase is dominated by the *nominating conventions*. In the past, candidates in the same party fought for the right to represent it in the fall elections, but the conventions now have a more ritualistic function. The primary season now yields the party's likely nominee; conventions merely confirm that choice. However, they still play an important part in defining the upcoming campaign and the issues that are likely to dominate it. In 1992 both of the parties' conventions were seen as symbols of the divisions and changes occurring in the United States. The Democrats met in New York City in a heavily stage-managed convention intended to impress the nation with a new, less liberal populist party. Those who were perceived as dissenters or potentially divisive—including Jerry Brown—were relegated to minor roles. Much of the convention used favored speakers such as former New York Governor Mario Cuomo to attack the "cynical" domination of the White House by the Republicans.[36]

In sharp contrast, the press largely portrayed the Houston meeting of the Republicans as a meeting that had been taken over by factions ready for a cultural and religious war. Speeches from Marilyn Quayle, Pat Buchannan and others sought to portray the Democrats as a party that had abandoned basic American values. Buchannan especially railed against change that would destroy "a nation we still call God's country." He was generally savaged by the press for his "slash and burn" rhetoric of polarization.[37]

The fourth stage, the *general election*, includes all of the traditional components of the political campaign. Strategic decisions are weighed and carried out, and scores of questions must be answered. Should the candidate avoid debates or welcome them? Should the emphasis of television advertising be on attacking the opponent—what consultants euphemistically call "raising the negatives of the opposition"—or ignoring him or her?[38] How much of the campaign should be carried on by surrogates who will make attacks on opponents that would be unseemly if delivered by the candidate? How much access will be given to members of the press? These and countless other questions are raised and dealt with in a campaign that frequently splits into separate and

Figure 11.1

**The Logistics of a Campaign:**

**Developing Basic Strategies and Resources**

No two campaigns are exactly alike. Even so, certain basic requirements for planning and executing political campaigns are quite predictable. This representative list applies to those seeking offices ranging from the Presidency to a seat in the House of Representatives.

| Period | Planning and Research | Campaign Activities |
|---|---|---|
| Pre-Primary: | Take the "benchmark polls" to measure visibility with potential voters; engage in issues research; make profile of strengths and weaknesses; learn about campaign finance and ballot requirements; seek advice of potential supporters. | Organize staff; begin fund-raising; seek assistance and support of party activitists; participate in newsworthy events; meet with local or national opinion leaders and editors; open and equip campaign office; establish campaign committees. |
| Primary: | Continue polling; identify contributors; research opposition; test basic camnpaign themes; "fine tune" basic speech, build "grassroots" organization. | Deliver basic campaign message, respond to attacks; hold fundraising events; begin directmail campaign to increase name recognition and to identify supporters and contributors. |
| Convention: | Identify supporters and potential workers; seek party help; purchase media time and space for the general election campaign. | Address delegate's concerns, identify issues for party support, seek roles for surrogates in public events and party hierarchy. |
| General Election: | Schedule events to target undecided voters; begin planning for "get out the vote" activities on election day; take series of "tracking polls" to measure efficiency of various messages and media; continue to refine basic themes. | Appear in "best chance" districts; seek "free" news media coverage of appearances; (if behind in polls) challenge opponent to public debates; seek newspaper endorsements; ask contibutors for additional support; (if affordable) use television for late campaign "blitz;" increase campaign appearances to five to ten each day. |

uncoordinated fronts. From late August to election day, presidential candidates operate extensively from an airplane—accompanied by members of the national press and a close cadre of advisers. In Washington and other major cities, scores of additional workers "advance" future appearances, coordinate efforts with local leaders of the political parties, and continue to contract for television, radio, and print advertising. In this final period, campaigns take on a character that is quite unlike anything else: partly a well-designed machine that is suddenly beyond anyone's control, partly an intellectually empty exercise in self-praise, and sometimes a chance to catch glimpses of the nation's collective will.

## Emphasis on Character, Concerns, and Issues

Electoral campaigns usually exploit three distinct types of content. The first and arguably most dominant message that comes across in any campaign involves cues and appeals that represent the kind of persons the would-be officeholders seem to be. "*Character*," in journalist Charles Peter's words, "is the ability to rise above all the forces that keep us from thinking clearly—not only about what will work, but about what is right."[39] We expect that election campaigns will provide evidence of the fitness of a candidate's character and will give us reason to put our faith in their judgments. As important as specific issues are, we realize that they will change over time, while the fundamental capacities and good sense of a leader will remain essentially unchanged. When we talk about particular politicians, it is usually not in terms of their ideas but rather in terms that describe the kind of person we think they are. We see them as generous, ambitious, serious, calculating, friendly, obsessed, self-serving, or hundreds of other traits. Political commercials in election campaigns generally feature candidates in the same way that dramatists might introduce a character as a film or play unfolds. We see them making statements and taking positions, but many of the statements are secondary to the image or *public persona* that is projected. In 1976, for example, political commercials for presidential candidate Jimmy Carter often featured the former rancher and governor at his home, clad in jeans and a western shirt. While Carter made suitably presidential comments about the state of the nation and the economy, the deepest impression the commercials left was of a competent, grass-roots leader far removed from official Washington. Carter's effective campaign slogans emphasized the need to build a "government as good as its people" and fostered the image of a leader who was still close to his Georgia roots.

Even though thirty-second political commercials are superficial, character remains an important aspect of political dialogue. As presidential scholar James David Barber has noted, "The issues will change, the character of the president will last."[40]

A second form of rhetorical content in campaigns involves *concerns*—expressions of awareness about general priorities or values. Statements of concern are often used to symbolize a person's awareness of a problem, frequently in place of more specific plans or policies. They are intended to show solidarity with a segment of the population that needs reassurance that a threat to the welfare or safety of some group has not been forgotten. A president, for example, may use many different public occasions to demonstrate his compassion and sensitivity: by expressing concerns about the breakdown of order in the Middle East, the decline of an industry such as textiles, or the fate of farm families who can no longer manage their debts. In many ways, these kinds of statements are the bread and butter of politics. General expressions of interest on certain issues are important to audiences who want evidence that their priorities are shared by their leaders. A question-and-answer session between Ronald Reagan and a group of farmers worried about Japanese restrictions on imports in 1982 presents a typical case.

> **Question**: Mr. President, I'm in the cattle business. I'd like to know what is being done to help cut down the barriers for foreign trade, especially in Japan. Now, they've sent all their products over in the area, and we do not put any restrictions on their products, and yet they put the restrictions on our products. . . . I feel that your administration . . . is doing a lot, but I feel that there should be a lot more done.

The farmer's comment was an invitation for the president to declare a firm policy of reciprocal restrictions on Japanese goods. However, because he had gone on record in opposition to a formal policy of tariffs on foreign goods, Reagan answered with an empathetic restatement of the problem and an expression favoring "quiet diplomacy" rather than "protectionist" legislation. His measured response focused on responding to the concerns of his listeners, not on the policy solutions sought by his audience.

> **The President**: This gentleman is talking about cattle farming and the restrictions that are put on our exported cattle, for example, to Japan, and yet the unlimited way in which they can come in here. He says he knows we're doing something but [he is] not sure it is enough. Well, maybe one of the reasons is because we believe in quiet diplomacy. Instead of putting some fellow on the other side on the spot, and holding him up to public view, we have been working very hard . . . to change some of these and to tell them that the only alternative is start to go down the road to protectionism, which we don't want to do.[41]

As President Kennedy once noted, "Every presidential speech cannot reveal a major decision."[42] There are clearly many times when a political message is more a ritual of reassurance than a call for action.

The third form of campaign content is perhaps the most important. It includes statements that propose specific *policy* objectives. A policy is a specific plan of action, or a set of guidelines or rules which are intended to alleviate a problem. As we noted in chapter 2, one of the most important functions of a democracy is to provide an orderly means for public discussion of rules that will govern the population. Before an election, only a small number of proposed policy issues will gain public attention. Debates over a candidate's positions on such questions form— or ought to form—the prime issues of a campaign. The complete agenda of issues that emerges is determined in part by the candidates and in part by the mass media. How does a candidate feel about restricting lumber harvests in areas where endangered species exist? Does he or she support using trade sanctions to encourage Japan to open up its markets? Is the candidate willing to raise taxes in order to pay for government services? Voter studies generally conclude that many Americans have only a vague sense of where candidates stand on a variety of issues.[43] This is sometimes because candidates are evasive, and other times because voters lack the will to learn what the candidates are thinking. Even so, Americans remain convinced that issues are the proper focus of elections.

## Politics as Expression

Thus far, we have described political persuasion in practical and pragmatic terms. Campaigns and discussions of policy seem to be about gaining or using power to achieve certain specific goals. As obvious as this observation is, it should not obscure the equally compelling fact that the realm of political discourse is actually much broader. Like all of the popular arts, political discussion sometimes exists more for the gratification or emotional "lift" it gives its participants than for the specific effects it may produce in the nation's governmental and civil life.[44] Politics has an *expressive* as well as an *instrumental* function in any society. A Memorial Day tribute to troops killed in battle—filled with music, flags, and soldiers—hardly lends itself to a discussion of the possibly disastrous foreign policy decisions that caused the deaths being commemorated. The cross, the flag, and their verbal counterparts are not instruments of discussion as much as expressive symbols of affirmation. Political language defines who we are or want to be as often, or more often, than it contributes to social change. Several dimensions of this expressive function are important to consider.

### Political Issues and Status

Sometimes an issue matters less for how it might evolve into legislative proposals than for what our position on it says about who we are. In his insightful discussion of what he calls "status politics," sociologist Joseph Gusfield has noted that we tend to combine our attitudes toward specific *issues* with stereotyped attitudes about certain kinds of people. A topic becomes a status issue when a group collectively makes the judgment that where other people stand on a question demonstrates their superiority or inferiority. The "right" position indicates stronger morals and higher social prestige. The "wrong" side of an issue may be interpreted as a sign of the moral weakness of its misguided advocates. Gusfield cited two examples.

> In the election of 1960, Protestant-Catholic conflict was a major source of candidate loyalties. Were Protestants protecting the White House

*Politics serves an expressive function in society. The Vietnam Memorial, the flag, and the cross are all symbols of affirmation.*

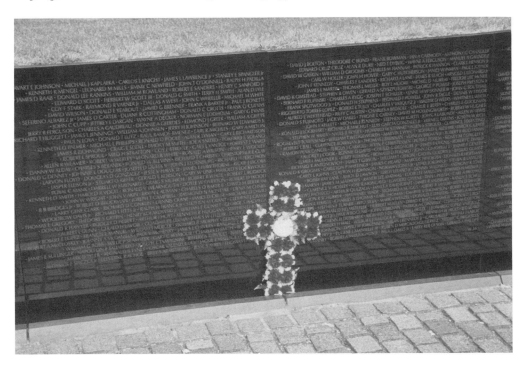

from papal domination? Were Catholics trying to enhance Catholic doctrines by a Catholic President [John F. Kennedy]? Only the naive and the stupid will accept either of these suggestions. At stake, however, was the relative prestige of being Protestant in American life. The ability of a Catholic to break the traditional restriction in American politics does mean . . . the prestige of being Catholic is enhanced. . . . In a similar fashion the current [1963] school desegregation struggle is symbolic rather than instrumental. Whether or not most [blacks] will actually be attending integrated schools in the near future is not the issue. Northern cities have developed little more than token integration. Public acceptance of the principle of integration, expressed as token integration, is an act of deference which raises the prestige of . . . [blacks]. Whether better educational conditions . . . will result is not the significant issue. It is that of equal rights.[45]

More recently, pressure from various civil rights groups prompted the Professional Golfers Association to withhold sponsorship of tournaments at country clubs that barred membership to nonwhites. The decision came in response to publicity in 1990 that a PGA tournament planned for Birmingham, Alabama, would take place at its whites-only Shoal

*Political persuasion addresses social recognition and legitimacy in addition to changes in policy.*

*Tribune* photo by Nancy Stone

Creek Country Club.[46] It is far from certain that the association's new policy will affect the access of African-Americans to the nation's most prestigious country clubs. However, as do heated debates about gay rights, women's issues, and the relative absence of Hispanics and Asian Americans in prime-time television, the stance of the PGA speaks to the vital issue of self- and group-esteem. The concept of status politics is a potent reminder that political persuasion is not only about objective changes in policy, but also about social recognition and legitimacy. Many issues remind us of our solidarity with certain groups and our estrangement from others. When statements are made that confirm the prestige of groups with which we identify, our own sense of self-worth and importance is confirmed.

## Politics as "Mediated," One-Way Expression

Public knowledge of issues and advocates today is undeniably shaped by the mass media, especially television. The role of the media in shaping political beliefs has both obvious and subtle aspects. In a simpler and more community-centered America, the average citizen's understanding of government was based on membership in a party and face-to-face contacts with local politicians. In many cities, the party's presence was (and in some instances, still is) made known by the neighborhood "ward healer," whose connections in city hall made it easier to get streets cleaned or potholes repaired. Between the Civil War and the advent of broadcasting in the 1920s, it was routine for the major parties and cultural organizations to hold large public gatherings to give the ordinary citizen a chance to hear the words of major political and social leaders. The popular temperance speaker John B. Gough, for example, spoke to over 9 million people in 9,600 separate addresses over the course of his career.[47] Leaders such as Teddy Roosevelt, Senator Robert LaFollette, and union leader Samuel Gompers depended on a network of theaters and lecture halls to tie even remote American towns to national issues.

There still are thousands of local officeholders such as mayors and school board members who are personally known to many individual residents, but different kinds of information-saturated networks now link most Americans to the political world. We know them by their familiar initials—CNN, ABC, WTBS, NPR, and so on. While these networks broadcast images rich in expressive content, including people reacting to events that have affected them, they naturally cast us more as observers than as participants. Ironically, our relationship to political events still mimics the intimacy of personal contact but ultimately denies it. Dan Rather and Peter Jennings are people we "know," and their familiar presence serves as much to reassure as to inform. In reality, they are part of a complex information web that has made us spectators to global events over which we have little influence. Television, rather than the party organization, now binds the nation together. No institution, including the political parties, the Congress, or even the presidency, can match the ability of the three networks to convey attitudes and information to the nation. Within minutes of a crisis, such as the 1981 attempt on the life of Ronald Reagan or the suicide of White House adviser Vincent Foster, citizens all over the continent and much of the developed world had access to the same information (or misinformation).

Television and other forms of rapid mass communication deliver political information in a way that is fundamentally different from how listeners used to acquire information from "live" speakers. Television presents the impression of unfiltered reality, but it and other mass media exclude far more than can be included. We, in fact, are recipients of secondhand reports. The routine processes of news gathering and reporting necessarily *mediate* between us and actual events. There is admittedly nothing new about this fact of life. Even President Lincoln had to deal with American public opinion that was shaped to a large extent by the nation's magazine and newspaper editors, many of whom hated him. What is unique about mediation is that it has partially

*In a more community-centered America, the average citizen's understanding of government was based on membership in a party and face-to-face contacts with local politicians. Today, reliance on mass media has shifted the balance from active participation to observation. We have become spectators—recipients of filtered reports. The danger of becoming consumers of political expression is that we abdicate our responsibility to participate and contribute.*

replaced direct political involvement with political expression. We no longer expect that political activism will flourish in local districts and neighborhoods. The political dialogue that does take place is carried on at a distance, some of it within the pages of newspapers and much of it within the narrow confines of thirty-second television commercials or video news headlines.[48] While people know at least a little about a lot of political issues, they feel more helpless about influencing the course of events surrounding an issue. To an extent, we have become a nation of political consumers rather than participants. A 1989 study, for example, indicated that 74 percent in a wide sample of Americans indicated that they regularly watched the news on television,[49] and yet Americans vote in fewer numbers now than fifty years ago. A "good turnout" is about 50 percent of all eligible voters, compared to 70 to 80 percent in many European democracies.[50]

## Political Messages in Nonpolitical Forms: A Critical Look

The persuasion discussed above comes from a fairly narrow sector of public discourse: direct involvement in the political institutions of government. Are other forms of American discourse—novels, film, television, and popular journalism—outside the realm of politics? To some extent all segments of popular culture—even those that seem light years away from presidential speeches and congressional debates—have a political context.

Persuasion is often most effective when it occurs in the context of *entertainment*. Even when we are entertained by watching television or feature films, we are receiving political messages with varying degrees of potency. Just as it is fair to conclude that all television educates— even television that is not "educational"—it is equally important to remember that the products of the entertainment industry carry at least some latent political messages.

Our point is not that there are secret or subversive attempts to "dupe" Americans with cleverly hidden political messages. Rather, the process of selection and choice inevitably forces the creators of all entertainment forms to reinforce perspectives that communicate praise or blame about institutions, values, and social priorities. Stories and screenplays, for example, must be fabricated to include specific details about settings, individuals, and lifestyles. In developing this detail writers, producers, and novelists insert their own visions of what we should fear or hope, honor or condemn, accept or reject. In Todd Gitlin's apt phrase, television and its content represent our "national dream factory." Its relentless presence in our living rooms gives it the power to "reproduce larger ideologies" and "grander fantasies" than might ever be communicated by less pervasive institutions.[51] Film theorist James Monaco has similarly noted that movies communicate the details of the "social contracts" that govern our lives, including challenges or affirmations of the "basic ideals of community, family, and relationships."[52]

"All movies, even those intended as pure entertainment," notes Terry Christensen, "send messages about politics and society."[53] As a form of vivid portraiture, for example, films naturally communicate what we collectively want to praise or condemn in our national life. They may celebrate heroes in the American military (i.e., *Patton, An Officer and a Gentleman, Top Gun*), or criticize American imperialism (*Apocalypse Now, Born on the Fourth of July*). Cities are often portrayed as islands of opportunity (*Manhattan, The Secret of My Success, Working Girl*) or as dangerous lairs filled with society's misfits (*Midnight Cowboy, Taxi Driver, Grand Canyon*). Businesses may be populated by cunning and corrupt figures (*Quiz Show, Philadelphia, Roger and Me, The Firm*) or occasional idealists (*The Paper, Tucker*). Some films provide portraits of feisty women who defy the limits of class or sexism (*Shadowlands, Norma Rae, Thelma and Louise*). Others offer implicit criticism of the limits of American tolerance (*Boyz in the Hood, Chaplin, Mississippi Burning*). Politics itself is frequently portrayed as a nominally corrupt enterprise (*Bob Roberts, The Candidate, The Distinguished Gentleman*).

The recurring fantasies of countless television series are usually more positive and idealistic than are feature films. We are subtly attracted to the social order and bedrock stability of the generally happy and adaptable families of prime time. The enduring success of *The Cosby Show* in syndication testifies to the tendency to find reassurance for the American dream in fictional situations. Cliff and Claire Huxtable remind us that education and wealth can be colorblind and that decades of racial discrimination in the United States has not necessarily scarred all its potential victims. As television critic Mark Crispin Miller asserts, there may be another message in *The Cosby Show* as well.

> As a willing advertisement for the system that pays him well, Cliff Huxtable also represents a threat contained. Although dark-skinned and physically imposing, he ingratiates us with his childlike mien and enviable lifestyle, a surrender that must offer some deep solace to a white public terrified that, one day, blacks might come with guns to steal the copperwear, the juicer, the microwave, the VCR, even the TV itself. On *The Cosby Show*, it appears as if blacks, in general, can have or do have what many whites enjoy, and that such material equality need not entail a single break-in. And there are no hard feelings, none at all, now that the old injustice has been so easily rectified. Cosby's definitive funny face . . . is a strained denial of all animosity.[54]

Films may offer a more challenging view of American race relations (*Ragtime, Do the Right Thing, Mississippi Massala*), but they are not burdened as directly by the need to attract audiences and advertisers who may prefer idealized portrayals of our hopes rather than more accurate evocations of entrenched realities. To be sure, some programs "play against type"; *Roseanne*, for example, portrays a less than perfect family. However, most television content is upbeat in order to function as a medium for selling the products of its sponsors.

The commercial structure of the mass media dictates that some of its activities are, indeed, "political." Fundamentally, we consume media content as "information," "news," or "entertainment," but in the United States it is essentially a product targeted to an *audience*. As such, the nature of the content is governed to a large extent by market forces centered on mass consumption. Whether the "manufacturer" is Disney or Viacom/Paramount, Gannett Newspapers or Rupert Murdoch's News Corporation, the end result is much the same. These industries have a "product" that must be sold as information, entertainment, or—increasingly—an uncomfortable combination of both. In the media there are many exceptions to this mass marketing logic; some publishing houses, newspapers, record companies, and television writers make valuable contributions to popular culture without imposing formulas that require appealing to a mass audience, but they are comparatively rare in terms of what Americans normally consume.

The tool that helps us discover the selective development of content with political overtones is sometimes called "negative evidence." It is an invaluable concept for the persuasion analyst, because sometimes the most interesting feature of a message is what is not present in it. Negative evidence develops in the course of a systematic search of communication content where there is an *absence* of something one might reasonably expect to find. As television's Linda Ellerbee has noted, "When we point the camera at one thing, we are pointing it away from another. Thus, one of the first things to look at when viewing the media is what you cannot see."[55]

In assessing the content of the broadcast networks' nightly newscasts, for example, one would expect to find stories on certain topics, such as the failures of savings and loan banks in the mid-1980s. Ironically, however, little was reported at the time, leading to discussions about how such an important event was ignored.[56]

Advertiser-supported media generally produce some interesting patterns of negative evidence. Many studies confirm that media content—in news or entertainment—generally plays to our fantasies and beliefs rather than our mistaken impressions.[57] More specifically, popular media content is usually about people rather than ideas, entertainment rather than information, "an interesting story" rather than the outline of a more subtle trend. Additionally, it is usually voyeuristic: exploring how people *feel* rather than what they *think*. The gaze that is favored most by television is the reaction shot, a close-up that allows us to watch how events register on the faces of people. The camera may linger on the face of a hapless bureaucrat caught in the crosshairs of a Mike Wallace interrogation on *60 Minutes.* The culprit's discomfort is far more vivid than the underlying social or political problems that gave rise to the segment. Success in the television marketplace is usually measured by whether the viewer or reader was amused by the drama of human conflict—not by an understanding of its complex causes.[58] The airwaves are flooded with a steady diet of talk shows where the private dysfunctions of ordinary people are put on display. *Oprah, Donahue, Geraldo,* and other shows present a "carnival culture": an almost continual national peepshow.[59] That culture is amplified in programs that mimic a hard news format but deliver soft tabloid gossip (*A Current Affair, Hard Copy, Inside Edition*); content is chosen to hook television grazers into the nine minutes of commercials that have been presold to advertisers at lucrative prices.

This argument that television and much of popular culture is "bubble-gum" for the mind is old and familiar. Yet the political effects of the "dummying down" of popular culture—especially at a time when the average American television is on for nearly seven hours a day—give reason for concern. Our search for distraction and escape through popular culture genres comes at the price of having less time and energy for competing messages with perhaps less entertainment value but far greater worth. To cite one instance, ABC has been forced to assess whether they can afford the half-hour discussions of social and political issues on *Nightline,* given the better audiences and economics of entertainment programming, including the late-night talk shows offered by the competition.[60]

The competitive environment of the media dictates content appealing to a mass audience, content that in many instances replaces more substantive discussion. As a result, our escapist popular culture has nearly swamped us in a media environment that has coarsened and debased public discourse.[61] Although we feel like we are consumers of a vast range of media choices, the price we may have paid is that we are less willing as a nation to attend to the portions of our civil life (presidential speeches, congressional debates, television documentaries on social issues) which serve as early warnings to future national problems. As television newscaster Edward R. Murrow warned over 30 years ago, "Surely we shall pay for using this most powerful instrument of communication to insulate the citizenry from the hard and demanding realities which must be faced if we are to survive."[62]

## The False Distinction between "Expedient" and "Principled" Messages

Finally, no overview of political persuasion would be complete without at least touching on the issue of our collective distrust of American political culture. If indeed we are political creatures, for most of us it is not a feature that bears witness to the greatness of our species. We like to see evidence that a politician has demonstrated political courage, but the more timeless image is of the corrupt opportunist aided by a cadre of consultants, ad agencies, and an invasive press. Thomas Nast's turn-of-the-century political cartoons still reflect this part of our folklore. In Nast's day as now, the politico is frequently a cynic, grossly overinflated with a misplaced sense of self-importance and greed.

Some of the most compelling figures in dramatic literature are characters caught between a sense of personal duty and the need to maintain a public face. Shakespeare made this a dilemma in many plays; strong and decisive heroes, such as Coriolanus, are forced to balance their private ideals against the need to say the correct political things to satisfy potential allies. Of the honest Coriolanus who says what he thinks even when it is impolitic, a friend observes that "his nature is too noble for the world." Because he has little interest in winning the support of others, he stands out as the nonpolitical hero, a man who "would not flatter Neptune for his Trident."[63] In more contemporary dramas, Alan Alda's senator in *The Seduction of Joe Tynan* and Kevin Kline's substitute president in *Dave* try to survive in an alien world of manipulators and politicos who lack principles but not ambition.

American attitudes toward politics are heavily shaped by such images. We seem to be guided by the assumptions that there are either expedient or principled forms of political behavior and that it is relatively easy to discern the differences. It is frequently believed that public servants are easily "bought off" by factions or special interests which effectively thwart what should be done to assure the greater public good. When examples contradict our expectations, we are surprised. For instance, a western senator who urges the breakup of large oil companies is taking a position that is thought to involve considerable political risk. The narrow interests of the oil industry in that state would seem to favor fewer and larger companies. Moreover, we would routinely conclude that campaign funds must regularly be replenished by "big oil" interests. To account for the failure to behave as we would expect, we might conclude that he or she was acting out of conviction to principle rather than political expediency. A midwestern senator who supports a presidential boycott of the sale of wheat to China provides another example. Wheat farmers are always helped when large surpluses of their crops are exported. Since the senator's support of a boycott helps to drive down the value of constituents' crops, we may conclude that he or she did not make the expedient choice, but instead the principled decision not to aid a communist state. These are the exceptions. By and large we expect politicians to be like the candidate in Tim Robbins' popular 1992 film, *Bob Roberts*—the kind of person who will say nearly anything to win support.

We explore the issue here because no image so clearly defines the political persuader as that of a human weathervane blown in the direction of the prevailing winds of public opinion. Like all stereotypes, there is some accuracy to the perception, and like many generalizations, this one falls apart when examined more closely. The reality is far more complex. In the examples above of senators who seem to be acting in accordance with higher principles, they could also be judged as negligent of the people who elected them. Would they have been less noble had they reflected the interests of their own constituents? Does the very idea of representation include the special interests of farmers, students, the elderly, or the oil industry? Democratic politics is a process for turning conflict into consensus; we should expect that the diversity of political opinions on any one question will reflect the diversity of opinion in society as a whole. It is easy to forget that democracies are based on the idea that pluralism is desirable and that the special interests of citizens deserve representation. On many political issues, there is no public consensus to be acted upon—only a collection of splintered opinions and opposing coalitions.

Political persuasion undoubtedly sometimes deserves its poor reputation. There are clearly instances when public opinion is ignored because of the excessive power of special interest lobbies. There are probably other times when public attitudes are so misinformed that they should be dismissed.[64] In either case, it would be simplistic to assume that every statement that defends a politician's known interests is a certain indicator of weak-willed opportunism. Politicians make decisions for many thoughtful reasons. Some believe they must serve as a *representative* of those who elected them, sacrificing their own feelings to vote the way they perceive public opinion at home. Others function more as **trustees**, prepared to ignore public opinion in favor of their own determination of what is the best course of action.[65] Perhaps we are too quick to label political arguments and attitudes we disagree with as expedient and too comfortable with the easy judgment that those who think as we do are principled.

## Summary

In this chapter, we have illustrated the scope of American political persuasion by surveying some of the communication patterns common to the politics of administrative, campaign, and policy-making activities. We have also explored some of the unique features of political communication, including its indirect role in defining social status in the United States and the submerged participation of the media. No single overview is adequate to describe the wealth of thought and research that has been directed to the processes involved in shaping public opinion. However, we have offered some broad conclusions that students of persuasion should keep in mind.

- We are all political, both as agents of groups seeking influence and as the recipients of the appeals of others.

- The low repute in which most political rhetoric is held probably says as much about the competence of the public as it does about the politician. Political appeals are a reflection of the society in which they are shaped.

- Unlike product advertising, political persuasion is concerned with portraying the positive and negative consequences that result (a) from the election of people with certain character traits and (b) from the choice of policies intended to deal with social or economic problems. Just as in product advertising, much political rhetoric is filtered through professionals trained in public relations and marketing.

- The processes of political communication can lead to deplorable decisions, such as occurred under Hitler in Germany's Third Reich. Those same basic processes placed at the disposal of decent leaders can remedy serious wrongs, such as the relatively recent actions against policies restricting the rights of women and minorities to vote.

- All of us have a considerable stake in political persuasion because it serves as an early warning about decisions that may alter our relationships with each other and with the state.

- In comparison to product advertising, political persuasion must overcome greater obstacles. While the subject matter of politics is more important, the abilities of advocates are limited by the necessity to communicate to constituents through the filters of the news media and by public apathy.

- It is a mistake to consider political activity as separate from other forms of popular culture, especially novels, films, and prime-time television. Popular media reflect the values and attitudes of our political culture.

## Questions and Projects for Further Study

1. Imagine that you are a lobbyist for a medical insurance company (i.e., Blue Cross). You are trying to win the approval of Congress for a change in how your company is regulated by a federal agency. Part of your work is talking to members of the House and Senate as the legislation moves through various committees. Given the experience of the Clinton administration's health care lobbying discussed in this chapter, select some lobbying strategies you might use, as well as several you would avoid. Explain your reasons.

2. In a discussion group, consider the ramifications of the following statement from the book on the electoral process: Politics is "mediated, one-way political expression."

3. An interesting way to experience firsthand the process of mediation is to attend a city council meeting, a session of the state assembly, legislative hearings, or an address given by a leading political leader. After observing one of these events, compare your overall impressions with the coverage provided by newspapers, radio, or television stations in your area. Did the mediation that occurred offer an accurate summary of what happened, or did it present a misleading picture?

4. Plan a group-viewing of the 1972 film, *The Candidate* (available on videocassette). This Academy Award-winning story of a political campaign—written by Jeremy Larner and starring Robert Redford—is widely regarded as one of the most accurate portrayals of modern electoral politics. After the film, compare your impressions. Specific questions to discuss might include:

   • Do you think the film is an authentic portrayal of the way modern election campaigns are run?

   • Who is responsible for the superficial nature of some political campaigns?

   • How did Bill MacKay convince so many voters to support him?

   • How would you like to see political campaigns change?

   • Which of the settings (political commercials, television news reports, rallies, and debates) offered the best opportunity to the public to access the candidates?

5. The authors argue that most forms of entertainment, such as films and television programs, have at least latent political content. After reviewing their arguments in the section, "Political Messages in Nonpolitical Forms," (a) argue against their position or (b) identify further examples that confirm their assertion.

6. The speeches of all modern presidents are available in most libraries as part of a continuing series of volumes collectively titled *Public Papers of the Presidents of the United States.* Using one volume from a recent presidency, find segments of speeches or remarks that illustrate the three subject areas of political persuasion.

7. Interview a local politician (council member, state representative or state senator) in person or by phone. Ask the politician to consider some of the persuasion approaches cited in the chapter. For example: What effect does he or she think lobbyists have on his or her own decision making? Do members of the local mass media do an adequate job of presenting new ideas and proposals to interested constituents and voters? Does the politician see him- or herself

primarily as a "trustee" or "representative?" Would he or she agree with Edelman and the text authors about the general low level of political information in the general public?

8. In this chapter we mention several social movements which have pushed for legislative action in civil rights, voter rights, abortion, and so on. What major social issues are highly visible now? Do the activists in those movements share any of the tactics cited in the 1920 campaign to secure the vote for women? Are any of the current movements justifiably seen as raising "status issues"?

# Notes

[1] Jonathan Lynn and Antony Jay, *The Complete Yes Minister: The Diaries of a Cabinet Minister.* Topsfield, MA: Salem House, 1987, p. 9.

[2] John H. Bunzel, *Anti-Politics in America.* New York: Vintage, 1967, pp. 7–8.

[3] Robin Toner, "Ads Are Potent Weapon in Health Care Struggle," *New York Times,* February 1, 1994, p. A14.

[4] *Ibid.*

[5] Michael Wines, "Sales Pitch for (Which?) Health Care Plan," *New York Times,* July 25, 1994, pp. A1, A13.

[6] Bob Woodward, *The Agenda: Inside the Clinton White House.* New York: Simon and Schuster, 1994, pp. 315.

[7] Catherine S. Manegold, "Health Care Bus: Lots of Miles, Not So Much Talk," *New York Times,* July 25, 1994, p. A12.

[8] Roger Simon, *Road Show.* New York: Farrar, Straus and Giroux, 1990, pp. 217–20.

[9] Peter Goldman and Tom Mathews, *Quest for the Presidency: The 1988 Campaign.* New York: Simon and Schuster, 1989, p. 306.

[10] "Memories and Apology by a Gravely Ill Atwater," *New York Times,* January 13, 1991, p. 16.

[11] Campaign flyer, New Jersey Republican State Committee, 1988.

[12] Goldman and Mathews, p. 306.

[13] Simon, p. 210.

[14] Goldman and Mathews, p. 306.

[15] See, for example, Michael Pfau and Henry C. Kenski, *Attack Politics: Strategy and Defense.* New York: Praeger, 1990, pp. 13–60.

[16] "Memories and Apology. . ," p. 16.

[17] Ann Firor Scott and Andrew M. Scott, *One Half of the People.* New York: J. B. Lippincott, 1975, p. 9.

[18] Sherna Gluck, ed. *From Parlor to Prison.* New York: Vintage, 1976, p. 22.

[19] Scott and Scott, p. 39.

[20] Franklin Roosevelt quoted in Emmet John Hughes, *The Living Presidency.* New York: Coward, McCann and Geoghegan, 1972, p. 184.

[21] Godfrey Hodgson, *All Things to All Men.* New York: Simon and Schuster, 1980, pp. 13–16.

[22] Woodward, p. 330.

[23] Michael Novak, *Choosing Our King.* New York: Macmillan, 1974, pp. 3–48.

[24] Paul D. Erickson, *Reagan Speaks: The Making of An American Myth*. New York: New York University, 1985, pp. 32–50.

[25] Lyndon Johnson, Address to a Joint Session of Congress, Washington D.C., March 15, 1965, in *Presidential Rhetoric (1961–1980)*, Second Edition. ed by Theodore Windt. Dubuque, IA: Kendall Hunt, 1980, p. 67.

[26] For a critical assessment of the power of Washington lobbyists see Jeffrey H. Birnbaum, *The Lobbyists*, New York: Times Books, 1992.

[27] William Safire, *Safire's Political Dictionary*. New York: Ballantine, 1978, pp. 383–84.

[28] An interesting case study of legislative lobbying is T. R. Reid's *Congressional Odyssey: The Saga of a Senate Bill*. San Francisco: W. H. Freeman, 1980.

[29] Stephen Hess, *The Ultimate Insiders: U.S. Senators in the National Media*. Washington: Brookings, 1986, p. 38.

[30] Richard F. Fenno, Jr., *Home Style: House Members in Their Districts*. Boston: Little, Brown, 1978, pp. 217–18.

[31] Congressional Quarterly, "House Democratic Whips: Massing Support," in *Inside Congress*, Second Edition. Washington: Congressional Quarterly, 1979, p. 29.

[32] Larry J. Sabato, *The Rise of the Political Consultants*. New York: Basic, 1981, p. 351.

[33] This four-part list is based on a discussion of campaigns in Judith S. Trent and Robert V. Friedenberg, *Political Campaign Communication*, Second Edition. New York: Praeger, 1991, pp. 17–48.

[34] Germond and Witcover, pp. 99–100.

[35] The extent to which political campaigns depend on fat war chests has been called a national disgrace. In 1990, for example, incumbents running for reelection to the House of Representatives and Senate raised over $262 million by October 17, about three weeks before the general election. Challengers raised a comparatively small $64.7 million. Political Action Committees contributed to these candidates in a very uneven 16 to 1 ratio; they gave $74.7 million to those already in office and only $4.7 million to their challengers. Despite efforts at campaign reform in 1993 and 1994, the need to raise large campaign war chests continues to suggest that elections are—among other things—events where the wealthy seek to buy access to legislators and executives. See "If Money Talks, Mr. Smith Won't Go to Washington," *Congressional Quarterly*, November 3, 1990, p. 3756.

[36] Germond and Witcover, pp. 334–346.

[37] *Ibid.*, p. 410.

[38] In the last 5 years a great deal has been written about campaign advertising denigrating opponents: what is often called "attack advertising." Estimates vary on how well attack ads work. One general strategy adopted by candidates who fear the effects of attack ads involves inoculating audiences against the effects of these ads. See, for example, Pfau and Kenski, *Attack Politics*.

[39] Charles Peters, *How Washington Really Works*. Reading, MA: Addison Wesley, 1980, p. 132.

[40] James David Barber, *The Presidential Character: Predicting Performance in the White House*. Englewood Cliffs, NJ: Prentice Hall, 1972, p. 446.

[41] Ronald Reagan, Remarks and a Question and Answer Session with Farmers From the Landenberg, Pennsylvania, Area, May 14, 1982, in *Public Papers of the Presidents of the United States, 1982*, Bk. I. Washington: U.S. Government Printing Office, 1983, p. 629.

[42] Quoted in Arthur Bernon Tourtellot, *The Presidents on the Presidency*. New York: Doubleday, 1964, p. 72.

43 For a discussion of voter awareness of issues see Thomas E. Patterson, *The Mass Media Election*. New York: Praeger, 1980, pp. 153–69.

44 For a broad discussion of this perspective see Jack M. McLeod and Lee B. Becker, "The Uses and Gratifications Approach" in *The Handbook of Political Communication*, ed by Dan D. Nimmo and Keith R. Sanders, Beverly Hills: Sage, 1981, pp. 67–99. A less technical discussion of this perspective is also developed in Murray Edelman, *The Symbolic Uses of Politics*, Urbana: University of Illinois, 1967, pp. 1–43.

45 Joseph R. Gusfield, *Symbolic Crusade: Status Politics and the American Temperance Movement*. Urbana: University of Illinois, 1963, p. 22.

46 Jaime Diaz, "Shoal Creek Club Agrees to Begin Admitting Blacks," *New York Times*, August 1, 1990, p. A13.

47 Kenneth G. Hance, Homer O. Hendrickson, and Edwin W. Schoenberger, "The Later National Period: 1860–1930," in *A History and Criticism of American Public Address*, Vol. 1, ed. by William Norwood Brigance. New York: Russell and Russell, 1960, p. 113.

48 For interesting discussions of political information presented via television news, print reports, and television advertising, see Michael J. Robinson and Margaret A. Sheehan, *Over the Wire and on TV: CBS and UPI in Campaign 80*, New York: Russell Sage, 1980; Robert M. Entman, *Democracy Without Citizens*, New York: Oxford, 1989; Dan Nimmo and James E. Combs, *The New Propaganda: The Dictatorship of Palaver in Contemporary Politics*, New York: Longman, 1993; Edward Jay Epstein, *News From Nowhere: Television and the News*, New York: Vintage, 1973; Martin Schram, *The Great American Video Game*, New York: Murrow, 1987; Kathellen Hall Jamieson, *Packaging the Presidency*, New York: Oxford, 1984; Tom Rosenstiel, *Strange Bedfellows: How Television and the Presidential Candidates Changed American Politics, 1992*, New York: Hyperion, 1993.

49 Alex S. Jones, "Study Finds Americans Want News but Aren't Well Informed," *New York Times*, July 15, 1990, p. A13. See also Michael A. Milburn, *Persuasion and Politics: The Social Psychology of Public Opinion*. Pacific Grove, CA: Brooks/Cole, 1991, pp. 131–51.

50 Eugene H. Rosenblum and Alfred E. Eckes, Jr., *A History of Presidential Elections*, Fourth Edition, New York: Macmillan, 1979, p. 336.

51 Todd Gitlin, ed., *Watching Television*. New York: Pantheon, 1987, pp. 4–5.

52 Quoted in Terry Christensen, *Reel Politics: American Political Movies From Birth of a Nation to Platoon*. New York: Basil Blackwell, 1987, p. 2.

53 *Ibid.*

54 Mark Crispin Miller, *Boxed In: The Culture of TV*. Evanston, IL: Northwestern, 1988, p. 74.

55 Quoted in Naomi Wolf, *Fire With Fire*. New York: Random House, 1993, p. 78.

56 Ellen Hume, "Why the Press Blew the S & L Scandal," *New York Times*, May 24, 1990, p. A25.

57 Robert Darnton, "Writing News and Telling Stories," *Daedalus*, 104, 1975, pp. 175–194.

58 See, for example, Neil Postman, *Amusing Ourselves to Death: Public Discourse in the Age of Show Business*. New York: Penquin, 1985, pp. 3–15.

59 James B. Twitchell, *Carnival Culture: The Trashing of Taste in America*. New York: Columbia University, 1992, pp. 193–251.

60 Ken Auletta, *Three Blind Mice: How the Networks Lost Their Way*. New York: Random House, 1991, p. 134.

[61] See, for example, Robert Hughes, *Culture of Complaint*. Oxford: 1993, pp. 1–8.
[62] Quoted in Gary C. Woodward, *Persuasive Encounters: Case Studies in Constructive Confrontation*. New York: Praeger, 1990, p. 85.
[63] William Shakespeare, *Coriolanus*, ed. by Reuben Brower. New York: Signet, 1966, pp. 244–55.
[64] For example, a paradox of many Congressional elections, including 1994, is that Americans who generally oppose the "gridlock" of divided national government—where the two parties split power between the White House and the Congress—tend to perpetuate it in their voting habits.
[65] William J. Keefe and Morris S. Ogul, *The American Legislative Process: Congress and the States*, Second Edition. Englewood Cliffs, NJ: Prentice Hall, 1968, pp. 63–65.

## Additional Reading

Terry Christensen, *Reel Politics: American Political Movies From Birth of a Nation to Platoon*. New York: Basil Blackwell, 1987.

Robert E. Denton Jr. and Gary C. Woodward, *Political Communication in America*, Second Edition. New York: Praeger, 1990.

Murray Edelman, *The Symbolic Uses of Politics*. Urbana: University of Illinois, 1963.

Joseph R. Gusfield, *Symbolic Crusade: Status Politics and the American Temperance Movement*. Urbana: University of Illinois, 1963.

Michael A. Milburn, *Persuasion and Politics: The Social Psychology of Public Opinion*. Pacific Grove, CA: Brooks/Cole, 1991.

Dan Nimmo and James E. Combs, *Mediated Political Realities*, Second Edition. New York: Longman, 1990.

David L. Paletz and Robert M. Entman, *Media Power Politics*. New York: Free Press, 1981.

T. R. Reid, *Congressional Odyssey: The Saga of a Senate Bill*. San Francisco: W. H. Freeman, 1980.

Larry J. Sabato, *The Rise of Political Consultants*. New York: Basic Books, 1981.

Martin Schram, *The Great American Video Game*. New York: Murrow, 1987.

Roger Simon, *Road Show*. New York: Farrar, Straus and Giroux, 1990.

Judith Trent and Robert Friedenberg, *Political Campaign Communication*, Second Edition. New York: Praeger, 1991.

# Issues and Strategies of Message Preparation

# IV

To this point we have approached persuasion with two general perspectives in mind. One is descriptive. We have described the history, past practice, and vocabulary of persuasion, all of which contribute to our understanding of how messages affect us. The second is theoretical. We have explored various models and theories that account for the social and internal processes that are sometimes triggered when influence is attempted. Because we are all the beneficiaries—as well as the occasional victims—of the efforts made by others to influence us, it is essential to be able to draw on the analytical processes provided by these two perspectives. Throughout our discussions, we have advocated (sometimes stated and sometimes implied) ethical intentions as the foundation for all persuasive efforts.

In this section, we will be directly concerned with the application of persuasive strategies and some of the ethical problems that arise when the strategies are practiced. Chapter 12 provides an overview of the dilemmas raised by the act of persuasion. Chapter 13 takes a step-by-step approach to the construction of several different forms of persuasion. Guidelines for preparing various discursive messages, such as speeches or presentational messages like those found in advertising, are presented.

# 12

# Ethical Considerations of Persuasion

## OVERVIEW

- ■ Communication, Ethics, and Society
    Persuasion and Communication Ethics
    Sources of Attitudes and Values
    Categories of Communication Ethics
- ■ Considerations for Ethical Communication
    Communicator Considerations
    Message Considerations
    Medium Considerations
    Receiver Considerations
    Ethical Values of Communicators
- ■ Areas of Special Concern
    Media and New Technologies
    News Journalism
    Politics and Political Communication
- ■ Summary
- ■ Questions and Projects for Further Study
- ■ Notes
- ■ Additional Reading

> Above all else, a man must study, not how to seem good, but to be so, both in public and in private life . . . And so rhetoric, like every other practice, is always to be used to serve the ends of justice, and for that alone.[1]
>
> —Plato

Since the beginning of time, humans have expressed a concern for ethics. Plato's *Republic* is essentially a work of political ethics, as is Aristotle's *Nicomachean Ethics*. For both Plato and Aristotle, the "good" person was a conscientious citizen contributing to the city-state. The notion of civic virtue implies a citizenry that is informed, active, selfless, enlightened and, above all, just.

Life today is more individualistic. We are concerned with self-actualization, comfort, convenience, property, and the pursuit of happiness. Contrast the opening quotation with the one that follows. "Everybody cheats. That's the way the world works." These were the words spoken by Jerry Plecki, advisor to a team of high school students in a national academic competition, as he handed out a stolen answer key to student participants. He resigned the following week after his team's extraordinary performance on the test was challenged and the cheating discovered.[2]

Society today can be overwhelming; we separate our world into personal, business, political, and religious realms. We tend to treat each realm with a different set of behaviors, whereas Aristotle and Plato defined individuals as members of society with a civic duty. Perhaps the segmentation has contributed to the problem. Deception and fraud abound in society across all occupations and socioeconomic groups. Individuals from the fields of entertainment, business, politics, and others too numerous to list are frequently in the news as a consequence of acts of deception. Paul Taylor reports that 61 percent of the public believe that there is something morally wrong in America, and 80 percent do not trust our leaders as much as they previously did.[3]

Ethical decisions are not always about life-and-death issues, scandals, or personal misconduct. On a daily basis we are confronted with choices and decisions that have ethical implications: Do I repeat a rumor I heard about another person? Do I answer a question honestly, even it if may hurt a friend's feelings?

It is indeed a sign of the times that nearly all textbooks, regardless of subject matter, now include a chapter on ethics. A cynic would argue that such a treatment is rather useless. How can a few pages and perhaps a class lecture or two succeed where years of religious instruction or family life have failed? Nevertheless, it is helpful to reflect on our own

*Civic virtue requires informed, active, selfless, and enlightened citizens contributing to the common good.*

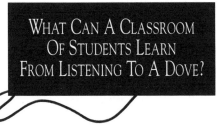

WHAT CAN A CLASSROOM
OF STUDENTS LEARN
FROM LISTENING TO A DOVE?

Plenty if it's Dr. Hood Frazier's Poetry class, and the "Dove" in question just happens to be Rita Dove, the Poet Laureate of the United States. Dr. Frazier's students studied Mrs. Dove's poetry and, after learning sophisticated camera equipment, conducted an interview with her on tape. Later, they presented the results to the class.

That was one of the many collaborative projects the students created with Dr. Frazier's help. Other projects included organizing poetry readings at local galleries and bookstores, creating a poetry writing workshop for elementary school students, and publishing a collection of poems from other high schools in the area.

Dr. Frazier believes the students "began to see themselves as writers and productive members of the community."

We couldn't agree more. And we're pleased to present Dr. Frazier with the State Farm Good Neighbor Award and to donate in his name $4,000 to Murray High School in Charlottesville, Virginia, and $1,000 to the Crossroads Waldorf School in Crozet, Virginia.

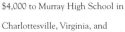
GOOD
NEIGHBOR
AWARD
STATE FARM INSURANCE COMPANIES
Home Offices: Bloomington, Illinois

The Good Neighbor Award
was developed in cooperation
with the National Council
of Teachers of English.

personal behavior and the potential consequences of our actions. According to the Hastings Center, instruction and discussion of ethics may result in stimulating the moral imagination, recognizing ethical issues, eliciting a sense of moral obligation, developing analytical skills, and tolerating disagreement.[4]   We realize that "ethics" and "morals" are open to a wide range of definitions and interpretations. In the limited scope of this chapter, we cannot address the philosophical questions of ethics such as: Do we judge actions (behavior, consequences, results) as ethical or do we judge the actor (the individual's intentions)? Do we consult principles or rules to judge whether a specific act is ethical, or must we look only at the consequences of the act? If we strictly follow rules, is morality reducible to authority? If we look only at consequences, do we reduce morality to expediency? Is there a universal right or wrong, or is all behavior relative?

Stephen Toulmin argues that the social function or purpose of ethics is to reconcile conflicts of interest and to prevent avoidable suffering. A simplified version of Toulmin's approach to ethics is to test individual actions by rules *and* to test those rules by their consequences.[5] Our position in this chapter follows his suggestions and could be rephrased as: ethical communication should be fair, honest, and designed not to hurt other people.

Our approach throughout this book has been to present ethical and responsible persuasion. Our goals in this chapter are to highlight and to explore some ethical issues and to summarize several rules governing ethical persuasion.

## Communication, Ethics, and Society

The disciplines of rhetoric and communication studies have long been interested in the subject of ethics. There is universal agreement that human communication demands concern for ethics. Richard Johannesen argues that "potential ethical issues are inherent in any instance of communication between humans to the degree that the communication can be judged on a right-wrong dimension, involves possible significant influence on other humans, and to the degree that the communicator consciously chooses specific ends sought and communicative means to achieve those ends."[6]

Because communication involves the process of symbol selection, choice, and creation, some scholars argue that all intentional communication transactions inherently involve some degree of persuasion.[7] As you may recall from chapter 3, language is the vehicle for social interaction, a practical tool for getting things done. It is also a form of social behavior. Through language, we define social roles and rules for behavior. Interaction with others creates the reality toward which we respond and act. Indeed, it does make a difference if we convince some-one that a glass is either half-full or half-empty. In the former, there is a sense of hope and optimism. The latter involves caution and perhaps even despair. Ethical choices about language are mandatory in a society which negotiates boundaries of conduct through communication.

Freedom of speech is a fundamental value of democracy.[8] With that freedom comes responsibility — responsibility for the form and content of our communication behavior. The importance of this point becomes clear when considering the essential characteristics of a democratic form of government.

The notion of *accountability* is essential to a representative democ-racy. Because citizens delegate authority to those who hold office, politicians must answer to the public for all actions and deeds. *Information* is critical for citizens to make informed judgments and evaluations of elected officials. Incomplete or inaccurate information can lead to bad public decisions. A *free marketplace of ideas* is vital to the concept of democracy. Diversity of thought and respect for dissent are hallmarks of the values of freedom and justice. When multiple viewpoints are heard and expressed, the "common good" prevails over "private interest." Finally, we enjoy a process of what Dennis Thompson calls *collective deliberation* on disputes about issues and fundamental values.[9] It is the national and public debate that determines the collective wisdom and will of the people.

Thus, at the very heart of democracy is public communication. The quality of that public communication directly impacts the quality of our democracy and society at large. According to philosopher Jack Odell, "A society without ethics is a society doomed to extinction. . . . Ethical principles are necessary preconditions for the existence of a social community. Without ethical principles, it would be impossible for human beings to live in harmony and without fear, despair, hopelessness, anxiety, apprehension, and uncertainty."[10]

## Persuasion and Communication Ethics

By its very nature, persuasion forces us to consider the ethical consequences of our own acts. When we communicate with a persuasive intent, we are usually seeking change in others rather than in ourselves. We expect those we address to risk changes in their attitudes or behaviors, even while we remain relatively comfortable in our own. Thus, the persuader gives up nothing while asking others to alter their lives. Under these circumstances, there is an understandable need to consider whether a communication transaction that places most of the risk on the receiver meets certain minimal standards of fairness and decency. The risks persuaders may ask others to accept may be financial ("This product is worth your hard-earned dollars"), psychological ("Your fear of large animals is irrational; you'll enjoy an afternoon of horseback riding"), social ("No one will think less of you for agreeing to serve as an unpaid volunteer"), or physical ("You haven't lived until you've tried hang gliding").

Two settings clarify the special ethical debt that persuaders may owe audiences. Television programs directed to children also sell to children. Advertisers seeking access on children's programs target their young audiences by using appeals that will motivate them to buy (or lobby their parents to buy) products such as cereals or toys. The ethical line here is a thin one. By their nature, children are not yet savvy consumers. The match between marketing experts and vulnerable four-year-olds is grossly uneven. Because children lack an adult's ability to discount the advertising puffery that is part of most product advertising, corporations obviously have special obligations to their young audiences.

Consider, too, the age-old ritual of sexual courtship. As Wayne Brockriede has pointed out, the relationships that can exist between communicators have some interesting parallels to various patterns of interaction that culminate in sex.[11] Love, seduction, and rape may all end in sexual union, but there is obviously an enormous difference in the motivations and sensitivities of the participants in each pattern. Lovers, in Brockriede's model, are conscious of each other's needs. They respect each other. They seek to give as much or more than they take. Comparable persuaders would understand the sacrifices that they are asking audiences to take and would be willing to change as much as they want others to change. In contrast, seducers are more manipulative. The objective of sexual conquest is planned carefully, with close attention paid to the steps necessary for one side to charm the other into acquiescence. Part of the art of seduction is concealing the planning that has gone into the effort. Like many instances of persuasion, plans work best when they take on the appearance of spontaneity. Rape is a far different matter; there is absolutely no respect for the other individual as an independent agent. Rapists act with only themselves in mind. They create victims; there is no interaction or exchange. The task facing persuaders, as Brockriede implies, is to find a path for persuasion that respects the audience and leaves its free will in tact.

Society's morals and ethics begin with individual citizens. Our individual morals and ethics are grounded in our beliefs, attitudes, and values. In chapter 6, we defined the concepts of beliefs, attitudes, and values and argued that attitude change is the core concept to nearly all theories of persuasion. But where do our attitudes, beliefs, and values originate? Louis Day identifies four influential sources that affect our attitudes and values: our family, peer groups, role models, and societal institutions.[12]

## Sources of Attitudes and Values

Early in our lives, parents provide our rules for behavior. Through instruction and discipline, we gain a sense of right and wrong. As we grow older, we learn not so much from what our parents tell us but from observing their behavior. We learn a powerful lesson about "acceptable deception" when we see Dad call in sick and then go fishing. As children we learn attitudes and form values somewhat from what parents tell us and more specifically from what our parents do.

As we reach adolescence, peer groups gain importance in developing our attitudes and values. We may have several peer groups, initially from our neighborhood, church, school, social clubs, and, eventually, our workplace. These groups exert pressure and challenge our core values.

Role models are another influence on our values and attitudes throughout our lives. By becoming psychologically involved with role models, we assume their ideas, attitudes, and behavior. Role models may be people we know, historical figures, or sports and media celebrities. Some social observers worry about the lack of genuine heroes today. Many parents are concerned about the influence of rock or media stars, such as Madonna or Howard Stern, on the values of their children. Even as adults, however, we are still influenced by real or fictionalized

*Role models influence our values and attitudes; they may be people we know, historical figures, or sports and media celebrities.*

*Tribune* photo by Chris Walker

characters. A telling moment for political observers was when President Ronald Reagan repeated Clint Eastwood's line, "Go ahead, make my day," to Congress in promising to veto a tax increase. The allusion was very clear. The statement portrayed Reagan as strong, defiant, even heroic. Likewise, Clinton's reference to the movie character Forrest Gump was used to praise the values and personal character of an earlier generation. Because of the powerful impact of celebrities, many citizens believe that media stars and athletes have a moral obligation to set higher standards of social conduct than does the public at large.

Social institutions are also important in influencing, changing, or reinforcing social values. We associate specific values and expectations of behavior with institutions such as churches, government, and various professional organizations. We are shocked and disappointed when we learn of corruption within government, the police, or the medical profession, for example.

The process of socialization begins early in life. Our beliefs, attitudes, and values are a product of all that we experience throughout our lives. They form the basis of our character as individuals and as a society. Our daily interactions, whether formal or informal, verbal or nonverbal, test our current beliefs and attitudes and shape our future values.

## Categories of Communication Ethics

Ronald Arnett reviewed studies related to communication ethics published from 1915 to 1985 in journals of the field. His review revealed five categories of or approaches to communication ethics: democratic ethics, universal-humanitarian ethics, procedural or code ethics, contextual ethics, and narrative ethics.[13]

Democratic ethical concerns, as already mentioned, focus on how to improve the functioning of democracy in America. Guidelines address the needs for openness, accuracy, mutual respect, and justice.

The universal-humanitarian approach to communication ethics goes beyond concerns for democracy. This approach attempts to identify universal (and rather concrete) guidelines for social interaction. Arnett uses terms like the following to characterize this approach: wisdom, morality, social and human values, rationality, character, commitment, and responsibility, to name only a few.[14] Such discussions often approach "Platonic idealism" but nevertheless recognize the importance of individual honesty, truth, and dignity.

Almost every organization and profession has developed a code or standards of conduct. They range from the very narrow and specific to the most broad and idealistic. Even a casual reading finds many of the guidelines rather optimistic, especially in light of contemporary practices.

---

#### CODE OF PROFESSIONAL ETHICS

As a member of the American Association of Political Consultants, I believe that there are certain standards of practice which I must maintain as a member of my profession. I, therefore, pledge to adhere to the following Code of Ethics:

- I shall not indulge in any activity which would corrupt or degrade the practice of political campaigning.
- I shall treat my colleagues and clients with respect and never intentionally injure their professional or personal reputation.
- I shall respect the confidence of my client and not reveal confidential or private information obtained during our professional relationship.
- I will use no appeal to voters which is based on racism or discrimination and will condemn those who use such practices. In turn, I will work for equal voting rights and privileges for all citizens.
- I shall refrain from false and misleading attacks on an opponent or member of his family and shall do everything in my power to prevent others from using such tactics.
- I will document accurately and fully any criticism of an opponent or his record.
- I shall be honest in my relationship with the press, and candidly answer questions when I have the authority to do so.
- I shall not support any individual or organization which resorts to practices forbidden in this code.

---

Signature                                          Date

Used by permission of the American Association of Political Consultants.

---

For example, members of the American Association of Political Consultants sign a code pledging to "use no appeal to voters which is based on racism or discrimination," to "refrain from false and misleading attacks on an opponent or member of his family," and to "be honest in my relationship with the press." In light of such guidelines, few political ads would qualify. As you may recall from chapter 11, many political pundits characterized the Bush campaign's "Willie Horton" ad as racist. Of course, the value of professional codes for an organization or profession is a public acknowledgement of standards of behavior. The codes serve as ideal standards for decision making about ethical practices when peer pressure or other concerns may cloud our judgments.

Several organizational and professional codes are presented throughout this chapter. A quick reading reveals great similarity in the

---

### THE ADVERTISING CODE OF AMERICAN BUSINESS*

1. *Truth*. Advertising shall tell the truth, and reveal significant facts, the concealment of which would mislead the public.

2. *Responsibility*. Advertising agencies and advertisers shall be willing to provide substantiation of claims made.

3. *Taste and Decency*. Advertising shall be free of statements, illustrations or implications which are offensive to good taste or public decency.

4. *Disparagement*. Advertising shall offer merchandise or service on its merits and refrain from attacking competitors unfairly or disparaging their products, services or methods of doing business.

5. *Bait Advertising*. Advertising shall offer only merchandise or services which are readily available for purchase at the advertised price.

6. *Guarantees and Warranties*. Advertising of guarantees and warranties shall be explicit. Advertising of any guarantee or warranty shall clearly and conspicuously disclose its nature and extent, the manner in which the guarantor or warrantor will perform and the identity of the guarantor or warrantor.

7. *Price Claims*. Advertising shall avoid price or savings claims which are false or misleading, or which do not offer provable bargains or savings.

8. *Unprovable Claims*. Advertising shall avoid the use of exaggerated or unprovable claims.

9. *Testimonials*. Advertising containing testimonials shall be limited to those of competent witnesses who are reflecting a real and honest choice.

---

* This code was developed by the American Advertising Federation and Association of Better Business Bureaus International and has been endorsed by many trade organizations. Reprinted by permission.

---

values and goals espoused in the various statements. Many of the statements could work for nearly any profession or social endeavor.

Contextual ethics in some ways counter the universal orientation. Proponents from this perspective argue that one must consider the dynamics and elements of the situation when rendering ethical judgments. Audience adaptation, symbolic choice, and flexibility become key issues. Lying may even be acceptable if the contextual requirements dictate such a strategy. While there may be problems identifying and articulating absolute ethical standards, few scholars totally favor a situational approach to communication ethics.

Of the various approaches, narrative ethics is the newest and most theoretical. In many ways, it is a combination of all the others. At the heart of this approach is the belief that community values and actions result from social drama, vision, and storytelling. A code emerges from public discussion and interaction. Public narratives provide the rationale for action and social definitions. In essence, this approach recognizes the process and dynamic nature of ethical considerations resulting in and from a constant "public/private dialectic."[15]

These five categories of approaches to ethics represent attempts to understand a complex topic from varying perspectives. While the categories may seem artificially segmented, they need not be viewed as mutually exclusive. Descriptive labels should not be confused with prescriptive rules. If we are attuned to our communication behaviors and attempts at persuasion, we will confront ethical dilemmas rather frequently. Attempting to classify the dilemma will probably not be our first concern (but knowledge about how others have analyzed other situations may help us assess our current situation).

# Considerations for Ethical Communication

There are several basic suggestions or procedures we might use to help in our decision making or to explore the ethicality of persuasive appeals. First, one could appeal to one's own conscience. We could reflect upon the lessons and values of our upbringing. Would we tell our parents of the prescribed action? Would our grandparents approve? How would our favorite teacher react to our behavior? A second test is peer consultation. We can discuss our ideas, appeals, or approaches with valued friends, mentors, or other people we respect and trust. Interpersonal discussion may help us sort out our own motives, suggest our own biases, and help focus issues of conflict. Third is the test of publicity. Here you test ideas or arguments with representatives of the people most likely to be affected by your opinions. For example, one may suggest solutions about smoking to a smoker or gun restrictions to an avid hunter. Finally, one can always resort to the use of professional, personal, or religious guidelines. Many samples are provided throughout this chapter. Of course, if all else fails, some ethicists argue that one can always rely on the golden rule, "do unto others as you would have them do unto you."

A casual survey of communication textbooks and codes provides a wide range of "dos" and "don'ts" to ensure ethical persuasive communication. Below we identify and summarize some of the most common standards in relation to the communicator, the message, the medium, and the receiver. We conclude by providing a list of desired ethical values of communicators.

## Communicator Considerations

1. Do not misrepresent personal knowledge, experience, or skills.
2. Do not conceal personal motives or purposes for persuasive appeals.

---

### NATIONAL VICTIM CENTER'S SUGGESTED MEDIA CODE OF ETHICS

I SHALL:

• Provide the public with factual, objective information about crime stories concerning:

the type of crime that has occurred;

the community where the crime occurred;

the name or description of the alleged offender if appropriate under existing state law; and

significant facts that may prevent other crimes.

• Present a balanced view of crime by ensuring that the victim and the criminal perspective are given equal coverage when possible;

• Advise victim and survivors that they may be interviewed "off the record" or "on the record" if they desire such an interview, and advise them that they have a right not to be interviewed at all;

• Quote victims, families and friends fairly and in context;

avoid photographing or filming crime scene details or follow-up activities such as remains of bodies or brutality, instruments of torture, disposal of bodies, etc., and

• Notify and ask permission from victims and their families before using pictures or photographs for documentaries or other news features.

I SHALL NOT:

• Photograph, film or print for publication photographs of victims, graphic crime scenes or victims in the courtroom without permission;

• Print or broadcast unverified or ambiguous facts about the victim, his or her demeanor, background or relationship to the offender;

• Print facts about the crime, the victim or the criminal act that might embarrass, humiliate, hurt or upset the victim unless there is a need to publish such details for public safety reasons;

• Print, broadcast, photograph or film lurid or graphic details of the crime; and

• Promote sensationalism in reporting crime or criminal court cases in any way.

---

This code was developed in a 1985 symposium co-sponsored by *Women in News* of Seattle and Seattle University and is strongly endorsed by the National Victim Center for journalists in contact with crime victims.

3. Do not misrepresent, distort, or ignore consequences of actions advocated.

4. Do not advocate ideas, positions, or actions in which you do not believe.

5. Do not advocate actions or behaviors of others that are dangerous, illegal, or unethical.

6. Do not use coercion or manipulation to achieve ends.

7. Respect the diversity of opinions.
8. Encourage full discussion and debate of issues.
9. Provide the very best thinking and reasoning based on the most current evidence in developing an argument.
10. Respect individuals' right to privacy.
11. Recognize that during moments of utterance, you are the sole source of argument and information.
12. Select and present facts and opinions fairly.
13. Reveal sources of information and opinions.

## Message Considerations

1. Do not use false, fictitious, distorted, or irrelevant information or evidence to support arguments or claims.
2. Do not intentionally use misleading or illogical reasoning.
3. Do not oversimplify complex issues, positions, or situations into polar views or choices.
4. Do not artificially link ideas or arguments to emotional appeals or claims.
5. Do not use language that is confusing or misleading to an audience.
6. Do not attack the personal character of opponents.
7. Do not use sexist or racist language or appeals.
8. Do not make false or misleading comparisons.
9. Do not offer quotations from testimonies of others out of context or in such a way as to distort original intent.
10. Avoid offensive appeals or materials.
11. Utilize the most timely and accurate information available in presentations.
12. Clearly distinguish among assumptions, opinions, and facts.

## Medium Considerations

1. Do not use "subliminal perception" or other techniques that convey information or views without the full awareness of the audience.
2. Do not use visual devices, effects, or techniques that distort information or deceive the audience (for example, exaggerated camera angles, lighting, etc.).
3. Do not use sound effects or devices that distort or deceive the audience (for example, the use of compressed speech, background music, etc.).

---

### ASSOCIATED PRESS SPORTS EDITORS ETHICS GUIDELINES

1. The newspaper pays its staffers' way for travel, accommodations, food and drink.
   (a) If a staffer travels on a chartered team plane, the newspaper should insist on being billed. If the team cannot issue a bill, the amount can be calculated by estimating the cost of a similar flight on a commercial airline.
   (b) When services are provided to a newspaper by a pro or college team, those teams should be reimbursed by the newspaper. This includes providing telephone, typewriter or fax service.

2. Editors and reporters should avoid taking part in outside activities or employment that might create a conflict of interest or even appearance of a conflict.
   (a) They should not serve as an official scorer at baseball games.
   (b) They should not write for team or league media guides or other team or league publications. This has the potential of compromising a reporter's disinterested observations.
   (c) Staffers who appear on radio or television should understand that their first loyalty is to the paper.

3. Writers and writers' groups should adhere to Associated Press Managing Editors and APSE standards: No deals, discounts or gifts except those of insignificant value or those available to the public.
   (a) If a gift is impossible or impractical to return, donate the gift to charity.
   (b) Do not accept free memberships or reduced fees for membership. Do not accept gratis use of facilities, such as golf courses or tennis courts, unless it is used as part of doing a story for the newspaper.
   (c) Sports editors should be aware of standards of conduct of groups and professional associations to which their writers belong and the ethical standards to which those groups adhere, including areas such as corporate sponsorship from news sources it covers.

4. A newspaper should not accept free tickets, although press credentials needed for coverage and coordination are acceptable.

5. A newspaper should carefully consider the implications of voting for all awards and all-star teams and decide if such voting creates a conflict of interest.

6. A newspaper's own ethical guidelines should be followed, and editors and reporters should be aware of standards acceptable for use of unnamed sources and verification of information obtained other than from primary news sources.
   (a) Sharing and pooling of notes and quotes should be discouraged. If a reporter uses quotes gained secondhand, that should be made known to the readers. A quote could be attributed to a newspaper or to another reporter.

7. Assignments should be made on merit, without regard for race or gender.

Guidelines can't cover everything. Use common sense and good judgment in applying these guidelines in adopting local codes.

Adopted June 22, 1991

4. Do not use visual, symbolic artifacts such as flags, children, or animals that generate emotional support or divert attention away from the issue or evidence presented.

5. The technology of or the access to the medium should not be the determining factor of influence, information, or message understanding.

## Receiver Considerations

1. Be open to dissent and the opinions of others.

2. Listen critically in order to analyze, synthesize, and properly interpret and evaluate ideas or arguments presented.

3. Be prepared to provide a response or feedback to the ideas or arguments presented.

4. Do not be defensive or ego-involved in responses.

5. Do not judge an argument or position based upon the speaker's race, religion, sex, or cultural heritage.

## Ethical Values of Communicators

Ethical persuasive discourse is essentially identical to all other ethical communication. A synthesis of various texts and essays reveals the following values or characteristics of an ethical communicator.

1. honesty—individuals are truthful, open, sincere, and objective.

2. integrity—individuals are principled with a sense of values and willing to take a stand.

3. caring—individuals are empathetic and concerned about the feelings and circumstances of others.

4. respectful—individuals believe in the dignity and value of all humans.

5. fair—individuals are committed to the expression of diversity of opinion and equal justice for everyone—even if expressed opinions are radically different.

6. democratic—individuals advocate the values of liberty, equality, and the process of open debate and discussion of ideas and issues.

7. responsible or accountable—individuals are willing to take responsibility for actions and ideas advocated.

8. civic virtue—individuals are committed to public service and the exercise of responsible citizenship.

9. competent—individuals are knowledgeable, intelligent, and capable to perform or complete tasks as claimed.

10. reliable—individuals are dependable, consistent, and loyal.

## Areas of Special Concern

As we have seen, ethical communication behaviors are critical for interpersonal relationships and individuals. They are also essential elements of any professional endeavor. In addition, some professions or communication industries tend to generate special ethical concerns. These include media and new technologies, news journalism, and politics. While the "sins" are easy to describe and illustrate, our purpose here is to illustrate general concerns and to suggest some actions.

## Media and New Technologies

Computers, fiber optics, and satellites have introduced an era of high-speed communication that greatly impacts the creation, collection, and dissemination of information. Our laws and social expectations have not kept up with the rapid changes in communication technologies. The Internet is becoming one of the defining scientific and social innovations of this century. The "information superhighway," as labeled by politicians and the media, has the ability to link people and resources in a way that was never previously possible. Users can share data, communicate messages, transfer programs, discuss topics, and connect to computer systems all over the world. The potential of the Internet as a tool for retrieving information is almost limitless. As a result of the freedom of expression allowed on this unique network, the possibilities for learning and enrichment are endless. But with a network so large (and a territory so uncharted), there is great concern about the material readily available to anyone accessing the "Net."

The Internet is unique; every individual connected to it defines his or her corner of "cyberspace." There is no Internet, Inc., no board of directors, no president, and very few rules, if any. Each person logging on to the system is generally given access through a service provider—a large company or organization that has paid to install and maintain a high-speed Internet connection and either give or sell that access to users. Whether the service provider is a commercial on-line service such as CompuServe or Prodigy, or an organization such as General Electric or a university, the service provider's obligation usually ends when its customer opens a connection. From that point, it is up to each user to seek out information and transfer it to the user's own computer.

Although the vast majority of data on the Internet is of great value, there does exist a certain segment of users that choose to make obscene text, graphics, and video available to others. Generally, any resource on the Internet is available to any user and it is difficult to restrict a user's access. The problem is that minors have full access to the items made public by individual users. Furthermore, misrepresentation and outright lying are rather commonplace on the "information highway."

*The freedom of expression available on the Internet creates endless possibilities for enrichment—and for possible confusion. During the 1996 campaign, this home page was as easily accessed as were official campaign sites.*

**Bill Clinton, America's 37th President:**
**"I can count the changes I've made on one hand; I got elected"**

Well, campaign season is getting started. This page is here to offer information about Bill Clinton's campaign and what you can do to help.

You can check out our <u>campaign theme song</u>, or choose one of the following:

<u>aiken@clinton96.org</u>

Individuals in discussion groups who seek on-line conversations and computer friendships may encounter others who lie about their age, sex, looks, income, or occupation. There is special concern for child and teenage safety on the Internet. Some of the risks include exposure to inappropriate material, emotional vulnerability from sharing personal information with strangers, or harassment from demeaning or belligerent e-mail or bulletin board messages. With the increased placement of Internet connections in public schools, educators are faced with numerous issues and concerns.

Most services providers and user organizations have created guidelines for acceptable Internet usage. Likewise, many public schools have found it necessary to develop both student and parental agreements outlining rules and risks of Internet usage (see figures 12.1 and 12.2). You will note that the guidelines cover a wide range of behaviors from language usage to copyright permission.

In the workplace, questions of privacy and ownership of communication are becoming issues of discussion and policy formation. Is computer e-mail private and confidential? Does your host system or organization keep records of your destinations on the Internet? Do computer files on office machines belong to you or to your organization?

Another example of technology's impact on communication is the increasing use of "photo manipulation" in advertising displays and new feature print presentations. Today's technology makes photo manipulation virtually impossible to detect. Some manipulations may seem rather harmless and even humorous. *Spy* magazine superimposed First Lady Hillary Clinton's face on a model dressed in leather, holding a whip. *TV Guide*, in doing a cover story on Oprah Winfrey, superimposed Oprah's face on the body of Ann-Margret. These examples may be in bad taste or disrespectful, but are they dishonest? Consider *National Geographic* publishing a picture of the pyramids of Giza with one moved closer to another for a "tighter shot composition," or a manipulated photo printed in *Newsweek* depicting figure skaters Nancy Kerrigan and Tonya Harding on the ice together for the first time since the assault on Kerrigan, or the removal of a soft-drink can from the photo of a Pulitzer prize-winning photographer.

Some editors and publishers argue that manipulated photos or videos are a disservice to history. People do not have the right to alter what is true and actual. Others argue that manipulated photos do not convey accurate information and thus, by definition, distort reality. Such photos are simply false and misleading. At the very least, scholars and observers contend that all manipulated photographs should carry proper disclosure and explanation.

Some examples of outright distortion are obvious. Others are more subtle. The arrest of O.J. Simpson for the murder of his wife and an acquaintance became a fast-breaking news story in 1994. The mug shot of Simpson became the cover photo for both *Time* and *Newsweek* magazines. However, the photo used by *Time* was a darkened image of Simpson which led to a storm of controversy. The differences between the two magazine covers was vivid. Many black journalists described *Time* magazine's image as racist, making Simpson look more sinister, and thus "guilty." *Time* magazine denied any racial implication or

Figure 12.1

## Acceptable Use of Information Systems at Virginia Tech

### General Principles

Access to computer systems and networks owned or operated by Virginia Tech imposes certain responsibilities and obligations and is granted subject to University policies, and local, state, and federal laws. Acceptable use always is ethical, reflects academic honesty, and shows restraint in the consumption of shared resources. It demonstrates respect for intellectual property, ownership of data, system security mechanisms, and individuals' rights to privacy and to freedom from intimidation, harassment, and unwarranted annoyance.

### Guidelines

In making acceptable use of resources you must:

- use resources only for authorized purpose;
- protect your user-ID and system from un-authorized use. You are responsible for all activities on your user-ID or that originate from your system;
- access only files and data that are your own, that are publicly available, or to which you have been given authorized access;
- use only legal versions of copyrighted software in compliance with vendor license requirements;
- be considerate in your use of shared resources. Refrain from monopolizing systems, overloading networks with excessive data, or wasting computer time, connect time, disk space, printer paper, manuals, or other resources.

In making acceptable use of resources you must NOT:

- use another person's system, user-ID, password, files, or data without permission;
- use computer programs to decode passwords or access control information;
- attempt to circumvent or subvert system or network security measures;
- engage in any activity that might be harmful to systems or to any information stored thereon, such as creating or propagating viruses, disrupting services, or damaging files;

- use University systems for commercial or partisan political purposes, such as using electronic mail to circulate advertising for products or for political candidates;
- make or use illegal copies of copyrighted software, store such copies on University systems, or transmit them over University networks;
- use mail or messaging services to harass, intimidate, or otherwise annoy another person, for example, by broadcasting unsolicited messages or sending unwanted mail;
- waste computing resources, for example, by intentionally placing a program in an endless loop or by printing excessive amounts of paper;
- use the University's systems or networks for personal gain; for example, by selling access to your user-ID or to University systems or networks, or by performing work for profit with University resources in a manner not authorized by the University;
- engage in any other activity that does not comply with the General Principles presented above.

### Enforcement

The University considers any violation of acceptable use principles or guidelines to be a serious offense and reserves the right to copy and examine any files or information resident on University systems allegedly related to unacceptable use. Violators are subject to disciplinary action as prescribed in the honor codes and the student and employee handbooks. Offenders also may be prosecuted under laws including (but not limited to) the Privacy Protection Act of 1974; The Computer Fraud and Abuse Act of 1986, The Computer Virus Eradication Act of 1989, Interstate Transportation of Stolen Property, The Virginia Computer Crimes Act, and the Electronic Communications Privacy Act. Access to the text of these laws is available through the Reference Department of the Newman Library.

## Figure 12.2
### Acceptable Use Policy for Internet Access
### Auburn High and Middle School

Auburn High and Middle School provides access to the Internet for all students, faculty, and staff. Students must have permission from at least one of their parents or guardians to access the Internet at school.

The use of an Internet account is a privilege, not a right, and inappropriate use will result in the cancellation of those privileges and/or disciplinary action by school officials. A student's activities while using the Internet in this school must be in support of education and research and consistent with the educational objectives of the Montgomery County Public Schools. In addition, a student accessing the Internet from a school site is responsible for all on-line activities which take place through the use of his or her account. When using another organization's network or computing resources, students must comply with the rules appropriate for that network.

**I AGREE** that the following actions (which are not inclusive) constitute unacceptable use of the Internet, whether that use is initiated from school or any other site:

- using impolite, abusive, or otherwise objectionable language in either public or private messages;
- placing unlawful information on the Internet;
- using the Internet illegally in ways that violate federal, state, or local laws or statutes;
- using the Internet at school for non-school related activities;

- sending messages that are likely to result in the loss of the recipient's work or systems;
- sending chain letters or pyramid schemes to lists of individuals, and any other types of use which would cause congestion of the Internet or otherwise interfere with the work of others;
- using the Internet for commercial purposes;
- using the Internet for political lobbying;
- changing any computer file that does not belong to the user;
- sending or receiving copyrighted materials without permission;
- knowingly giving one's password to others;
- using another person's password;
- using Internet access for sending or retrieving pornographic material, inappropriate text files, or files dangerous to the integrity of the network;
- circumventing security measures on school or remote computers or networks;
- attempting to gain access to another's resources, programs, or data;
- vandalizing, which is defined as any malicious attempt to harm or destroy data of another user on the Internet, and includes the uploading or creation of computer viruses;
- falsifying one's identity to others while using the Internet.

**Student's Agreement**

I have read the policy on Acceptable Use of Information Systems at Virginia Tech and I understand fully and agree to abide by the principles and guidelines it contains. In addition, I have read and agree to refrain from those actions listed above which are considered unacceptable to the proper use of Internet resources.

| | |
|---|---|
| Student's Signature | Date |

**Parent's Agreement**

As the parent or guardian of this student, I have read the Acceptable Use Policy for Internet Access as outlined above, as well as the Acceptable Use of Information Systems at Virginia Tech. I understand that this access is designed for educational purposes. I also recognize that employees of the school or school system may not be able to restrict access to all controversial materials on the Internet. I will not hold them responsible for materials my son or daughter acquires as a result of the use of the Internet from school facilities. I accept full responsibility for supervision if and when my child's use of the Internet is conducted outside the school setting. I hereby give my permission to Auburn High and Middle School, to the Montgomery County Public Schools, and to Virginia Tech to issue an Internet account for my child and/or to permit my child to access the Internet without an account on equipment provided on the school site.

_____        _____
Signature of Parent or Guardian                  Date

**School Verification**

I verify that this document was signed in my presence by the parent listed above.

_____        _____
Signature of School Official                     Date

imputation of guilt associated with the cover photo. While they used the technique of "photo-illustration" in creating the cover, the managing editor argued that "photojournalism has never been able to claim the transparent neutrality attributed to it. Photographers choose angles and editors choose pictures to make points. . . . And every major news outlet routinely crops and retouches photos to eliminate minor, extraneous elements, so long as the essential meaning of the picture is left intact. Our critics felt that Matt Mahurin's work changed the picture fundamentally; I felt it lifted a common police mug shot to the level of art, with no sacrifice to truth."[16]

Some of the problems associated with technology may be regulated. However, as is the case with most questions of ethics, they become issues of human judgment. As we enter the twenty-first century, ethical implications of the use of technology will increasingly dominate public debate.

## News Journalism

There is a growing concern about the practice of broadcast journalism in America. Criticisms of the press range from distortion to outright lying. Generally, the public increasingly thinks that the press has become too powerful, too negative, and too biased in its news coverage.

### ASSOCIATED PRESS MANAGING EDITORS CODE OF ETHICS

This code is a model against which newspaper men and women can measure their performance. It is meant to apply to news and editorial staff members, and others who are involved in or who influence news coverage and editorial policy. It has been formulated in the belief that newspapers and the people who produce them should adhere to the highest standards of ethical and professional conduct.

#### Responsibility

A good newspaper is fair, accurate, honest, responsible, independent and decent. Truth is its guiding principle.

It avoids practices that would conflict with the ability to report and present news in a fair and unbiased manner.

The newspaper should serve as a constructive critic of all segments of society. Editorially, it should advocate needed reform or innovations in the public interest. It should vigorously expose wrongdoing or misuse of power, public or private.

News sources should be disclosed unless there is clear reason not to do so. When it is necessary to protect the confidentiality of a source, the reason should be explained.

The newspaper should background, with the facts, public statements that it knows to be inaccurate or misleading. It should uphold the right of free speech and freedom of the press and should respect the individual's right to privacy.

The public's right to know about matters of importance is paramount, and the newspaper should fight vigorously for public access to news of government through open meetings and open records.

#### Accuracy

The newspaper should guard against inaccuracies, carelessness, bias or distortion through either emphasis or omission.

It should admit all substantive errors and correct them promptly and prominently.

#### Integrity

The newspaper should strive for impartial treatment of issues and dispassionate handling of controversial subjects. It should provide a forum for the exchange of comment and criticism, especially when such comment is opposed to its editorial positions. Editorials and other expressions of opinion by reporters and editors should be clearly labeled.

The newspaper should report the news without regard for its own interests. It should not give favored news treatment to advertisers or special interest groups. It should report matters regarding iteslf or its personnel with the same vigor and candor as it would other institutions or individuals.

Concern for community, business or personal interests should not cause a newspaper to distort or misrepresent the facts.

#### Conflicts of Interest

The newspaper and its staff should be free of obligations to news sources and special interests. Even the appearance of obligation or conflict of interest should be avoided.

Newspapers should accept nothing of value from news sources or others outside the profession. Gifts and free or reduced-rate travel, entertainment, products and lodging should not be accepted. Expenses in connection with news reporting should be paid by the newspaper. Special favors and special treatment for members of the press should be avoided.

Involvement in such things as politics, community affairs, demonstrations and social causes that could cause a conflict of interest, or the appearance of such conflict, should be avoided.

Stories should not be written or edited primarily for the purpose of winning awards and prizes. Blatantly commercial journalism contests, or others that reflect unfavorably on the newspaper or the profession, should be avoided.

No code of ethics can prejudge every situation. Common sense and good judgment are required in applying ethical principles to newspaper realities. Individual newspapers are encouraged to augment these guidelines with locally produced codes that apply more specifically to their own situations.

Adopted 1975

Much of the criticisms focus on the coverage of politics and political campaigns. According to Larry Sabato, "It has become a spectacle without equal in modern American politics: the news media, print and broadcast, go after a wounded politician like sharks in a feeding frenzy. The wounds may have been self-inflicted, and the politician may richly deserve his or her fate, but the journalists now take center stage in the process, creating the news as much as reporting it, changing both the shape of election-year politics and the contours of government."[17] During the 1992 presidential campaign, negative coverage dominated network news. More than 80 percent of the network news stories on the Democratic party were negative as well as 87 percent of all references to the Republican party. Such negative coverage was not limited to the candidates and political parties. Ninety-three percent of the references to the federal government and 90 percent of those to Congress were also negative.[18]

This negative, antipolitical bias of the press is an alarming historical trend. A study by Thomas Patterson shows that "candidates of the 1960s got more favorable coverage than those of the 1970s, who in turn received more positive coverage than those of the 1980s."[19] The overall change is dramatic. Of all the evaluative references to Kennedy and Nixon in 1960, 75 percent were positive. In contrast, in 1992 only 40 percent of reporters' evaluative references to Clinton and Bush were favorable. This trend of negative coverage has occurred in news magazines as well.

Patterson argues that the rules of reporting changed with Vietnam and Watergate. Members of the press felt that both Johnson and Nixon had lied to them. As a result, the press had let the nation down by perpetuating lies and falsehoods. In the end, an attitude developed among the press that no politician can be trusted. Thus, for Patterson, "there can be no doubt that the change in the tone of election coverage has contributed to the decline in the public's confidence in those who seek the presidency."[20]

Much has been written about the media and media ethics. We want to emphasize that broadcast news is a human communication endeavor. "News" is selected, created, and communicated by people. News is much more than just facts. It is a story, an argument, a process of the "symbolic creation of reality" as explained in chapter 2. News stories influence how readers and viewers perceive reality. As observed by Kathleen Jamieson and Karlyn Campbell, "news is gathered, written, edited, produced, and disseminated by human beings who are part of organizations and who have beliefs and values. . . . These beliefs, values, functions, and interests are bound to influence the messages these networks publish and broadcast."[21]

As television viewers, we need to recognize that news broadcasts contain very persuasive messages. News and the truth are not the same thing. News reporting is just one version of the facts—a created sequence. Some aspects are magnified, others are downplayed. Likewise, the notion of objectivity does not address the issue of truth. Rather, it simply acknowledges the *attempt* to present both sides or perspectives of an issue.

Some of the persuasive dimensions of the news include technology (i.e., camera angles, editing, special effects, etc.), the newsgathering process (i.e., deadlines, reliability and truthfulness of sources, etc.), story structure (i.e., drama, conflict, action, novel, etc.), interpretation (i.e., personal bias, ideological orientations, etc.), and social action (agenda setting, initiating public debate, etc.).

Without question, there are special and unique ethical considerations for the press: good news versus bad news, issues of privacy, objectivity, degree of explicitness of video footage, use of hidden cameras and recorders, use of unnamed sources, "off-the-record" versus "on-the-record," to name only a few. While our intent is not to provide a laundry list of ethical journalistic rules and practices, we do suggest that the practice of journalism should reflect the social values of our nation. Such values include honesty, justice, humaneness, social responsibility, stewardship, and freedom.

## Politics and Political Communication

Historically, there has always been great skepticism about the practice of politics and, above all, about politicians. In most public opinion polls, politicians rank below car salespeople and attorneys as the most dishonest profession. Part of the problem is the continual string of "bad" actions of many politicians: the resignation of Richard Nixon, Gary Hart and the allegations of sexual misconduct in the 1988 presidential contest, and questions of Bill Clinton's avoidance of the draft, to name only a few instances that generate concern among voters. Some ethical dilemmas arise because of the difference between campaigning and governing. George Bush's reversal of his pledge not to raise taxes was portrayed as an act of willful deception and outright lying, not as an act of leadership and conscience. Other concerns are raised about the actual process of getting elected. Many citizens assume that politicians will say or do almost anything to get elected. For many, the critical question becomes, is ethical politics possible or is the notion simply an oxymoron?

In essence, the ethical concerns or issues associated with politics and political campaigns are no different than those of other areas of life. They revolve around a speaker, a message, and an advocated behavior (i.e., "vote for me"). Because campaigns result in granting an individual public trust and social power if elected, they lend themselves to special concerns and judgments.

Bruce Gronbeck developed a model to assess ethical issues of presidential campaigns.[22] He views campaigns as corporate rhetorical ventures in which it is becoming increasingly difficult to place blame on individuals. Gronbeck argues that in order to make ethical assessments, citizens reduce campaigns to comprehensible dramas where they examine the action (motives), people (character), and thought (competence as politicians) of the candidates. These ethical pivot points can be assessed from four moral vantages: that of the message makers, message consumers, messages themselves, and situation expectations. In constructing a 3 x 4 matrix (see figure 12.3), Gronbeck generates 12 questions voters may ask in assessing the ethical dimensions of presidential candidates.

Of course, we do not witness campaigns firsthand. We form judgments and answer the proposed questions from the bits and pieces gleaned from friends and the media. For Gronbeck, "ethical assessment is a complex negotiatory process, whereby the causes and effects, rights and wrongs that politicians, the press, and other public commentators isolate and assess are framed in sociodramas that each of us views and judges in terms of our individual experiences."[23]

Political advertising has come under strong attack in recent years. Today, political ads are the primary source of campaign information for the vast majority of voters. Research indicates that political ads educate viewers about issues, influence voter perceptions about candidates, and especially influence late-deciding or undecided voters.[24] In addition, scholars have found that attack or negative political ads influence voters because they are more compelling, more memorable, and believable.[25]

Lynda Kaid raises several ethical concerns about political advertising.[26] First, the use of political ads is essentially purchasing media access to promulgate a point of view. Without adequate funding, you are restricted in getting your message to voters. Thus, the relative cost of ads raises the issue of fairness in terms of equal access to voters. Second, some scholars argue that ads deal more with images than with

## Figure 12.3
### Questions That Can Guide Voters' Ethical Judgments in Presidential Campaigns

| Moral Vantages | Ethical Pivots | | |
| --- | --- | --- | --- |
| | Motives | Character | Competence |
| Message Makers | Are candidates' motives acceptable? | Are candidates' characterological styles acceptable? | Have candidates demonstrated political competence? |
| Message Consumers | What political motives do sets of voters find acceptable? | What characterological styles do sets of voters find acceptable? | What measures of political competence are used by particular sets of voters? |
| Messages | Are candidates' motives expressed in acceptable ways? | Are candidates' characterological styles depicted in acceptable ways? | Are candidates illustrating their political competence in messages and in responses to opponents' messages? |
| Situations | What motives are acceptable in various situations? | What characterological styles are expected in various situations? | Are candidates handling various political situations competently? |

issues and hence rely more on emotional appeals than logical appeals. Political ads do not provide adequate information for informed decision making. Related to this concern, Kaid warns that the time constraints of commercial spots oversimplify political issues, debasing and even trivializing political argument and the democratic process. Many of the ads are misleading because they fail to disclose sources of information and sponsorship. Finally, concerns are growing about the use of technology such as creative editing techniques, special effects, visual imagery/dramatizations, computerized alteration techniques, and subliminal techniques.

While there may be many ethical issues and concerns about political campaigns and communication, we believe strongly that democratic life carries responsibilities for audiences and citizens as well as politicians. The polity must share the praise or blame that it heaps on its leaders. Their failures are, in many ways, our failures. An informed, educated, and critical voter is our best safeguard against unethical political advertising.

## Summary

Louis Day makes a case that all societies need a system of ethics.[27] A system of ethics provides for social stability. According to Day, "ethics is the foundation of our advanced civilization, a cornerstone that provides some stability to society's moral expectations."[28] A system of ethics serves as a moral gatekeeper by identifying and ranking the norms and morals of a society. A system of ethics also helps societies resolve conflicts and establishes rules and laws for behavior. Finally, a system of ethics helps clarify competing values and new social dilemmas. The current debate over the uses and role of genetic engineering and "suicide machines" are examples of new ethical and moral issues confronting America.

Ethical considerations are also an essential element of human communication. Human interaction gives meaning to our world, places, and events while it creates the reality toward which we act. Social interaction is at the core of human existence. Language usage is always selective, involving individual choice, values, and motives. Statements of policy or opinion, according to Kenneth Andersen, "conscious or not, relevant or not, provide a basis upon which an inference can be made as to the ethics and values of the individual making the choice."[29]

Throughout this book, we have identified and explained various "tools" of persuasion. We have also attempted to note problems and abuses of the practice of persuasion. Like any instrument, the tools of persuasion can be used for good or bad. In this chapter we explored ethical considerations of persuasion and summarized some of the specific rules of application. However, we believe that if there is a problem with ethics in America, it begins with each individual interaction. We cannot depend on teachers, politicians, the media, or religious leaders to correct the real or perceived problems of American ethics. The task is ours. Only as citizens can we alter or affect the quality of our society. As Ronald Arnett observes, "If we are to be concerned about ethical issues in communication and do not wish to place ourselves at the mercy of expert opinion, then argument, debate, and public discourse over what is and is not ethical must continue. If we are to be good choicemakers, we must actively pursue opportunities to ask ethical questions about the process and the content of communication."[30]

Your study of persuasion may well be a significant factor in your ethical growth. Learning how to find good reasons to support your ideas, learning how to present your opinions so that an audience will listen, and learning to express yourself clearly and intelligently will help you become an active, contributing member to society. Ethics is not a separate subject for study; it is an integral part of each individual and every action. Likewise, persuasion is not an isolated topic; it occurs constantly. We are both receivers and creators of persuasion—just as we both experience and create ethical behavior.

## Questions and Projects for Further Study

1. What values do you think your parents taught you? Friends? Teachers? Role models? How do they compare and contrast?

2. Select five magazine ads and analyze them according to the Advertising Code of American Business. How do they conform to the specified standards?

3. Reflect upon the list of ethical values of communicators provided in the chapter. Do you think it is possible for someone always to reflect these values? Why or why not?

4. Share with the class your current or childhood heroes. What makes them special? What do you emulate in them?

5. Describe the main values of democracy. Give a concrete example of each and explain how ethical communication contributes to each value.

6. Videotape two evening news broadcasts for the same day. Compare the broadcasts: order of story topics, length of time of stories, visuals used, etc. Compare and contrast reports on the same topic or story. How are they similar? How are they different?

7. Should the media treat rape as any other crime, i.e., give names of victims and names of alleged rapists? Should newspapers report the cause of death in the obituaries if the cause is AIDS?

8. You interviewed three people for a position in your company. How much detail do you provide to those not selected for the position? What influenced your decision?

## Notes

1 Plato, *Gorgias*, trans. by W. C. Helmbold. New York: Liberal Arts, 1952, 106–7.
2 *Newsweek*, April 10, 1995, p. 19.
3 Paul Taylor, *See How They Run*. New York: Alfred A. Knopf, 1990, p. 226.
4 James Jaksa and Michael Pritchard, *Communication Ethics: Methods of Analysis*. Belmont, CA: Wadsworth, 1994, p. 12.

[5] As quoted in Andrew G. Oldenquist, *Moral Philosophy.* Prospect Heights, IL: Waveland Press, 1978, pp. 16–17.

[6] Richard Johannesen, *Ethics in Human Communication,* Fourth Edition. Prospect Heights, IL: Waveland Press, 1996, p. 2.

[7] For this argument, see Johannesen, pp. 4–5.

[8] For a detailed discussion of democratic values and communication, see Robert E. Denton, Jr., "The Primetime Presidency: The Ethics of Teledemocracy" in *Ethical Dimensions of Political Communication,* ed. by Robert E. Denton, Jr. New York: Praeger, 1991, pp. 91–114.

[9] Dennis Thompson, *Political Ethics and Public Office.* Cambridge: Harvard University Press, 1987, p. 3.

[10] As quoted in John Merrill and Jack Odell, *Philosophy and Journalism.* New York: Longman Press, 1983, pp. 2, 95.

[11] Wayne Brockriede, "Arguers as Lovers," *Philosophy and Rhetoric,* Winter 1972, pp. 1–11.

[12] Louis Day, *Ethics in Media Communications: Cases and Controversies.* Belmont, CA: Wadsworth, 1991, pp. 11–13.

[13] Ronald Arnett, "The Status of Communication Ethics Scholarship in Speech Communication Journals from 1915 to 1985" in *Conversations on Communication Ethics,* ed. by Karen Joy Greenberg. Norwood, NJ: Ablex, 1991, pp. 55–72.

[14] *Ibid.,* p. 60.

[15] *Ibid.,* p. 68.

[16] "To Our Readers," *Time,* July 4, 1994, p. 4.

[17] Larry Sabato, *Feeding Frenzy.* New York: The Free Press, 1991, p. 1.

[18] Thomas Patterson, *Out of Order.* New York: Vintage Books, 1993, p. 18.

[19] *Ibid.,* p. 20.

[20] *Ibid.,* p. 22.

[21] Kathleen Jamieson and Karlyn K. Campbell, *The Interplay of Influence.* Belmont, CA: Wadsworth, 1992, p. 30.

[22] Bruce E. Gronbeck, "Ethical Pivots and Moral Vantages in American Presidential Campaign Dramas" in *Ethical Dimension of Political Communication,* ed. by Robert E. Denton, Jr. New York: 1991, pp. 49–68.

[23] *Ibid.,* p. 66.

[24] Montague Kern, *30-Second Politics.* New York: Praeger, 1989, p. 5.

[25] Michael Pfau and Henry Kenski, *Attack Politics.* New York: Praeger, 1990, p. xiii.

[26] Lynda Lee Kaid, "Ethical Dimensions of Political Advertising" in *Ethical Dimension of Political Communication,* ed. by Robert E. Denton, Jr. New York: Praeger, 1991, pp. 145–69.

[27] Day, pp. 19–21.

[28] *Ibid.,* p. 19.

[29] Kenneth Andersen, "The Politics of Ethics and the Ethics of Politics," *American Behavioral Scientist,* Vol. 32, 1989, p. 482.

[30] Arnett, p. 69.

## Additional Reading

Norman E. Bowie, *Making Ethical Decisions.* New York: McGraw-Hill, 1985.

Joan C. Callahan, ed. *Ethical Issues in Professional Life.* New York: Oxford University Press, 1988.

Louis Day, *Ethics in Media Communications: Cases and Controversies.* Belmont, CA: Wadsworth, 1991.

Robert E. Denton, Jr., ed. *Ethical Dimensions of Political Communication.* New York: Praeger, 1991.

Conrad Fink, *Media Ethics.* Boston: Allyn & Bacon, 1995.

Karen Joy Greenberg, *Conversations on Communication Ethics.* Norwood, NJ: Ablex, 1991.

James A. Jaska, James A. Pritchard, and Michael S. Pritchard. *Communication Ethics: Methods of Analysis,* Second Edition. Belmont, CA: Wadsworth, 1994.

Richard Johannesen, *Ethics in Human Communication,* Fourth Edition. Prospect Heights, IL: Waveland Press, 1996.

Thomas Patterson, *Out of Order.* New York: Vintage, 1993.

Larry Sabato, *Feeding Frenzy.* New York: The Free Press, 1991.

Philip Seib, *Campaigns and Conscience: The Ethics of Political Journalism.* Westport, CT: Praeger, 1994.

Dennis Thompson, *Political Ethics and Public Office.* Cambridge: Harvard University Press, 1987.

# 13

# Constructing and Presenting Persuasive Messages

## OVERVIEW

It is a great matter to know what to say . . . but how to say it is a greater matter still.[1]

—Cicero

Persuasive situations range from advertisements in the mass media to one-on-one encounters within a family, from direct mail letters soliciting support for groups like Greenpeace or Common Cause to speeches asking for commitments from audiences. One recent random sample study indicates that over half the adults surveyed gave at least one speech in a two-year period, with almost three-fourths of them giving four or more. The percentage rose dramatically for people with more years of education.[2] Even if you do not anticipate a career as a public communicator, a look at how persuasive messages are put together provides a useful opportunity to see how specific strategies of persuasion can produce concrete results.

In this chapter we will explore the basic elements of composition in several different settings. Most of our emphasis is on practical guidelines for preparing discursive messages such as speeches—statements which depend primarily on verbal arguments rather than visual images or emotional symbols. There are several reasons for this emphasis. First, face-to-face meetings with interested audiences continue to represent the most attractive chance for advocates to present their ideas. Second, the process of putting a speech together involves many of the same strategies that other forms of persuasion require. The strategies for successful public address adapt easily to other settings and media. The final sections of this chapter explore several strategic considerations for the process of organizing discursive messages and suggestions for constructing nondiscursive messages for print and broadcast advertising.

## Constructing a Persuasive Speech

People often say that they are "writing a speech," but a speech on paper is only a guide for what really matters—the actual presentation to an audience. Just as the building produced by an architect is more than the blueprints, a speech is more than words on paper. It is the communication that takes place between listeners and speakers at a particular point in time. What we actually write is a plan for that moment.

*A speech is more than words on paper—it is the communication between listeners and speakers at a particular point in time.*

*Tribune* file photo

In the basic but vital procedure described below, there is more thinking than writing. The suggested steps produce an extemporaneous sentence outline that serves as a flexible guide to every key idea, appeal, and phrase you want to use. This process avoids the tedious task of writing down every word, but it provides a sequence for locating the essential points that are right for you and the audience. The sentence outline provides built-in flexibility. While the extemporaneous speech is planned, the outline allows enough freedom to adapt to unexpected situations and opportunities. As you read through these steps, it will also be apparent that this plan is a practical application of the logic of the good reasons approach discussed in chapter 4.

## Know the Audience

Persuading an audience is similar to a journey over unfamiliar terrain. Your route has to be adjusted to fit the landscape of existing attitudes. As indicated in chapter 7, a fundamental requirement of communication is an awareness of whom you wish to influence. It is admittedly

*Persuasion begins with an assessment of your audience and their interest in or attitudes toward your topic. The fundamental step in preparing your presentation is questions about the audience.*

*Tribune* photo by Nuccio DiNuzzo

difficult to be precise about the attitudes, values, and interests of groups because people are too complex to be reduced to simple stereotypes. Because persuasion involves "adjusting ideas to people and people to ideas,"[3] thorough preparation starts with questions about the audience.

- How will they respond to your point of view?
- Will they consider you "well qualified" to talk about your topic?
- How interested are they in your topic?
- How much do they know about your topic?
- Has anything happened recently that would affect the audience's interest and attitudes?
- What position have opinion leaders in the audience taken on the topic?

- What feelings or values will you have to challenge when explaining and defending your position?
- Which audience values can be used as good reasons?

Questions like these will help you assess the audience to decide what you can hope to accomplish in the speech. If you know that a respected member agrees with your position, for example, make reference to that fact during the speech. Conversely, if you know that many disagree, find areas of common agreement and document all assertions thoroughly.

## Determine Your Objectives

After determining the makeup of your audience and their attitudes toward your topic, you are in a position to set realistic goals about what you can achieve. In some cases you may want an audience to give money, volunteer time, pass on a message to others, or buy a product. For example, in the last few years there have been a number of huge outdoor concerts on behalf of starving Africans, American farmers, victims of AIDS, and political prisoners. The audiences drawn by the entertainers heard many messages urging them to make financial contributions, write letters, or join organizations. In other cases, your goal may be to make listeners think differently about a topic—for example, to agree with the need for a new law or to accept or reject a person or idea. You have successfully found the objective for a speech when you know exactly what you want from your contact with the audience. Here are some examples.

### Behavioral outcomes

- To get a jury member to vote for a "not guilty" verdict
- To sign up volunteers or pledges for a campus organization
- To have listeners vote for an all-Republican ticket
- To make a sale
- To discourage the purchase of products that your group is boycotting
- To flood legislators with letters in support of a bill
- To encourage changes in the eating, drinking or smoking habits of friends

### Attitude-centered outcomes

- To encourage an audience to appreciate the work of a controversial author, artist, or musician ("The economist, John Kenneth Galbraith, is one of America's most gifted writers.")
- To win supporters for a different philosophy ("Everyone could benefit from the values held by vegetarians.")

- To encourage people to consider the merits of an unpopular position ("The gap between what we pay professional athletes and what we pay those in areas such as teaching and the military is an indictment of American priorities.")

- To convince an audience to lower or raise their attitudes toward a figure in the present or the past ("George Washington has been overrated as a president.")

- To redirect an audience's frustrations against one group toward another group ("The American public must share the blame for declining standards in television journalism.")

- To remind people that the beliefs they already hold are worth keeping ("Walt Disney was a great and innovative filmmaker.")

- To move listeners incrementally closer to accepting an attitude they still reject ("George Bush was a good president.")

Some desired purposes, such as a complete reversal of a group's opposition to a proposed law, may be impossible to achieve in one speech. Base your expectations on the fact that a single persuasive event will have limited impact. It is unlikely, for example, that a current member of the United States Senate could convince her colleagues that they should press for an end to the long-standing economic boycott of Cuba. Every recent president and many Americans support the boycott. Even so, the hope that she might weaken support for the boycott in the Senate may not be out of the question. Good objectives consider what is realistically possible given the specific circumstances. Even though you probably will not state them to your audience, write down your objectives and keep them in mind.

## Determine Your Thesis

To this point, your preparation has been largely concerned with thinking about the persuasive situation. Now that you have determined the nature of the audience and have one or more objectives in mind, you are ready to draft the most important sentence of the speech. Write the *thesis* (the central idea, the primary point of view) that you want to communicate. It may take some time to arrive at a satisfactory thesis, but by doing so you will eventually have a guide to construct everything else in the speech. The main parts of the message, the support you select, and even the introduction should follow the drafting of the thesis statement. *Think of this statement as the primary conclusion of the speech, the statement to which everything else in the speech is subordinate.* It should be the one idea listeners will recall weeks later.

Inexperienced communicators are tempted to skip the thesis-writing stage and begin preparing the rest of the speech, or they may substitute a one- or two-word topic for a genuine thesis statement. Failure to

*The thesis statement should be the one idea listeners will recall weeks later. Advertising relies on strong central statements.*

# BE LESS PRODUCTIVE AT THE OFFICE.

The office has always been a place to get ahead. Unfortunately, it's also a place where a lot of natural resources start to fall behind. Take a look around the next time you're at work. See how many lights are left on when people leave. See how much paper is being wasted. How much electricity is being used to run computers that are left on. Look at how much water is being wasted in the restrooms. And how much solid waste is being thrown out in the trash cans. We bet it's a lot. Now, here are some simple

*It takes 95% less energy to manufacture products from recycled materials.*

ways you can produce less waste at work. When you're at the copier, only make the copies you need. Use both sides of the paper when writing a memo. Turn off your light when you leave. Use a lower watt bulb in your lamps. Drink your coffee or tea out of mugs instead of throwaway cups. Set up a recycling bin for aluminum cans and one for bottles. And when you're in the bathroom brushing your teeth or washing your face, don't let the faucet run. Remember, if we use fewer resources today, we'll save more for tomorrow.

*Drink out of mugs instead of throwaway cups.*

Which would truly be a job well done. This message brought to you by the 43 environmental charities that make up Earth Share.

*For more tips or information on how you can help, write Earth Share, 3400 International Drive NW, Suite 2K (AD3), Washington, D.C. 20008.*

Earth Share

IT'S A CONNECTED WORLD. DO YOUR SHARE.

Reprinted by permission of Ad Council

establish one central idea in your planning can result in much wasted time and disorganization. A general topic does not present enough guidance to prepare the rest of the speech. For example, think about a message centered on phrases such as "federal standards for automobile fuel economy" or "trash-to-steam recycling"—where does it lead? Both topics are ripe for advocacy, but persuasive attempts on these issues should be constructed from sharply defined declarative sentences, so the audience has no question about the direction the message takes. Consider the following thesis statements, all of which are far more explicit.

- The federal government should dramatically raise its minimum standards for automobile fuel efficiency.

- Most state-of-the-art facilities for burning solid waste pose serious health risks for those living nearby.

- The recording of compact disks or tapes onto audiotape cassettes amounts to theft and is morally wrong.

- The television networks neglect the needs and interests of older Americans.

- Beer and wine advertising should be banned from all radio and television broadcasts.

- Colleges and universities should do a better job of helping students find suitable off-campus housing.

- The summer Olympic games should always be held in Greece.

Although no two people will develop identical speeches from the same thesis statement, the construction of a clear thesis is essential to trigger the mental processes necessary for the next stage—constructing the "good reasons" or main points that are the framework for the body of the message.

## Develop Main Points

The strongest persuasion combines a logical (well-supported and well-argued) structure with appeals appropriate to the audience. We are attracted to ideas that satisfy personal needs and build on the attitudes we cherish. The basis of a thirty-second television commercial for a "no frills" chain of budget hotels may appeal to our desire to save money and our admiration for a new company challenging the established giants. However, persuasion concerned with ideas and policies cannot take its appeals solely from the listener's self-interest. While advertising has limited time to be completely rational, we are less likely to accept lengthy messages unless an extensive case has been made. The best persuasive speaking requires evidence in the form of justifications which can be accepted by a diversity of people.[4] Aristotle stated the maxim that "it is not difficult to praise the Athenians to an Athenian audience,"[5] but it is a dangerous underestimation to assume that we can win over an audience with a few self-serving appeals.

After determining your thesis, the next step is to locate the *good reasons* which justify the thesis. As we noted in chapter 4, reasons are good when they make sense to you and are likely to make sense to your audience as a defense for the thesis. One person's good reasons for a position may not be another's. One of the intriguing features of human communication is that reasonable people can disagree about what makes good sense. However, you should work to establish reasons that are consistent with what you believe and what you think an audience will accept. For example,

*Thesis:* The summer Olympic games should always be held in Greece.

*because . . .*

I. Greece is the traditional home of the games.

II. Moving the games around to different countries has created enormous political problems and boycotts.

III. Unlike some other locations, Greece is neither too hot nor at too high an altitude for most competitors.

IV. Politically and culturally, Greece is a good neutral site, with ties to both the East and West.

In this preliminary outline, the main points are worded as declarative sentences, making their relationship to the thesis clear and apparent. The insertion of "because" between the thesis and each of the main points is a useful test of this relationship since main points should make sense when bridged by this word. If a main point does not seem to follow, it may not be a good reason. Imagine, for instance, a fifth and sixth point for the above example.

*Thesis:* The summer Olympic games should always be held in Greece.

*because . . .*

V. Greece is the setting of many impressive ruins.

VI. It was a mistake to allow professionals in sports such as basketball to compete in the Olympic games.

In relation to the thesis, both statements are non sequiturs. They fail to make sense when combined with the thesis. Unlike the other points, a listener may agree with the fact that Greece is a virtual museum of ancient culture and yet continue to disagree with the thesis. Changes in the rules about who is eligible to compete are not relevant to where the games should be held. Good main points should advance your thesis. It would be far more difficult for a listener to accept any of the first four points without moving closer to acceptance of the central idea of the message. Point five may provide interesting background for the introduction of the message, but it is not a good reason for moving the Olympic games to Greece.

If you are satisfied at this stage that you have located major points that defend your attitude, you are on your way to creating the super-structure of a persuasive message. When the main points are located, the preparation of the body of the speech involves filling in this frame-work with details that will clarify each main point.

## Clarify, Amplify, and Support the Main Points

The few sentences developed so far are essential to the successful pre-paration of the speech, but general assertions by themselves lack the impact of specific evidence and examples. Many listeners will remember only two parts of your message: your general point of view and your most interesting example or illustration.

There are three ways to make ideas vivid and memorable: clarification, amplification, and concrete evidence. These forms of support fill out the body of the speech, appearing as sub-points (A, B, C, and so on) under the main points already designated with Roman numerals. For example:

*Thesis*

    I. Main point

        A. Clarification, amplification, or evidence

            1. Further explanation

Although we treat these three items separately, some of the best pieces of support clarify, amplify, and prove all at once. Clarification makes complex or unfamiliar statements understandable; amplification drama-tizes the familiar or ordinary; evidence seeks to prove what may be doubted.

### Clarification and Understanding

Too often we confuse stating a point with making it clear. Simply saying what you think does not guarantee that understanding will follow. Ideas must be sufficiently explained so their relevance and implications are instantly apparent. Examples, extended illustrations, comparisons, and analogies are the basic explanatory tools. Inexperienced communicators frequently overestimate the ability of a few sentences to clear away confusion; they forget that their own familiarity with a topic is not shared by the audience. A good teacher, for example, does not simply talk about a subject, but *teaches* it—making the unfamiliar comprehensible, while watching for signs of comprehension from the audience. New words, technical relationships, and unfamiliar ideas all need explanation.

*Class of '80 average cost: about $10,800 for four years of college*

*Class of '95 average cost: about $26,000*

*Class of '10 projected cost: about $60,000*

# Reality is expensive.

**Prepare yourself for college with U.S. Savings Bonds.**

Today, parents shell out *over twice* what tuition and fees cost in the early 80s. Those $300 typewriters have been replaced by $1,900 computers. So what will it cost when your children are ready? And what will replace the computer — a virtual reality college simulator?

Better start saving now for those future college costs with U.S. Savings Bonds. They're guaranteed safe, earn Treasury-based rates, are guaranteed to earn interest for 30 years, and you can get them through most banks or through employers offering the Payroll Savings Plan. And families and individuals who use Savings Bonds for college tuition may qualify for a special tax exclusion.*

For your copy of the <u>Savings Bond Investor Information</u> pamphlet, write U.S. Savings Bonds, Washington, DC 20226.

*Maximum income and other limitations apply; read IRS Publication 550 and Form 8815 for details.

Take Stock in America — U.S. SAVINGS BONDS

A public service of this magazine

The following excerpts from a speech about the necessity to establish controls to curb acid rain illustrate why more details are required for a complex subject. The speaker had discussed emissions from cars, power plants, and industries that produce pollution which eventually returns to earth in rain. However, the solutions presented are somewhat difficult for a lay audience to understand.

> The clean air act is presently before the Congress and, when it acts, we hope it will pay heed to our proposals and require, at a minimum:
>
> —An emissions cap for sulfur dioxide from coal-fired power plants contributing to the acid rain problem;
>
> —A national coal washing program requiring coal with a sulfur content greater than three percent to be cleaned before burning;
>
> —Installation, where feasible, of low nitrogen oxide burners on existing power plants to cut down on emissions.[6]

For a speech to people familiar with the problem, it would be a reasonable assumption that each of these briefly summarized recommendations could be understood. For most other audiences, this summary of legislative steps to reduce acid rain would require more explanation. The average listener may ask: What is the relationship between the sulfur content in coal and the production of acid rain? How is coal washing done? What is a "low nitrogen oxide burner?" How would this burner cut down on sulfur dioxide? Audience members are unlikely to accept a new point of view if they do not understand it.

### Amplification as Dramatization of the Familiar

A point needs amplification when it is too familiar or general. When we become accustomed to certain assertions, their full meanings may no longer register with any impact. "Children today have to grow up faster," "Too many American families rely on television for entertainment," and "We can learn a great deal about industrial productivity from the Japanese" are good examples of claims that have lost their urgency. All of these have been part of the national dialogue for so long that they need to be dramatized and amplified in order to reestablish their importance. Few statements are so novel or fresh that merely stating them will command our attention. Listeners discover the significance of ideas through application to specific situations. In an address to prisoners of a Chicago jail in 1902, the famous trial lawyer Clarence Darrow asserted his belief that justice in the United States was class-conscious. It was a familiar charge.

> When your case gets to court it will make little difference whether you are guilty or innocent, but it's better if you have a smart lawyer. And you cannot get a smart lawyer unless you have money. First and last it's a question of money.

These claims were easy to understand, but they were stale and vague. Darrow was too good a criminal lawyer to let them pass without dramatizing them. He followed the general claims with vivid amplifications to show the audience that these ideas were significant.

> Let me illustrate: Take the poorest person in this room. If the community had provided a system of doing justice, the poorest person in this room would have as good a lawyer as the richest, would he not? When you went into court you would have just as long a trial and just as fair a trial as the richest person in Chicago. Your case would not be tried in fifteen or twenty minutes, whereas it would take fifteen days to get through a rich man's case. Then if you were rich and were beaten, your case would be taken to the Appellate Court. A poor man cannot take his case to the Appellate Court; he has not the price. And then to the Supreme Court. And if he were beaten there he might perhaps go to the United States Supreme Court. And he might die of old age before he got to jail. If you are poor, it's a quick job.[7]

Darrow's amplification of his point no doubt produced many nods of agreement from his prison audience. He used a general illustration that could fit the circumstances of many different cases, but the vividness of his details made the general point fresh again.

The primary benefit of explanations that dramatize points is that they strike chords of recognition in listeners. An assertion that takes on concrete form in an extended illustration has the advantage of allowing the listener to visualize the impact of an idea on real events.

## Using Evidence as Support

Evidence aspires to providing proof—sometimes factual, sometimes informed opinion—for a controversial claim. It is designed to reduce doubts and reservations in a skeptical audience.[8] Since the qualities of credible sources of evidence were thoroughly discussed in chapter 5, our focus here is on what evidence can and cannot do in overcoming audience resistance.

The word proof sometimes implies undeniability and certainty. While it is rare that evidence produces such certainty, persuaders usually attempt to cite evidence that may be hard for opponents to dismiss. A 1983 speech on problems in American public school education uses statistics which seem to function as proof for the claim that our schools have failed many of our students.

> The statistics are . . . chilling. . . . Among the most alarming: 13 percent of all seventeen-year-olds are functionally illiterate; among minority youngsters, the figure may be as high as 40 percent; . . . nearly 40 percent of seventeen-year-olds cannot draw inferences from written material; only 20 percent can write a persuasive essay; only a third can solve mathematics problems that require several steps.

American children go to school, on average, only 180 days a year, with another twenty days usually lost to absences, while children in Japan attend for 240 days. Our school day is about five hours long, while in many other countries it is eight hours long. And much of the American school day for the teacher is taken up with activities that have little to do with education—attendance, grading papers, maintaining discipline.[9]

With statistics and a comparison to a major economic competitor, the speaker offers a selective but compelling case. If we accept the accuracy of the percentages and numbers, it would be difficult to argue that the education of American public school students is adequate.

Using evidence to reduce listener resistance is a reasonable goal, but it is also important to remember that overcoming objections is sometimes not simply a matter of providing irrefutable proof. Evidence is frequently used to support preferences and judgments as well as known (and seemingly undeniable) truths.

We noted in chapter 4 that assertions that are preferences or personal judgments rather than facts can never be proved with certainty. Judgments have their roots in values; facts have their roots in observable events. Many judgmental claims are misinterpreted as claims that should have some basis in fact. It may be difficult to ''prove,'' for example, the statement that ''abortion is murder.'' Although the verb ''is'' has the effect of making the claim appear to be a matter of truth or falsity, it is actually a matter of judgment and value. ''Murder'' is the killing of one human being by another, but it remains unsettled within the medical, religious, or judicial worlds when a fetus becomes a human being. Is it in the first stages of cell division or when the fetus can survive without extraordinary medical care outside of the womb? The grammatically induced certainty of ''abortion is murder'' must (and has) given way to a wide variety of conflicting interpretations made by reasonable people who have differences that cannot be settled by appeals to ostensibly self-evident ''facts.''

Does this mean that we cannot use evidence effectively to support a thesis that makes a judgment? Not at all, but we must use the term ''proof'' with care. We can ''prove'' beyond doubt that water freezes at zero degrees Centigrade and that one of George Washington's most successful revolutionary war battles was fought on Christmas in 1776. Nevertheless, certain truth must give way to reasonable judgment when we use evidence to support issues where scientific or historical certainty is impossible. Should animals be sacrificed in medical tests? Was Jimmy Carter a better president than George Bush? Should medical and other professional schools reserve places for minority students? These questions have been the basis of passionate speeches reflecting different views, and evidence has at times furthered the case for all sides. The evidence rarely produces ironclad proof because all of these questions involve values as well as certain facts. The qualities that make good presidents or fair college entrance requirements, for instance, are not defined by everyone in the same way.

In a landmark speech Newton Minow challenged an audience of television network executives and broadcasters to do better than they were doing in serving the public interest requirements enforced by the FCC. He included statements of judgment as well as fact. "When television is good," he noted, "nothing—not the theater, not the magazines or newspapers—nothing is better. But when television is bad, nothing is worse." He began with an amplification of his basic point.

> I invite you to sit down in front of your television set when your station goes on the air and stay there without a book, magazine, newspaper, profit and loss sheet or rating book to distract you. . . . I can assure you that you will observe vast wasteland.
>
> You will see a procession of game shows, violence, audience participation shows, formula comedies about totally unbelievable families, blood and thunder, mayhem, violence, sadism, murder, western badmen, western good men, private eyes, gangsters, more violence, and cartoons. And, endlessly, commercials—many screaming, cajoling, and offending.

Rarely has a government bureaucrat (Minow had been chairman of the Federal Communications Commission) given such a lively and persuasive speech. In the course of making his case to the National Association of Broadcasters, Minow resorted to several forms of evidence, some of which are highlighted below.

*[Testimony supporting a judgment]*

> What do we mean by "the public interest"? Some say the public interest is merely what interests the public. I disagree.
>
> So does your distinguished [N.A.B.] president. . . . In a recent speech he said, "Broadcasting to serve the public interest must have a soul and a conscience, a burning desire to excel, as well as to sell; the urge to build the character, citizenship, and intellectual stature of people . . ."

*[Statistics supporting a judgment]*

> Is there one person in this room who claims that broadcasting can't do better?
>
> A glance at next season's proposed programming can give us little heart. Of 73.5 hours of prime evening time, the networks have tentatively scheduled 59 hours to categories of "action adventure," situation comedy, variety, quiz, and movies.

*[Examples supporting a judgment]*

> Television in its young life has had many hours of greatness—its Victory at Sea, its Army-McCarthy hearings, its Peter Pan, its Kraft

Theaters, its See it Nows, its Project 20, the World Series, its political conventions and campaigns. . .

*[Statistics supporting a fact]*

The best estimates indicate that during the hours of 5 to 6 P.M. 60 percent of your audience is composed of children under 12. And most young children today, believe it or not, spend as much time watching television as they do in the schoolroom.

*[Statistics supporting a judgment]*

There are estimates that today the average viewer spends about 200 minutes daily with television, while the average reader spends about 38 minutes with magazines and 40 minutes with newspapers. Television has grown faster than a teenager, and now it is time to grow up.[10]

Minow's speech was unusual in its adventurous attack on the audience; it was typical in the ways it used evidence to support a variety of factual and judgmental assertions. His effort is a useful reminder that evidence is often more than numbers and statistics; support for a claim must frequently include the use of materials that defend a reasonable—but maybe not provable—point of view.

# Write the Introduction

After the main and supporting points of the speech have been outlined, the remaining task is the completion of the introduction. While the introduction is the first part of a speech, it is the last to be written. Just as it would be difficult to introduce a person you did not know, so it is awkward to write an introduction before the body of a message has been completed. At this stage, you know what attitudes or behaviors you want the intended audience to accept. Now you are in a position to build a bridge between the audience's existing attitudes and those you want them to hold at the end of the message. A good introduction prepares an audience to accept the main points that you will present, reducing resistance to your ideas and arguments.[11] Each of the following is worth considering, although it is unlikely every introduction will need to achieve all of these objectives.

## Gain Interest and Attention

An audience cannot be motivated to accept an idea until it has been motivated to listen. Stories, relevant personal experiences, or vivid statistics are good ways to begin speeches. A detailed example offers an interesting approach to a topic. Abstract ideas are more accessible when explained through the actions of particular people. Here is the effective opening that illustrates the dangers of stereotyping people:

> In the local newspaper of my community recently, there was a story about a man named Virgil Spears. He lived in a small town about 40 miles from my home. He had served five years in the Missouri State Penitentiary for passing bogus checks. When he returned to his family, Mr. Spears couldn't find a job. Everyone knew he was an ex-con and everyone knew that ex-cons aren't to be trusted. Finally in what was described as calm desperation, he walked into a local barbershop where he was well known, pulled a gun, and took all the money the barber had. Up to this point it had been a fairly routine robbery, but then something unusual happened. Mr. Spears didn't try to get away. He got into his car, drove slowly out of town, and waited for the highway patrol. When they caught him, he made only one request. He turned to the arresting patrolman and said: "Would you please ask that the court put my family on welfare just as soon as possible?"
>
> To the people of Clarkston, Missouri, Virgil Spears wasn't to be trusted because he was an ex-con.[12]

The concrete images of this case gained the audience's interest while portraying the negative consequences of stereotyping.

### Establish Goodwill

The greater the gulf that separates speaker and audience, the greater the need to say something that will establish a sense of goodwill between the two. A speaker may start by noting that differences should not overshadow common values and goals. One of the strengths of an open society is the belief that differences of opinion can be productive and can flourish without producing walls of hostility. For example, members of the United States Senate may oppose each other in speeches given from the floor, but many continue to be friends in less partisan settings. The custom of addressing even vehement opponents as distinguished colleagues is not merely good politics but part of a healthy framework for persuasion.

One common device for gaining goodwill is to refer to values the audience and speaker hold in common. Expressing the fact that differences should not obscure similarities helps to put disagreements in perspective. Ronald Reagan used this approach in 1985 while addressing the Soviet people on radio. "Americans," he said, "will never forget the valor, the pain and at last the joy of victory that our people shared. I remember President Roosevelt's praise for the Russian people's heroism."[13] Another technique is to appeal to the audience's sense of fair play. Audiences can be complimented on their willingness to hear a position that is different from their own. This was the strategy of a *Playboy* editor at the beginning of a speech to Southern Baptists, few of whom could be counted on to share the "*Playboy* philosophy." He tactfully combined references to shared concerns with comments on the spirit of openness within the audience:

I am sure we are all aware of the seeming incongruity of a representative of *Playboy* magazine speaking to an assemblage of representatives of the Southern Baptist Convention. I was intrigued by the invitation when it came last fall, though I was not surprised. I am grateful for your genuine and warm hospitality, and I am flattered (though again not surprised) by the implication that I would have something to say that could have meaning to you people. Both *Playboy* and the Baptists have indeed been considering many of the same issues and ethical problems; and even if we have not arrived at the same conclusions, I am impressed and gratified by your openness and willingness to listen to our views.[14]

### Preview the Scope of the Message

Any human activity that requires work—and listening to a speech is hard mental work—needs to have its limits clearly defined. Just as runners pace themselves according to the distances that are set in advance, listeners should understand the length and scope of the topic in which they are investing their attention. Lack of information about the length of the speech and the range of topics to be considered is as frustrating as not knowing the distance of a foot race until the finish line.

Your introduction should tell the audience what topics you will discuss, what topics will be excluded, and how long the presentation will take. The effect of an overview is to make the logical relationship between your thesis and your major contentions more apparent to a listener. By mentioning what will be *excluded*, for example, you can lay to rest misunderstandings about the scope of your speech and provide a better match between what an audience expects and what they will hear. In a speech attacking the National Rifle Association's persuasion tactics, for example, Raymond Rodgers provided an initial indication of the framework of his remarks. He stated his thesis, referred to what he did not have time to talk about, and concluded with a summary of his main points.

I would like to have a closer look at some of the arguments offered by the National Rifle Association in their ongoing opposition to handgun control legislation.

I hasten to add the disclaimer that all of the arguments raised on all sides of the handgun control debate stand in need of improvement, but limitations of time and fully admitted personal bias dictate that today I will scrutinize only "The Rhetoric of the NRA."

In the brief time available today, I would like to discuss several standard arguments of the NRA against handgun control by measuring them against some standard logical and rhetorical fallacies. Those fallacies are: (1) failure to define terms; (2) use of the "Big Lie"; (3) the fallacy of the "slippery slope"; (4) Bully Tactics; and (5) the fallacy of Improper Appeals to authority.[15]

This overview not only communicated the thesis and main points, but also signaled that the speaker was aware of the limits he imposed on his subject.

### Define Key Terms

Successful communication sometimes depends on the way words or phrases are used. Some terms are misunderstood because they are technical and others because ordinary usage may not coincide with the meanings you have in mind. In either case, definitions are useful. The meanings associated with special language can work for or against a position. The average listener, for example, thinks of rhetoric as trivial communication that is far less concrete than reality. The original meaning of the term rhetoric was the art of using words effectively in speaking or writing. The average listener may now identify rhetoric as showy and elaborate speech empty of clear ideas or sincere emotion. The same can be said for other terms such as legalized gambling, brainwashing, recreational drugs, welfare rights, law and order, corporate monopolies, mercy killing, reverse discrimination, and child abuse. Each of us has a general idea of what these terms imply, but we are unlikely to define them in precisely the same way. Even very common terms can benefit from definitions that will prepare an audience to accept a new point of view. In the following example, the speaker begins an address on the relationship between sports and television with a redefinition of two familiar words that imply two different worlds.

> Sport, I am convinced, is the best known yet least understood phenomenon in American society. Much of our misunderstanding and misconceptions about sports stems from our failure to make meaningful distinctions among the various components of the sports world. . . .

*Successful communication depends on the way words or phrases are used.*

**DOONESBURY**

DOONESBURY © 1996. G. B. Trudeau. Reprinted with permission of Universal Press Syndicate.

> One is sport. Sport is an extension of play involving two or more persons. Sport turns on games and contests which are highly organized, competitive, characterized by the established rules; but like play, sport has as its primary purpose fun for the participant.
>
> Athletics, on the other hand, derives not from play at all, but from work. Athletics, as they have been referred to from the ancient Greeks on, refers to intensely competitive confrontation between specially trained performers whose primary objectives are (a) spectator entertainment and (b) victory. Although the game involved in sport and athletics may be the same, as, for example, basketball, the two activities are worlds apart in terms of purpose and attitude. . . . I would simply call your attention to the obvious difference that we understand between intramural sport and intercollegiate athletics.

The speaker then uses the distinctive meanings of the two terms to state his thesis: "The telecommunications industry is interested in athletic contests, not sporting events."[16]

Finally, it may appear that an introduction containing all four elements discussed above would consume half the allotted time for a speech. Even if this assessment were accurate, the minutes would be well spent if the receptivity of the audience was increased. The more unfamiliar an audience is with a topic or the more hostile they are toward your thesis, the greater the need to take the time to establish an appropriate foundation for the persuasive appeals.

### Preparing an Outline

As the outline is completed, it will contain key ideas and concepts you want to cover. Organize it clearly; type it; make the major ideas and divisions of the speech easy to locate at a glance. Every outline is different. The number of major and supporting points will differ. Some speakers use full sentences throughout, while others may work out a system of key words or topics below the main point (I, II, etc.) level. The following model is a general guide:

INTRODUCTION
A.
B.
C.

Thesis:

BODY
  I.
    A.
    B.
      1.
      2.

II.

    A.

    B.

III.

    A.

    B.

SUMMARY

Restate main points and close with a final capstone example, illustration, or quote.

# Delivery of an Outline Speech

Practice a speech by giving it several times orally, but do not memorize or rely on a manuscript. Memorization and reading short-circuit the thought processes that give feeling to our words. Only a skilled professional actor can make a printed speech text seem spontaneous. "Because variety has an almost constantly positive effect upon listener reactions," notes Jeffrey Auer, "the reading aloud from a manuscript, which is almost inherently more static, is understandably less effective than lively, direct, and extemporaneous delivery."[17]

An outline contains all of the essential points that should be raised in the speech but avoids the problem of the speaker who is *reading to* but not *communicating with* an audience. Because an outline can be read at a glance, the actual explanation of points can be made by direct eye contact with the audience. It provides all of the landmarks that are necessary to talk your way through the speech in an oral style that is closer to everyday conversation than to oral reading. As Otis Walter and Robert Scott have noted, we tend to be more expressive in voice and gesture if we *think about our ideas as we say them*. Good delivery involves thinking and speaking at the same time, creating the same mood and intensity that comes when convictions are expressed for the first time.[18]

Several additional suggestions:

1. Be flexible about cutting or adding items to the outline. The actual circumstances of delivery (running out of time, unanticipated comments made by a previous speaker) may force you to vary your speech from its original form. The outline can easily accommodate change.

2. Use a systematic pattern of indenting so that key points can be easily located along the left-hand margin. If you lose your place, for example, you can always restate the main points of the speech by searching them out on the left margin. Note that, for this reason, main points in the introduction are identified with capital letters

# A Sample Outline

The sample speech outline represents the organizational style extemporaneous speakers should develop. (We have made the illustration outline slightly more complete than an actual working outline to illustrate the reasoning behind the points. Some speakers reduce their notes to an outline of key words and phrases.) The following basic organizational style works well in speech preparation: a limited number of points; the expectation that the specific language, transitions, and some detail will be added during delivery; and a system of indentation that allows the speaker to see at a glance major ideas and their support.

## The Advantages of Being a "Near Vegetarian"

*Introduction*

A. A friend of mine says she won't eat anything that has eyes . . . unless it's potatoes. Actually, she eats some fish, but she is in good company, sharing a diet with millions around the world, from Paul Newman to Paul McCartney, from Pythagoras to Plato.

B. We can no longer dismiss vegetarians as skinny people who live on twigs and berries.

   1. A diet based on little or no meat is no longer a fad.
   2. And you don't need to be a customer of juice bars or health food stores to take advantage of what we now know about how to eat well without loading your body and your veins down with the residues caused by high-fat diets centered on meat.

C. We are what we eat: some medical specialists estimate that half of the people occupying hospital beds are in them because of problems brought on by their diets. Among the most common: colon cancer, heart disease, obesity, and perhaps the sharp rise in the number of instances of breast cancer in the United States.

   a. My point is not to convince you to become a particular kind of vegetarian, or even a total vegetarian.

   (But the evidence continues to build demonstrating that . . .)

*Thesis*: You can live a healthier life—and one that makes less demands on the resources of the planet—by eating a largely vegetarian diet.

I. We pay a heavy personal and global price for meat consumption.

   A. The personal cost of eating meat is a diet rich in fat.

      1. Dr. Bonnie Liebman writes in *Nutrition Action*, "The meat industry may insist on denying the health benefits of vegetarian diets, but research on heart disease, cancer, high blood pressure, diabetes, and obesity argues otherwise."[1]
      2. The *New York Times*' Jane Brody, a widely respected food writer in the mainstream of nutrition, has come to the same conclusion. She recently wrote, "The central question about vegetarian diets" is no longer whether it is "healthy to eliminate meat . . ." "The answer," she notes, "seems to be yes."[2]

   B. The global price of meat consumption is the depletion of range and forest land, and the inefficient use of our grain harvests.

      1. You need 16 pounds of grain to produce one pound of beef. But you need just one pound of grain to produce a large loaf of bread.[3]
      2. Food advocate John Robbins estimates that it takes nearly four acres to feed a meat eater for a year, but only one acre to feed a vegetarian.[4]

II. Vegetarians eat well.
   A. A vegetarian diet offers most of the variety and taste available to nonvegetarians.
      1. Most of our current cravings can be met without meat.
         a. Green Giant and other leading companies have developed good vegetable forms of meat items.
         b. Some "veggie-burgers" and "chicken" patties made by these companies are nearly indistinguishable from meat, but contain less saturated fat and calories.
      2. Most of the world's great cuisines are built on flavors and textures that occur in vegetable form:
         -pastas and pasta sauces.
         -the wonderful tastes and textures of grains used in Chinese, Middle Eastern and American southwestern cooking, especially rice and wheat.
         -grains used in great French and English breads and beers.
      3. The sweetest and most intense flavors we know are herbal and vegetable.
         a. When you use mustard, salsa, or ketchup, you are using vegetable and herbal flavoring frequently to cover the "off taste" of animal flesh.
   B. Vegetarians and near vegetarians consume food with a better nutritional balance.
      1. The enemy is saturated fat, so common in most kinds of meat.
         a. There is no doubt that cholesterol contributes dramatically to deaths from heart disease.
         b. Animal fats are major contributors of cholesterol; they also tend to retain pesticide residues with their own side effects.[5]
         c. Vegetables, including grains, have virtually no cholesterol.
      2. Vegetarians generally have cholesterol levels that make heart attacks extremely unlikely, according to researchers in the well-known Framingham, Massachusetts heart study.[6]

III. Life is sacred: We don't have to sacrifice other mammals to feed ourselves.
   A. All of us would be horrified to see the conditions we create for the 9 million animals we slaughter every day.
      1. A person doesn't have to be a die-hard animal lover to recognize how inhumane it is to subject animals to factory farming methods.
         a. A short life in a cage in a darkened building is all that most chickens, pigs and calves raised for their meat have.
         b. Cattle are injected with hormones to stimulate meat production, only to be shipped, often wounded or crippled, to feedlots and then to their deaths.
   B. It seems reasonable to extend our basic wish for quality of life to other living creatures, especially the mammals we now consume.

*Conclusion:* (Restate main points, and add closing:)

I was at a restaurant in Florida with a friend . . . She saw "dolphin" on the menu and was horrified . . . The waiter assured us that we "weren't eating 'Flipper.'" "Dolphin" can also mean a kind of scale fish. But the moment struck me as odd. Many of the animals we raise for food don't have cute names, but they are intelligent creatures living lives that—I believe—should only come to natural rather than violent ends.

**NOTES**

[1] B. Liebman, "Are Vegetarians Healthier Than the Rest of Us?" *The Nutrition Debate: Sorting Out Some Answers*, ed. by Joan Dye Gussow and Paul R. Thomas. Palo Alto, CA: Bull Publishing, 1986, p. 192.

[2] Brody quoted in A. C. Prabhupada, *A Guide to Gourmet Vegetarian Cooking.* Los Angeles: Bhaktivedanta, 1983, p. 1.

[3] F. Lappe, *Diet for a Small Planet*, New York: Ballantine, 1982, p. 9.

[4] J. Robbins, *May All Be Fed*, New York: William Morrow, 1992, p. 33.

[5] Orville Schell, "Modern Meat," in *The Nutrition Debate*, pp. 181–84.

[6] Liebman, p. 193.

rather than Roman numerals. Roman numerals are reserved for major contentions in the body of the speech that will be repeated several times.

3. Avoid writing a conclusion that introduces new ideas that have not been developed in the body. The real conclusion of the speech is the thesis. An extended conclusion may involve a review of all main points and perhaps a closing story or illustration.

4. Remember that oral communication is more idiomatic than formal written prose. Do not be overly concerned about pauses, the urge to rephrase an idea, or the desire to make another attempt to clarify a point. These are natural features of all oral communication. It is more unnatural to read to someone in a way that makes their presence seem marginal rather than central to your reason for speaking.

## Strategic Considerations for Discursive Messages

To this point, we have described a general method for translating a persuasive intent into an actual message. We turn now to several additional concerns about persuasion strategies in longer, discursive forms of communication.

## When to Reveal the Thesis

Ideally, you should state the thesis in the introduction to give direction to the remarks that follow. Most speechmakers have been taught to explain the key idea of a message clearly in the first few moments. In some instances, however, this strategy might alienate the audience. As Gary Cronkhite notes, a persuader who lays all the cards on the table in the introduction may find that "his hostile audience refuses to listen to the rest of his speech."

> Henry Grady, for example, after waiting for General Sherman to finish his speech and after waiting for the audience to stop singing "Marching Through Georgia," might have clearly stated his thesis that the northerners must forget the Civil War and help rebuild the South. He might have done that, but he would probably have ended up spending his next paycheck from the Atlanta Constitution on tar solvent. Instead, he chose a second type of introduction designed to emphasize the interests he and his listeners had in common . . .[19]

If your audience's hostility to the thesis is known to be very strong, you might withhold it until you have established a basis of support and evidence. The option to withhold the thesis until the end is an "inductive" method of development because the thesis is the conclusion that logically follows from everything you have said prior to it. A delay in stating an attitude may avoid an early rejection of your message before you have established the reasoned basis for it. In his famous "Funeral Oration," for example, Marc Antony begins by praising Brutus, one of the assassins of Caesar, as an honorable man. He does so because Brutus has just given his speech in which he has convinced the crowd that Caesar deserved to die. As Shakespeare writes his part, Antony begins with the famous lines that give no hint as to the eventual conclusion he wants his audience to reach:

> Friends, Romans, countrymen, lend me your ears;
> I come to bury Caesar, not to praise him.

Only later in the speech is it evident that he has actually come to bury Brutus and to praise Caesar. Antony concludes that Brutus is the true villain. This attitude gradually emerges from the signs of Caesar's goodness that Antony weaves into his observations seemingly as afterthoughts. Finally, the repeated phrase that Brutus was an honorable man takes on a calculated irony that is not lost on the audience.

> When that the poor have cried, Caesar hath wept;
> Ambition should be made of sterner stuff;
> Yet Brutus says he was ambitious;
> and Brutus is an honorable man.[20]

The pattern of Antony's speech is similar to television advertisements which withhold the tagline or pitch for the product until after they have established an entertaining context.

## Whether to Recognize Opposing Views

When we think of a persuader or a passionate advocate, we usually assume that the ideas to be presented will be one-sided. Few persuaders, whether they are consumer advocates testifying in a congressional hearing or people selling cars, will give equal time to ideas or attitudes they oppose. Successful persuasion frequently requires commitment to one side of a case because the communicator's conviction must be apparent. The ringing certainty of "Give me liberty or give me death" would not be as stirring if Patrick Henry had conceded that the British in colonial America had some legitimate complaints against the local inhabitants. Part of what makes a persuader credible is the evident passion he or she has for a cause.

Yet audiences do not live only in the persuader's world. In many cases, their awareness about a topic includes significant information about the other side of a controversial question. They have been subject to *counterpersuasion*—persuasion intended to weaken the impact of opposing advocates—and will be subject to it again. In the case of heavily advertised products such as beer and automobiles, for example, counterpersuasion frequently occurs within a matter of hours or even minutes. The newspaper reader or news viewer is similarly subjected to thousands of persuasive claims that may be retained and recalled on a vast range of social and political issues.[21] Thus, while a persuader must make a strong case for one side of an issue, it may be necessary to deal with some of the counterarguments a listener has retained and may recall as a topic is discussed.[22] Even if members of an audience lack knowledge of counterarguments, it may be beneficial to present some of what the other side thinks in order to control the way opposing ideas are raised. This interesting strategy is called *inoculation*.

> [J]ust as we develop the resistance to disease of a person raised in a germ-free environment by pre-exposing him to a weakened form of a virus so as to stimulate, without overcoming, his defenses, so also we can develop the resistance to persuasion of a person raised in an "ideologically clean" environment by pre-exposing him to weakened forms of counterarguments or to some other belief-threatening material strong enough to stimulate, but not so strong as to overcome, his defense against belief.[23]

Many experimental studies measuring how attitudes are affected by single and both-sides persuasion have been done. For example, a classic study conducted by Carl Hovland and his associates found that a two-sided presentation may not be as effective for an audience that already agrees with your point of view as for an audience that is initially opposed.

> (1) Presenting the arguments on both sides of an issue was found to be more effective than giving only the arguments supporting the point being made, in the case of individuals initially opposed to the point of view being presented.
>
> (2) For men who were already convinced of the point of view being presented, however, the inclusion of arguments on both sides was less effective, for the group as a whole, than presenting only the arguments favoring the general position being advocated.[24]

*Inoculation is the process of presenting some of the arguments of the opposition in order to control how opposing ideas are raised.*

*Tribune* photo by Ernie Cox, Jr.

Individuals hostile to a speaker's thesis were evidently impressed by the recognition and awareness given the other side of a question. This was especially evident in "better-educated" listeners.[25]

Overall, we think three guidelines are useful for longer, discursive messages. First, in this age of "objective" journalism and "objective" science, it may seem fair and natural to deal with both sides of an issue. However, extensive attempts at balance within a persuasive speech may weaken your impact on the audience. We expect persuaders to be partisans for their causes. There are usually numerous others anxious to carry the burden of presenting opposing views on your topic. The demands for strong advocacy are somewhat at odds with the requirements of balanced presentation. As a persuader, you should see yourself as a person with deep convictions rather than neutral observations. Second, it is never enough to prepare a message by knowing only your side. The best way to know what to anticipate from a hostile audience is to know their grounds for disagreement. Refer briefly to some objections, but spend most of your time as a forceful advocate for your own ideas. Third, remember that any time you spend dealing with the "cons" in opposition to your "pro" position may produce the unintended effect of planting the seeds for objections that otherwise might not have existed.

Finally, the consideration of the subject of one-sided arguments raises an important ethical issue that has plagued persuaders for centuries: should an advocate deliberately ignore information that goes against his or her point of view? We think the answer is yes. Although it is wrong to distort information to fit a belief, we do not think there is an inherent ethical problem in focusing on only one side of an issue if a speaker's belief is genuine. Passionate advocacy is preferable to timid neutrality. Even if a speaker knows that there is a good case to be made for a different point of view, we think it is ethical to concentrate on making the best possible case for one side. An open society functions better when there are many competing voices on issues rather than single voices trying to represent all sides.

## How to Use Persuasive Language

When Richard Nixon was running for the presidency in 1960, he frequently campaigned with his wife, Pat, at his side. A favorite story among reporters was that Nixon was fond of a political cliché that he later realized carried an unintended meaning. "America," he liked to say, "cannot stand pat." After receiving icy stares from his wife, the story goes, he decided to talk about how "America cannot stand still."[26] Nixon's problem is a fitting reminder that the language of persuasion needs to be considered carefully. We may get so involved in the structure of the outlined speech that we overlook the importance of key terms. A finished speech outline is like a completed but unpainted car. The basics are in place, but how we react to it depends to a great extent on the exterior color that is applied. Just as paint color can make a car acceptable or unacceptable in our eyes, so can the semantics of the speech make a difference in our attitudes toward an idea. Look closely at adjectives, nouns, and verbs that make up the major headings. Phrase them in ways that contribute forcefully to your appeals and arguments.

Here are two main points of a rough-draft outline for a speech arguing that employers should not use lie detectors to assess the honesty and performance of employees:

   I. Lie detectors are unreliable, and

   II. Lie detectors violate our personal liberties.

While these ideas may be well chosen, their wording could be greatly improved. First, a speech that is arguing against these devices should not use the inexact and misleading phrase "lie detector." Although the term is a common one, its use works against a main point of the speech (that these machines do not detect lies). A less loaded term is polygraph. Second, you could intensify the impact of the main points with more vivid and specific language. Consider, for example, the nouns, adjectives, and verbs added to these points to increase their impact:

I. Polygraphs are supposed to detect "lies," but the outdated machine is itself a notorious liar.

II. Imposed use of the polygraph destroys our rights to privacy, freedom, and honor.

Although the ideas in the original and revised drafts are essentially the same, the wording of the second attempts is more compelling. A fallible machine is a more obvious threat to our liberties. Every persuader should carefully choose evocative language to build the ideas through reasoned argument.

# Strategic Considerations for Nondiscursive Persuasion

Although our primary concern has been with the organization and presentation of reasoned, language-centered forms of persuasion, it is obvious that we are exposed to countless appeals that must work in a shorter time frame. For example, advertising and direct mail messages which encounter constant competition from other sources must be brief and vivid. The orderly and sequential process of development that works for a speech or written opinion must be greatly condensed in a magazine advertisement, television commercial, or requests for support received through the mail. The same search for good reasons should apply, as do the processes for identifying key audiences and realistic objectives. However, the nondiscursive messages of advertising and public relations must also reduce abstract ideas into specific, easily identifiable symbols. Although some of the items below will not be relevant to certain applications, consider the following checklist as a suggestive guide to persuasive settings (television, radio, billboards, posters, print ads, etc.) where time is short and the possibility for distraction is very high.

## Set Modest Goals

In direct one-on-one communication with another person, it may be possible to produce relatively high rates of success. It is far less likely that any brief encounter with a nondiscursive message will have a dramatic effect on attitudes.[27] Therefore, the key audience you need to reach must be exposed repeatedly to many messages. Our discussion of advertising and political campaigns in Part III of this book cites extensive evidence that such persuasion works only in the context of a sustained campaign that exposes audience members to several opportunities to see or hear the same message. A successful direct mail campaign in a political contest, for example, may generate a response rate of only 3 percent.[28] In order to achieve the final goal of raising money or support for a candidate, it must be duplicated several times.

## Keep It Simple

With some exceptions, the human attention span is notoriously short and subject to a good deal of external "noise." Watching anyone peruse a magazine or newspaper can be a sobering experience for an advertiser. A full-page ad may get little more than a glance as it competes for attention with photographs, human interest stories, editorials, attention-grabbing headlines, and other advertising. The popular media are so cluttered with messages that a persuader must think in terms of simple messages and vivid imagery. Speech-writers for politicians often try to write in "sound bites" or catchphrases finding brief ways to make a point. In 1984 presidential candidate Gary Hart attacked the foreign policies of Ronald Reagan by asking, "What will this president have for a foreign policy when he runs out of Marines?" In 1992 George Bush attacked the environmentalism of Al Gore by dismissing him as "Ozone Man."[29]

## Make Your Message Aural or Visual

Aural and visual information create an instant shorthand for feelings and moods that print cannot easily match. We live in an age dominated by fast-paced visual and aural references. Happiness, anger, or fear carry universal cues. We learn them early and quickly, and their physical signs will be recognizable to us almost any place on the globe. Unlike learning a foreign language, we do not need to master special access codes to understand many forms of aural and visual information.[30] For these reasons charities, social action organizations, and politicians have learned to seek out visually interesting events. Concrete images of persuaders engaged in enjoyable activities reinforces their similarities to us and enhances the likelihood that we will find them—and their requests—appealing.

## Position Your Message as Entertainment or Newsworthy Information

We are selective in what we expose ourselves to and, having been exposed, additionally selective in actually granting our attention. In this cluttered environment, any message framed in the form of entertainment or interesting information has a possible advantage. Commercials thus pose as mini-dramas featuring character, conflict, and denouement. Print ads appeal to our innate curiosity about the personal details of a particular personality (Does this guy really drink Scotch?). Health-oriented public service announcements offer "ten ways" or "five tests" for a person to determine if they suffer from an addiction or an undiagnosed medical condition. In American society, the creation of awareness about problems—whether on television, radio, or in the print media—often occurs when the ostensible function is to entertain or inform. The lines are increasingly blurred between news, entertainment, information, and advertising. Any single hour of *Larry King Live*, for example, will contain each of these elements. Authors sell their latest books in their roles as experts; tough questions frame issues as dramatic encounters; victims "entertain" us with vivid accounts of their harrowing experiences. Advertisers are pleased to sponsor this riveting forum that is part town meeting and part tabloid gossip, using their ten minutes of commercial time to sell everything from soap to diet aids.[31]

## Use a Sympathetic Figure or Powerful Image to Enact Your Central Idea

The literary device of the synecdoche has a potent counterpart in most short forms of persuasion. A *synecdoche* is a thing or person that symbolizes, embodies, or represents the much larger universe. The statements "Woody Allen is the embodiment of the craziness that is New York City," "Tom Hanks is the perfect 'everyman' in American films," or "Chicago represents the best and worst of American life" speak to our impulse to identify reality in the features of specific people, places, or events. Kenneth Burke described the synecdoche as one of four "master tropes," or one of the thought patterns we use to discover and describe basic truths.[32]

Many advocates find that the most direct way to touch a responsive chord with a viewer or listener is to find a symbol or image that can represent a much larger universe. The creators of commercials and print ads will carefully cast potential actors with an eye to how well they can stand in either for the average person or the idealized consumer. Some actors have a middle-aged, middle-class, American look that is right for selling financial services, toothpaste, or breakfast cereal. Others convey a younger, urban, and professional appearance that is right for selling high-performance cars, expensive clothes, and liquor. They are often meant to represent an idealized symbol of a product's users. The Dewar's scotch ad, for instance, communicates its basic themes quickly and clearly. The well-known profile series prepared by the company's ad agency, Leo Burnett, puts the product in the context of a real person who is attractive but more than a model; young, but moving toward middle age; well-groomed, but obviously not too fussy about clothes; and

*Advocates frequently try to touch a responsive chord with the audience by establishing a universal image with which to identify.*

accomplished, with a careful mix of intellectual and athletic talents. We are asked to identify with Mark Salzman not necessarily because he is like us but because his appearance and carefully summarized biography epitomize the Dewar's user in ways we admire.

## Frame the Discussion in the Imagery of Heroes, Villains, and Victims

Storytelling is a universal, familiar method of both presenting information and illustrating a point of view. The essence of storytelling is the portrayal of specific characters as they negotiate life's obstacles. We could accurately describe the human being as *homo narrans*, the only living creature who naturally frames an understanding of the world in terms of narratives and related characters.[33] In Sharon Lynn Sperry's words, the human being is "an incorrigible imagist," knowing and giving order to the world by devising and sharing stories.[34] We communicate our impressions of events by selectively arranging particular facts and features according to the formulaic requirements of storytelling. There must be action that requires others to respond; the plot must build. Responses must be characterized as appropriate or problematic. Characters must be sorted out as creators of the problem (villains), bystanders who have been harmed (victims), or protagonists who may solve the problem (heroes). Finally, there must be a wrapping up—a conclusion that resolves the problem justly. While it is not always possible, we usually want the closure and finality that most storytelling implicitly promises.

It is easy to forget how innate the narrative impulse is. Consider one of the most common and widely distributed forms of promotional communication from businesses, organizations, and political figures: the press release. Virtually every institution that deals with the public has a public relations staff that cranks out good news about their organization for the local press. Press releases are written as stories. While maintaining the basic journalistic style of a running narrative, the releases gently promote the official views or accomplishments of the organization. They are meant to spur media interest in events the organization would like to publicize. Many news outlets insert the contents of these statements as legitimate news stories, sometimes with only minor changes.

Press releases are a common way to try to influence the daily news agenda. Their journalistic style sometimes conceals their true intent: to call attention to an individual's (or organization's) positive actions. In many releases, those issuing the statement are portrayed as agents for positive change (heroes). Their thoughtful words and actions are intended to suggest that the end of a significant problem is in sight. Directly or by implication, these statements also imply who will be helped by the efforts of the individual (potential victims) and who may attempt to disrupt their successful intervention (potential villains).

## Summary

In this chapter, we explored a number of recommendations for constructing persuasive messages. With a primary emphasis on highly organized discursive messages such as speeches, we reviewed a development sequence of six steps: (1) know the audience, (2) determine your objectives, (3) determine your thesis, (4) develop main points, (5) develop clarification, amplification, and evidence, and (6) write the introduction. We made two basic claims about persuasive speaking. The first is that it is important to think of a speech as more than a written copy of what you intend to say. Preparing to persuade an audience is as much a process of thinking about the event as it is about writing words on paper. Everything done before the speech should make the contact between you and your listeners as successful and satisfying as possible. The single most important consequence of this conclusion is that no speech is completed when it is written—only when it is delivered. The outline contains the basic ideas needed to keep you on track; it should not get in the way of the spontaneous and flexible communication expected when we meet others face-to-face. Our second claim is that the preparation of a speech requires careful attention to detail—how to defend and to explain points, how to introduce controversial ideas, and what kind of language will evoke the right response.

We also explored conventional message-building guidelines used by persuaders who have less time or space to develop their views. The shorter, nondiscursive persuasion of advertising and television news relies much more on visual and aural symbols that can serve as shorthand expressions of attitudes that persuaders want audiences to share. These kinds of messages depend heavily on the creation of interesting stories, praise- or blameworthy agents, and vivid symbols to carry their meanings. Such short-form persuasion builds on our natural tendency to frame events in terms of narratives about good and evil.

## Questions and Projects for Further Study

1. Assess the speech outline entitled "The Advantages of Being a Near Vegetarian." Estimate how a skeptical audience of nonvegetarian college students might react to the arguments and the evidence. What are the flaws of the speech? Given its thesis statement, what would strengthen the speech for that audience?

2. In discussing "one-sided" versus "two-sided" presentations, the authors note that there is no inherent ethical problem in focusing on only one side of an issue. Agree or disagree with the authors, citing real or hypothetical examples to support your point of view.

3. As an exercise in generating good reasons for an assertion, (1) write a thesis statement that presents an attitude that a partner disagrees with and (2) identify two or three good reasons in support of the thesis. These are steps 3 and 4 in the six-step sequence for writing a persuasive speech. Working alone, write down the strongest case that you can.

   Ask the partner questions about the "bare bones" logical structure you have developed. Your questions may include the following: Does this seem like a strong argument? If not, where are the flaws? Do you accept any of the good reasons? If so, does your acceptance of a good reason make you feel uncomfortable about rejecting the thesis? Is there a major objection that the outline overlooks?

4. Locate and analyze the evidence used (or missing) in the arguments of a newspaper columnist. A sample of nationally syndicated writers may include Ellen Goodman, Mike Royko, Jimmy Breslin, James Kilpatrick, William Buckley, and David Broder. Identify the kinds of evidence the writer employs using the categories developed in this chapter and the types of sources cited in chapter 5.

5. Amplification is an important type of development in almost any message. Write vivid hypothetical examples (one or two paragraphs) to amplify three of the following familiar contentions:

   • Enormous medical costs can ruin a family.
   • Higher education today is still a matter of privilege rather than a right.
   • Travel in another country is the best form of education.
   • Americans watch too much television.

6. Considering our comments on "good" and "bad" delivery, analyze and evaluate a persuasive presentation (i.e., at a campus forum, in Congress over cable television's C-SPAN, in church, or in a persuasion class). Some questions to consider: What kind of notes is the speaker using? Are the notes a help or a hindrance in promoting successful communication with the audience? If the speaker were to ask you, what could you suggest to improve his or her delivery?

7. Working with a partner and using some of the recommendations for constructing nondiscursive forms of persuasion, design a newspaper ad for a social action group that interests you (Greenpeace, Mothers Against Drunk Driving, Planned Parenthood, animal rights, etc.). Consider the role of photos, headlines, key symbols, and additional persuasive copy.

8. Good examples of contemporary speeches can be found in the weekly periodical *Vital Speeches* and the yearly compilation *Representative*

*American Speeches.* Using one of these sources, locate a persuasive speech that contains an especially effective introduction. Explain why you think the introduction was successful in preparing the audience to listen to the speaker's ideas.

# Notes

[1] Cicero, quoted in Harold Croft, *A Guide to Public Speaking*, Labour Party Publication. Leicester, England: Leicester Printers, n.d., p. 34.

[2] Kathleen Kendall, "Do Real People Ever Give Speeches?" *Spectra*, December 1985, p. 10. See also Kathleen Kendall, "Do Real People Ever Give Speeches?" *Central States Speech Journal*, Fall 1994, pp. 233–35.

[3] Donald C. Bryant, "Rhetoric: Its Function and Scope," *Quarterly Journal of Speech*, December 1953, p. 401.

[4] See Karl R. Wallace, "The Substance of Rhetoric: Good Reasons," *Quarterly Journal of Speech*, October 1963, pp. 239–49; and Walter R. Fisher, "Toward a Logic of Good Reasons," December 1978, pp. 376–84.

[5] Aristotle, *The Rhetoric* in *The Basic Works of Aristotle*, ed. by Richard McKeon. New York: Random House, 1941, p. 1356.

[6] Robert F. Flack, "Acid Rain: Controlling the Problem," *Vital Speeches*, November 1, 1982, pp. 49–50.

[7] Clarence Darrow, "Address to the Prisoners in Cook County Jail," in *The Rhetoric of No*, Second Edition, ed. by Ray Fabrizio, Edith Karas, and Ruth Menmuir. New York: Holt, Rinehart and Winston, 1974, p. 140.

[8] Audiences do not always respond to the presence of strong evidence as a basis for accepting claims, but we believe that ethical persuasion requires reasoning from available evidence. For more discussion of research in this area see Michael Burgoon and Erwin P. Bettinghaus, "Persuasive Message Strategies," in *Persuasion: New Directions in Theory and Research*, ed. by Michael E. Roloff and Gerald R. Miller. Beverly Hills: Sage, 1980, pp. 146–48.

[9] W. Ann Reynolds, "What is Right With Our Public Schools?" in *Representative American Speeches: 1983–1984*, ed. by Owen Peterson. New York: H. W. Wilson, 1984, pp. 16–17.

[10] Newton Minow, "The Vast Wasteland," in Glen E. Mills, *Reason in Controversy*. Boston: Allyn and Bacon, 1964, pp. 271–82.

[11] There is surprisingly little research on how audiences respond to various tactics for introducing controversial topics to audiences. For a dated but useful survey of research on introductions see Gary Cronkhite, *Persuasion: Speech and Behavioral Change*. New York: Bobbs-Merrill, 1969, pp. 192–95.

[12] Sally Webb, "On Mousetraps," in Contemporary American Speeches, ed. by Will A. Linkugel, R. R. Allen, and Richard Johannesen. Belmont, CA: Wadsworth, 1965, p. 216.

[13] "Transcript of President Reagan's Address Broadcast to the Soviet Union," *New York Times*, November 10, 1985, p. A18.

[14] Anson Mount, "The Playboy Philosophy-Pro," in *Contemporary American Speeches*, Fourth Edition, ed. by Will Linkugel, R. R. Allen, and Richard Johannesen. Dubuque, IA: Kendall-Hunt, 1978, p. 182.

[15] Raymond S. Rodgers, "The Rhetoric of the NRA," *Vital Speeches*, October 1, 1983, p. 759.

[16] Larry R. Gerlach. "Sport as Part of Our Society," in *Representative American Speeches, 1983–1984*, pp. 106–7.

[17] J. Jeffrey Auer, "The Persuasive Speaker and His Audience," in *The Rhetoric of Our Times*, ed. by J. Jeffery Auer. New York: Appleton-Century-Crofts, 1969, p. 272.

[18] Otis M. Walter and Robert L. Scott, *Thinking and Speaking*, Fifth Edition. New York: Macmillan, 1984, pp. 292–93.

[19] Cronkhite, pp. 192–93.

[20] "Marc Antony's Funeral Oration," *The Dolphin Book of Speeches*, ed. by George W. Hibbitt. New York: Dolphin, 1965, pp. 10–11.

[21] Estimates that reveal our constant exposure to persuasive messages are fascinating. In *How to Talk Back to your Television Set*, New York: Bantam, 1970, p. 11, former FCC Commissioner Nicholas Johnson estimates that the average sixty-five-year-old American male will have spent the equivalent of nine full years of his life in front of a television set. In *Processing the News*, New York: Longman, 1984, p. 1, Doris Graber notes that available news sources on just one day present a wealth of material that would tax even the most committed news junkie: between 50 to 100 pages of newsprint . . . 25 to 50 stories served up at dinner and bedtime by national and local television newscasts, plus assorted bulletins on radio throughout the day, not to mention news magazines and journals . . ."

[22] For an interesting discussion of strategies for increasing resistance to persuasion, see Gerald R. Miller and Michael Burgoon, *New Techniques of Persuasion*. New York: Harper and Row, 1973, pp. 18–44.

[23] Arthur R. Cohen, *Attitude Change and Social Influence*. New York: Basic Books, 1964, p. 122.

[24] Carl I. Hovland, Arthur A. Lumsdaine, and Fred D. Sheffield, "The Effects of Presenting 'One Side' Versus 'Both Sides' in Changing Opinions on a Controversial Subject," in *Experiments in Persuasion*, ed. by Ralph L. Dosnow and Edward J. Robinson. New York: Academic Press, 1967, pp. 224–25.

[25] *Ibid.*, p. 225.

[26] William Safire, *Before the Fall*. New York: Doubleday, 1975, p. 530.

[27] Like so many general rules describing human conduct, this one is subject to exceptions. The feature film is a nondiscursive form that holds the potential for significant audience impact. It would be dangerous to underestimate the power of a narrative film with the potency of Steven Spielberg's 1993 drama, *Schindler's List*.

[28] Larry J. Sabato, *The Rise of Political Consultants*. New York: Basic Books, 1981, p. 228.

[29] Howard Fineman, "The Torch Passes," *Newsweek*, Election Issue, November/December, 1992, p. 9.

[30] Joshua Meyrowitz, *No Sense of Place*. New York: Oxford, 1985, pp. 93–109.

[31] The marriage of information and entertainment in *Larry King Live* and similar programs is discussed in Gary C. Woodward, *Persuasive Encounters: Case Studies in Constructive Confrontation*. New York: Praeger, 1990, pp. 99–131.

[32] Kenneth Burke, *A Grammar of Motives*. New York: Prentice Hall, 1954, p. 503.

[33] This is Walter R. Fisher's phrase in *Human Communication as Narration: Toward a Philosophy of Reason, Value, and Action*. Columbia: University of South Carolina, 1987, p. 62.

[34] Sharon Lynn Sperry, "Television News as Narrative," in *Understanding Television: Essays on Television as a Cultural Force*, ed. by Richard P. Adler. New York: Praeger, 1981, pp. 297–98.

## Additional Reading

J. Jeffery Auer, "The Persuasive Speaker and His Audience," in *The Rhetoric of Our Times*, ed. by J. Jeffery Auer. New York: Appleton-Century-Crofts. 1969, pp. 255–76.

Michael Burgoon and Erwin P. Bettinghaus, "Persuasive Message Strategies," in *Persuasion: New Directions in Theory and Research*. Beverly Hills: Sage, 1980, pp. 141–69.

Ruth Ann Clark, *Persuasive Messages*. New York: Harper & Row, 1984.

Arthur R. Cohen, *Attitude Change and Social Influence*. New York: Basic Books, 1964.

Bruce Gronbeck, Alan Monroe, and Douglass Ehninger, *Principles and Types of Speech Communication*, Twelfth Edition. New York: HarperCollins, 1994.

Carl I. Hovland, ed., *The Order of Presentation in Persuasion*. New Haven: Yale, 1957.

Michael Osborn and Suzanne Osborn, *Public Speaking*, Third Edition. Boston: Houghton Mifflin, 1994.

Karl R. Wallace, "The Substance of Rhetoric: Good Reasons," *Quarterly Journal of Speech*, 49. 1963, pp. 239–49.

Otis M. Walter and Robert L. Scott, *Thinking and Speaking*, Fifth Edition. New York: Macmillan, 1984.

# Index